How Can the Petrine Ministry Be a Service to the Unity of the Universal Church?

Edited by

James F. Puglisi

WILLIAM B. EERDMANS PUBLISHING COMPANY

GRAND RAPIDS, MICHIGAN / CAMBRIDGE, U.K.

© 2010 Wm. B. Eerdmans Publishing Co.
All rights reserved

Published 2010 by
Wm. B. Eerdmans Publishing Co.
2140 Oak Industrial Drive N.E., Grand Rapids, Michigan 49505 /
P.O. Box 163, Cambridge CB3 9PU U.K.

Printed in the United States of America

16 15 14 13 12 11 10   7 6 5 4 3 2 1

Library of Congress Cataloging-in-Publication Data

How can the Petrine ministry be a service to the unity of the universal church? /
    edited by James F. Puglisi.
        p.   cm.
    Proceedings of two conferences held 2003-2004
    at the International Bridgettine Centre of Farfa.
    ISBN 978-0-8028-4862-8 (pbk.: alk. paper)
    1. Papacy and Christian union — Congresses.   I. Puglisi, J. F.

    BX9.5.P29H68   2010
    262'.13 — dc22

                                                            2010016207

www.eerdmans.com

*How Can the Petrine Ministry Be a Service
to the Unity of the Universal Church?*

Contents

Preface   ix

   James F. Puglisi, SA

Introduction   1

   Peder Nørgaard-Højen

SCRIPTURE AND PATRISTICS

Petrine Ministry in the New Testament
and in the Early Patristic Traditions   13

   John P. Meier

The Petrine Ministry in the Early Patristic Tradition   34

   Archbishop Roland Minnerath

The Petrine Ministry in the New Testament
and in Early Patristic Tradition   49

   John Reumann

POST-REFORMATION DEVELOPMENT

Protestant Reaction to the Post-Reformation
Development of Papal Authority   81

   Günther Gassmann

Contents

Historical Development of Forms of Authority and Jurisdiction:
The Papal Ministry — an Ecumenical Approach   98

   Hermann J. Pottmeyer

Did Vatican I Intend to Deny Tradition?   108

   Hermann J. Pottmeyer

Vatican I and the Development of Doctrine:
A Lutheran Perspective   124

   Michael Root

SYSTEMATICS

What Ecclesiology for the Petrine Ministry?   145

   Joseph A. Komonchak

Papal Ministry in a Communication Ecclesiology:
A Search for Some Possible Themes   155

   Sven-Erik Brodd

The Future Exercise of Papal Ministry in the
Light of Ecclesiology: An Orthodox Approach   169

   Metropolitan John (Zizioulas) of Pergamon

Infallibilitas Papae — Indefectibilitas Ecclesiae:
A Systematic and Ecumenical Approach   180

   Johannes Brosseder

Is Papal Infallibility Compatible with Ecclesial Indefectibility?   194

   Peder Nørgaard-Højen

ECUMENICS

Introductory Considerations in the Ecumenical Dialogue
on the Petrine Ministry from a Catholic Viewpoint   213

   Walter Cardinal Kasper

Papal Primacy — a Possible Subject of Lutheran Theology?   225

   Harding Meyer

Universal Episkopē and the Papal Ministry:
A Critical Overview of Responses to *Ut unum sint*   237

   Peter Lüning

Does the Joint Declaration on the Doctrine of Justification
Have Any Relevance to the Discussion of the Papal Ministry?   251

   André Birmelé

A Ministry of Unity in the Context of Conciliarity
and Synodality   269

   Eero Huovinen

A Primatial Ministry of Unity in a Conciliar
and Synodical Context   284

   Geoffrey Wainwright

Towards a Common Understanding of Papal Ministry:
A Catholic Critical Point of View   310

   Hervé Legrand, OP

Towards a Common Lutheran/Roman Catholic
Understanding of Papal Ministry   335

   Harding Meyer

How Can the Petrine Ministry Serve the Unity
of the Universal Church?   354

   Jared Wicks, SJ

Preface

James F. Puglisi, SA

The Farfa Project

The Petrine ministry has been at the center of the modern ecumenical discussion, for it concerns the very question of the unity of the church. The International Bridgettine Centre in Farfa Sabina has seriously undertaken a study of the theological, historical, and dogmatic issues that underlie the issues of Christian unity dealing with the role of unity as exercised by the Bishop of Rome.

This current work represents only part of the work that the Centre has been engaged in during these past ten years. The texts published in this volume give a "snapshot" of the situation when they were presented during the series of colloquia, study groups, and consultations that have taken place. Therefore there has been no attempt to update the bibliographical information. It is important to note that the work is still "a work-in-progress."

In addition, for the past five years a dialogue group of Lutherans and Catholics have dealt in depth with the questions of infallibility and jurisdiction. They have met faithfully on the weekend surrounding the Feast of All Saints in November. The Farfa group of theologians, canonists, ecumenists, ecclesiologists, sociologists, and Scripture experts have completed their study. That dialogue document will be published with their conclusions in the near future. This present volume serves as an "appetizer" for that final statement. It forms the backdrop of their work.

It is our hope that this volume itself will provoke critical reactions to the studies found herein. Only in this way will we be able to go forward with the dialogue that John Paul II invited us to in his monumental encyclical, *Ut unum sint*. His was an invitation to the churches for a fraternal dialogue concerning the issues and obstacles that the Petrine ministry may pose. Finally, it is hoped that the wide implications that the Petrine question has for the church, its unity, and its mission will be seen with new eyes thanks to insights coming from this group of scholars' utmost efforts to bring forward this fraternal dialogue.

Introduction

Peder Nørgaard-Højen

The Problem

For centuries the papal ministry has not ceased to cause uneasiness and even bewilderment among Christians. As much as it is by its very nature a ministry of unity, it has in fact equally been a stumbling block and a reason for severe divisions and insurmountable tensions between churches and confessions — even within the ranks of the Roman Catholic Church. The Reformation created an unbridgeable gap between the Protestant churches and the see of Rome, as did even earlier the Great Schism with regard to the churches of the East, and not least since the First Vatican Council and, in many ways, its misunderstandable doctrine of papal infallibility, the papacy has more often than not been the preferred object of immediate rejection or even hatred in non-Catholic circles around the globe.

The doctrine of 1870 sharpened the traditional conflicts and seemed to confirm and cement the most detrimental prejudices against the Roman Catholic Church and its alleged autocracy. Any dialogue was blocked, and any attempt at building a bridgehead and forming a platform, from which positive and innovative approaches in either direction could be launched, was condemned to fail, as long as erroneous interpretations and malicious and outdated assumptions defined the agenda.

This situation was not changed until the Second Vatican Council paved the way for a modification in ecclesiology that could at its best possibly allow for a revised view of papacy, to which the ecumenical movement in turn responded all the more constructively — not by adopting the Roman

1

understanding of papacy, but rather by acknowledging that what is intended in the Catholic doctrine on papacy and even infallibility is a common theological concern of all churches. The object of disagreement is not *that* a ministry of unity is indispensable and that the unified church is in need of an authoritative instrument to express the one, catholic, and apostolic truth — at least not in ecumenically open parts of our churches.

The question, however, as to how and by whom this truth is to be formulated as well as the issue of the criteria of unity tear Christianity apart. Catholics and non-Catholics alike share, on the other hand, the conviction that the church of Christ *perpetuo mansura est* and that no demonic powers shall ever overcome it (Matt. 16:18). Christ has promised to be with his church always until the end of the world (Matt. 28:20) and that his Spirit shall lead it into all truth (John 16:13). Thus it is the common conviction of both Catholics and Lutherans that the church as a totality of believers *(communio)* shall be held in and never fall out of the truth *(sensus fidelium)*. It may fall victim to all kinds of errors and defeats and even betray its Lord and Savior, but it will never cease to be the church. This fact of faith is expressed in the traditional concept of *indefectibilitas,* that is, *perennitas ecclesiae,* in the Lutheran context in the notion of *ecclesia mansura.* The certainty of *indefectibilitas ecclesiae* is a strong persuasion of all Christians. Yet, thus far they failed in getting closer, when it came to adequately and concretely defining their belief in the ecclesial indefectibility — or even to agree that an understanding of *infallibilitas papae* in terms of *indefectibilitas ecclesiae* is a proper, and indeed the only and authoritative interpretation of the disputed doctrine of the First Vatican Council.

However, apart from and indeed in spite of the many problems that still remain unsolved, a certain will to rapprochement on both sides can be observed, not least on the Catholic part, and numerous dialogues since the Second Vatican Council have directly and indirectly dealt with issues pertaining to papal primacy. Recognizing his call to exercise the office of unity in terms of "a brotherly fraternal communion of faith and sacramental life,"[1] as it had existed throughout the first millennium, the late Roman Pontiff John Paul II in his encyclical *Ut unum sint* (1995) took a remarkable and thus far unseen step to appeal to leaders and theologians of Catholic and non-Catholic churches "to engage with [him] in a patient and fraternal dialogue" on "the forms in which this ministry may accomplish a service of love recognized by all con-

---

1. Second Vatican Council, *Lumen gentium* 27.

cerned."² At the same time the pope did not deviate from the basic Catholic principle that "the communion of the particular churches with the Church of Rome, and of their Bishops with the Bishop of Rome, is — in God's plan — an essential requisite of full and visible communion"³ as the Roman point of departure in the reflections and negotiations that the pope wanted to launch. He insisted indisputably on the continuation of the function of Peter in the church "so that under her sole Head, who is Jesus Christ, she may be visibly present in the world as the communion of all his disciples."⁴

John Paul II was courageous enough to challenge his own church and other churches on a difficult but necessary point, but he was also sufficiently honest to indicate the Roman Catholic point of departure. He did not facilitate the dialogue he wanted in a superficial manner, but pointed to the simple and evident fact that if Christian churches want to establish a ministry of universal unity, an exclusion of the Roman Catholic Church will, of course, not be possible — just as the exclusion of any other church would obviously be detrimental to the unity that we intend to gain and secure. Given the fact that a possible future office of universal unity thus requires faithfulness to the see of Rome (and for that matter faithfulness to any other criterion of unity), we are, indeed, left with a number of questions that need to be clarified, before any such universal ministry can be even thought of. The concern of the pope's encyclical is the search for new forms of papal primacy without abandoning what has so far been regarded as essential.

However, the distinction between what might be changed and what is not subject to alterations is exactly the problem. What is the very essence of the Petrine ministry, and what are the forms that could actually be changed? Not only practical issues, but a number of substantial theological questions are at stake. Is the Roman Catholic Church able to reinterpret the doctrines of papacy, especially that of papal infallibility, in such a way that other Christian communities could accept the papal ministry without betraying their own heritage?

Farfa Events

We are still far from having offered any conclusive solutions to such crucial difficulties, although the reactions to the pope's encyclical have been numer-

2. *Ut unum sint,* 96 and 95.
3. *Ut unum sint,* 97.
4. *Ut unum sint,* 97.

3

ous and remarkable. Modest reactions were given in the spring of 2003 in the form of a consultation as well as in May 2004 at a greater symposium at the International Bridgettine Centre in Farfa Sabina, where professional ecumenists and church officials of different denominational origin from the Nordic countries, Germany, France, Belgium, Italy, and the USA gathered in order to discuss the Petrine ministry as an instrument for universal church unity and other essential issues. The atmosphere of these events was extremely open, and the papers and discussions revealed a decisive consent and will on the part of all (Catholic and non-Catholic) participants to rethink and re-examine the doctrinal statements on papacy that continue to cause so much ecumenical difficulty. It was stressed that present Catholic theology finds a re-reception of Vatican I not only necessary, but also legitimate, simply because its definitions are commonly misunderstood even within the Catholic Church and imply obvious shortcomings due to historical circumstances. On the grounds of this basic conviction the concepts of universal jurisdiction and infallibility appear in a new critical light.

Thus, ecumenical progress is primarily to be achieved through *re-lecture* and re-reception of the First Vatican Council and the doctrines of papal primacy and infallibility. According to the hermeneutic rules, though, doctrines are to be understood in the sense in which they were declared. "... is sensus perpetuo est retinendus, quem semel declaravit sancta mater Ecclesia ..." (DS 3020). However, faith and understanding are interrelated to the effect that progress of insight into what has been once defined and handed down through history is possible. History of doctrine is also a history of interpretation and understanding. In this perspective a *re-lecture,* that is, a re-reception, does not question the validity of conciliar decisions, but interprets them in ever-new situations and contexts.

Four guidelines were mentioned as important for this process:

(a) The doctrine of papal primacy is to be integrated into the whole of Catholic ecclesiology. No doctrine must be seen in isolation, but always within the whole of the doctrinal system (cf. the *hierarchia veritatum*). This integration of primacy into ecclesiology was intended by both Vatican I and Vatican II. However, the former was interrupted by the Franco-Prussian War; the latter did not fully succeed in harmonizing the doctrines of primacy and infallibility with new ecclesiological tendencies (the concept of the church as *communio,* the significance of the local church, and the sacramental understanding of episcopacy).

(b) The doctrine of papal primacy is to be integrated into the whole of tradition. The church remains through all centuries and in all councils the same. The Holy Spirit does not contradict himself, and what was right in the first millennium cannot be wrong in the second. Therefore the *communio*-ecclesiology can possibly be seen as the hermeneutical framework for the interpretation of Vatican I.

(c) In terms of the hermeneutical principle of a new actual interpretation, the doctrine of primacy and infallibility is to be re-received with regard to the distinction between its historical form and its permanent authoritative content. The formulations of the Vatican doctrines are not the only possible expressions of what was meant to be of authentic validity for all future generations. The concept of absolute sovereignty, by which papal primacy was defined under the stress of severe political difficulties, is thus no longer receivable. The problem is not the dogma itself, but its maximalistic interpretation. What is permanently authoritative, however, is the conviction that the pope is free to act according to the actual and ever-changing necessities of the church. To that effect the juridical statements of Vatican I could be interpreted as aiming to identify the Petrine ministry as *episkopē*.

(d) The Petrine ministry must be interpreted according to the gospel. Authority in the church can only claim, not what is based only on human traditions, but that which can be traced back to Scripture itself (the problem of *ius divinum*). However, what is important is not merely the biblical foundation, but rather the understanding and practice of the Petrine ministry in accordance with the gospel, i.e., to conceive papal ministry as service and not as dominion (Matt. 20:28).

Lutheran participants, in turn, signaled a corresponding openness and readiness to listen to the Catholic concern of papacy and to re-examine their own tradition critically and constructively. At first Martin Luther saw no contradiction between his endeavors towards reform of the church and acceptance of papal ministry. After 1520, however, his statements on papacy were characterized by ferocious attacks on the papal institution and on the pope himself as Antichrist. But even then Luther seemed to regard papacy as a possibility in the church — on the condition of a reform and renewal according to the gospel. He was not just open in principle to the theme of papal ministry, but to this ministry itself. In short: radical rejection and conditional acceptance.

Luther's occasional openness must, however, be interpreted in relation to his extremely radical and devastating critique of papacy as an anti-Christian institution. The Antichrist-verdict can be seen as a biblical abbreviation for fundamental and precise theological reproaches against the papacy of his time. The pope was understood as Antichrist, because he claimed the exclusive right to interpret the Scripture and to add new doctrines and requests with the same authority as the Bible, and finally because Christians could not be saved without being obedient to him. These accusations did not reject papacy as such, but certain characteristics of the papal office as it was exercised at the time of Luther. His critique, therefore, did not imply a judgment in principle, but a judgment of facts. The possibility of a renewed papal ministry was not excluded.

Melanchthon criticized primarily the papal claim of *ius divinum*, especially in its maximalistic interpretation. This means that the *ius divinum* was not rejected in principle and under all circumstances. A papacy reformed and renewed in the light of the gospel still appeared to be possible. In conclusion, the Reformation looked upon the papal ministry within the framework of a *Kontroverstheologie*, within which a positive, principal acceptance of papacy still appeared to be possible.

This perspective has changed in the ecumenical dialogues of our time. The prevailing principle is now the idea of universal church unity and the search for a ministry through which this unity may be promoted. Should a personal ministry possibly be established as an instrument for such unity, and could the papacy, as we now know it, possibly serve and further the unity among Christians? Because the visible unity of the universal church is at stake, the issue of the Petrine ministry and its shape according to the gospel is not only a possible, but a *necessarily possible* theme with regard to both the Reformers and the Catholic-Lutheran dialogue.

However, a fundamental difference between Catholic and Lutheran understanding of this Petrine ministry seems to remain: Whereas Catholics interpret papacy to be necessary, Lutherans would rather concede this ministry to be of an optional nature and to have a possible function. Here also the problem of the possibility of revision of papal decisions arises. This raises the question: Is it conceivable that papal authority (primacy) be exercised in and extended to different churches while these communities still maintain different forms of ecclesiality (as is the case, e.g., with regard to the Eastern Catholic churches having their own canonical rite)? However, if yes, what does that mean *in concreto*?

Although the Farfa conferences thus manifested a decisive readiness of both Catholics and Lutherans to re-examine their respective traditions in the light of biblical and historical research with the aim of possibly reaching a common understanding of the Petrine ministry,[5] tendencies to support alternative solutions were also clearly voiced. This seemed all the more natural, as the Lutheran as well as the Protestant tradition as a whole in the last analysis resorts to the indefectibility of the church in matters of ultimate definitions of truth rather than to an infallible teaching ministry (cf. the scanty remarks above). From this indefectibility results the obligation of the church to actually define what it means *in concreto* to be held in the truth.

The Roman Catholic Church responds to that challenge through the infallible teaching ministry, the Lutherans by means of calling a *status confessionis*. Thus both confessions, though differently, teach authoritatively and testify to their Christian faith over against the world. The theological concern of the doctrine of papal infallibility — parallel to the institution of *status confessionis* — is to underline the necessity of having an authority able to authentically formulate ultimate binding definitions of truth. Among Lutherans and Catholics it is not controversial that authoritative teaching is necessary, but the way in which this is actually done is highly disputed. Whereas Catholicism ties the *sensus fidelium* so vehemently to papal infallibility that the prophetic office of the church is at risk of becoming a voice immanent to the ecclesial system, the Lutheran churches are in danger of individualizing the *sensus fidelium,* with the result that authoritative teaching becomes impossible.

Both extremes are to be avoided. Papal infallibility appears to be theologically meaningful and ecumenically acceptable only when interpreted in the hermeneutic context of ecclesial indefectibility and thus applied to the church. To that effect, *indefectibilitas ecclesiae* and *infallibilitas papae* are not

---

5. Especially the 2004 symposium explored the roots of the Petrine ministry on the basis of a study of the Scriptures and early church traditions and examined the historical development of papal authority and jurisdiction and the Protestant reaction to the post-Reformation development of papal authority. Furthermore, the implications of the Lutheran-Catholic dialogues (on justification, ministry, and church) for the understanding of the Petrine ministry were considered. The conference took a look at the preliminary reactions to the papal encyclical *Ut unum sint* and reflected on differently balanced ecclesiology(-ies) as parameter for the concept and practice of papal ministry from a Catholic and Lutheran as well as from an Orthodox perspective. On these solid grounds the symposium finally ventured to move *towards* a preliminary attempt to formulate what Catholics and Lutherans are able to state *in common* on the nature and function of Petrine ministry — although the formulation of such a definition is evidently still premature.

compatible concepts. From the indefectibility of the church results the universal council as the forum, in which the truth-finding process takes place and the church ever anew identifies herself as the *communio sancta et apostolica,* remaining in the truth and living towards the truth. This points to a way of finding and defining the truth other than that of infallible papal decisions, a way that shows more coherence with the common faith in the indefectibility of the church and takes the *sensus fidelium* and the historical character of truth seriously. Ultimate definitions of truth are taken in and by the council, but not without the pope. He would, however, fail to define such ultimately binding doctrines without the council. In short, the Farfa gatherings showed an amazing readiness among Lutherans and Catholics to somehow reach a common position with regard to papacy and infallibility, yet it did so by pointing unmistakably to the indispensable dependence of any papal decision on the conciliar nature of the church.

This kind of reflection has been initiated in the hope that the Farfa Centre in cooperation with professional university and seminary ecumenists may offer — unofficially, though not without the participation of church officials and ecclesial institutions — its modest contribution to the unity of our churches that is now needed more than ever in order that the world may believe. In the firm conviction that ecclesial unity is many-faceted and dependent on a number of different factors and above all deeply conditioned by the different church traditions, the Farfa Centre, however, does not want to attain church unity without penetrating and delving thoroughly into the serious theological problems that remain keep dividing us. Ecumenical dialogue never ceases to be a dialogue on faith and truth. *Tolle assertiones, et christianismum tulisti,* as Luther confrontationally pointed out in his dispute against Erasmus. This does not make the dialogue any easier, but by never neglecting to speak the truth in love it renders interconfessional endeavors more trustworthy and — in the longer perspective — prospective of more serious rapprochement.

Farfa Continuation

The positive outcome of the events of the years 2003 and 2004 has encouraged the Academic Committee of the Farfa Centre to initiate a more permanent dialogue on the Petrine ministry and its bearing on Catholic-Lutheran fellowship. Therefore the decision was taken to create a *Permanent Working Group on the Petrine Ministry* and to give it a five-year assignment. The Farfa

Foundation provided subsequently the financial means necessary for this period. This initiative is doubtless in keeping with the original vision of the Centre to reconsider the theological grounds of church fellowship and to develop possible models for re-establishing the unity between Rome and the churches of the Reformation. Several conferences and symposia sponsored by the Centre have reflected on the practical implications for church unity of what has truly developed in the theological field since the Second Vatican Council between the Roman Catholic Church and the Lutheran churches. To be sure, the last four decades have not been without success, and much progress has certainly been made with respect to overcoming traditional obstacles to church fellowship. Yet, this very fellowship in terms of eucharistic communion is still impossible. Even more than ever since the conclusion of the Second Vatican Council, it presently seems to fade away and disappear into a distant and uncertain future marked in both Catholicism and Lutheranism by church political opposition to a closer drawing together between the confessions. *Grosso modo,* it may be maintained that in reality only the one complex of ordained ministry, including essentially papal infallibility and universal jurisdiction, blocks the road to fellowship between Catholics and Lutherans.

Theologically the Lutherans argue that once an agreement is reached in the understanding of justification by faith (for them the *articulus stantis et cadentis ecclesiae*), the re-establishment of the broken unity follows by necessity. This has in fact been the case since the *Joint Declaration on the Doctrine of Justification.* The Catholics, on the other hand, maintain that there may be other criteria and other *articuli* by which the church stands and falls, first and foremost the understanding of the ordained ministry and, more specifically, the office of episcopacy, including in the last analysis the papal ministry.

In the Catholic-Lutheran dialogue there is a growing awareness that Catholics will not welcome Lutherans at the eucharistic table unless some sort of common understanding of the Petrine ministry and some kind of Lutheran recognition of papal authority are reached. This, in turn, is rejected by wide circles of world Lutheranism. Lutheran theology in recent years has shown serious efforts to conceive episcopal office as an integrated and necessary element of ecclesiology, although heavy deficits with regard to an actual and concrete shaping of the indefectibility of the church are vividly experienced. Lutheran churches have not been left unaffected by the Roman claim that for the sake of unity a top-level — papal — ministry is necessary, possibly even endowed with some sort of infallibility, much less however with universal jurisdiction. Papal authority is clearly not only *an*, but rather *the* important *quaestio disputanda* in the area of Lutheran-Catholic encounter.[6]

However, commitment to traditional thought patterns promotes the immobility and inertness in both confessions and prevents them from really taking courageous steps to surmount church political resistances and walk towards new forms of common life. As little as the official dialogues have achieved so far in providing a breakthrough, so much more effort is needed to achieve Christian unity in an increasingly secularized world.

Under these circumstances it may be appropriate and promising to launch a dialogue on private initiative, yet not — as already stated — without connection to official conversations as sponsored by the Vatican Council for Promoting Christian Unity and the Lutheran World Federation. In calling renowned scholars from Scandinavia and Italy to form a Permanent Working Group on the Petrine Ministry, the Farfa Centre hopes to pave the road to a rapprochement between the Christian confessions in an area that increasingly proves to be theologically and ecclesially crucial and at the same time poses an impediment to Christian unity. A doctrinal dialogue with the aim of clarifying the fundamental and critical theological questions regarding the Petrine ministry raised by the Reformation would convincingly promote a common Catholic-Lutheran understanding of the Petrine ministry and its possible role in a future united church — evidently all the more so, because the Reformers certainly criticized, yet do not seem to reject papacy and papal authority in principle. The following papers, given at the conferences in 2003 and 2004, are intended to serve as background material for the Permanent Working Group.

---

6. Karl Rahner proclaimed already thirty years ago provocatively that all church-dividing issues in terms of theology ("auf der Ebene der hohen Fachtheologie") were in fact solved — with the explicit exception of the Roman Primacy, Karl Rahner, *Schriften zur Theologie* (Zürich: Benziger, 1975), vol. 12, p. 559.

SCRIPTURE AND PATRISTICS

Petrine Ministry in the New Testament and in the Early Patristic Traditions

John P. Meier

Introduction

The theme of our symposium is posed as a question: *How* can the Petrine ministry serve the unity of the universal church? The focus of this first session is the Petrine ministry in the New Testament and the early patristic traditions.[1] And the concrete context of our meeting here at Farfa is the mis-

---

1. The bibliography on Peter, both the historical person and the theological symbol, is vast. A few works that can supply the reader with an overview of the problems and further bibliography are Oscar Cullmann, *Peter: Disciple — Apostle — Martyr*, 2nd ed. (London: SCM, 1962); Raymond E. Brown, Karl P. Donfried, and John Reumann, eds., *Peter in the New Testament* (Minneapolis: Augsburg; New York: Paramus; Toronto: Paulist, 1973); Wolfgang Dietrich, *Das Petrusbild der lukanischen Schriften* (Stuttgart: Kohlhammer, 1972); Jack Dean Kingsbury, "The Figure of Peter in Matthew's Gospel as a Theological Problem," *JBL* 98 (1979): 67-83; Rudolf Pesch, *Simon-Petrus. Geschichte und geschichtliche Bedeutung des ersten Jüngers Jesu Christ* (Stuttgart: Hiersemann, 1980); Arthur H. Maynard, "The Role of Peter in the Fourth Gospel," *NTS* 30 (1984): 531-48; Rudolf Schnackenburg, "Petrus im Matthäusevangelium," *A cause de l'évangile*, Jacques Dupont Festschrift (LD 123; Paris: Cerf, 1985), pp. 107-25; Carsten Peter Thiede, *Simon Peter: From Galilee to Rome* (Grand Rapids: Academie/Zondervan, 1986); Kevin Quast, *Peter and the Beloved Disciple: Figures for a Community in Crisis* (Sheffield: JSOT, 1989); Arthur J. Droge, "The Status of Peter in the Fourth Gospel: John 18:10-11," *JBL* 109 (1990): 307-11; Arlo J. Nau, *Peter in Matthew* (Collegeville, MN: Liturgical Press, 1992); Pheme Perkins, *Peter: Apostle for the Whole Church* (Columbia: University of South Carolina Press, 1994); João Tavares de Lima, *"Tu serás chamado Kēphas." Estudo exegético sobre Pedro no quarto evangelho* (Rome: Gregorian University, 1994); Christian Grappe, *Images de Pierre aux*

sion of this International Centre to foster the unity of the church, especially within an emerging united Europe.

Granted therefore this question, this focus, and this context, I would like to preface my own presentation with a general observation. In the last hundred years or so, Christianity in Western Europe and North America has faced a relatively new phenomenon: the mass education of the Christian — or post-Christian — laity. While knowledge of history on the part of the general population is not what one would wish — especially in the United States — still, the general populace is imbued, at least in a vague way, with a historical-critical sensibility. Hence a church's theological claims about its past history will not receive today the same sort of uncritical acceptance by the laity that such claims might have received from medieval or early modern peasants. This modern critical sensibility as a product of mass education will no doubt spread increasingly to Eastern Europe as the European Union expands and matures.

Now all this is to the good. Only an ecclesiastical leader who felt insecure about the historical veracity of his own tradition would be threatened by this increase of a historical sensibility on the part of the general population. At the same time, we would be naïve to ignore the challenge that this heightened historical sense creates. In the early modern period, the churches of Western Europe had to struggle to find an effective way to proclaim the Christian faith to educated elites in the Age of Reason, then in the Enlightenment, and then in an age marked by ever-accelerating scientific, social, and economic developments. For the last hundred years or more, this challenge has become ever more severe as the churches have had to address no longer just an educated elite but an educated general population knowledgeable of history.

I mention this widespread and obvious challenge in order to frame a more specific challenge posed by this state of affairs to the Roman Catholic Church. The challenge is this: Granted the phenomenon of mass education and the general knowledge of history that such education instills, how is the Roman Catholic Church today to articulate a historically responsible account of the origins of the papacy to a laity that is better educated than any laity in the first 1800 years of the church's history? A papacy that cannot give a credible historical account of its own origins can hardly hope to be a catalyst for unity among divided Christians.

---

deux premiers siècles (Paris: Presses Universitaires de France, 1995); Joachim Gnilka, *Petrus und Rom* (Freiburg: Herder, 2002); Fred Lapham, *Peter: The Myth, the Man and the Writings* (London: Sheffield Academic Press, 2003).

Fortunately, progress has already been made in this area. For decades now, ecumenical studies like *Peter in the New Testament* (1973), produced by biblical scholars in the United States, and serious monographs by Catholic scholars such as Rudolf Pesch's *Simon-Petrus* (1980) and Joachim Gnilka's *Petrus and Rom* (2002), have prepared the way on the academic front. One cannot and should not expect that all of this scholarship would immediately be taken up by Catholic authorities into official documents of the magisterium. In my opinion, though, it is not without significance that neither the *Catechism of the Catholic Church* nor Pope John Paul II's groundbreaking encyclical *Ut unum sint* employed certain problematic assertions like "St. Peter was the first Pope." Granted, academics may smile at such an assertion, yet it is still often heard in the popular media, to say nothing of homilies and catechetical instruction. Hence it is at least noteworthy that some recent authoritative documents of the Roman Catholic Church have avoided certain types of claims that would not hold up under the scrutiny of critical historical research.

The question I pose in my presentation this morning is whether this experiment in nuance, in historically responsible articulations of Rome's claims, can be pursued further by the Roman communion. To rephrase my own question in light of the grand question of our meeting: How can the Petrine ministry serve the unity of the universal church by presenting to educated persons of the twenty-first century an account of the origins of the papacy that is both historically credible and faithful to Catholic convictions?

I would suggest that one approach would be for the Roman church to adopt a catechesis that honestly presented the multiple historical matrices out of which the phenomenon of the papacy arose. Such an admission and explanation of these multiple matrices would demonstrate to an educated audience, Catholic and non-Catholic alike, that, while insisting on the essential importance of the Petrine ministry for the life of the church, Rome was not engaging in historical obfuscation or in some historical fantasy labeled "tradition."

In making this suggestion, I use the word "matrix" rather than words like "source," "influence," "factor," or "origin" to stress an organic, generative process that may in some ways be likened to procreation, gestation, and full birth. The image of "matrix" avoids the notion that the papacy suddenly appeared on the scene or was created all at once within a given day or year or decade. Like any other grand and long-lived historical institution, its coming to be or coming to birth involved a laborious process. At the same time, the image of "multiple matrices" is purposely paradoxical. The developed papacy arises not from a single source but from the interaction of several sources over the span of a century or more. Needless to say, as a Catholic I view this century-long process not as some historical accident or mistake but as the expression of God's will and providence active in history, as he directs the course of events according to his saving purpose over the centuries. We need not be surprised that, just as Rome was not built in a day, neither was the Roman papacy.

What, then, are the multiple historical matrices that give birth to the papacy? While different scholars would no doubt offer different enumerations, for the sake of convenience I distinguish — however artificially — the following six matrices: (1) the Simon of history; (2) the Peter of faith presented in the canonical books of the New Testament; (3) the continuing memory of Simon Peter, as reflected in the earliest patristic literature, which gives us the first indications of the prominence and/or leadership of the church of Rome; (4) the rise of the monepiscopate in the Roman church sometime in the second century; (5) the striking assertion of Roman leadership by its bishop Victor toward the end of the second century; and (6) at the end of the second century, the beginning of theological reflection on and argument about the key Petrine texts of the New Testament.

The Six Historical Matrices of the Papacy

Within the time allotted, I can sketch only briefly the nature and interaction of these six matrices:

The Simon of History

If scholars rightly distinguish between the Jesus of history and the Christ of faith — however that distinction is more precisely defined — then they likewise should distinguish between the Simon of history and the Peter of faith.[2] The New Testament writings present us with a portrait of Peter shaped by Christian faith and history, and the same methods used to construct a hypothetical historical Jesus can be used to construct a hypothetical historical Si-

2. This distinction is followed in Gnilka's treatment. The historical Simon's career is traced in Gnilka, *Petrus und Rom,* pp. 31-141; then the theological portrait of Peter in each of the four gospels is outlined on pp. 142-78.

mon as the starting point of our inquiry. If the impact of Jesus Christ on all subsequent history is due at least in part to the fact that faith in Jesus Christ is not faith in a timeless deity or mythic hero but in a historical Palestinian Jew of the first century, the same is analogically true of Simon Peter. We are not dealing with shadowy figures like Philip or Bartholomew, whose names were hijacked by later Christian apocrypha.

In volume three of my series, *A Marginal Jew*, I try to lay out what can be reasonably affirmed of the historical Simon.[3] Simon (or "Shimeon," to use the Hebrew form of his name)[4] was a first-century Galilean fisherman who, perhaps like his brother Andrew, originally came from the town of Bethsaida east of the Jordan. Simon seems to have settled with his wife and mother-in-law in the Jewish town of Capernaum on the northwest coast of the lake. He may have first come to know Jesus of Nazareth when both spent some time in the circle of the disciples of John the Baptist. Around A.D. 28, Jesus called Simon away from his fishing business to follow Jesus as a permanent disciple. Interestingly, all the various gospel stories present Simon as being called to discipleship not in splendid isolation but as part of a larger group being called at the same time. Nevertheless, *Simon did function as the spokesman and/or leader of the inner circle of disciples established by Jesus, namely, "the Twelve." Presumably this is why all four New Testament lists of the Twelve, for all their differences, always name Simon first.*

At some point during the public ministry, Jesus conferred or confirmed Simon's second name or nickname or title, i.e., *Kēp'* in Aramaic (transliterated as *Kēphas* in Greek and translated as *Petros*). The Aramaic

3. John P. Meier, *A Marginal Jew: Rethinking the Historical Jesus*, Anchor Bible Reference Library; 3 vols. (New York: Doubleday, 1991, 1994, 2001), vol. 3, pp. 221-45.

4. Joseph A. Fitzmyer, "Aramaic *Kēpha* and Peter's Name in the New Testament," in *To Advance the Gospel* (New York: Crossroad, 1981), pp. 112-24, esp. p. 112, supports the commonly held view that "the use of both Symeon and Simon [of Peter in the NT] reflects the well-known custom among Jews of that time of giving the name of a famous patriarch or personage of the Old Testament to a male child along with a similar-sounding Greek/Roman name." Theoretically possible, though less likely, is the view that, during his fishing days in Galilee in the 20s and 30s of the first century, Peter simply bore the Semitic name of Symeon *(Šimōn)*, while the Greek Simon was introduced to designate him when the Gospel story was first told in Greek. On Simon as a common name for Jews around the turn of the era, see Joseph A. Fitzmyer, "The Name Simon," in *Essays on the Semitic Background of the New Testament* (Missoula, MT: Scholars, 1974), pp. 105-12. For a full listing of the occurrences of "Simon," "Symeon," "Peter," and "Simon Peter" in the gospels, see Pesch, *Simon-Petrus*, pp. 25-27.

noun *kēp'* means "rock," "rocky crag," or "stone," and is attested around the time of Jesus in the Dead Sea documents.[5] Scholars sometimes miss the point that *kēp'* was not a proper name in first-century Jewish Palestine; rather, it was simply a common noun meaning rock or stone. Unlike the name *Boanerges,* given by Jesus to the sons of Zebedee, *Kēp'* turned out to have a long and fateful history. In this it resembled the Aramaic word *mšî* ("anointed one"), which was applied to Jesus and which in Greek was both transliterated as *Messias* and translated as *Christos.* As *Christos* became Jesus' second name in Greek, so did *Petros* for Simon. So important was the Aramaic title in each case that its meaning as well as its Aramaic form had to be preserved.

Not a great deal more can be said about the historical Simon during the public ministry. As spokesman of the Twelve, Simon Peter made a powerful profession of faith in Jesus at some critical moment in the public min-

---

5. Pre-Christian documentation of the meaning of Aramaic *kp* can be found in various Qumran fragments: 11QtgJob 32:1 (translating Hebrew Job 39:1); 11QtgJob 33:9 (translating Hebrew Job 39:28); 4QEn^e 4 iii 19; 4QEn^c 4:3; 4QEn^a 1 ii 8. The Greek feminine noun *petra* means "a large and solid rock." Strictly speaking, therefore, *petros* and *petra* should be distinguished in meaning; however, some scholars claim that they were often used interchangeably. Sustaining this position is Oscar Cullmann, *"petra,"* in *TDNT* 6 (1968): 95-99; cf. Fitzmyer, "Aramaic *Kepha,*" pp. 121-32, esp. p. 131; and emphatically Chrys C. Caragounis, *Peter and the Rock* (Berlin/New York: De Gruyter, 1989), pp. 9-16. However, Peter Lampe argues by way of a corrective that the use of *petros* in the sense of "rock" was not all that common in ancient Greek; see his "Das Spiel mit dem Petrusnamen — Matt. xvi.18," *NTS* 25 (1978-79): 227-45, esp. 240-41; see also Pesch, *Simon-Petrus,* pp. 27-34 (notably under the influence of Lampe). As for the use of these words as proper names, Fitzmyer ("Aramaic *Kepha,*" pp. 127-30) points to an occurrence of *kp* in an Aramaic papyrus from Elephantine in Egypt that dates from the late fifth century B.C. He argues forcefully that the word is used in this text as an Aramaic proper name; but, as he notes, not all scholars are convinced of this position. More to the point, no occurrence of *kp* as an Aramaic proper name for a man has been so far documented in Palestine around the turn of the era. As for *petros,* despite the claims of Caragounis (*Peter and the Rock,* pp. 17-25), no firm and unambiguous evidence for its use as the proper name of a man can be dated to the first half of the first century A.D. For critiques of Caragounis's positions, see the reviews of his book by Gérard Claudel, *Bib* 71 (1990): 570-76; John P. Meier, *CBQ* 53 (1991): 492-93. On Peter's name in its various forms, see Cullmann, *"petra,"* pp. 95-99; Cullmann, *"petra,"* pp. 100-112; J. K. Elliott, "*Kēphas: Simn Petros: ho Petros:* An Examination of New Testament Usage," *NovT* 14 (1972): 241-56; Fitzmyer, "Aramaic *Kepha,*" pp. 121-32; Caragounis, *Peter and the Rock;* Timothy Wiarda, "Simon, Jesus of Nazareth, Son of Jonah, Son of John: Realistic Detail in the Gospels and Acts," *NTS* 40 (1994): 196-209.

istry. Yet Peter's role in the inner circle was not all positive. We have an isolated saying in which Jesus assails Peter with the withering rebuke, "Get behind me, Satan, for your mind is set not on divine but on human things." This chiaroscuro picture of Peter, worthy of Caravaggio, continues into the last days of Jesus (around the year 30) and into the early days of the church. Peter was present at the Last Supper and at Jesus' arrest in Gethsemane. When questioned about his relationship with Jesus, Peter panicked and denied he ever knew Jesus. Yet not many days later, this discredited Peter claimed that he had seen the risen Jesus. Within short order, Peter regathered the scattered disciples and became the leader of a nascent group of "Messianic Jews" or "Nazoreans" in Jerusalem. His leadership soon involved journeys around Judea and Samaria. During the 30s and early 40s, Peter's activity as leader attracted the unhealthy attention of other-minded Jewish leaders, including the high priest and King Herod Agrippa I. After a couple of incarcerations in Jerusalem, Peter apparently found it expedient to spread the Christian gospel at a greater distance.

While he was still in Jerusalem, Peter was visited for two weeks by Saul alias Paul after the latter had become a Christian (Gal. 1:18). For a while in Jerusalem, Peter formed a kind of *troika* with James the brother of Jesus and John the son of Zebedee; it was with this *troika* in particular that Paul, around the year 49, brokered the agreement that acknowledged his circumcision-free mission to the Gentiles (Gal. 2:6-10). Some time later, during a visit to Syrian Antioch, Peter was embroiled in a dispute with Paul over table fellowship between Jewish Christians and Gentile Christians (Gal. 2:11-14). After that, with the possible exception of a sojourn in the church at Corinth in the early 50s, the historical Peter, as far as he is knowable from the pages of the New Testament, disappears from view,

The Peter of Faith

Closely interconnected with this first matrix and not always distinguishable from it is the second matrix, the faith portraits of Simon Peter presented by various New Testament books. The pattern of light and dark that we found in the historical Simon continues in the Peter of faith. His high profile in the gospels and epistles is not always a positive one. Mark and Matthew go out of their way to make him a negative archetype of failed discipleship in a number of scenes. The "Get behind me Satan" logion is positioned right after Peter's profession of faith in Jesus' messiahship. Jesus' walking on the water is paralleled by Peter's sinking into the same. The embarrassing historical fact of Peter's denial becomes a dark drama of Jesus' dire prophecy at the Last Supper, fulfilled by Peter's *triple* denial in the courtyard of the high priest just as Jesus is confessing the truth.

All the more startling, then, are the various ways in which the gospels give Peter unparalleled prominence in a positive sense. Even stark, dark, laconic Mark makes Peter, along with Andrew, the first to be called by Jesus. Peter is the first absolutely in the list of the Twelve and the first disciple to understand the dangerous half-truth of Jesus' messiahship during the public ministry. Even the young man at the empty tomb in Mark 16 gives the former denier special attention as he orders the women: "But go tell his disciples and Peter. . . ."

Much more weighty are the three distinct solemn charges that Jesus gives Peter, charges found respectively in Matthew, Luke, and John. Perhaps sufficient reflection is not given to the paradox that all three evangelists include a special saying about Peter and yet each saying is strikingly different from the other two. The most famous of the three, Matthew 16:17-19,[6] which

---

6. For a survey of opinions in the various periods of interpretation of Matthew 16:16-19, see Joseph Ludwig, *Die Primatworte Mt 16,18.19 in der altkirchlichen Exegese* (Münster: Aschendorff, 1952); Franz Obrist, *Echtheitsfragen und Deutung der Primatsstelle Mt 16,18f. in der deutschen protestantischen Theologie der letzten dreissig Jahre* (Münster: Aschendorff, 1961); Joseph A. Burgess, *A History of the Exegesis of Matthew 16:17-19 from 1781 to 1965* (Ann Arbor, MI: Edwards Brothers, 1976). For a sampling of present-day approaches, see Anton Vögtle, "Messiasbekenntnis und Petrusverheissung. Zur Komposition Mt 16,13-23 par.," *BZ* 1 (1957): 252-72; "Zum Problem der Herkunft von 'Mt 16,17-19,'" *Orientierung an Jesus* (Freiburg/Basel/Vienna: Herder, 1973), pp. 372-93; Oscar Cullmann, "L'apôtre Pierre instrument du diable et instrument de Dieu," in A. J. B. Higgins, ed., *New Testament Essays* (Manchester: Manchester University Press, 1959), pp. 94-105; Johannes Ringger, "Das Felsenwort," in Maximilian Roesle and Oscar Cullmann, eds., *Begegnung der Christen* (Stuttgart: Evangelisches Verlagswerk; Frankfurt: Knecht, 1959), pp. 271-347; Josef Schmid, "Petrus 'der Fels' und die Petrusgestalt der Urgemeinde," in Roesle and Cullmann, *Begegnung*, pp. 347-59; André Legault, "L'authenticité de Mt 16:17-19 et le silence de Marc et de Luc," in *L'église dans le bible* (Bruges: Desclée de Brouwer, 1962), pp. 35-52; Ernst Haenchen, "Die Komposition von Mk vii 27–ix 1 und par.," *NovT* 6 (1963): 81-109; Kenneth L. Carroll, "'Thou Art Peter,'" *NovT* 6 (1963): 268-76; Robert H. Gundry, "The Narrative Framework of Matthew xvi 17-19," *NovT* 7 (1964): 1-9; Jacques Dupont, "La révélation du Fils de Dieu en faveur de Pierre (Mt 16,17) et de Paul (Ga 1,16)," *RSR* 52 (1964): 411-20; François Refoulé, "Primauté de Pierre dans les évangiles," *RevScRel* 38 (1964): 1-41; Erich Dinkler, "Petrusbekenntnis und Satanswort. Das Problem der Messianität Jesu," *Zeit und Geschichte* (Tübingen: Mohr [Siebeck] 1964), pp. 127-53; Reinhart Hummel, *Die Ausein-*

Matthew situates near Caesarea Philippi during the public ministry, felicitates Simon Bar Jona as the recipient of a special revelation from Jesus' heavenly Father. Just as Simon has conferred the titles Messiah and Son of God on Jesus, so Jesus reciprocates by conferring the title *Petros* on Simon and by

---

andersetzung zwischen Kirche und Judentum im Matthäusevangelium, 2nd ed. (Munich: Kaiser, 1966), pp. 59-64; Brown et al., *Peter in the New Testament*, pp. 83-101; André Feuillet, "'Chercher à persuader Dieu' (Ga 1:10a). Le début de l'Epître aux Galates et la scène matthéenne de Césarée de Philippe," *NovT* 12 (1970): 350-60; Günther Bornkamm, "The Authority to 'Bind' and 'Loose' in the Church in Matthew's Gospel," in Dikran Hadidian et al., eds., *Jesus and Man's Hope*, 2 vols. (Pittsburgh: Pittsburgh Theological Seminary, 1970, 1971), vol. 1, pp. 37-50; Georg Strecker, *Der Weg der Gerechtigkeit*, 3rd ed. (Göttingen: Vandenhoeck & Ruprecht, 1971), pp. 201-6; Paul Hoffmann, "Der Petrus-Primat im Matthäusevangelium," in Joachim Gnilka, ed., *Neues Testament und Kirche* (Freiburg/Basel/Vienna: Herder, 1974), pp. 94-114; Max Wilcox, "Peter and the Rock: A Fresh Look at Matthew xvi.17-19," *NTS* 22 (1975-76): 73-88; Christoph Kähler, "Zur Form- und Traditionsgeschichte von Matth. xvi.17-19," *NTS* 23 (1976-77): 36-58; Franz Mussner, *Petrus und Paulus — Pole der Einheit* (Freiburg/Basel/Vienna: Herder, 1976), pp. 11-22; Ferdinand Hahn, "Die Petrusverheissung Mt 16,18f.," in Karl Kertelge, ed., *Das kirchliche Amt im Neuen Testament* (Darmstadt: Wissenschaftliche Buchgesellschaft, 1977), pp. 543-61; John P. Meier, *The Vision of Matthew* (New York/Ramsey/Toronto: Paulist, 1979), pp. 106-21; Lampe, "Das Spiel"; J.-M. van Cangh and M. van Esbroeck, "La primauté de Pierre (Mt 16,16-19) et son contexte judaïque," *RTL* 11 (1980): 310-24; Stephen Gero, "The Gates or the Bars of Hades? A Note on Matthew 16.18," *NTS* 27 (1981): 411-14; M.-A. Chevallier, "'Tu es Pierre, tu es le nouvel Abraham' (Mt 16/18)," *ETR* 57 (1982): 375-87; J. Duncan M. Derrett, "Binding and Loosing (Matt 16:19; 18:18; John 29[sic]:23)," *JBL* 102 (1983): 112-17; Bernard P. Robinson, "Peter and His Successors: Tradition and Redaction in Matthew 16.17-19," *JSNT* 21 (1984): 85-104; Pierre Grelot, "L'origine de Matthieu 16,16-19," in *A cause de l'évangile* (Paris: Cerf, 1985), pp. 91-105; Richard H. Hiers, "'Binding' and 'Loosing': The Matthean Authorizations," *JBL* 104 (1985): 233-50; Herbert W. Basser, "Derrett's 'Binding' Reopened," *JBL* 104 (1985): 297-300; Augustine Stock, "Is Matthew's Presentation of Peter Ironic?" *BTB* 17 (1987): 64-69; Joachim Gnilka, "'Tu es, Petrus.' Die Petrus-Verheissung in Mt 16,17-19," *MTZ* 38 (1987): 3-17; P. Grelot, "'Sur cette pierre je bâtirai mon Eglise' (Mt 16,18b)," *NRT* 109 (1987): 641-59; Gérard Claudel, *La confession de Pierre* (Paris: Gabalda, 1988); Joel Marcus, "The Gates of Hades and the Keys of the Kingdom (Matt. 16:18-19)," *CBQ* 50 (1988): 443-55; Hildebrecht Hommel, "Die Tore des Hades," *ZNW* 80 (1989): 124-25; Caragounis, *Peter and the Rock*, pp. 61-119; W. D. Davies and Dale C. Allison, *The Gospel According to Saint Matthew* (Edinburgh: T. & T. Clark, 1988), vol. 2, pp. 602-52; Ulrich Luz, "Das Primatwort Matthäus 16.17-19 aus wirkungsgeschichtlicher Sicht," *NTS* 37 (1991): 415-33; A. del Agua, "Derás narrativo del sobrenombre de 'Pedro' en el conjunto de Mt 16,17-19," *Salmanticensis* 39 (1992): 11-33; François Refoulé, "La Parallèle Matthieu 16/16-17 — Galates 1/15-16 réexaminé," *ETR* 67 (1992): 161-75; Christian Grappe, "Mt 16,17-19 et le récit de la Passion," *RHPR* 72 (1992): 33-40.

declaring that on this rock Jesus will build *his* church, firmly established against the powers of sin and death. Like the major-domo Eliachim in Isaiah 22:22, Peter is invested with the keys to the king's palace and so with the divinely ratified power to declare actions licit or illicit.

Quite different is the charge of the Lucan Jesus to Peter at the Last Supper (Luke 22:31).[7] As the prelude to Jesus' prediction of Peter's denial, Jesus reveals that Satan has sought from God the power to throw all the apostles into a crisis of faith as the eschatological struggle between good and evil reaches a climax in Jesus' passion and death. Faced with this threat to all the apostles, Jesus considers it sufficient to pray for Simon alone, that his faith may not fail completely. Once Simon repents and turns from his denial of Jesus, he is charged with the duty of strengthening the brethren in general.

The Fourth Gospel places its special Petrine logion in a resurrection appearance, after the miraculous catch of fish, in which Peter exercises a leading role.[8] Within the overarching symbolic context of a worldwide mission, of a church whose unity is strained by so many various members, and of a meal with eucharistic overtones, the risen Jesus three times gives a charge to Simon, who denied Jesus three times. Peter is to be the shepherd who feeds, tends, and guides *(poimaine)* the sheep of Jesus — even to the point of laying down his life in martyrdom like Jesus. This pastoral charge is all the more startling because the Fourth Evangelist insisted in chapter 10 of his gospel that Jesus alone is the Good Shepherd, no one else. The final redactor, to whom we probably owe chapter 21, is willing to have Peter continue this role of Jesus in the church, provided he also imitates Jesus' death for the flock. In all this, there is a curious echo of the Petrine tradition found in 1 Peter 5:1-2, where Peter, or more likely a disciple writing in his name, charges his fellow presbyters to shepherd *(poimanate)* the flock of God in a context of suffering and possible death.

In light of the very different images and emphases in the three Petrine logia of Matthew, Luke, and John, certain common elements are all the more striking. It is Jesus who always takes the initiative and speaks directly to a Pe-

---

7. For an overview of the problems in the text, see Meier, *A Marginal Jew*, vol. 3, pp. 238-42. My remarks are aimed especially against the position of Günter Klein, "Die Verleugnung des Petrus," in *Rekonstruktion und Interpretation* (Munich: Kaiser, 1969), pp. 49-98.

8. For detailed treatments of the many problems connected with John 21, see Raymond E. Brown, *The Gospel According to John (xiii–xxi)* (Garden City, NY: Doubleday, 1970), pp. 1066-1130; Rudolf Schnackenburg, *Das Johannesevangleium. III. Teil* (Freiburg: Herder, 1975), pp. 406-48.

ter who, in the larger context, has failed or will fail. Jesus charges Peter with a duty vis-à-vis not some local congregation but the body of believers at large: "*my* church," "*my* sheep," "the brethren" in general. *In my opinion, all three Petrine logia are post-Easter sayings of the risen Lord, reflecting what different streams of first-century Christianity expected from or saw in Peter.* This in turn raises a further question: Since all three gospels are written after Simon Peter has died, what is the point of inserting these weighty Petrine sayings at key points in the plot of each gospel?

These Petrine memories or expectations are not limited to the gospels. The Acts of the Apostles elaborate Luke's portrait of Peter in the post-Easter church. Of the Twelve, only Peter is allowed by Acts to deliver sermons on the Christian faith, always with resounding success when it comes to the common people. Acts makes sure that Peter steals Paul's thunder in converting the first Gentile, namely Cornelius. This conversion, not unlike Paul's, is recounted or remembered three times. Indeed, it is Peter's conversion of Cornelius, not the conversion of Paul, that is invoked by both Peter and James (Acts 15:7-9, 14) at the so-called council of Jerusalem to provide the necessary divine approval and precedent for Paul's circumcision-free mission.

Even Paul, for all his problems with Peter, testifies to Peter's special position in the early church. The creed Paul teaches his converts at Corinth and elsewhere testifies to Peter's special position in the early church as the first witness to see the risen Lord (1 Cor. 15:3-5). It is with Peter that Paul spends two weeks on his first visit to Jerusalem after his acceptance of Christian faith. It is with Peter that Paul instinctively ranks and measures himself when he insists that he is a true, "first-class" apostle. Indeed, even in his fiercely polemical description of his confrontation with Peter at Antioch, Paul cannot hide the fact that Peter's influence is able to draw every Christian leader except Paul to Peter's side, including Paul's closest partner Barnabas.[9] And it is by no means clear that Paul finally wins the debate at Antioch. Granted Paul's argument in Galatians, his silence on the pivotal point of who won the debate, as well as his speedy and long-term departure from Antioch to points West, may be telling.

Part of the irony of the fight at Antioch is that, in due time, Peter may have imitated Paul's missionary thrust to the West. That, at least, is a likely interpretation of the existence of a Cephas group alongside an Apollos group and a Paul group in the church of Corinth, founded by Paul himself. Indeed, if we may read between the lines of some late New Testament books,

---

9. On the dispute at Antioch, see Raymond E. Brown and John P. Meier, *Antioch and Rome* (New York/Ramsey, NJ: Paulist, 1983), pp. 36-44.

Peter may have imitated Paul more than either had intended or wanted. Both the charge to Peter in John 21 and some allusive references in the First and Second Epistles of Peter point to knowledge of Peter's martyrdom, and the symbolic reference to the church in Babylon, together with the mention of "my son Mark," may be the first glimmer of the tradition of Peter's martyrdom in Rome.[10] To be sure, his martyrdom in Rome is never directly mentioned in the New Testament. But then, neither is Paul's, though this silence has not kept most New Testament scholars from treating Paul's martyrdom in Rome as a given fact of history.

One final point of imitation lies beyond the lives of both apostles. In my opinion, Colossians, Ephesians, and the Pastoral Epistles are pseudepigraphic works produced by different disciples of Paul — or students of his epistles — who were active in Asia Minor between A.D. 70 and 100. Similarly, and perhaps in conscious imitation of this phenomenon of apostolic pseudepigraphy, various disciples or admirers of Peter composed two pseudepigraphic letters in his name, speaking most likely from Rome to the churches of Asia Minor or simply to churches in general. The phenomenon of authoritative apostolic teaching being continued and developed by disciples of an apostle in the apostle's name is thus found in both Pauline circles in Asia Minor and Petrine circles in Rome. Perhaps the greatest irony of all, in this example of imitation being the sincerest form of flattery, is the fact that the Second Epistle of Peter, probably the last canonical book of the New Testament to be written (possibly as late as A.D. 120-30), concludes with the iconic Peter supplying the authoritative interpretation of all of the epistles written by "our beloved brother Paul" (2 Peter 3:15-16). The Peter of faith, though hardly the Simon of history, gets the last word in the canonical process.[11]

The Earliest Patristic Witnesses to the Prominence of the Roman Church

(a) As we move to our third matrix, it is important to remember that moving outside the New Testament canon does not necessarily mean moving to

---

10. For a spirited defense of the view that "Babylon" symbolizes Rome, see John H. Elliott, *1 Peter* (New York: Doubleday, 2000), pp. 880-90; similarly, Paul J. Achtemeier, *1 Peter* (Minneapolis: Fortress, 1996), pp. 353-54. For a brief survey of 1 Peter, see Gnilka, *Petrus und Rom*, pp. 179-87.

11. For a brief treatment of 2 Peter, see Gnilka, *Petrus und Rom*, pp. 188-97.

chronologically later writings. One is surprised, for instance, to see Joachim Gnilka entitle his chapter that treats of 1 Clement and the letters of Ignatius of Antioch "The Importance of Peter and Rome in the Early Post-New Testament Period." We must remember that 1 Clement and even Ignatius' letters were being written at a time when the latest New Testament books had not received their final form (e.g., perhaps the Gospel of John and the Johannine Epistles) or had not yet been written (e.g., 2 Peter). Significantly, witnesses to Peter's importance in late New Testament writings (e.g., John 21, 1 Peter) and the earliest non-canonical writings (e.g., 1 Clement) overlap.

At the same time, the focus of our investigation necessarily shifts as we move to the non-canonical writings. In the New Testament, the focus is on Simon Peter, with at best a fleeting hint of a connection with Rome in 1 and 2 Peter. In the earliest patristic literature, our focus is necessarily on indications of the leadership or prominence of the Roman church, with only fleeting references to Peter (and, regularly, to Paul). This state of affairs is especially clear in 1 Clement.[12] The situation itself — the Roman church taking the initiative to call the church of Corinth to order — is a remarkably early witness to the "high self-esteem" the Roman church possessed. Since 1 Clement was still reverently read in Corinth, along with the Scriptures, as late as A.D. 170 (according to Bishop Dionysius of Corinth), this high self-esteem and sense of leadership apparently found a receptive audience outside Rome, indeed, in a church that could boast of being founded by Paul (and perhaps visited by Peter).

In striking contrast to 1 and 2 Peter, where individual teachers speak not only in the name of Peter but as Peter, the anonymous author of 1 Clement speaks as "we," as the whole church of Rome, which presumably, like Corinth, is led by a group of presbyter-bishops assisted by deacons. There is no sign of the monepiscopate soon to be championed by Ignatius. It is rather "the church of God sojourning in Rome" as such, and not Peter, and not some individual claiming to be the successor of Peter, that implicitly exercises authority over a distinguished Pauline church in Greece. Indeed, the final blessing of the epistle is extended not only to the Corinthians but also "to all those called by God everywhere" (1 Clement 65.2). When Peter is mentioned, it is not in splendid isolation but rather in the company of Paul. In fact, Peter and Paul are mentioned together as martyrs — the first

---

12. For a brief overview of 1 Clement and the way it reflects the situation of the church in Rome at the end of the first century, see Brown and Meier, *Antioch and Rome*, pp. 159-83.

time this happens in Christian literature (chap. 5). First Clement does not explicitly state in chapter 5 that the two apostles died in Rome, but the seamless transition to the martyrs of Rome in chapters 6-7 at least implies a connection of place as well as of fate. Peter and Paul are not explicitly invoked as the basis and source of the authority of the Roman church, but chapter 6 does explicitly join the Roman martyrs to the two apostles, thus at least indirectly bathing the Roman church in the glow of the two apostolic martyrs. It is perhaps accurate to say that in 1 Clement the honor and authority of the Roman church are founded upon the glorious witness of all its martyrs, with Peter and Paul — Peter being named first in chapter 5 — as the first and most famous.

This implicit placing of Peter and Paul at the origins of the Roman church is not connected by our author with another claim he makes later in the letter; but the two claims, present in the same letter, contain great potential that would be exploited in later theology. In chapters 42-44, "Clement" makes his famous assertion that the apostles *(hoi apostoloi)* appointed bishops and deacons in the cities where they preached in order to provide successors when they died. "Clement" makes no connection between this claim and the implicit one about "the good apostles" [*tous agathous apostolous*], Peter and Paul, in chapter 5. Yet, if "Clement" intends to claim that these two apostles are somehow involved in the origins of the Roman church, then the logic of his argument in chapters 42-44 would seem to demand that Peter and Paul were the apostles who appointed the presbyter-bishops and deacons of Rome. I stress, though, that this connection is never explicitly made by our author, and the authority of the Roman church is never grounded explicitly on the primordial authority of Peter and Paul.

(As an aside, we might also note that, from the practical and *Realpolitik* point of view, the position of the Roman church in the capital of the empire no doubt added authority to its exhortation to a city that had been refounded by Julius Caesar as a Roman colony. But such a consideration is never brought up in the letter.)

(b) As we move from 1 Clement to Ignatius of Antioch, the terrain shifts seismically.[13] We are now dealing with the first appearance of the monepiscopate, operating in supposed harmony with a council of presbyters and assisted by deacons. The sole direct connection of this new three-tier hi-

---

13. For a brief overview of the letters of Ignatius of Antioch and his relation to Rome, see Brown and Meier, *Antioch and Rome,* pp. 73-86, 202; William R. Schoedel, *Ignatius of Antioch* (Philadelphia: Fortress, 1985), pp. 14-15, 165-67.

erarchy with our particular concern is Ignatius' *Epistle to the Romans*, written somewhere around the end of the first decade of the second century. Of the seven authentic letters of Ignatius, the *Epistle to the Romans* stands out in a number of ways. While the other letters dwell on the double theme of the necessity of the three-tier hierarchy for the unity of the church and the necessity of avoiding docetic or Judaizing errors, these two themes are absent in *Romans*. Instead, in *Romans* Ignatius spends most of his time expatiating on his desire for martyrdom and pleading with the Romans not to impede it. There is something quite striking about the absence of the first theme that dominates the other letters, namely, the necessity of the triple hierarchy with one bishop as leader. In his other letters, Ignatius cannot conceive of a true church without the one bishop; obedience to and harmony with the bishop are essential. Yet Ignatius is totally silent about the existence of this pivotal office in the Roman church, probably because — as we can see from 1 Clement — it did not exist in Rome at the time.

We have here, then, a curious backhanded compliment, a curious deference to the Roman church. Despite the fact that it fails to meet Ignatius' primary requirement for genuine church life, he passes over this glaring deficit in silence. In fact, he begins *Romans* with the most fulsome praise he gives any church in any *praescriptio* of his seven letters. Within this longest of all his *praescriptiones,* Ignatius uses twice the verb *prokathēmi,* "to preside": the Roman church "presides in the region of the Romans" and it "presides in love." One should not press these phrases into a later canonical meaning, but it is intriguing that Ignatius should apply the idea of "presiding" — which elsewhere he uses only of bishops and presbyters[14] — to a church that lacks the triple hierarchy that, according to his theology, is necessary for a true church.

Despite his high self-esteem as "bishop of Syria" (*not* just of Antioch, *Romans* 2.2), Ignatius does not presume to command but rather beseeches (*parakal,* 4.1) the Roman church not to hinder his martyrdom. He pointedly abjures any attempt to command the Roman Christians. At this point, he makes a telling contrast (4.3): "I do not command you as Peter and Paul [did]; they were apostles, I am a condemned [convict]." Clearly, therefore, Peter and Paul — again, as in 1 Clement, in that order — are connected with Rome. That both of them are said to have commanded or ordered the Roman church presumes the presence of both of them in Rome. Moreover, Ignatius' distinction between them as free men and himself as a slave until

---

14. See *Magnesians* 6.1-2.

he is martyred intimates their martyrdom in Rome, though it does not explicitly affirm it. Thus, the Roman church is esteemed by Ignatius because it was in some sense governed or directed by Peter and Paul, who, it seems, shed their blood there, making it the fit place for Ignatius himself to consummate his journey to martyrdom.

Interestingly, Peter and Paul are mentioned as active in no other church, though Paul is mentioned in passing in *Ephesians* 12.1. To be sure, the unique dignity of the Roman church, arising from its special relation with Peter and Paul, is not connected by Ignatius with its activity of "presiding in the region of the Romans." Still, the emphasis on Peter and Paul commanding the *Roman* church remains somewhat curious, since Ignatius, the bishop of Antioch, never mentions the activity of the two apostles in Antioch in particular or in Syria in general. He connects the two of them only with Rome, though without forging a juridical link, à la 1 Clement, by invoking the idea of apostolic succession. But perhaps, in the end, Ignatius' final contribution to the Roman church was an existential rather than a merely theoretical one. Perhaps the impressive witness given by Ignatius, bishop and martyr, was the Roman church's first and formative encounter with the monepiscopate. But, obviously, at this point, we are left with mere surmises.

The Rise of the Monepiscopate

Be that as it may, a fourth and vital matrix of the Roman papacy was the appearance of the monepiscopate in Rome. Except for suggesting that the transition from a college of presbyter-bishops to the one-bishop model was probably a gradual one, we are left largely in the dark about the details of this mutation in Rome.[15] As we have seen from 1 Clement, at the end of the first century, the Roman church was governed by presbyter-bishops assisted by deacons. At the end of the second century, single bishops like Victor I seem firmly in control.

The few documents we have from Rome during the second century leave us unsure about exactly when and how the transition took place. The *Shepherd of Hermas* seems to reflect the older order of governance by presby-

---

15. On the whole question of the development of the Roman church in the first two centuries, see Peter Lampe, *Die stadtrömischen Christen in den ersten beiden Jahrhunderten*, 2nd ed. (Tübingen: Mohr [Siebeck], 1989).

ters, though the complicated tradition history of *Hermas*'s composition, perhaps spanning decades, lessens the usefulness of this work for our purposes.[16] There is a slight possibility that Justin Martyr's description of the Roman Eucharist in his *First Apology,* with the sole presider preaching, offering the eucharistic prayer, and most notably receiving and controlling all the donations of the faithful, may point to a Roman monepiscopate around mid-century.[17] However, Justin's text need not be read this way.

In the second half of the second century, the clear affirmation of a monepiscopate in Rome as well as its connection with the apostles is supplied, interestingly, not by Rome itself but by church writers from elsewhere who visit Rome. The exact import of the statement of Hegesippus (c. A.D. 160) concerning episcopal succession in Rome, cited by Eusebius (*Ecclesiastical History,* 4.22.3), is disputed; but Hegesippus seems at least to attest to the existence of the monepiscopate in Rome circa A.D. 160. Much clearer and explicit evidence is offered by Irenaeus, a theologian of the East who became bishop of Lyons. Somewhere around A.D. 180, Irenaeus visited Rome when Eleutherus was bishop. Irenaeus testifies to the existence of a succession-list of bishops, reaching back to Linus, the first leader of the Roman church supposedly appointed by the apostles Peter and Paul, who are said to have founded the church at Rome (Greek text in Eusebius, *E.H.* 5.5.8–5.6.1-5; Latin text in *Adversus Haereses,* 3.3.3). Tellingly, Peter and Paul are not counted among Rome's bishops. Indeed, the title "bishop" *(episkopos)* is absent from the list proper; the abstract noun *episkopē* is used instead. In the larger context of the list, Irenaeus seems to use interchangeably the titles "bishop" and "presbyter"; elsewhere he speaks of the succession of presbyters in the churches.

Hence, while the names of the Roman leaders in Irenaeus's list may well record historical figures, the idea that they actually functioned as single bishops in Rome throughout the second century is anachronistic — anachronism being a common failing not only of ancient theologians like Irenaeus but also of ancient historians like Josephus and Tacitus. What Irenaeus's testimony shows, alongside that of Hegesippus, is that church writers from outside of Rome knew of the monepiscopate existing in Rome from the second half of the second century onwards. Its existence in Rome

---

16. On the *Shepherd of Hermas,* see Brown and Meier, *Antioch and Rome,* pp. 203-4; Robert Joly, ed., *Hermas. Le Pasteur,* 2nd ed. (Paris: Cerf, 1997), pp. 34-41; Carolyn Osiek, *Shepherd of Hermas* (Minneapolis: Fortress, 1999).

17. *First Apology* 65-67; Justin speaks in the singular of *ho proests.*

is not reliably attested before that time. With the convergence of the Simon of history, the Peter of faith, the prominent leadership role of the Roman church, and finally the appearance of the monepiscopate in Rome, we can begin to speak of the emergence of the papacy in Rome toward the end of the second century.

The Quartordeciman Controversy

In a sense, this emergence of the Roman papacy was consecrated, in hardly a happy fashion, by Victor I's conflict with the churches of Asia Minor over the date of Easter, our fifth matrix. (I should note as an aside that I do not accept the view that the controversy was merely a local dispute within the Roman church, a dispute that Eusebius later misunderstood or misrepresented.)[18] In Victor (governed c. 189-98), we see for the first time the one bishop of the Roman church claiming authority over the churches in both East and West. Specifically, and somewhat amazingly, Victor claimed the authority to order the churches of Asia to change their observance of Easter to make it coincide with the date observed by Rome. Though the details of the controversy are unclear, apparently the intervention of Irenaeus was able to bring the dispute to a peaceful conclusion. Somewhat prophetically, Irenaeus emphasized that Rome had to distinguish between the unity of faith, which must be preserved, and the differing customs of local churches, which should be respected. This distinction is all the more remarkable since it is Irenaeus in his *Adversus Haereses* (3.3.2) who insists on the need for every church to agree with the Roman church on matters of faith. He bases this necessity on the unique position of the Roman church. According to Irenaeus, this church was founded by Peter and Paul (mentioned together, as in 1 Clement and Ignatius' *Epistle to the Romans*); their apostolic tradition has been preserved in the succession of leaders appointed by them. Irenaeus sees these bishops of Rome as the successors of Peter *and* Paul, who are not themselves called bishops of Rome.

It is on the basis of this most distinguished apostolic pedigree that Irenaeus makes his weighty claim, whose precise meaning is much debated: "*Ad hanc enim ecclesiam propter potentiorem principalitatem necesse est*

---

18. Eusebius' account is found in his *E.H.*, 5.23-24. On the Quartordeciman controversy and the interpretive problems connected with it, see Gnilka, *Petrus und Rom*, pp. 226-41.

omnem convenire ecclesiam."[19] Whatever one makes of this statement, which unfortunately we have in a Latin translation, not in the original Greek, one should remember two points: (1) Irenaeus recognizes other great churches as enjoying apostolic foundation and tradition. (2) Irenaeus is making this statement in regard to the essential apostolic faith, not liturgical customs that vary among local churches. As the fight over the date of Easter shows, Irenaeus did not think that other churches had to obey Rome in questions that did not touch on the apostolic faith. It is this faith that Peter and Paul and the church founded by them guarantee. A similar point is made slightly later by the Roman presbyter Gaius, who appeals in a dispute with some Montanists to the *tropaia* (victory monuments) of the apostles Peter and Paul, who founded the Roman church (Eusebius, *E.H.,* 2.25.6-7). Whatever one thinks of the debate surrounding the excavations under St. Peter's Basilica,[20] the archaeological findings plus the text of Gaius make it likely that from about the middle of the second century onwards, the graves, cenotaphs, or places of martyrdom of Peter and Paul were venerated in Rome, providing a very concrete expression, by way of popular devotion, of the historical and theological claims implied as far back as 1 Clement. To what extent the veneration of the apostolic *tropaia* was connected with the emergence of the monepiscopate in Rome must remain a matter of speculation.

Theological Reflection on the Petrine Texts

Our sixth and final matrix brings us full circle back to the New Testament texts on Peter with which we started. Remarkably, none of the patristic texts

19. In *Irénée de Lyon. Contre les Hérésies. Livre III* (Paris: Cerf, 1974), pp. 32-33, Adelin Rousseau and Louis Doutreleau translate the phrase "potentiorem principalitatem" as "more excellent origin"; the hypothetical Greek original supplied is *dia tēn hikanteran archēn.*

20. On the whole question of Peter's connection with Rome and the excavations under St. Peter's Basilica, see Jocelyn Toynbee and John Ward Perkins, *The Shrine of St. Peter and the Vatican Excavations* (New York: Pantheon, 1957); Erich Dinkler, "Die Petrus-Rom-Frage. Ein Forschungsbericht," *TRu* 25 (1959): 189-230, 289-335; 27 (1961): 33-64; Margherita Guarducci, *The Tradition of Peter in the Vatican in the Light of History and Archaeology* (Vatican City: Vatican Polyglot Press, 1963); Daniel W. O'Connor, *Peter in Rome* (New York: Columbia University, 1969); Engelbert Kirschbaum, *Die Gräber der Apostelfürsten. St. Peter und St. Paul in Rom,* 3rd ed. (Frankfurt: Societäts-Verlag, 1974); Pesch, *Simon-Petrus,* pp. 113-34; John E. Walsh, *The Bones of St. Peter* (Garden City, NY: Doubleday, 1982); Gnilka, *Petrus und Rom,* pp. 126-41.

we have examined so far makes any direct appeal to the great Petrine texts of the New Testament — though, admittedly, we lack direct attestation of the arguments put forward by Victor I. In a sense, though, we should not be surprised by this lack of argument from what we consider key texts. From 1 Clement onwards, the claims of Rome were based on the witness and martyrdom in Rome of both Peter and Paul. Granted that way of looking at things, New Testament texts — and let us remember that the New Testament canon was still in process — that focused solely on Peter were not quite suited to the type of theological claims being made in the second century.

Ironically, when, at the end of the second and the beginning of the third century, theologians in the West begin to draw key Petrine texts into reflection on church power, bishops, and Rome, the initiative is taken not by theologians in Rome but rather in North Africa. Tertullian (d. 220) and Cyprian (d. 258) are the first notable thinkers to argue over what Petrine texts like Matthew 16:17-19 or John 21:17 have to do with the authority of bishops in general or of the Roman bishop in particular. They begin a tradition of theological reflection on Petrine texts that will continue to be developed throughout the fourth and fifth centuries, reaching a certain climax in the claims of Pope Leo the Great. With this final step, all the matrices that helped produce the historical phenomenon of the papacy are in place and have begun to interact. The rest, as they say, is history.[21]

Conclusion

What conclusions might we draw from this all-too-brief survey of the historical matrices of the Roman papacy?

(1) First and foremost, to return to my initial observations, a Catholic Church that seeks to address an educated audience of the twenty-first century must articulate a doctrine of the papacy that acknowledges and incorporates the lengthy and complicated historical development outlined in this presentation. This is not to say that basic catechesis on the subject should engage in detailed historical reconstructions and speculation. Still, even ba-

---

21. In recent years, greater attention has been paid to the treatment of Peter in the New Testament Apocrypha; see, e.g., Gnilka, *Petrus und Rom*, pp. 263-72; Lapham, *Peter*. While the various portraits are important for a complete history of Christian theology and piety in the patristic period, the apocryphal writings do not contribute anything of significance to the topic pursued in this presentation.

sic catechesis can speak of God's providential guidance of the church, leading by a series of steps to the emergence of the bishop of Rome as a center and servant of church unity and apostolic faith. More detailed instruction to educated adults, theological students, and seminarians could expand on this basic insight. In my view, there is nothing in this approach that is threatening to a genuine Catholic vision of revelation and doctrinal development in and through history. Whether we think of Vincent of Lérins or Cardinal Newman, development of doctrine is an accepted principle of Catholic theology, clearly exemplified in such doctrines as the seven sacraments or the Immaculate Conception, two doctrines that took much longer to come to clear articulation than the papacy.

(2) In a historically grounded theology of the papacy, emphasis should be given to the fact that early patristic witnesses considered the Roman church and its leadership to be based on the preaching and martyrdom of *both* Peter *and* Paul in Rome. First Clement, Ignatius, Irenaeus, and Gaius think in terms of the two apostles Peter and Paul, not just Peter.

(3) A historically grounded theology of the papacy should make clear that, in the beginning, leadership was seen to be embodied in the Roman church as such, not in a single leader. In due time, this Roman leadership came to be embodied in the one bishop who emerged from the college of presbyter-bishops and who therefore presided over the Roman church. To put the point in modern terms, Benedict XVI is not bishop of Rome because he is the pope; he is the pope because he is the bishop of Rome, embodying Rome's ancient role of leadership.

(4) The balanced two-part teaching of Irenaeus must be stressed because the mistake of Victor I, the mistake that identifies unity with uniformity, remains a constant temptation for any pope. On the one hand, in essential matters of faith, it is necessary for every local church to agree with the Roman church. On the other hand, provided that the faith is not in question, Rome should not impose its own customs, ways of doing things, and theological perspectives on local churches that have developed legitimate differences in such matters. Subsidiarity, so lauded today in the secular sphere, needs to be practiced in the church as well — and not as some modern invention or accommodation but rather as the retrieval of the ancient teaching of Irenaeus. If the Petrine ministry is to serve the unity of the universal church in the twenty-first century, it would do well to imitate Victor I not in his heavy-handed power-grab but in his eventual bowing to the wisdom of that doctor of the universal church who was and must remain in a special way the doctor of the Roman church, Irenaeus.

The Petrine Ministry in the Early Patristic Tradition

Archbishop Roland Minnerath

1. The question of a Petrine ministry in the church, which until now has divided the churches of East and West, is linked with the interpretation of the New Testament data. The question is twofold: Did Peter receive from the Lord a specific mission within the group of Twelve, and within the whole Christian community? The second question is whether this mission was to be perpetuated in the church along its history.

Modern New Testament scholarship points out that the traditions on Peter were received independently by Matthew (Matt. 16:18-19), John (John 21), and Luke (Luke 22:32). It is generally admitted that in Matthew 16:18 *petra* means the person of Peter and not only his faith. Luke shows clearly in the first chapters of Acts that Peter exercised a real leadership in the apostolic community until the persecution by Herod Agrippa around A.D. 42. In the last writings of the New Testament, while James, John, and Paul created around them rather separate and even mutually hostile movements, Peter appears as a figure able to bring back to the mainstream apostolic church the community of John (John 21), and to recommend to his Jewish-Christian readers to accept Paul also as an apostle and a brother (2 Peter 3). Moreover the New Testament suggests that Peter as well as Paul had come to Rome, and had suffered there a martyr's death (Rom. 15:20; 1 Peter 5:13; Apoc. 11:3). Nothing is said of a successor in his office. We learn that the apostles settled after them collegial leaders called presbyters. The collegial and presbyterial structure of the local churches prevailed until the last quarter of the second century.

The First Three Centuries

2. The first document after the New Testament, essential for our topic, is 1 Clement. This document is a collective letter of the presbyters of the Church of Rome to the presbyters of the Church of Corinth. It appears to be an answer to a request for help on behalf of the Church of Corinth. It is striking that this letter deals with authority with a problem risen in another apostolic church, Corinth. Yet it does not invoke the authority of Peter, but the authority of the Church of Rome, which refers to Peter and Paul as "the columns" who suffered martyrdoms in Rome together with many others (5:2–6:1). Over eighty years later the letter, attributed to Clement by bishop Denis, was still read with respect in Corinth, and revered as a scripture according to Eusebius.[1]

In the Christian literature of the second century, the first hints about a special position of the Church of Rome come from outside witnesses: Ignatius of Antioch, Irenaeus, Hegesippus; Tertullian and Cyprian. As did Paul in writing to the Romans, Ignatius uses only words of consideration when he addresses the Roman church, a church that has received "orders from Peter and Paul" (Rom. 4:3). The Roman church "teaches the others" (Rom. 3:1-2). This church is called to "preside the agape," understood as to "gather in unity." We should bear in mind that agape is a title for the whole Christian communion. About the widowed Antiochene church he says that it has "Christ as a bishop and the Romans' agape" (Rom. 9:1).[2]

In his refutation of all the heresies, Irenaeus relies on the argument of the apostolic tradition. If you are looking for an apostolic church, go to Rome, he says — this church has been founded by the two glorious apostles Peter and Paul. It enjoys a *"potentior principalitas,"* a more outstanding origin and authority. This church always and everywhere proclaimed the faith preached by the apostles — so much so that all the churches have kept the apostolic tradition in accordance with the Church of Rome. "Towards that church," says Irenaeus, "all the churches should converge."[3] The church of

---

1. Eusebius, *Hist. eccl.* IV, 23,11.16.

2. The pseudepigraphic literature around James clearly subordinates Peter to James, called *episcopus episcoporum*. It argues that James had ordained Peter bishop of Rome and that Peter ordained Clement. This writing is the first one that witnesses that the prerogatives of Peter have been transmitted to his successors in the see of Rome. Cf. *Epistula Clementis ad Jacobum* 1,2-3; 2,5; 17,1; 19,1, in Bernhard Rehm, ed., *Die Pseudoklementinen, Homilien* (Leipzig: Hinrichs, 1953), vol. 1, pp. 5-22.

3. Irenaeus, *Adv. haer.* III, 3,3.

Peter and Paul is "the unique mouth" that proclaims in the name of all churches "the tradition received from the Apostles."[4]

Hegesippus around 160, traveling through the main churches founded by the apostles, collects the names of the bishops who succeeded to those established by the apostles. As for Rome, he says that the founder apostles transmitted the episcopate to Linus.

With these second-century witnesses, attention is drawn not on the person of Peter or on a successor in a time when monarchical episcopacy was only beginning to emerge. The general consideration is that the Church of Rome is the apostolic church par excellence, and the reference for the apostolic teaching. Indeed during the second century, it was the apostolic origin of a church that conferred on it a particular authority in the transmission of the "rule of faith."

3. There is an attempt at a Petrine theology with the two Africans Tertullian and Cyprian. As the first patristic commentator on Matthew 16:18, Tertullian interprets *petra*/"on this rock" as referring to the person of the apostle. Peter is the type of the one Church of the origins. This one Church has developed and is now present in the variety of local churches, "which are all this one primitive apostolic Church from which they all proceed."[5] Even when he became a Montanist, Tertullian considered Peter as the type of the church of the Spirit. Tertullian never thought that a successor of Peter in Rome would exercise a jurisdiction over the whole Christian world. But he is the initiator of a Petrine theology. Peter is an active symbol for all times, inviting the churches to grow in unity as they consider themselves the continuation of the one Church built on the rock of Peter. In *Pud.* 16, Tertullian deepens his exegesis of Matthew 16:18-19. He argues that the power to bind and unbind has passed from Peter to the apostles and prophets of the Montanist church, not to the bishops.[6] It is interesting to note that Matthew 16 is used as a support for the power to forgive sins, not to support a particular power of a successor of Peter in Rome.[7] It is disputed whether Tertullian had Pope Calixtus in mind or Agrippinus the bishop of Carthage, when he challenged him on the question of forgiving capital sinners. He mocked this

---

4. Irenaeus, *Adv. haer.* I, 10,2.

5. Tertullian, *De praescr.* 22,3; cf. *Praescr.* 20,5-7; *Scorp.* 10; *Ieun.* 15.

6. Tertullian, *Pud.* 21,9.10.

7. During the same period, Pope Calixtus began to admit penance even to those guilty of adultery. He used to quote not Matthew 16, but rather Matthew 13:29-30 or Romans 14:4. It is not impossible that for that time in Rome Matthew 16 was already used to support the idea of a Petrine succession to the benefit of the Roman bishop.

"bishop of bishops" who pretended to "derive to himself the power of the keys given to Peter personally."[8]

As a disciple of Tertullian, Cyprian is the first theologian to elaborate on Peter as a permanent archetype of the church of Christ. His views are summarized in the two versions he successively wrote of chapter 4 of his treaty *De unitate ecclesiae,* the first stressing the uniqueness of the figure of Peter. Unity, says Cyprian, is given by Christ to the church in its origin. The church's beginning goes back to the words of Jesus announcing that he will build his church on Peter the Rock. So all existing churches draw their origin from that starting point. The churches are one in reference to their common origin.

The apostle Peter continues to foster the unity of the church in shaping the unity of all the bishops who derive their office from the words of Jesus to Peter. All the bishops together make up a unique *"collegium sacerdotale."*[9] Among them the bishop of Rome occupies the *"locus Petri,"* the place of Peter. Before Cornelius was elected, he writes, the *"locus Petri"* and the *"cathedra sacerdotalis"* were vacant.[10] Now the college of the bishops is united by the *"cathedra Petri"* itself, "from which derives the unity of the episcopate."[11] The see of Rome is a permanent witness that the Lord built one united church, of which each local church acts a part of the whole. Cyprian is also the first to use the word *primatus,* a position given by the Lord to Peter as the first of the apostles, who concentrates in himself the church to come.[12]

For Cyprian, the apostle Peter plays permanently a role in shaping the unity of the whole episcopacy derived from the words of the Lord to Peter. Moreover the bishop of Rome takes the place of Peter: Cornelius is elected when the *"locus Petri"* and the *"cathedra sacerdotalis"* were vacant. Cyprian developed the idea that all bishops, regardless of the territorial entity to which they belong, make up a unique *"collegium sacerdotale."* This college is united by the *"cathedra Petri."*

4. The consciousness of a global responsibility for the whole church appears for the first time with bishop Victor (186-97) in his conflict with the

---

8. Tertullian, *Pud.* 21,9. See Roland Minnerath, "L'exégèse de Mt 16,18.19 chez Tertullien," *Revue d'histoire et de philosophie religieuses* 72 (1992): 61-72.

9. Cyprian, *Ep.* 55,1.21.24.30.

10. Cyprian, *Ep.* 55,8

11. Cyprian, *Ep.* 59,14.

12. Cyprian, *De unitate* 4.

Asian churches about the celebration date of Easter. This is the first case in which a Roman bishop claims authority over the affairs of a whole region far beyond Italy. Eusebius says that Victor considered excommunicating the Asian bishops on the ground that they did not wish to follow the Roman and universal custom of celebrating Easter the Sunday after the 14th of Nisan.[13] The Asian bishops did not comply, but neither did they challenge Victor's right to intervene.

5. The figure of Peter was often interpreted by ecclesiastical writers in a mystical sense. So Origen says that each believer who proclaims the true faith, each true gnostic, bears the name of Peter.[14] Until Pope Stephen (254-57), there is no Roman bishop claiming to exercise the Petrine office in the church. What we know about his claim is induced from the reaction of his opponents. Stephen pretended to rally all the churches to the practice of the Roman church in matters of readmission of heretics and schismatics, founding his intervention on the words of Matthew 16:18. The pretension of Stephen was harshly rebuked by both Cyprian and Firmilian of Caesarea in Cappadocia. The latter protests that Stephen declares himself to have succeeded in the *"cathedra Petri"* and to occupy his *"locus."*[15] Stephen seems to have drawn the consequences of Cyprian's first version of *De unitate* 4. As for Firmilian, he must have been upset by the fact that Stephen planned to excommunicate the Asian churches. The synod of Carthage of 256 rejected such a pretension as coming from one who claims to be "the bishop of the bishops." Firmilian adds that no bishop should be judged by another bishop, each one being accountable only to God.[16] There seems to come quite a clash between the Roman and the African-Oriental interpretation of the Petrine character of the see of Rome. Up to our own times, the issue raised by this controversy would receive different answers.

6. Nevertheless, during the third century, the apostolic Church of Rome was universally recognized as a reference in matters of doctrine and order. When Origen was excommunicated by his bishop Demetrius the latter forwarded the verdict to the other bishops, also to Pontianus of Rome, who held a synod to confirm his verdict.[17] The synod of Antioch that excommunicated Paul of Samosata in 268 forwarded its decision to Denis the

---

13. Eusebius, *Hist. eccl.* V, 24,2-6.
14. Origen, *Commentary on Matthew* XII, 14, where *petra* is Christ himself.
15. Cyprian, *Ep.* 75,17.
16. Cf. Cyprian, *Ep.* 72,3,2.
17. Eusebius, *Hist. eccl.* VI, 8,4.

bishop of Rome, who also confirmed the sentence in his own synod. Interesting here is the decision of Emperor Aurelius, to whom Paul had appealed. He ruled that the bishop's house of Antioch should belong to those "who write to the bishops of Italy and specially the bishop of Rome."[18] Not much later, Denis the bishop of Alexandria asked the Roman bishop for his advice in Trinitarian questions related to the Sabellian heresy. Pope Denis answered with an exhaustive exposition on the Trinity issue.[19] Even for the bishops in the East, the apostolic Church of Rome was a symbol of the whole church and a mirror of its unity in faith and order, as long as Rome respected their own traditions and procedures of communion.

Rome and the Territorial Primacies

7. The Fathers of the fourth and fifth centuries generally understood the Petrine passages of the gospels as applicable to all the bishops. In Peter all the bishops have received the powers of the keys. Most of the Oriental Fathers interpret *petra* as referring to the faith of Peter, not to his person. St. John Chrysostom, for instance, has nice developments on Matthew 16 and John 21, but he has no idea of a personal successor to Peter in Rome. Rather, all bishops receive the mission to pasture the cattle of the Lord.[20] He praises Rome for keeping the relics of the two apostles Peter and Paul.[21] Together with him Theodoret of Cyr, John Damascene, and Theodore of Mopsuestia share the same approach. A second line of interpretation of Matthew 16:18 prevailed in the West as well as in the East. Origen and Augustine, for instance, consider *petra* as referring to Christ himself. So Christ builds his church on himself. There is a third category arguing that *petra* clearly takes into consideration the person of the apostle Peter (Ambrose, Hilarius, Jeronimus) as suggested, but also finding significance in the nickname *Kēpha* given by Jesus to Peter. Hilarius takes up this view with an important nuance: it is Simon Peter, open to God's revelation, who becomes *petra* — rock — in the moment when he confesses the true faith of the whole church. So the rock on which Jesus builds his church is the enlightened witness of the Easter faith of the whole church. Peter is not seen as an individual in his

18. Eusebius, *Hist. eccl.* VII, 30,19.
19. Eusebius, *Hist. eccl.* VII, 6.
20. John Chrysostom, *De sacerdotio* II, 1.
21. John Chrysostom, *Hom.* 32 on the Epistle to the Romans.

own human weakness, but as the one who points at the true cornerstone, the *petra* of salvation, who is Christ himself.[22]

8. Already towards the end of the second century, the church had begun to develop means of strengthening communion between communities. Following a practice of the Montanists, synods began to be celebrated on a provincial level. The second Eastern conflict witnesses meetings of bishops in such areas as Palestine, Rome, Pontus, Gaul, Osroene, Achaia.[23] Bishops of a single province used to recognize a precedence in the bishop of the capital city. So the metropolitan structure gradually arose. After the administrative reforms of Diocletian and Constantine, with smaller provinces, the civil diocese became the natural framework for ecclesiastical exchanges. Canon 6 of Nicea (325) refers to an "ancient custom" when speaking of the regional primacy of Rome in Italy as a model for the primacy of Alexandria in Egypt, Libya, and Pentapolis, and for the primacy of Antioch in Syria. The second canon of Constantinople I (381) confirms the administrative autonomy of the churches within the civil dioceses, and explicitly mentions Egypt, Syria, Pontus, Asia, and Thrace, stressing the importance of the over-metropolitan or regional jurisdiction. Thus was reinforced the notion of the local church: at the metropolitan, exarchal, and later patriarchal levels. The structure of government was subsidiary. Bishops were elected, ordained, and judged by their metropolitan synod (Const. I, can. 2; Antioch, can. 16 and 19). According to the same logic, the Council of Chalcedon (451) fixed the territorial limits of the patriarchal jurisdiction of Constantinople to the Pontic, Asian, and Thracian dioceses, and to the churches among the barbarians. Later the patriarchs would vindicate the right to ordain and judge their metropolitans.

The central notion of territorial administrative autonomy was summed up in its form and doctrine by the 34th canon of the apostles, taken up by canon 2 of the council in Trullo of 692: "The bishops of every nation must acknowledge him who is the first among them and account him as their head, and do nothing of consequence without his consent; but each may do those things only which concern his own parish, and the country places which belong to it. But neither let him who is the first do anything without the consent of all; for so there will be unanimity, and God will be

---

22. See Joseph Ludwig, *Die Primatsworte Mt XVI 18-19 in der Altkirchlichen Exegese* (Münster: Aschendorff, 1952), and Jean M.-R. Tillard, *The Bishop of Rome* (Wilmington, DE: Glazier, 1983).

23. Eusebius, *Hist. eccl.* V, 23 3-4.

glorified through the Lord in the Holy Spirit." In Eastern ecclesiology the church is synodical by essence. Synodality requires the service of a *prōtos*.

The whole tradition considered the Roman bishop as the first of all bishops and later the first of the five patriarchs. This position was granted him through the canons of the ecumenical councils. In considering the Roman bishop as having a *presbeia tēs timēs*, a privilege of honor, the holy canons did not make any link with a special mission entrusted by the Lord to Peter. The pope was the first by canonical prescription, not by divine law. Yet the notion of *honor (timē)* implied a specific responsibility, that of the *prōtos* in his territory.

In this territorial organization of the church, no reference was made to the apostolic principle. The original insistence on the see founded by the apostles vanished. The church adapted its structures to the administrative divisions of the Roman Empire. Constantinople was no apostolic foundation. Ephesus and Corinth were apostolic foundations and received no major rank other than that of a metropolitan.

After Chalcedon, the idea of a pentarchy of patriarchs was initially shaped and diffused by Justinian. The word "patriarch" was first given by the imperial chancery to the Roman bishop in 450, then by Emperor Zenon to Constantinople (476). The five patriarchs are listed for the first time in the Novels 81 and 123 of Justinian (545 and 546), "the pope of the city of Rome being the first of all."

If we look at churches established outside the patriarchal territories of the Roman Empire, we find amazing support for the primacy of the see of Rome on the ground of the Scriptures and not of the synodical canons. So a Persian collection of 73 canons attributed to the Council of Nicea and composed around the year 400 develops a mystique of the four patriarchates of Rome, Alexandria, Ephesus, and Antioch, where the patriarchs are called "successors of Christ and of the Apostles." The Syriac version says "the patriarch of Rome will have authority over all the patriarchs, as Peter had over the whole community."[24]

9. On the precise issue of the foundation of the major episcopal sees came a strong reaction from the West. It is around the years 380-82 that a first serious dispute takes place. Canon 3 of Constantinople I elevated the see of the new capital city immediately after Rome "because Constantinople is New Rome." This decision and its motivation not only opened a long period

---

24. Oskar Braun, *De Sancta Nicaena Synodo. Syrische Texte des Maruta von Maipherkat* (Münster: Schöningh, 1898), p. 68.

of hostility between Constantinople and Alexandria, but also between Rome and Constantinople. What was at stake was the indirect statement of this canon that Rome enjoyed its position of first ranking see in the Christian world, and thus received a *presbeia tēs timēs,* because it was the old and first capital of the empire.

The Council of Constantinople was recognized as ecumenical only by Chalcedon. When canon 28 was proposed to this latter assembly, with the objective of renewing and furthering canon 3 of Constantinople, the Roman legates left the assembly and protested that the canons of Constantinople were not inserted among the synodal canons, and were unknown in Rome. Still in the fifth century, Leo the Great,[25] and at the end of the sixth, Pope Gregory I would regret that the Church of Rome never received notification of these canons.[26] The popes Vigilius, Pelagius II, and Gregory the Great would acknowledge the holy creed of Constantinople I, but not its canons.

So the *Decretum gelasianum* (a work of the early sixth century), which contains a list of authorities recognized by the Roman church, does not mention Constantinople among the ecumenical councils. The *Decretum* contains an important statement on how Rome sees the rank granted to Constantinople and the reason invoked to justify it. Scholars assume that chapter 3 of the *Decretum (De primatu Romano et de sedibus patriarchalibus)* goes back to Pope Damascus (366-84). It is reported that Damascus held a synod in Rome a year after Constantinople I, and although he never received officially the acts of this council, he reacted without quoting it by name, against the elevation of Constantinople to the same level of honor as Old Rome. It is probably the Roman assembly of 382 that declared the Roman church does not owe its pre-eminence among all churches to the decisions of a synod, but to the Lord's will when he decided to build his church on Peter.[27] The *Decretum* rejects the political principle chosen as a criterion in settling the hierarchy of sees. It is the apostolic principle that should continue to prevail. The *Decretum* even says that the first sees are all Petrine: Rome, Alexandria, and Antioch. It applies to the see of Rome the promise made by the Lord in Matthew 16:18-19. In this writing, the Roman see is considered as the see of Peter. Paul is only associated. The topic of the *triada petrina* would

---

25. Leo I, *Ep.* 106.

26. Gregory I, *Ep.* I, 25.

27. Decretum III,1: "quamvis . . . sancta tamen romana ecclesia nullis synodicis constitutis ceteris ecclesiis praelata sit, sed evangelica voce Domini et Salvatoris primatum obtinuit: 'Tu es Petrus, inquiens' [Mt 16,18-19]."

remain in the Roman discourse. So Gelasius against Acassius, Gregory the Great, and Nicolas I.

One of the projects of Constantine was to gather relics of the twelve apostles in the church he built for that purpose, he himself to be buried in their midst. As early as 357, the relics of St. Andrew were brought to this church, thus enforcing the legend of the foundation of that church by the apostle protochytos. Constantinople also tried to find an apostolic legitimation.

Further, the *Decretum gelasianum* argued that the see of Rome has always maintained the purity of faith,[28] and communion with Rome and its bishop is a criterion for communion with the whole church catholic.

The Appeals to Rome

Under the holy canons of the united church, the Roman see had a special position in matters of appeal. When a metropolitan synod was not able to judge a case, the second council (can. 2) and the Constantinopolitan synod of 382 expressly[29] foresaw the possibility of resorting to "a greater synod of that diocese," namely the exarchal synod, mentioning Asia, Pontus, and Thracia. The Arian crisis proved that this still was not enough. The canons 3-6 of Sardica (343) envisaged resorting to a higher level, namely to Rome. At Sardica, bishop Ossius suggested appealing to Rome in consideration of "the memory of the blessed Peter." So it was decided that a bishop could appeal to the Roman pope for a judgment of his provincial synod. The pope would then choose another provincial synod and defer the case to it. If the charges were still not settled, he would delegate his envoys to preside in synod and meet the ultimate decision.

In line with the former usage to consider Rome as a universal reference on doctrinal matters are the appeals directed to Rome by some Eastern bishops during the Arian crisis. Both parties, the Eusebians and Athanasius, turned to Rome with different goals. The former was eager to obtain Julius's

28. Decretum gelasianum III,1: "est ergo prima Petri apsotoli sedes romana ecclesia 'non habens maculam nec rugam nec aliquid eiusmodi'" (*Ep* 5,27); Ormisdas, *Ep.* 7: "quia in sede apostolica immaculate est semper catholica servata religio" (Andreas Thiel, *Epistolae Romanorum pontificum genuinae et quae ad eos scriptae sunt A. S. Hilaro usque ad Pelagium II. Tomus I, A. S. Hilaro ad S. Hormisdam, ann. 461-523* [Brunsbergae: E. Peter, 1868], p. 755).

29. So-called canon 6 of Constantinople I.

approval for the deposition of Athanasius, the latter to be recognized as innocent of the charges proffered against him. Pope Julius was asked to settle the
controversy between Athanasius and his synod on the one hand, the
Eusebians and their synod of Tyr, on the other. Both parties were interested in
having Rome on their side. Athanasius visited Julius himself and gave as a
motivation the relationship of the see of Rome with Peter, the first to proclaim in the name of all the apostolic faith.[30] The synod of Rome in 341 reha-
bilitated Athanasius and recalled the antique usage that synods should be free
to express the apostolic sentence, not to be overruled by political intrigues.[31]
In the views of Athanasius, however, there was no idea of the bishop of Rome
playing in the universal church the role of Peter in the apostolic college.

Later, Basilius of Caesarea in Cappadocia himself requested Athanasius to intervene in Rome in order to settle the schism of Antioch.[32] The only
way to get out of the crisis was to seek communion with the bishops of the
West. Pope Damascus should send some representatives able to reconcile the
parties or at least declare its communion with Meletius. Basilius would be
utterly disappointed by Damascus. He had sought the help of Rome only in
order to activate the communion between Western and Eastern bishops.
Communion with Rome was the sign of effective communion with all the
catholic bishops. Again, John Chrysostom looked for Pope Siricius's agreement in the election of Flavianus of Antioch and so resolved the schism. In
all these examples there is nothing that goes beyond the canons of the
church. Rome was a center of communion, the last reference to resort to.
The recourse to Rome was generally considered in the East when the administrative autonomies of the local churches and the imperial interferences
were unable to resolve the local problems.

Roman Petrine Theology in the Fifth Century

Since the time of Damascus, the papal chancery had adopted the style and
language of the imperial curia. The popes began to issue normative statements for the West in the form of decretal letters. The *Decretum* was an authoritative answer with general force to a request of a bishop. The pope began to develop a legislative activity for the West, parallel to the canons of the

---

30. Athanasius, *Pro fuga* 21-22.
31. Athanasius, *Historia Arianorum* 35-36.
32. Basilius, *Ep.* 66; 67; 69; 80; 82.

councils. The first collection of canons by Dionysius the Little lists the papal decretals after the canons of the councils. Canons of the councils could even be modified unwillingly under the influence of papal legislation.

A specific Petrine theology developed in Rome in the second half of the fourth century. The first point put into new light was again the notion of *cathedra Petri,* the word *cathedra* being understood as the episcopal office. Now it was stressed that Peter continued to sit in the cathedra of Rome, the bishop of Rome being his *vicar.* In the middle of the fourth century Rome celebrated the annual feast of the *Natale Petri de cathedra* on February 22, as the birthday of the Church of Rome through the cathedra given by Jesus to Peter, first in Jerusalem and later in Rome. So the episcopal see of Rome was the see of Peter successively occupied by the bishops of Rome. The title *Vicarius Petri* would be held by the pope during the rest of the first millennium. At the Council of Ephesus, the papal legate spoke of the "successor and vicar of Peter."[33] From 354 onwards, the expression *sedes apostolica* was currently used for Rome.[34] The Roman synod of 378 stressed that this see had a particular *praerogativa,* or privilege, to rank the first among all.[35] This point was rejected by the Arian synod of Aquileia three years later, saying that the see of Peter had passed equally to all bishops.[36] As Augustine stated in 396, it was generally admitted in the West that in the Roman church "the primacy of the apostolic see has always existed."[37]

Coming to concrete terms, the kind of primacy exercised by the popes during the first millennium did not exceed what the Eastern patriarchs operated in their own territories. The only new development was the legislative activity of the see of Rome, and the appeals coming from the Western provinces on doctrinal and disciplinarian matters. Gradually, the Roman bishops produced canonical norms binding ecclesiastical life in the whole Western sphere, just as the canons of the councils. From that time on, parallel developments between East and West in disciplinarian questions are to be noted, for instance in matters of clerical continence.

Pope Leo the Great in his sermons on the occasion of the feast of Saints Peter and Paul and for the anniversary of his own ordination gives a

---

33. Athanasius, *Pro fuga* 21-22
34. Pope Liberius to Eusebius of Vercelli, in PL 8, 1350.
35. PL 13, 582.
36. Fragments from Palladius, in Roger Gryson, ed., *Scolies ariennes sur le Concile d'Aquilée,* Sources chrétiennes 267 (Paris: Cerf, 1980), p. 306.
37. Augustin, *Ep.* 43,3,7, in CSEL 34, p. 90.

full theology of the Petrine office perpetuated by his successor the bishop of Rome. The idea of Petrine succession is stressed. Peter is at the same time apostle and bishop of Rome. His follower collects his heritage. According to Roman law, the heir receives the goods and the rights of the testator, and constitutes with him the same legal person.[38] Pope Siricius states that Peter continues to operate in his own ministry.[39] The apostolic see of Peter has authority over the whole church. The model is the relationship of Peter to the other apostles. Leo says that Peter governs also the pastors of the church, being himself governed by Christ.[40] Then Leo uses the juridical concept of *principatus.* The primacy of Peter's successor consists in a principatus, a jurisdiction over the whole church. The whole episcopacy is a corporate entity. It has the pope as its head.[41]

The successors of Pope Leo — Siricius, Zosimus, Innocent, Bonifacius — would develop the same thematic. Again in the schism provoked by the imperial edict Henotikon of 482, Pope Felix III reacts: it is Peter, not the emperor, who received the promise of Jesus in Matthew 16:18. When the schism of Acasius is settled, Pope Hormisdas asks the Orientals to recognize that the apostolic see has always kept the true faith under the promise of Matthew 16:18.[42]

By the end of the fifth century, Roman theology had effected a shift of emphasis, moving from the common, traditional, canonically established assumption that Rome was the first see in the Christian world, and its bishop the first in honor. The new outlook was that the bishop of Rome, now alone called *papa,* was the successor and the heir of the apostle Peter. So the image of Peter, head of the group of Twelve, imposed itself as the major reference or key to understanding the relationship of the pope to the other bishops.

Conclusion

The Eastern church has never taken into account the developments about the Roman bishop as vicar, successor or heir of the apostle Peter, but the

38. Justinian, *Novel* 48, ed. Schoell-Kroll, p. 286.

39. PL 13, 1153.

40. Leo I, *Serm.* 95, 2.

41. So Siricius to Himerius of Tarragona (PL 13, 1146, "utpote ad caput tui corporis").

42. Libellus Ormisdae, in Otto Günther, ed., *Epistvlae imperatorvm pontificvm aliorvm inde ab a. CCCLXVII vsqve ad a. DLIII datae Avellana qvae dicitvr collectio* (Vindobonae: F. Tempsky, 1895-98) = CSEL 35, pp. 520-22.

connection of the see of Rome with the apostle Peter was never totally forgotten in the East. When Emperor Theodosius imposed Nicean Christianity as the official religion of the empire he gave as a reference "the religion that the divine Apostle Peter brought to the Romans and now professed by bishop Damascus. . . ."[43] When the Fathers of Serdica considered establishing Rome as supreme court of appeal, they mentioned the memory of Peter, even though this did not imply in their eyes any universal jurisdiction attributed to the see of Rome.

In the ecumenical councils, the representatives of the bishop of Rome did not play an outstanding role, except for Chalcedon and later Constantinople III (680). In these particular circumstances, the dogmatic letters of the popes were acclaimed and adopted, but after discussion. Only with Nicea II (787) would it be clear that one of the formal criteria for a council to be ecumenical is the active cooperation, or "synergeia," of the bishop of Rome, while the other patriarchs have to give their assent.[44] Nevertheless even with a strong Petrine consciousness the bishop of Rome continued to act according to the traditional forms of communion established in the church. It is worth mentioning that the Petrine claims of the popes were never invoked as a cause for schism by the Eastern church during the first millennium.

Pope Gregory the Great (+604) refused for himself the title of "universal pope," stressing that his honor was to strengthen the honor of his brethren bishops.[45] In the first millennium there was no question of the Roman bishops governing the church in distant solitude. They used to take their decisions together with their synod, held once or twice a year. When matters of universal concern arose, they resorted to the ecumenical council. Even Leo, who struggled for the apostolic principle over the political one, acknowledged that only the emperor would have the power to convoke an ecumenical council and protect the church.

At the heart of the estrangement that progressively arose between East and West, there may be a historical misunderstanding. The East never shared the Petrine theology as elaborated in the West. It never accepted that the *prōtos* in the universal church could claim to be the unique successor or vicar

---

43. Codex Theodosianus XVI, I, 2: "quam divinum Petrum apostolum tradidisse Romanis religio usque nunc ab ipso insinuata declarat quamque pontificem Damasum sequi claret et Petrum Alexandriae episcopum."

44. Giovanni Domenico Mansi, *Sacrorum conciliorum* (Paris: Expensis Huberti Welter, 1903-27), vol. 13, p. 208.

45. Gregory the Great, *Ep.* 8,30, in PL 77, 933C.

of Peter. So the East assumed that the synodal constitution of the church would be jeopardized by the very existence of a Petrine office with potentially universal competencies in the government of the church.

Maybe the future will tell us whether synodality and primacy are not only compatible,[46] but mutually necessary, and that primacy and synodality are both implied in the words the Lord directed to the apostle Peter.

46. See Roland Minnerath, *Le pape, évêque universel ou premier des évêques?* (Paris: Beauchesne, 1978).

The Petrine Ministry in the New Testament and in Early Patristic Tradition

John Reumann

"Simon called Peter" has been the object of a variety of approaches and studies for his life and ministry, including ramifications for church office in Rome over subsequent centuries.[1] The major part of this presentation will be (1) a research report on Petrine studies over the last fifty years, indicating nine trends in biblical scholarships; (2) probes into specific texts, documents, and possible turning points, in summary only; and (3) treatments of "Petrine ministry" ecclesiologically. There is much that time and space do not permit treating here, but some suggestions are often indicated in the notes and bibliography.

Peter — Life, Faith, Work

An Overview

As baseline we shall employ *Peter in the New Testament: A Collaborative Assessment*, 1971-73, by eleven New Testament scholars — four Roman Catholics, five Lutherans, one Reformed, one Anglican — sponsored by the United States Lutheran–Roman Catholic dialogue.

---

1. Research reports: Erich Dinkler, "Der Petrus-Rom Frage: Ein Forschungsbericht," *Theologische Rundschau* NF 25 (1959): 189-230, 289-335; 27 (1961): 33-64; 31 (1965-66): 232-53; on "narrative criticism," Wiarda, pp. 9-33; Gnilka 2002, pp. 9-18.

An earlier alternative is the pioneering book, prior to Vatican II, by Oscar Cullmann, *Peter: Disciple, Apostle, Martyr,* 1952,[2]1960.

The U.S. volume is a decade more recent, from a number of scholars, and specifically related to ecumenical dialogue through the American volume V of "Lutherans and Catholics in Dialogue," on *Papal Primacy.*[2] Moreover, *Peter in the New Testament* is available in a number of languages and was reprinted in 2002.[3] In many ways the U.S. volume represents a climax in agreement on use of historical-critical methods (see chaps. 2, 7-9), before other approaches to Scripture emerged. That does not mean that all of its collaborators agree on every finding; I have always had questions over the use of the term "trajectories." There is probably no subsequent volume on Peter that has had the breadth of use and assent the 1973 one did, as a template for comparing subsequent studies.[4]

A number of those who collaborated in the 1973 project have since done further work on Peter, helpful for seeing how they develop the topic and assess later trends.[5] Of particular importance is the work of Raymond E. Brown from 1973 till his death in 1998.

Especially significant for our interests is *Antioch and Rome: New Testament Cradles of Catholic Christianity,* by Brown and John Meier. The approach posits "at least" four diverse groups among Christians with regard to the Jewish law and circumcision. Paul and Peter (and James) are placed together in group three, somewhat left of center.[6] It was in this "moderate center," worked out in Antioch and Rome, that the future of Christianity lay (214-15). This proposal for Peter and for Rome seemed to some "sophisti-

2. Paul C. Empie and T. Austin Murphy, eds., *Papal Primacy and the Universal Church* (Minneapolis: Augsburg, 1974), a volume related to "Lutherans and Catholics in Dialogue, IV," in *Eucharist and Ministry* (New York: U.S.A. National Committee of the Lutheran World Federation; Washington, DC: United States Catholic Conference, 1970).

3. German, French, Dutch, Spanish, Japanese. London: Geoffrey Chapman, 1974. Reprinted, Eugene, OR: Wipf & Stock, 2002.

4. Cf. Kessler, pp. 175-78.

5. Among them, Paul Achtemeier 1986, 1987, and *1 Peter,* Hermeneia (Minneapolis: Fortress, 1996); Joseph A. Burgess, "Lutherans and the Papacy: A Review of Some Basic Issues," in Peter J. McCord, ed., *A Pope for All Christians? An Inquiry into the Role of Peter in the Modern Church* (New York: Paulist, 1976), pp. 17-47; Karl P. Donfried, *ABD* 1992; Joseph A. Fitzmyer, *The Gospel According to Luke,* 2 vols. (Garden City, NY: Doubleday, 1981, 1985); *The Acts of the Apostles* (1998); Karlfried Froehlich, "Petrus. II. Alte Kirche," *TRE* 26: 273-78; Gerhard Krodel, *Acts* (Minneapolis: Augsburg, 1986).

6. Cf. pp. 2-8 and Brown, "Not Jewish Christianity and Gentile Christianity, but Types of Jewish/Gentile Christianity," *CBQ* 45 (1983): 74-79.

cated apologetics for Roman primacy," to others "an antipapist plot" (215). One reviewer saw a "programme . . . essentially that of F. C. Baur and his 'Tübingen School,'" a "Petrine *via media . . .* happily ascendant."[7] The reconstruction of development in Antioch, by Meier (11-86), and of continuity in Rome, by Brown (87-216), depends, of course, on the sources assigned to each place. Neither picture is without its problems; the variety was probably greater than indicated. At issue for Antioch is the jump from Matthean ecclesiology to Ignatius, with the Didache placed elsewhere than in Syria (compare and contrast Minnerath, 90, 298-306). How was the egalitarian Matthean community (23:8-12) that disapproved of charismatics (7:21-23) and was led by "prophets, sages, and scribes" (23:34) moved to adopt monepiscopacy and an almost divinized threefold office of ministry under a charismatic Ignatius (*Philadelphians* 7:1-2; cf. *Romans* 7:2)? For Rome, the assumption of ties to Jerusalem, James, and Peter from the outset and "normative Judaism" of the Mishnah; Hebrews as a radical position (group 4) versus 1 Clement, are among the issues.

Brown's reconstruction of the Johannine community shows considerable dissension in the "community of the Beloved Disciple," but in 3 John and beyond, a "transition" into "a structure or ecclesiastical polity" of Ignatius and "the church catholic" (159-61) — but, he adds, we need, especially in Roman Catholicism, "an inbuilt conscience against the abuses of authoritarianism" that the "disciple whom Jesus loved more than he loved Peter" (164) symbolizes.[8]

Subsequent work by Brown dealt less extensively with Peter and Rome. In his two-volume analysis of the Passion Narrative (1994), Peter's denial (1:587-626), e.g., is treated more on the level of each gospel than on a source- or historical Jesus- or Peter-level.[9] Factual basis is defended for the denial but not with the "exaggerated conclusions" that the tradition came from Peter himself (Papias, Vincent Taylor),[10] let alone a written Petrine source while

---

7. Wayne A. Meeks, *Heythrop Journal* 27 (1986): 455.

8. *The Community of the Beloved Disciple* (New York: Paulist, 1979); *The Epistles of John,* Anchor Bible 30 (Garden City, NY: Doubleday, 1982); perhaps less vigorously, pp. 47-115: "the Secessionists" move toward gnosticism, not the Great Church.

9. *The Death of the Messiah: From Gethsemane to the Grave. A Commentary on the Passion Narratives in the Four Gospels* (New York: Doubleday, 1994).

10. Vincent Taylor, *The Gospel According to St. Mark* (London: Macmillan, 1952), pp. 550, 572. Rudolf Pesch, "Die Verleugnung des Petrus," in Joachim Gnilka, ed., *Neues Testament und Kirche* (Freiburg: Herder, 1992), pp. 42-62; Pesch 1980, p. 43, "auf Petrus selbst zurückgehen muß."

Caiaphas was high priest (Rudolf Pesch), or that it arose as anti-Petrine propaganda in rival church circles.[11] Brown's "working hypothesis" concludes for "a brief mention [in the passion narrative] of Peter's particular failure in denying that he was associated with Jesus when challenged by a woman servant"; this developed into "a self-standing *narrative* . . . as Peter's role in Christianity became more visible," then "pre-Marcan and pre-Johannine forms" (621), used by each evangelist somewhat differently (622-26). As this example suggests, Brown's Passion analysis is light on Peter historically, concerned mostly with the evangelists, and in its own way "reader response" ("persecuted Christians of the 1st cent. . . . would have understood Peter's testing in light of their own," 626).

Brown's approach and the results are not different with Peter, James, and John in Gethsemane[12] or John 18:10, where "there is serious reason to doubt that John's identification of the sword-wielder as Simon Peter need stem from history."[13] The tendency is to be non-committal about the historical, more emphatic on the evangelists.

A final aspect of Brown's work stands out: strong opposition to the non-canonical Gospel of Peter, where Simon Peter speaks in the first person (14:60; cf. 7:26), a document "known to have been in circulation in the Antioch area before A.D. 200," extant in Greek fragments recovered in 1886-87 at Akhmin, Egypt.[14] This apocryphon was the basis on which John Dominic Crossan reconstructed an earlier "Cross Gospel"[15] which, though

11. With Robert W. Herron, Jr., *Mark's Account of Peter's Denial of Jesus: A History of Its Interpretation* (Lanham, MD: University Press of America, 1992), against Kelber, Weeden, K. E. Dewey, "Peter's Curse and Cursed Power (Mark 14:53-54, 66-72)," in Werner H. Kelber, ed., *The Passion in Mark: Studies on Mark 14–16* (Philadelphia: Fortress, 1976), pp. 96-114; and Günther Klein, "Die Verleugnung des Petrus," *ZTK* 58 (1961): 285-328, reprinted in his *Rekonstruktion und Interpretation: Gesammelte Aufsätze* (Munich: Kaiser, 1969), pp. 49-98.

12. 1:146-62, "impossible to decide with surety whether the mention of Peter, James, and John is a Marcan creation, stems from pre-Marcan tradition, and/or is historical" (p. 151).

13. 1:267-68. John 18:11 is "from tradition" (p. 278). In 1970, *The Gospel According to John (xiii–xxi)*, Anchor Bible 29A (Garden City, NY: Doubleday, 1970), p. 816, Brown allowed that "no one can establish the veracity of the details narrated by John alone . . . ; but they are not implausible."

14. *The Death of the Messiah*, 2:1317-49; earlier and more polemically in his Presidential Address to the Studiorum Novi Testamenti Societas, "The *Gospel of Peter* and Canonical Gospel Priority," *New Testament Studies* 33 (1987): 321-43.

15. *The Cross That Spoke: The Origins of the Passion Narrative* (San Francisco:

Docetic, featured Peter.[16] This passion narrative, Crossan and others claim, was used by all our canonical gospels. Just the reverse, Brown says: the Gospel of Peter was composed A.D. 100-150, drawing on the canonical gospels.[17]

Trends

There are other books about Peter that we shall note below, but we can already begin to list some observations on trends in recent years.

1. *Seeking Simon Peter in many ways parallels the "quest(s) for the historical Jesus."* It is a subset of *Leben-Jesu Forschung.*[18] Hence the questions of "criteria" and "development," post-Easter and "church" influences on the historical figure. Some authors do a "life" of Peter after having written one on Jesus and perhaps on Paul.[19]

2. Over the last thirty years there has been *a lessened emphasis* on a "theology of Peter." Ethelbert Stauffer had emphasized a "paidology" or Servant-Son Christology, built around material from the historical disciple, his speeches in Acts, and 1 Peter.[20] So also Cullmann.[21] Although the idea oc-

---

Harper & Row, 1988). See also John Crossan's *The Historical Jesus: The Life of a Mediterranean Jewish Peasant* (San Francisco: Harper, 1991), pp. 367-94.

16. E.g., at Jesus' death, "I with the companions was sorrowful . . . we were in hiding . . . sought after by them as wrongdoers . . . fasting . . . mourning and weeping" (7:26-27).

17. *The Death of the Messiah,* 2:1341-42, probably in Antioch (p. 1344), by someone familiar with Matthew, Luke, and John (pp. 1334-35).

18. So, among others, Pesch 1980, p. 2, but also part of church history and theology; Böttrich, pp. 23-25; Gnilka 2002, pp. 9-11.

19. So, e.g., Gnilka, *Jesus von Nazaret: Botschaft und Geschichte,* Herders theologischer Kommentar zum Neuen Testament, Supplementband 3 (Freiburg: Herder, 1990; Taschenausgabe ⁶2000), trans., *Jesus of Nazareth: Message and History* (Peabody, MA: Hendrickson, 1997); *Paulus von Tarsus: Apostel und Zeuge,* Herders theologischer Kommentar zum Neuen Testament, Supplementband 6 (Freiburg: Herder, 1996); *Petrus und Rome* (2002). Michael Grant, a classicist, *Saint Paul* (New York: Scribner, 1976); *Jesus: An Historian's Review of the Gospels* (New York: Scribner, 1977); *Saint Peter, A Biography* (New York: Scribner, 1995).

20. *New Testament Theology* (London: SCM, 1955), pp. 30-55, 244-46, Greek *pais, paidos;* Petrine formulae, stressing the OT "Joseph tradition," pp. 339-42; German ⁴1948.

21. *Peter* (1962), pp. 66-70, "a place of honour at the beginning of all Christian theology"; Acts 3:13 = Isa. 52:13; 3:26; 4:25-30; 1 Peter 2:21ff. *The Christology of the New Testament* (London: SCM, 1959), "Jesus and the *Ebed Yahweh,*" pp. 60-75, esp. 73-74; 1963 ed., pp. 69-78.

casionally lingers on,[22] the notion has met with increasing rejection, not least by Catholic scholars.[23] This does not mean, in the ups and downs of biblical theology, a total loss of theological interest in recent decades[24] but simply that Peter is now less frequently given a distinctive voice in New Testament theology.[25]

3. Given the trends already noted, there have been *warnings by Roman Catholic authorities, but also by others, against historical criticism applied to Scripture.* Thus in 1988, at the one-day "Ratzinger Conference on the Bible and the Church" in New York City, there was a targeting of unfounded hypotheses, putative sources, and philosophical presuppositions, especially in Bultmann and Dibelius (i.e., in form criticism). But fundamentalism or over-literalism was rejected. At a press conference that followed, moderate critical scholars were praised.[26] More positive is a 1993 International Biblical Commission document from Rome on biblical interpretation.[27] Within the Catholic Biblical Association of America, a 1997 paper by Luke Timothy Johnson, on "What's Catholic about Catholic Biblical Scholarship?" charged that over the last century it had changed from "being Catholic but not very scholarly, to . . . being scholarly but not markedly Catholic."[28] Responses especially drew attention to the 1993 Biblical Commission document.[29]

22. Cf. A. D. Kroger, Jr., "The Question of a Distinctive Petrine Theology in the New Testament," diss., Baylor University, Waco, TX, 1988. Dschulnigg, p. 180 n. 33.

23. Rudolf Pesch, "The Postion and Significance of Peter in the Church of the New Testament," *Concilium* 64 (1971): 31; Josef Blank, "The Person and Office of Peter in the New Testament," *Concilium* 83 (1973): 83.

24. Cf. John Reumann, "Profiles, Problems, and Possibilities in Biblical Theology Today," *Kerygma und Dogma* 44 (1998): 61-85, 145-69.

25. In a book-by-book approach to New Testament theology, 1 and 2 Peter will, of course, be profiled, but with various appraisals and often not traced to Peter's authorship.

26. Richard J. Neuhaus, ed., *Biblical Theology in Crisis: The Ratzinger Conference on the Bible and the Church*, Encounter Series 9 (Grand Rapids: Eerdmans, 1989), including Joseph Ratzinger, "Foundations and Approaches of Biblical Exegesis," *Origins* 17, no. 35 (1988): 595-602; R. E. Brown on how historical criticism contributes to ecumenical discussion; William H. Lazareth, on Luther; George Lindbeck, "Scripture, Consensus, and Community," also in *This World* (Rockford, IL) 23 (1988): 5-24, on reappropriating "classical hermeneutics"; plus discussion inspired by the papers.

27. Joseph Fitzmyer, *The Biblical Commission's Document: "The Interpretation of the Bible in the Church,"* Subsidia Biblica 18 (Rome: Pontifical Biblical Institute, 1995).

28. Cited from Peter S. Williamson, "Catholic Principles for Interpreting Scripture," *CBQ* 65 (2003): 327.

29. See note 27; Williamson (note 28), *CBQ* 65 (2003): 327-49, and his *Catholic*

It is not impossible to find similar outcries from non–Roman Catholics, particularly when the plethora of "new methods" to be noted in point 4, below, are included and terms like "postmodern" are invoked.[30] One may observe that anguish will be even greater if and when these new methods take over that attempt through critical study to remove historicity from the agenda.

4. For all attention to historical criticism, which continues to one degree or another in subsequent treatments of Peter, like Pesch 1980 and 2001, Perkins, Dschulnigg, Böttrich, and Gnilka 2002, *new methods for interpretation have proliferated in the last thirty years or so.*[31] They have often been touted as replacing "historical criticism." They may involve older approaches, even ancient ones, like *rhetoric,* but sometimes in the form of the "new rhetoric."[32] They may involve aspects long present in good exegesis, like attention to *literary* features, but now refined and applied in new ways, as with *narrative criticism.*[33] Some clearly have philosophical and linguistic underpinnings, as with *structuralism.*[34] Concern for *social setting* of a text or author or audience has been taken under the aegis of various modern sociological theories as part of the "social world."[35] Emphasis on the biblical canon has led to several forms of *canonical criticism.*[36] Other examples can be added to the list.[37]

These several approaches have been hailed since the 1970s as "revolu-

---

Principles for Interpreting Scripture: A Study of the Pontifical Biblical Commission's "The Interpretation of the Bible in the Church," Subsidia Biblica 22 (Rome: Pontifical Biblical Commission, 2001), reviewed by Dale Launderville in *CBQ* 65 (2003): 460-62.

30. Cf. Lindbeck (n. 26, above); David C. Steinmetz, "The Superiority of Pre-Critical Exegesis," *Theology Today* 37 (1980): 27-38; Brevard S. Childs, *Biblical Theology of the Old and New Testaments: Theological Reflection on the Christian Bible* (Minneapolis: Fortress, 1993), pp. 524-29.

31. Overview in Brown, *Intro.,* pp. 24-28, who begins with source, form, and redaction criticism, and adds to categories we shall note, "advocacy criticism."

32. Brown, *Intro.,* pp. 26-27; Reumann, *JES* (1992): 69-70; Chaïm Perelman and Lucie Olbrechts-Tyteca, *The New Rhetoric* (Notre Dame: University of Notre Dame Press, 1971; French 1958).

33. Brown, *Intro.,* pp. 25-26; Reumann, *JES* (1992): 71-73; Perkins, pp. 52-59 and passim.

34. Or Semiotics. Brown, *Intro.,* pp. 24-25; Reumann, *JES* (1992): 67-68.

35. Brown, *Intro.,* pp. 27, 55-73; Reumann, *JES* (1992): 68-69. On 1 Peter, cf. John H. Elliott, *A Home for the Homeless: A Sociological Exegesis of 1 Peter, Its Situation and Strategy,* 2nd ed. (Philadelphia: Fortress, 1981). Jerome H. Neyrey, *2 Peter, Jude,* Anchor Bible 37C (New York: Doubleday, 1993) reflects more "cultural anthropology."

36. Brown, *Intro.,* p. 24; Reumann, *JES* (1992): 73-74.

37. See above, n. 32; discourse analysis, feminist approaches, liberation theology (= advocacy).

tionary change," removing historical criticism with its interest in "what happened" from the picture, in a "paradigm shift."[38] To generalize, most of these new methods take up the biblical text "as is," in the canon or amid all the documents and artifacts of Christian origins, and emphasize subsequent readings of the biblical text, rather than penetrating behind it to written or oral sources and what occurred in Jesus' lifetime or Peter's career.[39] To this extent these methods are usually "ahistorical."[40] Most of them have thus far been applied to Peter only sporadically (some examples are indicated in the notes above), except for literary-narrative criticism.

Results of the "shift" since structuralism can be seen in Pesch 2001. He stresses (16-18), in a seemingly canonical-critical approach, the final text (Endtext) within the canon and the "Autorenwillen" that stands behind the canon. But it is not so much the approach of Brevard Childs or James Sanders that is followed, but the proposals by David Trobisch, an admittedly controversial view on development of the canon, a canon that emerged quickly, already in the second century.[41] From a "school of Peter" in Rome has come a unified Old Testament and New Testament, with Peter playing a key role in development from the Jewish-Christian foundation of the church, with its Jerusalem pillars, to the church of the Gentiles with Paul (19). Matthew, first in the New Testament canon, provides a link to the Old Testament (in Matthew, note 16:17-19). Mark, though containing only a part of the picture that Matthew provides on the primacy of Peter, has especial Petrine authority in the four-gospels canon, for the Papias tradition is now deemed likely.[42] The four gospels conclude with John 21,[43] a link to Peter in Acts (where Paul also ap-

---

38. Reumann 1992, pp. 57-58 gives references.

39. Reumann 1992, pp. 59-67 on texts as "window" to the past or "mirror" for the reader.

40. In *The New Interpreter's Bible* (Nashville: Abingdon, 1994), Carl R. Holladay, "Contemporary Methods of Reading the Bible," pp. 137-38, and Moisés Silva, "Contemporary Theories of Biblical Interpretation," p. 116.

41. Trobisch, *Die Endredaktion des Neuen Testaments. Eine Untersuchung zur Entstehung der christlichen Bibel,* NTOA 31 (Fribourg/Göttingen, 1996).

42. Pesch 2001, pp. 39-40, citing in n. 32 Martin Hengel, "Probleme des Markusevangelium," in Peter Stuhlmacher, ed., *Das Evangelium und die Evangelien,* WUNT 28 (Tübingen: Mohr Siebeck, 1983), pp. 221-66; Edward E. Ellis, "Entstehungszeit und Herkunft des Markus-Evangelium," in Bernhard Meyer, ed., *Christen und Christliches in Qumran?* Eichstätter Studien, N. F. 32 (Regensburg: F. Pustet, 1992), pp. 195-212; William R. Schoedel, "Papias," *ANRW* 2, no. 27/1 (1993): 262-67.

43. Trobisch 1996 (above, n. 41), pp. 150-51. Klaus Berger, *Formgeschichte des Neuen*

pears, in chapters 13-28); in this arrangement, Acts was followed not by the Pauline corpus but the General Epistles (including 1 and 2 Peter); then Paul and Revelation. In the canon a testament of Peter (2 Peter) corresponds to a testament of Paul (2 Timothy), both from Rome (cf. Knoch 1973, above n. 5). In the total New Testament canon, the Corpus Paulinum is placed within a structure *(Gefüge)* of Petrine texts. First Peter includes a Pauline inheritance (50-51) and shows Petrine authority in an area geographically Pauline.[44] Thus an encompassing *Petrusbild* structures *Primat* and *Kanon.* Having sketched this canon-criticism approach to Peter, Pesch nonetheless goes on using the historical-critical findings he had previously presented in 1980. Indeed, he builds some of them into his "canonical" case.

It is far from clear what results these "new methods," often apart from historical criticism, will have in ecumenical dialogue and interfaith conversation.[45]

5. Of all these new approaches the one so far most clearly applied to Peter is *narrative criticism* by, among others,[46] Timothy Wiarda, who seeks a literary pattern in the gospels that sets forth the apostle's personality and relationships, notably with Jesus. Wiarda classified treatments of Peter thus: (I) as if historical persons and events are involved; (II) symbolic presentations of ecclesiastical situations contemporary to the narrator; (III) the narratives as "story worlds."[47]

The pattern that Wiarda finds is a structure of "positive intention" on Peter's part ("he means well") and then a reversal (it turns out badly). E.g., Mark 8:31-33, "Peter tries to discourage Jesus from thinking in terms of suffering," but Jesus rebukes Peter as "Satan."[48] This pattern is analyzed in great

---

Testaments (Heidelberg: Quelle & Meyer, 1984), p. 80, termed John 21 a testamentary act of the exalted Lord, showing his authority through a miracle, more about "succession" than fish; Installatio (21:15-17) and personal Vaticinium (21:18-23).

44. Cf. Otto Knoch, *Der Erste und Zweite Petrusbrief. Der Judasbrief,* Regensburger Neues Testament (Regensburg: Pustet, 1990), p. 121; cf. pp. 217, 146.

45. Pesch 2001, p. 16, the consequences are still not visible; Reumann 1992. If these new methods come to dominate, probably each ecclesial group will learn how to employ various methods to its own advantage.

46. Gnilka 2002, pp. 13-15. Jack D. Kingsbury 1979 began with a theological concern that he never lost, but he increasingly moved into a narrative approach in the Synoptics.

47. The historical approach (I) may focus on (1) the time of Peter (Cullmann; Pesch 1980; Thiede 1986) or (2) an "impersonal Peter" with a church role (the U.S. dialogue's *Peter in the New Testament;* Dschulnigg; Nau on Matthew; Dietrich on Luke).

48. An "obvious" pattern also in Mark 9:5-7; 14:29-30; 14:54, 66-72; Matt. 14:28-31;

detail,[49] with the conclusion that, because of multiple attestation in Mark, M, L, and John, it must "reflect something of [Peter's] actual character and experience" (226). (Here, Wiarda has reverted to "historical grounding" for his "reversal structure" through a criterion in the quest for the historical Jesus.) The pattern, it is allowed, may provide a paradigm for the relationship of Christ and believers (232), but again and again Wiarda denies that his analysis shows any tie to a "special church role" for Peter (167, 181, 227, 230). While Wiarda holds that there is a "trans-episodic, unified Peter story" (7), he deals mainly with episodes or really parts of pericopes, rather than the whole gospel book — contrary again to much narrative criticism.

There is more to narrative-critical approaches on Peter than Wiarda's study provides. Some think narrative criticism especially reinforces what redaction criticism turns up.[50] Nau provides a striking example on Peter in Matthew's Gospel. Source, form, and redaction criticism, as well as rhetoric (see n. 33, above), are employed to point up how Matthew presents him. The net result is to view Peter in the sequence Matthew provides. Nau's visualization chart on what is actually said in Matthew (25; in Mark, 41) shows more than the "variegated" portrayal that the 1973 U.S. study saw, more than even "conflicting traditions." Aware of what Matthew omits from Mark (like 16:7) and carries over from Mark and Q, at times with changes, Nau depicts (not the "historical" but a "mythopoeic") Peter (103) as a figure marked by dramatic reversals (good beginnings, bad outcome; 14:28, 30; 16:16-19, 23). Traditional ascriptions are artfully shifted from Peter to the disciples (e.g., the confession at Mark 8:29, to all the disciples in the boat at 14:33; binding and loosing, in a tradition about Peter at 16:19, for all at 18:18) or from the disciples as "little faiths" (Q, Matt. 6:30 parallel Luke 12:28) or "stumbling blocks" (Mark 9:42-50; Q, Matt. 18:7 par. Luke 17:1) to Peter (14:31 and 16:23, respectively). Peter is listed as "first" at 10:2, but this term is unpacked in Matthew at 19:30 and 20:16, cf. 27, through the principles, "The last will be first, and the first last"; "whoever would be first among you must be your slave" (75-76). Each high spot about

---

Luke 5:8-11; John 13:6-7, 8, 9-10; 18:10-18; 21:15b-16a, 16b-17a. The pattern is perceived "more faintly" in Mark 1:35-38; Matt. 17:24-27; 18:21-22; John 13:36.

49. Mary R. Thompson, *CBQ* 64 (2002): 593-94, speaks of the "extensive categorizations" — which often lead to the obvious.

50. Perkins, pp. 53-55 contrasts them. Is, e.g., Matt. 16:17-19 to be understood as redactoral addition or at least in part redactoral creation? In the literary whole of the book, how is it to be understood within the framework of 14:33 and 18:18, where all the disciples confess Christ and receive power to bind and loose? Wiarda's analysis (97) offers little help on this old question.

Peter (walking on water, his correct confession of Christ) is followed by a negative extreme in the story (Peter sinks in the sea; he is "Satan . . . a hindrance," note 16:23, *skandalon ei emou* is added in Matthew). In keeping with the way Stock, 68, quoting B. van Iersel (cf. *TijdTheol* 25 [1985]: 402-9), summed up the "broad picture of Peter" in Matthew as "good beginning — poor ending," Matthew's final reference to Peter at 26:75 is of him weeping bitterly, after his denials of Jesus. There is no reference to Peter at the empty tomb or in a resurrection appearance story, as in Mark 16:7, Luke 24:34, or John 20–21.

Nau fits all this into a pattern of "encomiastic dispraise of Peter in Matthew" (138-40). The *stasis*, or statement of the problem, is his proposed rank and privilege ("first," 10:2). The result of all the contrasting pictures and comparisons is that at the end Jesus stands alone with all power and authority (28:18-20), Peter unmentioned by name after 26:75. He is just one of the eleven disciples. Matthew 28:17 ("when they saw Jesus, they worshiped him but some doubted"; or is it, "they saw Jesus, worshiped him, and doubted"?) suggests that for Matthew "even after the resurrection . . . in his own Antiochan community — there were still some who shared Peter-like doubts" (103; cf. 14:31). We need not trace out here how this dispraise or blame of Peter is fitted by Nau into the ecclesial situation at Antioch (122-28), where the choices may have included a charismatic approach, the family-of-Jesus model (James of Jerusalem, his brother), elder-presbyters, as in the synagogue, and rule of a single leader as in the empire or province. What Nau's careful reading of the references in Matthew, one by one, suggests is that too often 16:17-19 has been elevated, without 16:21-23 (compare *Ordo* assignments on separate Sundays in the lectionary). Many churches, not just Rome, suffer from "Matthew 16:17-19 syndrome" (22, 109).

For ecumenical work, a danger is that narrative literary criticism (unless coupled with other approaches, like source and redaction criticism) merges into reader-response, so that each party can find its own interpretation confirmed; texts have no meaning in themselves, criteria are subjective. Gnilka (2002:15) warns, "An exegesis that forgoes the historical dimension runs the danger of becoming play without results, art for art's sake (unverbindlichen Spiel, l'art pour l'art)."

6. In one way or another, usually via historical criticism, *New Testament studies have concluded for a number of "images of Peter" on which there is considerable agreement.*

Cullmann worked, as his subtitle shows, with Peter as disciple, apostle, and martyr, "in the apostolic period of revelation," but with "no trace" of a "chain of successors" (234).

The *U.S. dialogue volume* (1973) listed, beyond "minimal facts about Simon Peter of which we have some historical certitude" (158-62), some eight images (or roles; I avoid the term "trajectory" for these images), namely, "early and perhaps the first witness of the risen Jesus, the leader and spokesman of the twelve, the missionary," i.e., "the great Christian fisherman" (163). Further, "the shepherd (pastor) of the sheep" (John 21); "Christian martyr"; "receiver of special revelation" (1 Cor. 15:5; Luke 24:34; Mark 9:2ff.; add Matt. 16:17; "greatly developed in the apocrypha"); "confessor of the true Christian faith" (Matt. 16:16); guardian of the faith against false teaching (2 Peter); and weak and sinful man (Gal. 2:11ff.; Mark 9:5-6, etc.).[51]

Pesch 1980 included Peter as witness of the Easter faith, leader of the Jerusalem *Urgemeinde* and of the mission to the Jews. He of course discusses Peter's relationships with Jesus, Paul, etc. But most of Pesch's "development of the *Petrusbild*" is book by New Testament book, not image by image. Under significance for the whole church he presents Peter, like whom there is "no second apostle figure," as first disciple, spokesman for the disciples and the Twelve, "eyewitness of the *vita Jesu* from the beginning," and "chief guarantor of the Jesus-tradition" (161). In *Pesch* 2001 the *Bild* includes the "primacy" of Peter ("rock"; John 21, something "passed on," 30-46), and Peter as *Typus,* not just of discipleship but of *Amtstäger* (66-69). In the "heilsgeschichtliche Translation" from Jerusalem to Rome we see, from the New Testament *Bild,* Peter's power in mission, exorcisms and healings, teaching, discipline, mediation, and leadership (85-91).

Dschulnigg 1996 is interested in both *Petrusbild* and *Petrusdienst.* Elements in the *Bild* are summarized book by book. E.g., in Mark: the disciple most frequently named; speaker for the disciples; part of the three and four within the Twelve (a point Dschulnigg will later stress); mission proclaimer; with a by-name that means "precious stone," perhaps corner or foundation stone; literally in the first and last scenes in Mark (1:16; 16:7), three at the beginning of the book (1:16-39), three in the middle (8:27–9:8), and three at the end (14:26-72). There are also negative features: Peter didn't understand the theme of suffering and resurrection (8:27-30); he denied Jesus and fell asleep in Gethsemane, all in a broader picture of failure, yet acceptance into the

---

51. Donfried's book-by-book analysis in *ABD* (above, n. 6) does not include a trajectory of images; nor does Lampe in *RGG*[4]. Perkins 1994 speaks of "witness" and "martyr," especially in light of extra-canonical sources, plus "Peter's teaching as true tradition," opposing Simon Magus; spokesperson for conventional Christianity; gnostic apostle, and bishop of Rome (pp. 131-76), without using the term "images."

service of Jesus. Space does not permit spelling out here the careful summaries by Dschulnigg for each New Testament book that lead to a picture of Peter's great significance — but lack of a successor in the New Testament. His shoes were too big to fill till later "institutionalization" occurred (209-10). But there are New Testament guidelines for suggesting what *Petrusdienst* and its limits might be (212-14).

Böttrich 2001 offers a "profile" of Peter as a follower of Jesus, his collegial place in the Twelve, the four, and the three; spokesman; chief actor in some stories (87-96); then witness of Easter (with Mary Magdalene), organizer in Jerusalem, taking initiative in proclamation and responsibility in visiting Samaria and at the "Gentle Pentecost" in Acts 10 (132-72). He works miracles through faith, is an itinerant preacher, mediator in Antioch (Acts 15, *Apostelkonvent,* not "Council"), but is not above criticism in the controversy over table-fellowhip (Gal. 2; 173-211). Probably a martyr in Rome in a Christian pogrom in A.D. 64 (219), something no less likely historically than traditions about other ancient personalities (227). In addition to images in the New Testament, there are also images in apocryphal sources and legends *("quo vadis?").* Primacy for the pope, as *vicarius Christi* (or *Petri*), meet with the Reformers' criticisms (obedience to the pope is not necessary for salvation, the papacy is not an institution of "göttlichen Rechts"), but in the new ecumenical openness about *Petrusamt, -funktion,* and *-dienst,* there may be a common basis in the Peter of the Bible.[52]

Gnilka 2002, in his work on Peter and Rome in the first two centuries, finds no model for today but does see stimuli for finding together how to preserve the variety there (7). His New Testament findings offer data for a sketch of Peter's life where many of the items noted above in other treatments reappear (201-2, cf. 19-200). The *Petrusbild* (202-5) emerges especially in the gospels, as rock *(Fels),* first among the Twelve from the beginning and at Easter. The classic expression in Matthew 16:17-19 probably arose in Antioch, for the teacher with the keys as guarantor and surety *(Bürge)* of the gospel, with the task of strengthening brothers and sisters (Luke 22:31-32) and power to lead universally (John 21:15-17). First Peter bears out this authority for Asia Minor, 2 Peter for the universal church; both letters arose in Rome, or at least in a part of the community there. A personal succession in the New Testament is denied, but hints were there to make the *Dienst* necessary to continue. Yet dis-

---

52. Specifically listed are Peter's *Grundergestalt* (Matt.), *als Seelsorger* (Luke), *Hirte* (John), *Nachfolger und Bekenner, Initiator und Wortführer, Organisator und Missioner, Wegbereiter, Traditionsträger.*

ciples can also forgive sins (Matt. 18:18; John 20:23); it and teaching authority in Matthew 16:19 mesh together *(ineinander greiffen).* In the Fourth Gospel, Peter represents "office," the Beloved Disciple the immediacy of Christ *(Christusunmittelbarkeit).* In the two epistles of Peter, direction is given under his authority, false teachers corrected. Rome came to the fore as the chief city of the Imperium Romanum, where Peter the rock and Paul died. But the New Testament also sees a church built on apostles and prophets (Eph. 2:20); the heavenly Jerusalem has the names of twelve apostles on the foundation of its walls (Rev. 21:14). Christ is the foundation upon which an apostle builds (1 Cor. 3:10), the *Eckstein* (Mark 12:10-12, etc.).

Kessler focused on a single image: Peter as the first witness of the risen Lord and thus an Easter context for primacy and authority. First Corinthians 15:5, Luke 24:34, Mark 16:7, Luke 24:12, and John 21 point to an appearance to Peter (cf. Minnerath 13-15, 16, 30, 577), though, admittedly, such an event is never narrated in the New Testament. It is echoed in "retrojections" like Matthew 16:17-19 and Luke 22:32 and projected in 2 Peter 1:16-18, perhaps also in the Gospel of Peter (a lost narrative appearance? cf. Ps.-Clementine Homilies 17). But there was always ambiguity about an appearance to Peter (53-71; e.g., was Mary Magdalene really the first person to whom Jesus appeared, John 20? or James?). The appearance (reconstructed by Kessler, often in agreement with von Campenhausen 1960) faded in the patristic period and was abandoned from the second till the nineteenth century, often in favor of the pattern of "promise" (Matt. 16, during the ministry) and "conferral" (John 21:5ff., after Jesus' resurrection; cf. Bellarmine, *De Controversiis* 342). Recovery of the importance of the Easter appearance to Peter came, ironically, through "liberal Protestant," chiefly German, critics, notably Harnack 1893 and 1922 (Peter had two visions of Christ, at the Transfiguration and of the risen Lord, 1 Cor. 15:5). Catholics began to see an Easter context and its importance, e.g., in O'Collins 1973. But there was reticence on the part of many to pin so much on an appearance to a single person, let alone that Peter was then responsible for acceptance of "Easter faith" among other apostles and disciples. O'Collins qualified the picture by emphasis on Mary Magdalene as first to see the risen Jesus (cf. *Mulieris Dignitatem* 67-69; she is *apostola apostolorum,* "the first to bear witness to him before the Apostles, . . . Christ entrusting divine truths to women as well as men"; cf. *The Catechism of the Catholic Church* ##641-42) and by viewing Peter within a circle of apostles and disciples and "college of Easter witnesses" (Kessler 123, 127-29, 198-207).

While Vatican I reflected the "promise/conferral schema" (*Pastor aeternus,* DH [1969] 3053 = Tanner, *Decrees* 812), Kessler finds his emphasis on Easter witness reflected in Vatican II (". . . the sole Church of Christ . . . which our Saviour, *after his resurrection,* entrusted to Peter's pastoral care [John 21:17], commissioning him and the other apostles to extend and rule it [cf. Matt. 28:18, etc.], . . . a society in the present world," which "subsists in the Catholic Church," *Lumen Gentium* 8, Flannery translator, italics added; Kessler 182-83; 201-2). Hence, to the words on the cupola of St. Peter's Basilica in Rome (Matt. 16:18; John 21:15, 16, 17; *Peter in the New Testament* 83), one ought to add, "The Lord has risen indeed, and has appeared to Simon" (Luke 24:34; O'Collins 1973: 83; Kessler 206).

7. These lists of Petrine imagery vary. Some are more precise than others, some less irenic than others. Is there a single basic image? Can reconstruction together build on images today? Most treatments listing images of Peter are concerned to show him as defender of what became Christian orthodoxy. But some of the *figures used about him* invited application *in circles outside the New Testament canon* in literature to which only some studies of Peter have paid attention.[53] In particular, there were lines of development such as "recipient of revelation" and "Offenbarungsträger" that so-called gnostic texts picked up. These references are part of the picture for "Christian origins," if not part of "biblical theology," especially for the decades when orthodoxy and heresy were not clear opposites but part of a range of positions that existed, one blending into another.[54]

The seminal verse at Matthew 16:17 invited this, for it has no direct object after the verb "revealed": "Flesh and blood has not revealed *(apokalypsen)* . . . to you, but my Father who is in heaven." We supply "this" and understand Peter's confession from the Matthean context, but the statement is open-ended. The Transfiguration scene in 2 Peter is confirmatory about "the prophetic message" (1:19) and in the context revelatory about Peter's martyr death as Christ had made evident *(edēlōsen)* to him (1:14). Prophets receive revelation (1 Peter 1:12).

Peter's name was used to give authority to both orthodox and heterodox views. Gnilka suggests that in the post–New Testament period, "the East saw in Peter a charismatic, the recipient of revelations and divine secrets, who can be a model *(Vorbild)* for all Christian women and men striving after knowledge, spirituality, and wisdom," while the Western church, especially

---

53. *Peter in the New Testament* (1973), pp. 20-22.

54. Here Brown's picture of a continuum on positions concerning Jewish law (above, n. 6) may be applied to other issues, including the role of the Spirit, place of women, community organization, etc.

in North Africa (Tertullian) concentrated, through use of Matthew 16:18-19, on church office and "juridicized" it (2002: 276).

We cannot examine here all the Nag Hammadi documents or others long known, like the Gospel of Peter or Acts of Peter, nor do we mean to endorse all their sometimes wild speculations. But the Gospel of Thomas may contain versions of Jesus' sayings earlier than forms in our canonical gospels.[55] The Gospel of Peter has been pushed too far by the Jesus Seminar and J. D. Crossan, but it is part of the images of Peter in early Christianity. If one is going to conjecture a "Petrine School,"[56] some of these documents fit with a group interested in Peter, not just canonical texts. Perhaps, indeed, one should say "schools" devoted to Peter.

This whole area has been brought to the fore through Terence V. Smith's 1985 monograph on *Petrine Controversies in Early Christianity*. Certainly there were controversies involving Peter in the New Testament period, e.g., in Antioch (Gal. 2), in the community of the Beloved Disciple (in John at least against claims made for Peter), perhaps in Mark, and elsewhere. Certainly Petrine controversies continued later, involving Matthew 16, as can be seen in Tertullian's *De Pudicitia*,[57] or Cyprian against Pope Stephen.[58] There was material pro-Peter in certain Nag Hammadi documents,

---

55. Not to be confused with the Infancy Gospel of Thomas. Brown, *Intro.*, pp. 117-20, 220-21, 839-40, e.g., GTh 46 (Brown p. 248 n. 48).

56. D. H. Schmidt, "The Peter Writings: Their Redactors and Their Relationships," diss. Northwestern University, Evanston, IL, 1972; Terence V. Smith, *Petrine Controversies in Early Christianity*, WUNT 2, Reihe 15 (Tübingen: J. C. B. Mohr [Paul Siebeck], 1985), pp. 62-64; Marion L. Soards, "1 Peter, 2 Peter and Jude as Evidence for a Petrine School," *ANRW* 2, no. 25/5 (1988): 3827-49; Otto B. Knoch, "Die Petrusschule in Rom: Die Stellung des Petrus in der Kirche," in his *Petrusbrief* commentary, pp. 143-46; "Gab es eine Petrusschule in Rom? Überlegungen zu einer bedeutsamen Frage," *SNT* 16 (1991): 105-26; Pesch 2000; Thomas Schmeller, *Schulen im Neuen Testament?*, Herders Biblische Studien 30 (Freiburg: Herder, 2001).

57. In Tertullian's Montanist period, against the *pontifex maximus* and "bishop of bishops" who claimed power to remit the sins of adultery and fornication upon penance, citing Matthew 16:19 (*De Pud.* 21; perhaps Pope Calixtus, A.D. 217-22, but also "every church akin to Peter"); Smith, pp. 20-22; Johannes Quasten, *Patrology*, vol. 2 (Westminster, MD: Newman; Utrecht/Antwerp: Spectrum, 1953), pp. 312-15, cf. 164 on Hippolytus, against Calixtus' lenient treatment of penitents.

58. On whether baptized heretics should be rebaptized on return to the Catholic Church, see Cyprian, *Epp.* 71, 72, 74, 75, holding that bishops are of equal rank; Stephen in Rome appealed to Matthew 16:18-19 for supremacy and succession; Smith, pp. 22-24; G. Haendler, "Zur Frage nach dem Petrusamt in der alten Kirche," *ST* 30 (1976): 108-13;

the Acts of Peter and the Twelve,[59] the Epistle of Peter to Philip,[60] and the Apocalypse of Peter.[61] This Apocalypse and canonical 2 Peter, Smith suggests, may be "products of the same Petrine controversy." There were also gnostic documents against Peter.[62]

Smith points out that Peter was not "the exclusive property of 'orthodox' second century Christian groups" (214). Lack of references to him in writers of the first half of the second century (the Apostolic Fathers, Apologists, Justin) may be due to the fact that these Christians linked Peter with "'heretical' groups." Hence Papias, on Peter and Mark. Toward the end of the second century (Irenaeus), Peter is beginning to be recovered from "heretical" associations. "By the mid-third century" Peter is "firmly placed back inside the orthodox camp," perhaps "in *response* to use of Peter (and Matthew 16) by Gnostic groups." Smith's most striking claim is that 2 Peter, a second-century document, is part of a "controversy involving Gnostic themes" (99-100) and is itself somewhat gnostic, "not quite the orthodox document which it is often held to be" (100). If we speak of trajectories, they are multiple for Peter, groupings are in a spread; the categories are not simply "orthodox" or "heretical" in the murky second century.[63]

8. Biblical and patristic studies make clear that *historically* a gap occurs at the point where it has been claimed "the apostles were careful to appoint

---

Quasten (n. 57, above), 2:342, 348-53, on pro-Petrine "additions" (or deletions in a final form), p. 365.

59. Smith, pp. 119-21, Simon's proper confession of Christ (Matt. 16:16) gave him the name "Peter"; contrast Gospel of Thomas 13, where Peter's answer ("You are like a righteous angel") pales beside that of Thomas; James M. Robinson, ed., *The Nag Hammadi Library in English* (New York: Harper & Row, 1977), pp. 265-70 = Nag Hammadi Corpus (NHC) VI,1; Douglas M. Parrott, "Peter and the Twelve Apostles, The Acts of," in *ABD* 5:264-65, "one of the independent narratives about the apostles that began to appear in the 2nd century," not gnostic, but used by gnostics.

60. Smith, pp. 121-26. The author heightens Peter's significance, compared to Acts, his source; Peter is leader of the author's gnostic community. *Nag Hammadi Library,* pp. 394-98 = NHC VIII,2; Marvin W. Meyer, "Peter to Philip, Letter of," in *ABD* 5:265-66; Perkins, p. 161.

61. Smith, pp. 126-41, Peter receives visions that the Savior explains; Peter becomes "transmitter and guarantor of Gnostic traditions" (p. 131). *Nag Hammadi Library,* pp. 339-45 = NHC VII,3.

62. Smith, pp. 103-17. Perkins, pp. 157-59 and *The Gnostic Dialogue* (New York: Paulist, 1980). E.g., Gospel of Thomas 12 (James is to be leader); 13 (above, n. 59).

63. Gnilka notes Smith's monograph (pp. 264 n. 5; 269 n. 27; 272) but not his overall thesis on 2 Peter. Perkins, p. 129 n. 57 succinctly summed up, "Smith argues that 2 Peter has adopted Gnostic motifs so that the issue is not simply orthodoxy vs. heresy."

successors in" what is called "this hierarchically constituted society," specifically "those who were made *bishops* by the apostles . . . ," an episcopate *with an "unbroken succession going back to the beginning."*[64] For that, evidence is lacking, quite apart from the problem that monepiscopacy replaced presbyterial governance in Rome only in the mid- or late second century.[65] It has been noted above how recent treatments conclude that in the New Testament no successor for Peter is indicated.[66]

Pesch, in what may be the strongest of statements in the books on Peter being noted here, sees for Roman Catholics nothing less than the divine reality of the church as a whole to be at stake in opposition to papal primacy (2001: 13-15). He concluded in a careful statement for "the *catholic primacy* of Peter, in *apostolic* succession to the apostles in the office of bishop in service to the faith in *one, holy* church" (1980: 170, *factum theologicum*) and spoke further (2001) of those who bear the primacy as coming to further understanding (Matt. 11:27), in spite of weakness, and taking martyrdom upon themselves — in principle, collegially and synodically.[67]

Ohlig, in what Kessler (190) terms "perhaps as low an estimate of the Easter witness as we have found," denied that Jesus "commissioned Peter to a primatial role later in the church" (Ohlig 11); that includes his "temporary" leadership at Jerusalem after Easter (14). Position and "personal succession" cannot be claimed from the New Testament (20).

Dschulnigg (209-12) sees Rome's rise to prominence to have been based on historical and societal factors. Papal institutionalization and its hierarchical structure reflect the political structures of the Roman Empire.

---

64. *Lumen gentium* 20 (Flannery trans., *Vatican Council II* [Collegeville, MN: Liturgical Press, 1975], pp. 371-72; Abbott trans., *Documents of Vatican II* [New York: Guild Press, America Press, Association Press], pp. 39-40, "the episcopate in a sequence running back to the beginning"). Cited are Iren. *Adv. Haer.* 3,3,1 = PG 7:848; Tertullian, *Praescr. Haer.* 32 = PL 2:52f., and Ignatius of Antioch passim.

65. Gnilka 2002, p. 225. Ignatius had no "succession"; bishop and presbyter correspond to Christ and apostles, not successors to the apostles (p. 223); the "succession lists" in Rome were of presbyters and bishops (pp. 242-50).

66. Dschulnigg, p. 209, with Cullmann, citing G. Christ, "Das Petrusamt im Neuen Testament," in Georg Denzler et al., eds., *Zum Thema: Petrusamt und Papsttum* (Stuttgart: Hiersemann, 1970), p. 49; "a qualitative leap"; Erich Gräßer, "Neutestamentliche Grundlagen des Papsttums? Ein Diskussionsbeitrag," in die Arbeitsgemeinschaft ökumenischer Universitätsinstitute, ed., *Papsttum als ökumenische Frage* (Munich: Kaiser; Mainz: Grünewald, 1979), p. 54.

67. Pesch 1980, p. 168 speaks of office as service, bound to the Jesus-tradition, not formal authority but agreement with the believer/converted sinner.

Only later was Matthew 16:17-19 specifically applied. From the New Testament picture he adds limits as well as guidelines.[68]

More specific is Gnilka 2002 on Peter and Rome (15-17, 206-62, 273-76). Rome was not "spared severe [inner] disturbances" till "well into the second century," as some claim,[69] but was involved in various controversies in its many house churches. Especially significant was Pope Victor's assertion of authority against Polycrates of Ephesus. Victor does not "cut a good figure" in making ecclesial Rome, like imperial Rome, the place from which law goes forth (274-76). In the face of unity that was lost with the East and then with the Reformers, in a juridicized church, an *ecclesia numerus episcoporum*, how may a full unfolding of the heritages, Petrine and other images, now go forward?[70]

9. There has been some tendency to *group Peter and Paul together*, especially with regard to the heritage of the church in Rome and with ecumenical implications for the present day. In addition to references above, passim, note Farmer and Kereszty on this "forgotten potential" and the earlier titles they cite: Jean M. R. Tillard, *L'Évêque de Rome* (Paris: Cerf, 1982), translated as *The Bishop of Rome* (Wilmington, DE: Glazier, 1983); Yves M. J. Congar, "Saint Paul et l'authorité de l'église romaine d'après la Tradition," *Studiorum Paulinorum Congressus Internationalis Catholicus* 1961, *Analecta Biblica* 17-18: 491-516; Emmanuel Lanne, "L'Église de Rome a gloriosissimis duobus apostolis Petro et Paulo Romae fundatae et constitutae ecclesiae (Adv. Haer. III,3,2)," *Irénikon* 49 (1976): 275-322; Jean-J. von Allmen, *La primauté de l'église de Pierre et de Paul* (Fribourg/Paris: Editions Universitaires/Cerf, 1977).

68. Pages 213-14 list (1) *Petrusdienst* as totally oriented to proclamation of Jesus, the teaching of the apostles, prophets, and teachers, obligated to the beginnings of the church and biblical reflection of faith (as in Matthew, the *Vorzugsjünger* in the Gospel of John, 2 Peter), yet (2) with authority to enable, protect, and legitimate new impulses, ways, and developments (see Matthew, and in Acts the Gentile mission); (3) collegiality, the three and the Twelve (in the gospels and Acts); (4) not individually stamped concepts but ones widely supported, ecumenical, of the whole church (cf. 1 Peter, Luke/Acts); (5) defending biblical faith (Matthew, 2 Peter); (6) more important, pastoral, the unity of the church and its *Teilkirchen* (John); (7) representatives of this service are sinful believers; when a representative does not go the way of the gospel, opposition is justified (the gospels, Galatians).

69. Gnilka, p. 226, against Walter Bauer, *Rechtgläubigkeit und Ketzerei im ältesten Christentum*, BHTh 10 (Tübingen [2]1964), p. 132 = *Orthodoxy and Heresy in Earliest Christianity* (Philadelphia: Fortress, 1971), p. 128.

70. Cf. also Gnilka, p. 7, "daß wir von verschiedenen Standpunkten aus in der Christenheit bei Wahrung der Verschiedenheit besser zusammenfinden."

Possible Probes

A number of areas call for fuller treatment than can be given here. Some of them are the object of entire symposia and volumes of essays. Listed are passages or topics that arise in light of both agreements among scholars on Peter together with the questions such agreements raise and the disagreements seen in the survey above. The brief comments amount to items for further study and discussion.

A. Matthew 16:16-19 — Is this traditional flashpoint to be regarded as a unity or combination of sources and tradition? To what degree does it reflect controversy over Peter within and beyond the Matthean community (the problem of "mirror readings")? If taken only literarily, as part of a twenty-eight-chapter narrative, how do these verses fit with what is said about all disciples (14:23; 18:18)? What is to be made of the lack of a direct object for the verb "(God) revealed . . . to you"?

B. The Fourth Gospel — the Beloved Disciple in relation to Peter, especially John 21.

C. Galatians 2:1-10, 11-14 (or 21) — How do this account and the "incident at Antioch" fit with the depiction of Peter and Paul as leaders in agreement on issues like the Jewish law (cf. R. Brown, n. 7, above)? Did Peter "win" at Antioch? (So Achtemeier 1986: 25-26. Paul becomes "an isolated figure" who sought to go to Spain because he had lost in the East [1987]; but see the critical review by L. T. Johnson in *CBQ* 50 [1988]: 704f.) In the short run only (Böttrich 208)? Was there a Petrine dominance there, or was it the position of James that ruled?[71] Does not Paul's position on food laws eventually win out in the whole church? The question of relating theological principle and moderating leadership is raised.

D. 2 Peter — There is wide agreement that the document is pseudonymous (Pesch 1980: 150; Dschulnigg 189-91, 200-201; Böttrich 247-48; Ps.-Petrus). What of a "school of Peter" in Rome? So Pesch 2001: 53-55, with O. Knoch; contrast Gnilka 2001: 198-200 (above, n. 57). Is the Petrine group here posited somewhat gnostic? Note that there are other apostles in 2 Peter, notably Paul, but no reference to the Twelve. Many agree that the thought world and vocabulary of 2 Peter is Hellenistic (Dschulnigg 196, who adds,

---

71. John Meier, *Antioch and Rome*, pp. 40-44. After Paul left, there were probably separate meals and Eucharists, Peter's "moderating role" trying to prevent "complete schism"; but Hellenist Jewish Christians (Acts 7) were also likely active there. Antioch therefore had Christians from three or four of Brown's groups.

plus Jewish-Christian faith; Gnilka 2002: 196; Harrington 2003: 237). Gnostic (T. V. Smith)? Gnilka 2002: 192 sees a gnostic "realized eschatology" on the part of the opponents. The U.S. dialogue study in 1973 spoke of a "Petrine magisterium" at this point, based on "Peter's" judging (defending?) the writings of Paul; cf. Mussner 1976: 66, re "primacy," and Dschulnigg 200 (with limits) and his article, "Der theologische Ort des Zweiten Petrusbriefes," *Biblische Zeitschrift* N.F. 33 (1989): 161-77, reflecting the Matthean portrayal of Peter. Contrast Gnilka 2002: 197; to see an ecclesial *Lehramt* of a Petrine cast or *Frühkatholizismus* (Käsemann) in 2 Peter goes too far.

Peter, Rome, and Ecclesiology

Historically and in light of early images of him, Peter has long been connected with the church at Rome, e.g., in a traditional Roman Catholic position, now somewhat undergoing revision through biblical, patristic, and ecumenical studies (see I.8 and 9, above). There is an Orthodox position or positions on the bishop of Rome.[72] During the Reformation, Lutheran, Reformed, Anglican, and Anabaptist views emerged, not to mention stances on the papacy in subsequently developing churches, Methodist, Pentecostal, etc.

In ecumenical discussion the terms "Petrine function, ministry, *Amt*, and *Dienst*" have been used to sum up New Testament findings with an eye to later church developments. The meaning of each term may differ slightly and need further discussion.[73]

A. We shall look here at Peter and the church in light of "koinonia ecclesiology."[74] This will be done by surveying New Testament passages us-

72. Recently, Olivier Clément, *Rome autrement. Une réflexion orthodoxe sur la papauté* (Paris: Desclée de Brouwer, 1997), trans. *You Are Peter: An Orthodox Reflection on the Exercise of Papal Primacy* (Hyde Park, NY: New York City Press, 2003).

73. Scharfe in 1893 spoke of "die petrinishe Strömmung" in the New Testament. *Peter in the New Testament* (1973) put its closing emphasis on a "Petrine trajectory" of images (along with trajectories "of the Twelve and even of Paul," p. 167). The trajectory was not of each image (such as how "recipient of revelation" developed) but the continuing "trajectory traveled by Peter's image" (p. 168).

74. Gnilka speaks of the *communio*-Gedenke in 1 Clem. (p. 215) and in connection with second-century exchanges between churches to strengthen, encourage, and stress unity (p. 274). Böttrich, pp. 272-73 touches on the terms *Petrusfunktion*, etc., in connection with the German Lutheran-Catholic statement in 2000, *Communio Sanctorum. Die Kirche als Gemeinschaft der Heiligen* (Paderborn/Frankfurt), trans. *Communio Sanctorum: The*

ing words from the *koinon-* root.[75] They are limited in number, but at times can be considered in light of the even larger number of references in Paul using koinonia language, as well as verses in Hebrews and 1 John. We sketch the picture in a chronological order for Peter's career, without debating whether each reference is historically factual or later literary fictive development.

1. Simon had partners *(koinonoi)* in the fishing business, James and John, the sons of Zebedee (Luke 5:10).

2. The only other use of such vocabulary in the gospels came in the claim of scribes and Pharisees that, in the days of their ancestors, "we would not have taken part [*koinonoi,* had a share] with them in shedding the blood of the prophets" (Matt. 23:30) and in references to what defiles (*koinoi,* or makes common) a person according to Old Testament food laws (Mark 7:15 par. Matt. 15:11; 7:18, 20, 23 par. Matt. 15:18, 20; Mark 7:2, eating with "defiled" hands, *koinos*). This usage is reflected in Peter's position, asserted against the Lord, "I have never eaten anything that is profane *(koinon)* or unclean," and the divine command, "What God has made clean, you must not call profane" (*koinon,* Acts 10:14, 15, repeated at 11:9).

3. Did Peter know of the charge against Paul, at Acts 21:28, "This fellow has defiled *(kekoinōke)* the holy place, the Temple"?

4. In the Jerusalem community after Easter, *koinōnia* was one of the things that characterized the followers of Jesus, along with "the apostles' teaching, the breaking of bread, and the prayers" (Acts 2:42). This aspect of church life, not a name for the church itself, has been variously interpreted as fellowship with each other, with the apostles, table-fellowship liturgically,

---

Church as the Communion of Saints (2004), VI.4 Petrusdienst. The U.S. statement, Lutherans and Catholics in Dialogue, X, *The Church as Koinonia of Salvation: Its Structures and Ministries,* completed April 2004, treats the biblical references to koinonia in I.A-D and under "Biblical and Historical Foundations and Backgrounds," I.

75. In the considerable literature, sometimes oriented to ecumenical concerns, see especially George Panikulam, *Koinōnia in the New Testament: A Dynamic Expression of Christian Life,* Analecta Biblica 85 (Rome: Biblical Institute Press, 1979); Josef Hainz, *Koinonia: "Kirche" als Gemeinschaft bei Paulus,* Biblische Untersuchungen 16 (Regensburg: Pustet, 1982) and his article *"koinōnia, etc.,"* in *Exegetisches Wörterbuch zum Neuen Testament* (Stuttgart: Kohlhammer, 1981), 2:749-55 = *Exegetical Dictionary of the New Testament* (Grand Rapids: Eerdmans, 1991), 2:303-5; John Reumann, "Koinonia in Scripture: Survey of Biblical Texts," in Thomas F. Best and Günther Gassmann, eds., *On the Way to Fuller Koinonia,* Faith and Order Paper no. 166 (Geneva: WCC, 1994), pp. 37-69; and Norbert Baumert, *KOINONEIN und METECHEIN — synonym? Eine umfassende semantische Untersuchung* (Stuttgart: Katholisches Bibelwerk, 2003).

and increasingly as sharing of material goods, having all things in common (*koina*, 2:44), so that "everything they owned was held in common" (*koina*, 4:32) and no one was in need. Such a socio-economic interpretation, as a "communal form of life," echoed the Hellenistic world and perhaps Qumran but without the latter's communal structuring.[76]

5. We have no evidence that Peter knew of the numerous and theologically significant uses of *koinōnia* in Paul's letters. Perhaps the eucharistic wording at 1 Corinthians 10:16 was common knowledge, if it was a pre-Pauline formula, participation *(koinōnia)* in the body and participation in the blood of Christ, and behind it his death.

6. There is one exception. At Galatians 2:9, James, Cephas, and John gave Paul and Barnabas "the right hand of fellowship" *(dexias edōken . . . koinōnias),* to seal an agreement on spheres for mission work, to the circumcised and to the Gentiles, respectively, with the proviso to "remember the poor."[77] This proviso about caring for the poor led to the collection in Paul's churches for the "saints" in Jerusalem, an undertaking sometimes referred to in Paul's letters by *koinōnia* terms (2 Cor. 8:4; 9:13; cf. Rom. 15:27). Ironically we have no indication that Peter engaged in such fund-gathering for impoverished Jewish Christians in Palestine, an undertaking for the unity of the churches that led ultimately to martyrdom for Paul.

There are three important uses of *koinon*-terms in the Petrine epistles.

7. First Peter 5:1, paranesis for elders or presbyters in the church community, along with "youngers" (*presbyteroi* in 5:1; *neōteroi* in 5:5), is the only passage in the New Testament where Peter is brought into connection with church office via the term *koinōnos:* "Now as an elder myself *(sympresbyteros)* and a witness of the sufferings of Christ, one who shares *(koinōnos)* also in the glory that is going to be revealed, I exhort the elders among you: shepherd the flock of God that is among you *(poimanate to en hymin poimnion). . . .*" Some manuscripts add *episkopountes,* which, if read, should not be taken as a technical term about bishops, but simply as "seeing to it, caring for";[78] the emphasis is on how this is to be done: willingly, not under

---

76. Reumann 1994, pp. 59-60, summarizing Panikulam 123 and other views; Alan C. Mitchell, "The Social Function of Friendship in Acts 2:44-47 and 4:32-37," *JBL* 111 (1992): 255-72; Joseph Fitzmyer, *Acts* (above, n. 5), p. 270, "*communal form of life . . .* (communion). . . ."

77. Reumann 1994, pp. 51-52. Some think the words come from the protocol minutes of the meeting; note "Cephas," which Paul does not normally use of Peter.

78. Norbert Brox, *Der erste Petrusbrief* (Leipzig: St. Benno-Verlag, ²1986; EKKNT 21, Zürich: Benzinger, Neukirchen-Vluyn: Neukirchener Verlag, 1986), p. 230, supplies

compulsion; eagerly, not for gain; not domineering those allotted (by God, to your care).[79] Over all stands the *parousia* of the Chief Shepherd, Christ (5:4). Peter, the apostle of Jesus Christ, appears here with co-presbyters in the "royal priesthood" (2:9) of baptized believers.[80]

8. The theme in 1 Peter of sufferings (of Christ) and glory (to be revealed to Christians), present at 5:1, appears further in 4:13, "Rejoice as you share *(koinōneite)* the sufferings of Christ, so that at the revelation of his glory you will rejoice with exaltation." Not just Jewish tradition is involved about joy amid suffering, for it is specifically rooted in a passion-theology about Christ for all the community; cf. 2:21-25.[81]

9. Related is 2 Peter 1:4, where God's power, call, and promises point to those being addressed becoming "participants of the divine nature" *(theiois koinōnoi physeōs)* at their "entry into the eternal kingdom of our Lord and Savior Jesus Christ" (1:11), i.e., at his *parousia* (1:16; 3:4, something firmly promised, though delayed; 3:12, the day of our God).[82]

How such data from the New Testament on Peter might be further related to "koinonia ecclesiology" remains to be worked out, including any pertinent patristic references. The New Testament Petrine *Bild* connects Peter to the Hellenistic koinonia concept as apostle and presbyter in the household-church community, sharing with all its members in many aspects of life under Christ.

"tut diese Aufgabe" since the participle is not in ℵ, B, or patristic citations. Karl H. Schelke, *Die Petrusbriefe. Der Judasbrief* (Freiburg: Herder, ³1976), pp. 127-28, suggests it was added under the influence of 2:25. See the Bauer-Danker-Arndt-Gingrich, *Greek-English Lexicon of the New Testament* . . . (Chicago: University of Chicago Press, ³2000), p. 379 for the definitions **"give attention to, accept the responsibility for the care of,"** as well as the possible renderings above.

79. The genitive object *tōn klērōn*, after *katakyrieuontes,* is to be taken as a reference to people (not land or money, "the allotment"), parallel to *tou poimniou* ("but be examples [*typoi*] to the flock"), its various portions assigned to individual elders or shepherds (Bauer-Danker . . . *Lexicon* [above, n. 78], p. 548), geographically or by households(?).

80. The "Amts-Paränese" (Brox [above, n. 78], p. 226) reflects Hellenistic household codes (*hypotagēte,* youngers are to be subject to elders; cf. 2:13–3:7), with the church as *oikos* of God (2:5; 4:17); Elliott, pp. 810-11.

81. Brox (above, n. 78), p. 214; Reumann 1994 (above, n. 75), p. 57; Achtemeier (above, n. 5), pp. 306-7; Elliott, pp. 774-78, who, like others, notes parallels in Paul, esp. Philippians 3:10 (and Col. 1:24).

82. On 1:4, cf. Reumann 1994 (above, n. 75), pp. 57-58; Neyrey (above, n. 35), Hellenistic philosophy "cast in Christian terms, namely the end of the world"; similarly Karl H. Schelke, *Die Petrusbriefe. Der Judasbrief* (above, n. 78), p. 189.

B. Treatments of the *church as koinonia,* if they seek to relate ecclesiology to *ministry and church office,* must do so in some other way than through New Testament vocabulary using koinonia terms, since the terms do not turn up with regard to office holders; cf. III.A.7, above.[83] But do the many New Testament references, or most of them, have something in common?

It has seldom been noticed, let alone applied, that *New Testament passages about koinonia most frequently relate to all believers, the entire community, all who are in Christ.* They are the ones who are called into the fellowship of God's Son (1 Cor. 1:9), share in the gospel and mission (Phil. 1:5), in faith (Philem. 6), in Christ's body and blood in the Lord's Supper, and behind it at the cross (1 Cor. 10:16). They are the ones, every Christian, who share in the Holy Spirit (Phil. 2:1; 2 Cor. 13:14, the community created by the Spirit), in Christ's sufferings (Phil. 3:10; 1 Peter 4:13), in mutual sufferings and consolation (2 Cor. 1:7). They have fellowship with Father and Son and with one another (1 John 1:3, 6, 7). Hence they share what they have (Heb. 13:16), partnering with those maltreated (Heb. 10:33). Koinonia in the New Testament very often has to do with what we all share (Heb. 2:14; 2 Cor. 8:4; 9:13; Phil. 4:14-15; 1 Tim. 6:18; Rom. 12:13, 15:26). Even when *koinon*-terms, like the verb, are used in the singular, the individual Christian is being addressed as one within the whole community, to whom the precept applies.[84] Koinonia is again and again an aspect of life for the entire community (Acts 2:42, 44: 4:32; 2 Peter 1:4).

Does this mean that *koinonia ecclesiology* ought to begin with what is often asserted as primary in ecclesiology, namely *the whole people of God,*[85] but now needs to be followed through with regard to office? There is, then, place for Petrine ministry (see above on passages connecting Peter with koinonia), for Paul, for all the apostles, and for teaching ministry (Gal. 6:6), set within the whole people of God, in the gospel.

---

83. The U.S. Lutheran-Catholic dialogue, round 10 (above, n. 74), has done so using koinonia as the lens for examining structure and ministry.

84. 1 Tim. 5:22, to Timothy, "do not participate in the sins of others," can fit any Christian; cf. 2 John 11; Gal. 6:6, of teacher and those being taught; Rom. 15:27, mutuality.

85. Cf. *Baptism, Eucharist and Ministry,* Faith and Order Paper no. 111 (Geneva: WCC, 1982), Ministry I. ##1-6; *Lumen Gentium* II, ##9-17; *Church and Justification: Understanding the Church in the Light of the Doctrine of Justification* (Geneva: LWF, 1994), 3.2, ##51-62.

Select Bibliography

Abogunrin, S. O. "The three variant accounts of Peter's call: A critical and theological examination of the texts," *NTS* 31 (1985): 587-602.

Achtemeier, Paul J. "An Elusive Unity: Paul, Acts, and the Early Church," *CBQ* 48 (1986): 1-26.

——. *The Quest for Unity in the New Testament*. Philadelphia: Fortress, 1987.

Bauckham, Richard. "2 Peter: An Account of Research," *ANRW* 2, no. 25/2 (1988): 3713-52.

——. "The Martyrdom of Peter in Early Christian Literature," *ANRW* 2, no. 26/1 (1992): 539-95.

Berger, Klaus. "Unfehlbare Offenbarungsliteratur. Petrus in der gnostischen und apokalyptischen Offenbarungsliteratur," in *Kontinuität und Einheit,* Festschrift für F. Mußner, ed. Paul-G. Müller/Werner Stenger. Freiburg: Herder, 1981, pp. 261-326.

Best, Ernest. "Peter in the Gospel According to Mark," *CBQ* 40 (1978): 11-35.

Böcher, Otto/Froehlich, Karlfried. "Petrus I/II," *TRE* 26 (1996): 263-78.

Böhm, Martina. "Nachfolge aus Erfahrung. Redaktions-kritische Beobachtungen zur Berufung der ersten Jünger dei Markus und Lukas," in *Gedenk an das Wort,* Festschrift für Werner Vogler, ed. Christoph Kähler et al. Leipzig, 1999, pp. 24-33.

Böttrich, Christfried. *Petrus: Fischer, Fels und Funktionär.* Biblische Gestalten 2. Leipzig: Evangelische Verlagsanstalt, 2001.

Burnett, Fred W. "Characterization and Reader Construction of Characters in the Gospel," *Semeia* 63 (1993): 3-28.

Campenhausen, Hans von. 1960 (German), trans., "The Events of Easter and the Empty Tomb," in *Tradition and Life in the Church: Essays and Lectures in Church History*. Philadelphia: Fortress, 1968, pp. 42-89.

Caragounis, Chrys C. *Peter and the Rock.* Beihefte zur Zeitschrift für die neutestamentliche Wissenschaft und die Kunde der älteren Kirche, 58. Berlin/New York: de Gruyter, 1990.

Claudel, Gérard. *La Confession de Pierre: Trajectoire d'une Péricope Évangélique.* Paris: J. Gabalda, 1988.

Cullmann, Oscar. *Petrus. Jünger — Apostel — Märtyrer. Das historische und das theologische Petrusproblem.* Zürich: Zwingli Verlag, 1952, ²1960, ³1985. ET: *Peter, Disciple . . . Apostle . . . Martyr: A Historical and Theological Study*. Philadelphia: Westminster Press, 1953, ²1962. Cf. his article, *"petra, Petros, Kephas,"* *TDNT* 6 (1959): 95-112 (German).

Culpepper, R. Alan. *Anatomy of the Fourth Gospel: A Study in Literary Design*. Philadelphia: Fortress, 1983.

De Lima, João Taveres. *"Tu serás chamado* Kēphas," in *Estudo exegético sobre Pedro no quarto evangelho.* Analecta Gregoriana 265. Rome: Editrice Pontifica Università Gregoriana, 1994.

Denziger, Heinrich. *Echiridion symbolorum definitionum et declarationum de rebus fidei et morum,* re-edited by Peter Hünermann, 37th edition. Freiburg: Herder, 1991. Cited as DH.

Dietrich, Wolfgang. *Das Petrusbild der lukanischen Schriften.* BWANT 5/14. Stuttgart/ Berlin/Köln/Mainz: Kohlhammer, 1972.

Dinkler, Erich. "Peter's Confession and the Satan Saying: The Problem of Jesus' Messiahship," in James Robinson, ed., *The Future of Our Religious Past: Essays in Honour of Rudolf Bultmann* (New York: Harper & Row, 1971), pp. 169-202.

Droge, Arthur J. "The Status of Peter in the Fourth Gospel: John 18:10-11," *JBL* 109 (1990): 307-11.

Dschulnigg, Peter. *Petrus im Neuen Testament.* Stuttgart: Katholisches Bibelwerk, 1996.

Dunde, Siegfried R. "Simon Petrus — die erste autoritäre Persönlichkeit der (katholischen) Kirche?" in Raul Nieman, ed., *Petrus, der Fels als Anstosses.* Stuttgart: Kreuz-Verlag, 1994, pp. 21-25.

Elliott, John H. *1 Peter.* Anchor Bible 37B. New York: Doubleday, 2000.

Farmer, William R./Roch Kereszty. *Peter and Paul in the Church of Rome: The Ecumenical Potential of a Forgotten Perspective.* Theological Inquiries. New York: Paulist, 1990.

Feldmeier, Reinhard. "Der Darstellung des Petrus in den synoptischen Evangelien," in *Das Evangelium und die Evangelien. Vorträge vom Tübinger Symposium 1982,* ed. Peter Stuhlmacher, WUNT 28. Tübingen: Mohr Siebeck, 1983, pp. 267-71.

Frisch, Helga. "War Petrus eine Frau? Die Geschichte von der Jüngerin Simone," in Raul Nieman, ed., *Petrus, der Fels als Anstosses.* Stuttgart: Kreuz-Verlag, 1994, pp. 976-1008.

Gnilka, Joachim. *Petrus und Rom. Das Petrusbild in den ersten zwei Jahrhunderten.* Freiburg/Basel/Wien: Herder, 2002.

———. "'Tu es Petrus.' Die Petrus-Verheißung in Mt. 16,17-19," *MThZ* 38 (1987): 3-17.

Goppelt, Leonhard. *A Commentary on 1 Peter.* Edited by Ferdinand Hahn. German 1978, MeyerKEK 12/1. Translated and augmented by John E. Alsup. Grand Rapids: Eerdmans, 1993.

Grappe, Christian. *D'un Temple à l'autre. Pierre et l'Église primitive de Jérusalem.* Études d'Histoire et de Philosophie Religieuses 71. Paris: Presses Universitaires de France, 1992.

———. *Images de Pierre aux deux premiers siècles.* EHPhR 75. Paris: Presses Universitaires de France, 1995.

Hahn, Ferdinand. "Die Petrusverheißung Mt 16,18f. Eine exegetische Skizze," in *Das kirchliche Amt im Neuen Testament,* ed. Karl Kertelge, WdF 189. Darmstadt: Wissenschaftliches Buchgesellschaft, 1977, pp. 543-63.

Hardt, Michael. "Petrus. II. Petrustradition. 4. Ökumenisch," *RGG*⁴ 6 (2003): 1168-69.

Harnack, Adolf von. *Bruckstücke des Evangeliums und der Apokalypse des Petrus,* TU 9. Leipzig, 1893.

———. "Die Verklärungsgeschichte Jesu, der Bericht des Paulus 1 Kor 15:3ff. und die beiden Christusvisionen des Petrus," *Sitzungsberichte der Preussischen Akademie der Wissenschaften* (1922): 62-80.

Harrington, Daniel J. 2003. *Jude and 2 Peter.* See "Senior, Donald P.," below.

Heiligenthal, Roman. "'Petrus und Jakobus, der Gerechte.' Gedanken zur Rolle der beiden Säulenapostel in der Geschichte des frühen Christentums," *Zeitschrift für Neues Testament* 2 (1999): 32-40.

Herzer, Jens. *Petrus oder Paulus? Studien über das Verhälnis des Ersten Petrusbriefes zur paulinischen Tradition,* WUNT 103. Tübingen: Mohr Siebeck, 1998.

Hill, R. M. "The Role of Peter in the Gospel of Mark: A Study of Authority in the Early Church." Diss., Drew University, Madison, NJ, 1994.

Hoffmann, Paul. "Der Petrus-Primat im Matthäusevangelium," in *Neues Testament und Kirche,* Festschrift für Rudolf Schnackenburg, ed. Joachim Gnilka. Freiburg: Herder, 1974, pp. 94-114.

Hofstetter, Karl. 1959. See "Stauffer, Ethelbert," below.

Kähler, Christoph. "Zur Form- und Traditionsgeschichte von Matt. XVI.17-19," *New Testament Studies* 23 (1977): 36-58.

Karrer, Martin. "Petrus im paulinischen Gemeindekreis," *ZNW* 80 (1989): 210-31.

Kessler, William Thomas. *Peter as the First Witness of the Risen Lord. An Historical and Theological Investigation.* Tesi Gregoriana, Serie Teologia 37. Rome: Editrice Pontificia Università Gregoriana, 1998.

Kingsbury, Jack Dean. "The Figure of Peter in Matthew's Gospel as a Theological Problem," *JBL* 98 (1979): 67-83.

Kirschbaum, Engelbert. *Die Gräber der Apostelfürsten. St. Peter und St. Paul in Rom,* 3rd rev. ed. Frankfurt: Societäts-Verlag, 1974. Translation of 2nd ed., *The Tombs of St. Peter and St. Paul.* London: St. Martin's Press, 1959.

Klein, H. "Christologie und Anthropologie in den Petruslegenden des matthäischen Sondergutes," in *Anfänge der Christologie,* Ferdinand S. F. Hahn, ed. Cilliers Breytenbach/Henning Paulsen. Göttingen: Vandenhoeck & Ruprecht, 1991, pp. 209-20.

Kuhn, Ulrich. "Petrusdienst und Papsttum — Überlegungen zu eienem 'heißen' ökumenischen Thema," *Amt und Gemeinde* 36 (1985): 33-39.

———. "Die ökumenische Verpflichtung der lutherischen Theologie," *TLZ* 122 (1997): 521-34.

———. "Papsttum und Petrusdienst. Evangelische Kritik und Möglichkeiten aus der Sicht reformatorischer Theologie," in his *Die eine Kirche als Ort der Theologie. Ausgewählte Aufsätze,* ed. H. Franke et al. Göttingen, 1997, pp. 213-44.

Lampe, Peter. "Petrus. I. Neues Testament," *RGG*[4] 6 (2003): 1160-65.

Lehmann, Karl, ed. *Das Petrusamt: Geschichtliche Stationen seines Verständnisses und gegenwärtige Positionen.* München: Schnell & Stein, 1982.

Maynard, Arthur H. "The Role of Peter in the Fourth Gospel," *New Testament Studies* 30 (1984): 531-48.

Meier, John P. "Surveying the Individual Members of the Twelve. 12. Peter," in his *A Marginal Jew: Rethinking the Historical Jesus,* vol. 3, *Companions and Competitors.* New York: Doubleday, 2001, pp. 221-45. Bibl., p. 266 n. 57, and on 16:17-19, p. 271 n. 76.

Miller, J. Michael. *What Are They Saying About Papal Primacy?* New York: Paulist, 1983.

Minnerath, Roland. *De Jérusalem à Rom. Pierre et l'unité de l'église apostolique.* Théologie Historique 101. Paris: Beauchesne, 1994.

Mussner, Franz. *Petrus und Paulus — Pole der Einheit. Eine Hilfe der Kirche.* QD 76. Freiburg/Basel/Wien: Herder, 1976.

Nau, Arlo J. "A Redaction-Critical Analysis of the Role of St. Peter in the Gospel of Matthew." Th.D. diss., Toronto School of Theology and the University of Toronto, 1983.

————. *Peter in Matthew: Discipleship, Diplomacy, and Dispraise . . . with an Assessment of Power and Privilege in the Petrine Office.* Collegeville, MN: Liturgical Press, 1992.

Nieman, R., ed. *Petrus, der Fels als Anstosses.* Stuttgart: Kreuz-Verlag, 1994.

O'Collins, Gerald. *The Easter Jesus* (London) = *The Resurrection of Jesus Christ.* Valley Forge, PA: Judson Press, 1973.

Ohlig, Karl-Heinz. 1973. *Braucht die Kirche einen Papst?* Translation: *Why We Need the Pope: The Necessity and Limits of Papal Primacy.* St. Meinrad, IN: Abbey Press, 1975.

Perkins, Pheme. *Peter: Apostle for the Whole Church.* Studies on Personalities of the New Testament. Columbia: University of South Carolina Press, 1994.

Pesch, Rudolf. "The Position and Significance of Peter in the Church of the New Testament," *Concilium* 4, no. 7 (1971): 21-35.

————. *Simon-Petrus: Geschichte und geschichtliche Bedeutung des ersten jüngers Jesu Christi.* Päpste und Papstum 15. Stuttgart: Anton Hiersemann, 1980.

————. *Was an Petrus sichtbar war, ist in den Primat eingegangen.* Freiburg: Herder, 2000.

————. *Die biblische Grundlagen des Primats.* Quaestiones disputatae 187. Freiburg/Basel/Wien: Herder, 2001.

————. *Il Primato del successore di Pietro nel mistero della chiesa: Considerazioni della Congregatione per la dottrina della fede: tesio e commenti.* Città del Vaticano: Libreria Editrice Vaticana, 2002.

Pfamatter, Josef. "Was Petrus nicht angeht. Ein Versuch, Joh 21,22 zu verstehen," in *Kirche Kultur Kommunikation,* Festschrift für P. Henrici, ed. U. Funk/R. Zihlmann. Zürich, 1998, pp. 87-94.

Quast, Kevin. *Peter and the Beloved Disciple: Figures for a Community in Crisis.* JSNTSup 32. Sheffield: JSOT Press, 1989.

Radlbeck-Ossmann, R. "Vom Papstamt zum Pertusdienst," diss. Regensburg, 2003.

Scharfe, Ernst. *Die petrinische Strömmung in der neutestamentlichen Literatur: Untersuchungen über die schriftstellerische Eigentümlichkeit des ersten Petrusbriefes, des Markusevangeliums und der petrinischen Reden der Apostelgeschichte.* Berlin: Reuter & Reichard, 1893.

Schnackenburg, Rudolf. "Petrus im Matthäusevangelium," in *A cause de l'évangile,* Festschrift für J. Dupont, LD 123. Paris: Cerf, 1985, pp. 107-25.

Schneider, Gerhard. "'Stärke deine Brüder!' (Lk 22,32). Die Aufgabe des Petrus nach Lukas," in his *Lukas, Theologe der Heilsgeschichte.* Aufsätze zum lukanischen Doppelwerk, BBB 59. Bonn: Hanstein, 1985, pp. 146-52.

Senior, Donald P. *1 Peter,* with Daniel J. Harrington, *Jude and 2 Peter.* Sacra Pagina Series 15. Collegeville, MN: Liturgical Press, 2003.

Shiner, Whitney T. *Follow Me! Disciples in Markan Rhetoric.* Atlanta: Scholars, 1995.

Simon, Lutz. *Petrus und der Lieblingsjünger im Johannesevangelium.* Amt und Authorität. EHS.T 489. Frankfurt/New York: Peter Lang, 1994.

Snyder, Graydon F. "Survey and 'New' Thesis on the Bones of St. Peter," *Biblical Archaeologist* 32 (1969): 2-24, repr. *The Biblical Archaeologist Reader* 3. Garden City, NY: Doubleday, 1970, pp. 405-24. *NTA* 13 #1074.

Stauffer, Ethelbert, and Karl Hofstetter. 1959. "Das Petrusamt in der Urkirche: Petrus und Jakobus in Jerusalem; Das Petrusamt in der Kirche des 1.-2. Jahrhunderts: Jerusalem — Rom," in *Begegnung der Christen: Studien evangelischer und katholischer Theologen,* ed. Maximilian Roesle and Oscar Cullmann. Stuttgart: Evangelisches Verlagswerk/Frankfurt: Josef Knecht, 1959, pp. 361-404.

Stock, Augustine. "Is Peter's Presentation of Peter Ironic?" *Biblical Theology Bulletin* 17 (1987): 64-69.

Testa, E. "S. Pietro nel pensiero dei giudeo-cristiani," in *San Pietro: Atti della XIX Settimana Biblica,* ed. Augustin Bea et al. Brescia: Paideia, 1967, pp. 459-500.

Thiede, Carsten Peter. *Simon Peter: From Galilee to Rome.* Exeter: Paternoster; Grand Rapids: Academie/Zondervan, 1986.

————, ed. *Das Petrusbild in der neueren Forschung.* Wuppertal: R. Brockhaus, 1987.

Thümmel, Hans Georg. *Die Memorien für Petrus und Paulus in Rom. Die archäologischen Denkmaler und die literarische Tradition.* AKG 76. Berlin/New York: De Gruyter, 1999.

————. "Petrus. II. Petrustradition, 1. Literarisch. 2. Archälogisch. 3. Ikonographische in der altchristlichen Kunst," *RGG*⁴ 6 (2003): 65-68.

Trilling, Wolfgang. "Zum Petrusamt im Neuen Testament. Traditionsgeschichtliche Überlegungen anhand von Matthäus, 1 Petrus und Johannes," in *Studien zur Jesusüberlieferung.* Stuttgart: KBW, 1988, pp. 111-40.

Vorster, Willem S. "Characterization of Peter in the Gospel of Mark," *Neotestamentica* 21 (1987): 57-76.

Wechsler, Andreas. *Geschichtsbild und Apostelstreit. Eine forschungsberichtliche und exegetische Studie über den antiochenischen Zwischenfall (Gal 2,11-14).* BZNW 62. Berlin/New York: De Gruyter, 1991.

Weeden, Theodore J. 1968. "The Heresy That Necessitated Mark's Gospel," *ZNW* 59 (1968): 145-58.

————. *Mark: Traditions in Conflict.* Philadelphia: Fortress, 1971.

Wehr, Lothar. *Petrus und Paulus. Kontrahenten und Partner. Die beiden Apostel im Spiegel des Neuen Testaments, der Apostolischen Väter und frühen Zeugnisse ihrer Verehrung.* NTA 30. Münster, 1996.

Wiarda, Timothy. "Peter as Peter in the Gospel of Mark," *New Testament Studies* 45 (1999): 19-37.

————. *Peter in the Gospels: Pattern, Personality and Relationship.* WUNT 2/127. Tübingen: Mohr Siebeck, 2000.

Wilckens, Ulrich. "Joh 21,15-23 als Grundtext zum Thema 'Petrusdienst,'" in *Wege zum Einverständnis,* Festschrift für Chr. Demke, ed. M. Beintker et al. Leipzig: Evangelische Verlagsanstalt, 1997, pp. 318-33.

Zimmermann, Heinrich. "Die innere Struktur der Kirche und das Petrusamt nach Mt 18," *Catholica* 30 (1976): 168-83.

POST-REFORMATION DEVELOPMENT

Protestant Reaction to the Post-Reformation Development of Papal Authority

Günther Gassmann

Introduction

Over thirty years ago — in 1975 — I wrote the Introduction for a publication of the Strasbourg Institute for Ecumenical Research where I worked at that time. *Papsttum und Petrusdienst — Papacy and Petrine Ministry —* was the title of the booklet.[1] I am grateful that after this long interval I am now returning to the issue of the ecumenical problem and possible significance of the papal office. Because the period of my survey extends from the time of Lutheran orthodoxy to the first half of the twentieth century, my presentation will not be a constructive, future-oriented reflection on this issue. Rather it will be a reminder of the historical stumbling blocks that are represented by both the papacy and Protestant reaction to it — reactions that are still operative both consciously in legitimate critical theological questions and subconsciously or simply emotionally as anti-Roman or anti-papal phobia in many Protestant minds. A number of Protestant reactions to the Lutheran-Catholic *Joint Declaration on the Doctrine of Justification* have their roots, I believe, in this slippery subconscious-emotional realm. The painful and deep-seated controversies of the past, I wrote thirty years ago, have made the papacy far beyond the limited field of theology and doctrine into a kind of shibboleth and symbol of the breach and struggle between the confessions.[2] Accordingly, it is the purpose of my paper to help us face this

---

1. (Frankfurt: Lembeck/J. Knecht, 1975).
2. Günther Gassmann, ed., *Papsttum und Petrusdienst*, p. 10.

controversial and divisive history, and not too quickly edify ourselves with the discovery of those wonderful irenical voices that can be heard as tiny counter-voices in the midst of the thunder of past controversy and polemics.

During the short time of preparation I have found a number of relevant texts and surveys of Protestant reactions in the books of Michael Hardt[3] and Wolfgang Klausnitzer[4]; several articles were also helpful. However, these surveys refer only to a very limited number of Protestant reactions and only from the German-speaking area. Furthermore they work with the methodology of "representative voices": one or two establish certain groups of reactions on the basis of only one example; they mollify also the harshness of vitriolic polemics by making generalizing summaries, or they jump from Luther and Melanchthon directly to the present ecumenical dialogues. I cannot rectify these weaknesses, but I have tried to broaden somewhat the choir of voices and let the judgments, polemics, irony, and sarcasm speak for themselves. In a more comprehensive survey I would have liked to include more non-German and non-Lutheran voices, more reactions from Lutheran and Reformed orthodoxy, and from the neo-Lutheran confessional awakening in the nineteenth century. Next time!

Lutheran Orthodoxy — Seventeenth and Eighteenth Centuries

Protestant, i.e., Lutheran critical reaction to the authority of the pope has found its fundamental and classical expression in the statements of Martin Luther and Philipp Melanchthon. Their verdict, that the understanding and exercise of papal authority contradict the *sola scriptura, solus Christus,* and *sola gratia,* and are without biblical foundation, has marked Lutheran and general Protestant reactions until today. Luther's critique was continued in Lutheran orthodoxy during the seventeenth and eighteenth centuries. Hans Jörg Urban[5] and Wolfgang Klausnitzer[6] present a survey by **Johann**

3. Michael Hardt, *Papsttum und Ökumene. Ansätze eines Neuverständnisses für einen Papstprimat in der protestantischen Theologie des 20. Jahrhunderts* (Paderborn: Schöning, 1981).

4. Wolfgang Klausnitzer, *Das Papstamt im Disput zwischen Lutheranern und Katholiken. Schwerpunkte von der Reformation bis zur Gegenwart* (Innsbruck/Vienna: Tyrolia, 1987).

5. Albert Brandenburg and Hans Jörg Urban, eds., *Petrus und Papst, Beiträge und Notizen* (Münster: Aschendorff, 1977), pp. 270-74.

6. Klausnitzer, *Das Papstamt im Disput,* pp. 239-57.

Georg Walch (1693-1775), whom they consider a typical representative of Protestant critique of the papacy in the succession of Luther and Melanchthon.[7] In the five volumes of his work, Walch put together the controversial points that marked the difference between Lutherans and other Christian traditions. (Walch also produced the significant twenty-four-volume edition of Luther's works, 1740-53.)

For Walch and the authors mentioned by him, the papacy is the main controversial point between Lutherans and Catholics.[8] The primary motivation for anti-papal polemics is for him clearly the papal claim to domination and power. Everything in the Roman church is directed towards the power of the pope.[9] The spiritual domination of the pope over the reason and will of the faithful leads to the captivity of consciences. One has, writes Walch, indoctrinated the people "that the pope is a divinely instituted monarch that infallibly has the power to make new articles of faith, decide theological controversies, interpret Holy Scripture, dispense indulgences. He is regarded as Jesus Christ who has all power in heaven and on earth, a representative and 'vice-deus' on earth. . . . One pretends that all grace that Jesus has gained is distributed by the pope and that the one who is not willing to recognize his highness cannot hope for salvation."[10] This dependence of salvation on the submission to the pope is for Walch the most negative expression of the papal claim to domination because, "if this were the case, the teaching about the pope would have to be the preeminent fundamental article of our faith. . . ."[11] How could the church be justified in attributing to a single human being such great power in matters of faith and salvation, in direct contradiction of the divine order?[12] In this regard the pope can rightly be called Antichrist because his reign is directly opposed to the reign of Christ.[13]

According to Walch the claim to papal dominating authority cannot be substantiated, for biblical as well as historical reasons.[14] Matthew 16:18

7. Johann G. Walch, *Historische und Theologische Einleitung in die Religions-Streitigkeiten ausser der Evangelisch-Lutherischen Kirchen* (Fak. Neudruck der Ausgabe Jena), 1733-1736, 5 vols., reprint (Stuttgart-Bad Cannstatt: F. Frommann, 1972).

8. Walch, *Historische und Theologische Einleitung*, vol. 2, p. 239.

9. Walch, *Historische und Theologische Einleitung*, vol. 2, p. 245.

10. Walch, *Historische und Theologische Einleitung*, vol. 2, p. 314.

11. Walch, *Historische und Theologische Einleitung*, vol. 2, p. 263.

12. Walch, *Historische und Theologische Einleitung*, vol. 2, p. 263.

13. Walch, *Historische und Theologische Einleitung*, vol. 2, p. 360.

14. Walch, *Historische und Theologische Einleitung*, vol. 2, p. 244.

and John 21:15 are not proofs for the primacy of Peter and the papacy.[15] In Matthew 16:18 the "rock" does not refer to the person of Peter but to his confession of faith.[16] It is also impossible to prove that Peter was the first pope at Rome and that he had successors in such a ministry.[17] Furthermore, church fathers and councils indicate that there was no papacy in the early church.[18] Rather, the succession of Peter means succession in teaching and life, "otherwise the Mufti of Constantinople would have to be the successor of Holy Chrysostom."[19] The papacy "has become the center and summit of Roman Catholic ecclesiology that could start with the article on the pope according to which nobody could be saved who did not accept the same [i.e., the pope]."[20]

In conclusion: For Walch the pope has been given the place and authority of Christ for salvation.[21] This directly contradicts and betrays the article of justification.[22] For this reason the Roman church cannot be the true church of Christ.[23] Accordingly, Walch considers attempts at Lutheran-Catholic union[24] as futile, because the two systems exclude each other.[25]

As a concrete example of critique of papal authority in Lutheran orthodoxy one could add the position of **Abraham Calov** (1612-86). For him the decrees of the popes and church councils cannot be considered sources of Christian doctrine. Furthermore, the Roman claim concerning the authority of the pope and of church councils sets aside the principle of Scripture.[26] This implies that the authority of pope and church is placed above Scripture. And if the pope speaks against Scripture, Calov argues, he comes under God's curse, but when he speaks in agreement with Scripture, he dif-

---

15. Walch, *Historische und Theologische Einleitung,* vol. 2, p. 263.

16. Walch, *Historische und Theologische Einleitung,* vol. 2, p. 274.

17. Walch, *Historische und Theologische Einleitung,* vol. 2, pp. 273 and 286.

18. Walch, *Historische und Theologische Einleitung,* vol. 2, pp. 264-65, 268.

19. Walch, *Historische und Theologische Einleitung,* vol. 2, p. 287.

20. Walch, *Historische und Theologische Einleitung,* vol. 2, p. 359.

21. Walch, *Historische und Theologische Einleitung,* vol. 2, p. 695.

22. Walch, *Historische und Theologische Einleitung,* vol. 2, p. 767.

23. Walch, *Historische und Theologische Einleitung,* vol. 2, p. 787.

24. E.g., Spinola, see Manfred Fleischer, *Katholische und Lutherische Ireniker* (Göttingen: Musterschmidt-Verlag, 1968), pp. 62-66.

25. Walch, *Historische und Theologische Einleitung,* vol. 2, pp. 211-12.

26. Abraham Calov, *Systema Locorum Theologicorum è sacrâ potissimum scripturâ, & antiquitate, necnon adversariorum confessione* (Wittenberg: A. Hartmanni, 1665), vol. 1, pp. 367ff.

fers in no way from any other ministers of God's Word. The countless instances where popes have fallen into pernicious error and heresy ought to show the absurdity of such extravagant claims for papal authority.[27]

Protestant Reaction in the Nineteenth Century

Protestant voices of the nineteenth century criticizing papal authority are of particular importance for our survey. First, they are shaped and influenced by the historical context before, at, and after the First Vatican Council, and second, they may have had a stronger impact on twentieth-century Protestant thinking than is generally recognized because of the prominence of the reaction against liberal theology and the emerging ecumenical movement during the first half of the century. **Wilhelm Löhe**, the great renewer of Lutheran diaconia, mission, liturgy, and spirituality, takes us back to the pre-Vatican I period. He is an example of how Protestant criticism of papal authority is not much different before and after Vatican I. It is only reinforced by Vatican I. In his famous *Three Books About the Church* of 1845, Löhe argues rationally, historically, and theologically when criticizing the power and authority of the pope. In the section on the understanding of tradition, he asks where the apostolic tradition is to be found. And he responds in quite a witty and popular manner:

> It is a poor attempt to answer the question when one points one's finger reverently at the breast of a man who is, humanly speaking, in a high position. It is ludicrous that a man who is just as human and no better than anyone else is supposed to be the repository of all the wisdom of the apostles and whose mouth is supposed to pour forth authoritative speech as often as the divining rod (Wünschelrute) of casual questions touches his breast. Such an arrangement has often left men in the lurch. This is proved not only by the many completely mistaken interpretations and applications of the Scriptures which may be found in the public writings of the Roman bishops but also by the many times those same judges kept silent when, if they really possessed the divine truth, they could and should have been able to speak. There are cases in which any ordinary man could undeniably have interpreted the Scriptures better

27. Robert D. Preus, *Theology of Post-Reformation Lutheranism* (St. Louis: Concordia, 1970), vol. 1, pp. 259-60.

than those men whose judgments and opinions are trusted by millions. Accordingly, the statements of popes and councils cannot be called a tradition, much less can they gain an aura of infallibility on the basis of such a tradition.[28]

The other argument of Löhe is directed against the Roman claim that the unity of the church is based on communion with the pope and apostolic succession. Arguing that "nothing can be a divine ordinance and bind men's consciences except what the Word of God commands and institutes," Löhe sarcastically argues against the claim that Roman unity rests on the primacy of Peter and its inheritance by the Roman bishops: "In the light of the divine Word the whole pompous sham of the Roman hierarchy and succession quickly dissolves into mist and nothingness."[29] Löhe continues to state that the Eastern church has stood as a witness against Rome and its primacy, and that not only the so-called Protestants but "the overwhelming majority of Christendom on earth will have nothing to do with a Roman primacy." And while some Protestants, or at least Melanchthon, would have allowed the pope to exercise a primacy according to human right, the Eastern Orthodox would not allow it at any cost.[30] The conservative Lutheran Löhe combines in an interesting manner rationalistic arguments so typical of his time with traditional Lutheran references to the normative authority of Scripture and adds to it a dose of sarcastic irony.

Much more in a rationalistic spirit, but now as part of the liberal theological and ecclesial flock, are several other reactions in the nineteenth century. One of them is church historian **Karl August von Hase** (1800-1890), whom Hans Jörg Urban presents[31] as a representative voice of Protestant anti-papal polemics in the nineteenth century. In his work on Protestant polemics against the Roman Catholic Church,[32] von Hase's critique, similar to Walch's, is primarily directed against the papal claim to spiritual power and domination. This criticism, however, is expressed in the historical as well as individualistic and pragmatic mold of his time that abhors any idea of infallibility and absolute authority.

28. Wilhelm Löhe, *Three Books about the Church* (Philadelphia: Fortress, 1969), pp. 77-78.

29. Löhe, *Three Books,* p. 132.

30. Löhe, *Three Books,* pp. 132-35.

31. Brandenburg and Urban, eds., *Petrus und Papst,* pp. 274-79.

32. Karl von Hase, *Handbuch der Protestantischen Polemik gegen die römisch-katholische Kirche* (Leipzig: Breitkopf und Härtel, [7]1900).

As an institution of human right, writes von Hase, the papacy has no foundation in Bible and apostolic church but has grown by means of the historical force of circumstances. Such an institution may for a pious regard on history nevertheless be a part of divine will, but not — von Hase immediately warns — in the narrow catholic sense of Christ having once instituted the primacy of Peter and his succession as a domination over the church for all time. Yet what has emerged in the encounters of historical conditions can and will also disappear under different circumstances.[33] This leads to the remarkable conclusion that the papacy is not really essential for Roman Catholicism, that "Catholicism does not yet stand or fall with the papacy."[34] Similarly, the claim to papal infallibility is without biblical foundation and based solely on tradition.[35] Papal infallibility, according to von Hase, is a barrier to the exercise of the infallibility of the church,[36] and he regards it as basically a private invention of Pius IX that is supported by Catholic naïveté and ignorance, and is thus nothing but an expression of human arrogance.[37] It is clear that the basis of von Hase's opposition to the pope's claim of spiritual power is not primarily grounded on a Lutheran emphasis on the sole authority of the Word of God and in the criterion of the doctrine of justification, but on the liberal and rationalistic understanding of the liberty and autonomy of the individual.[38]

Another representative voice from the nineteenth century is that of **Leopold von Ranke** (1795-1886). In his impressive *History of the Popes During the Last Four Centuries*,[39] the great historian presents in a detailed and comprehensive historical account the development of papal authority and power up to the First Vatican Council within the complex context of European history. He saw the overture to Vatican I, like others, in the first formalized test of infallibility in the form of the pope's lonely personal authoritative promulgation in 1854 of the dogma of Mary's immaculate conception.[40] During the preparation of the Council, the idea and divine institution of pa-

---

33. Hase, *Handbuch der Protestantischen Polemik,* pp. 143-44.

34. Hase, *Handbuch der Protestantischen Polemik,* p. 146.

35. Hase, *Handbuch der Protestantischen Polemik,* p. 150.

36. Hase, *Handbuch der Protestantischen Polemik,* pp. 172, 182.

37. Hase, *Handbuch der Protestantischen Polemik,* pp. 177, 180.

38. Cf. Brandenburg and Urban, eds., *Petrus und Papst,* p. 280.

39. Leopold von Ranke, *Die Geschichte der Päpste in den letzten vier Jahrhunderten* (Köln, [6]1877). ET *The History of the Popes During the Last Four Centuries* (London: G. Bell and Sons, 1913).

40. Ranke *Die Geschichte der Päpste,* pp. 546-47.

pal primacy was already in place when a free deliberation at the Council was excluded and the right of making propositions was attributed exclusively to the pope. The pope did not request the consultation of the council members, but their assent.[41] His intention was a re-justification and re-enforcement of the highest authority in its traditional sense by reinforcing and centralizing the power of his predecessors.[42] The pope, furthermore, clearly insisted on the superiority of papal power over conciliar power which, by necessity, led to papal infallibility.[43]

For von Ranke the question of the relationship of episcopal and papal, conciliar and papal authority that had marked with controversy the long sequence of past centuries was now decided in favor of the absolute power of the Roman see. This was regarded as "the recognition of a living authority, based on divine institution, in the midst of disputes and fights of the world, the origin of such disputes and fights being exactly the refusal to recognize an authority."[44] Referring to the outbreak of the Franco-Prussian War shortly after the proclamation of papal infallibility, von Ranke ends his book by commenting again on the repercussions of the unlimited expansion of papal power on the European states. In that war, he writes, a victorious nation (i.e., Prussia) had achieved power in its antagonism against the exclusive power of the pope and took now its influential place within the universal political and religious movement of the world. In a Hegelian vision von Ranke ends his book by saying: "A convinced Protestant would like to say: it [i.e., the victory of Prussia] was the divine decision against the arrogant claim of the pope to be the only interpreter on earth of the faith and the divine mysteries." As a consequence of the war, the pope retreated to the exercise of his spiritual power, and it would be up to the present and to the future in how far this exercise would be possible under changed circumstances.[45]

Two other influential texts from the late nineteenth and early twentieth centuries can be found in the *Realencyclopädie for Protestant Theology and Church*. In the second edition of 1885, **Theodor Wagenmann** writes that the definition of papal universal episcopate and papal infallibility is only the logical "conclusio" and practical consequence of the Tridentine-Jesuit premises that since the time of the Counter-Reformation have

41. Ranke, *Die Geschichte der Päpste*, p. 558.
42. Ranke, *Die Geschichte der Päpste*, p. 560.
43. Ranke, *Die Geschichte der Päpste*, p. 561.
44. Ranke, *Die Geschichte der Päpste*, p. 570.
45. Ranke, *Die Geschichte der Päpste*, p. 571.

achieved predominance, and it is the capstone of the whole hierarchical-papal system that has been erected since Pope Leo the Great. But it is also certain "that in this false 'conclusio' the falsehood of the premises and that in the untenable capstone the untenable foundation of the whole building have come to light. It is evident not only for each evangelical Christian but also for each reflective Catholic that an untrue opinion cannot be elevated to an affirmation of faith to which the whole Catholic Christianity is bound under threat of eternal condemnation — an opinion that is in itself not clear and true and that contradicts Scripture and tradition, reason and history like the one of the infallibility of the pope promulgated with the 'placet' of 533, not free, badly informed, partly even not capable to judge of formally unauthorized prelates."[46]

In the third edition of the same *Encyclopädie,* **Carl Mirbt** sees in the First Vatican Council the beginning of a new era in the history of the Roman Catholic Church. Not only has the power of the pope been heightened and the church, governed by the infallible pope, gained in strength, unity, and stability, but also by not declaring certain decisions as *ex cathedra* the pope has claimed the implications of the possession of infallibility for his whole activity.[47] Together with others, Mirbt sees in the definition of the universal primacy and infallibility of the Roman bishop the conclusion of the history of the emergence and development of this dogma. But he questions whether this dogma will really be respected and implemented for all times. "The history of dogma provides not a few examples of transvaluations and devaluations of individual dogmas . . . without being formally abandoned or changed." The Catholic Church with its great adaptability and elasticity would also cope with such a development.[48]

Like other historians, too, **Adolf von Harnack** traces and exposes the historical line and development that led with an inner consequence to the First Vatican Council. While, according to Harnack, Trent had not yet decided the issue of pope or council, papal decision or tradition, the post-Tridentine development led towards a decision. *The Professio fidei Tridentinae* already had smuggled the Roman church and the pope into its credo, and the Thomistic *Catechismus Romanus* (1566) taught papal autocracy as

---

46. Theodor Wagenmann, in Albert Hauck, ed., *Realencyclopädie für protestantische Theologie und Kirche* (Leipzig: J. C. Hinrichs, ²1885), vol. 20, p. 338.

47. Carl Mirbt, in Hauck, ed., *Realencyclopädie für protestantische Theologie* (Leipzig: J. C. Hinrichs, ³1908), vol. 20, p. 473.

48. Mirbt, in Hauck, ed., *Realencyclopädie für protestantische Theologie,* p. 474.

an article of faith.[49] The next step was that the church be seen as the living tradition, and consequently the pope as *the* tradition (Pius IX) who exercised it in 1854 with the dogma of the immaculate conception.[50] It marks "the definite exaltation of the papacy" and the expulsion of Augustinianism together with Gallicanism and Jansenism.[51] Thus, the church that, in union with political reaction and romanticism, "had exalted the pope to lordship over herself and proclaimed him as the living tradition was finally ripe for the dogma of the infallibility of the pope."[52] By means of the new dogma, "the Romish church has revealed itself as the autocratic dominion of the *pontifex maximus* — the old Roman empire taking possession of the memory of Jesus Christ, founded upon his word and sacraments, exercising according to need an elastic or iron dogmatic legal discipline. . . ."[53]

The Boston professor **Henry C. Sheldon** fits very well into this group of liberal Protestants. In his *System of Christian Doctrine* he declares that the monarchical concept of the church found its "culminating expression in the dogmas of papal supremacy and papal infallibility." The former "assigns to the pope the most unqualified lordship over the Church which can be conceived to be vested in a human being." In the light of this dogma "the biblical revelation has no right of direct impact upon human minds; that in truth for all, except the pope, it is no sun in the spiritual firmament, but a mere moon, having permission to shine upon the world at large only as it is reflected from the understanding of the vicegerent in the Vatican, who is alike the arbiter of faith and of conduct. Surely a dogma thus vitally related to salvation, and fundamentally determinative of the function of the biblical revelation, ought not to be ignored or left in the mist by that revelation."[54]

The response of Sheldon is definite: "The dogma of papal supremacy is not taught either clearly or obscurely in the Scriptures,"[55] and he concludes that to predicate a strict succession of the apostles, especially of Peter, "would be like assuming a continuous succession of the founders of

49. Adolf v. Harnack, *Outlines of the History of Dogma* (1885-89, [4]1909, reprint Boston: Starr King Press, 1957), pp. 518-19.

50. Harnack, *Outlines*, p. 521.

51. Harnack, *Outlines*, p. 525.

52. Harnack, *Outlines*, p. 527.

53. Harnack, *Outlines*, p. 528.

54. Henry C. Sheldon, *System of Christian Doctrine* (Cincinnati/New York: Jennings & Pry, 1903), p. 489.

55. Sheldon, *System*, p. 489.

the American Republic."[56] After further considering the historical data,[57] Sheldon finds: "It required centuries of industrious aggression and assertion, aided by great forgeries, to enthrone that theory [of papal authority] even within the limits of Latin Christendom."[58] In a similar way, Sheldon rejects the infallibility of the pope as not founded on biblical and historical facts.[59] For example, "the record of the early church showed that it had no idea that doctrinal disputes could be settled by the short method of appealing to him [i.e., the Roman bishop]. They were fought out in the arena of debate until carried before an ecumenical council."[60] After enumerating heresies and contradictions in papal utterances, Sheldon finishes with a form of rationalistic argumentation so characteristic of his whole approach. The suggestion, he says, that one "should refine on the precise way in which the pope must speak, in order to deliver himself infallibly, is to discredit the notion of his infallibility in the sight of clear practical intelligence. If we are not required to believe him when he faces to the west, there is minor occasion for reposing entire confidence in him when he faces to the east."[61]

Protestant Reaction in the Twentieth Century

I would like to open the group of twentieth-century examples of Protestant reaction to papal authority with two American voices. **George Park Fisher**, professor of ecclesiastical history at Yale University, comments in 1922 on Vatican I and writes that the decree on infallibility was not an act of the Council but of the pontiff and "the assent of the Council being the destruction of the doctrine of Episcopalism. It was so far an act of suicide on the part of the defenders of conciliar theory as to the seat of authority."[62] For Fisher, one formal indication for the shift is the formulation with which the decrees are introduced: while Trent still used formulations such as "the sacred and holy, ecumenical and general Synod teaches," Vatican I uses the

---

56. Sheldon, *System*, pp. 489-90.
57. Sheldon, *System*, pp. 490-93.
58. Sheldon, *System*, p. 493.
59. Sheldon, *System*, pp. 494-98.
60. Sheldon, *System*, p. 496.
61. Sheldon, *System*, p. 499.
62. George Park Fisher, *History of Christian Doctrine* (New York: Scribner, 1922), p. 542.

simple formulation "We [i.e., Pius IX] teach and define," adding sometimes "the sacred Council assenting."[63]

Forty years later **Otto W. Heick** commented in the same way on Vatican I as the definite victory of curialism over conciliarism. From now on the pope makes dogmatic decisions by virtue of his own power. The "Council thereby lost every dogmatic importance in the sense of the ancient, medieval, and even of the Tridentine Council. . . . What really occurred within Catholicism was the shifting of the seat of infallibility from a group (i.e., the church) to an individual." And he adds, that the stipulations (conditions) concerning the exercise of infallibility are too elastic so that it is extremely difficult to determine when the pope exercises this power.[64]

Klausnitzer and Hardt select Barth, Steck, Peter Brunner, and Althaus as representative Protestant voices of the German-speaking area. In relation to our focus on Protestant reactions to papal authority, **Karl Barth** argues on the basis of the absolute priority, authority, and primacy of God's revelation, of the Word of God.[65] Vatican I with its dogma has identified revelation with the church and its hierarchical head, the pope.[66] The divine I of the church receives its earthly counterpart in the office of God's representative in the Roman episcopal see. The Roman Catholic history of the teaching on Scripture and tradition is for Barth the history of infidelity of that church over against the authority of God in his Word and is thus the history of the usurpation of the authority of God, dissolved into the authority of the church, and handed over at Vatican I into the hands of the papacy.[67] The fundamental protest of the Reformers against the papacy aimed at the re-establishment of the authority of God.[68] Though Barth maintained his basic critique that the Catholic Church has put its and the pope's authority in the place of Christ's authority, the older Barth somewhat differentiated his judgments under the impact of Vatican II. He recognized the beginning of important new developments and rejected Protestant polemics: "The pope is not the antichrist."[69]

63. Fisher, *History,* p. 542.

64. Otto W. Heick, *A History of Christian Thought* (Philadelphia: Fortress, 1966), vol. 2, p. 314.

65. E.g., Karl Barth, *Die kirchliche Dogmatik* (München: Chr. Kaiser, 1932-70), I/2, p. 598.

66. Barth, *Die kirchliche Dogmatik,* I/2, pp. 606ff., 634.

67. Karl Barth, *Die Theologie und die Kirche. Gesammelte Vorträge* (Zürich: Evangelischer Verlag, 1928), pp. 329-69, 339, 357.

68. Barth, *Die Theologie,* p. 340.

69. Karl Barth, *Ad Limina Apostolorum* (Zürich: EVZ-Verlag, 1967), p. 18.

For **Karl Gerhard Steck** the controversial positions concerning the papal office belong to the broader context of the relationship of the authority of the church to the authority of Christ.[70] When the encyclical *Mystic corporis* speaks of the pope as vicar of Christ, the sole authority of Christ is questioned, even removed.[71] The claim of the pope to be the visible head of the church and the idea of his representation of Christ negate the exclusive rule of Christ over his church.[72]

Most interesting is the position of the conservative Lutheran theologian **Peter Brunner**. Among the fundamental Protestant-Catholic differences he mentions the double dogma of 1870. Accordingly, after Vatican I the door has definitely been closed with regards to the issue of the papacy. It remains part of the Lutheran confession to reject the claims of the papacy.[73] The Word of God in Scripture, Brunner writes, is indeed the criterion of the apostolicity of each minister in the church. According to this criterion the dogma of 1870 is not grounded in Holy Scripture and, consequently, the pope stands even outside of Christianity. The papal magisterium as defined at Vatican I also contradicts the doctrine of justification. This is in line with Luther's critique of the papacy, according to which the papacy obscures or puts aside the decisive article of justification. If a consensus in this article were achieved/reached, then there would be nothing that could separate the churches[74] — a remarkable prediction! The present authority of the bishop of Rome in the Catholic Church confirms for Brunner the critique of Luther.[75]

Brunner, in an article, accepts Peter's special place among the apostles and at the formation of the primitive church. He excludes, however, a primacy of the bishop of Rome.[76] He argues that an ecclesial structure in a certain area within which "several pastors and bishops are gathered around *one* of them" does not contradict Scripture[77] even though this ministry of unity can only be *iure humano*. Not in accordance with Scripture is the identifica-

---

70. Karl Gerhard Steck, *Der evangelische Christ und die römische Kirche* (München: Chr. Kaiser, 1952), p. 18.

71. Steck, *Der evangelische Christ*, pp. 40-45.

72. Karl Gerhard Steck, *Was trennt uns von der römischen Kirche?* (Wuppertal: Jugenddienst-Verlag, 1958), pp. 14-19.

73. Peter Brunner, *Bemühungen um die einigende Wahrheit* (Göttingen: Vandenhoeck & Ruprecht, 1977), p. 32.

74. Brunner, *Bemühungen*, pp. 35, 55.

75. Brunner, *Bemühungen*, p. 54.

76. Brunner, "Evangelium und Papsttum," *ELKZ* 10 (1956): 439-43.

77. Brunner, "Evangelium und Papsttum," p. 442.

tion of a leading pastor of the church with the respective bishop of Rome. This is an "enthusiastic" dogma because it lacks biblical as well as historical foundation. As long as "the bishop of Rome teaches doctrines that are not grounded in Holy Scripture and even contradict it, Christianity has to place him under the anathema."[78]

Paul Althaus, in his dogmatics, sees in the understanding of the church the deepest difference between Roman Catholicism and Protestantism.[79] The hierarchical structure of the Catholic Church, the claim to primacy of the pope, and the demand of submission to him as necessary to salvation do not find any justification in Bible and dogmatics.[80] Christ rules in his church through his Word and not through Peter and the pope as his successor/vicar.[81] It is the hierarchy and ecclesial authority that occupy the position of the rule of Christ and absorb the authority of the Word of God.[82] The difference is clear: "Over there is the papacy, canon law and thus a new law that imprisons the Gospel — over here is the Gospel of the New Testament in its purity."[83]

The most critical and extremely negative judgments concerning papal authority that I have encountered among serious and scholarly theologians are those of **Francis Pieper** (Franz August Otto Pieper). Pieper was the most important and influential theologian of the Lutheran Church–Missouri Synod in the twentieth century. His *Christian Dogmatics*[84] continues to this day to be a basic textbook for the theological teaching in his church. The fundamental criteria for Pieper's judgments throughout his three volumes are the normative and absolute authority of inspired Holy Scripture and the doctrine of justification by faith alone.

Already in the Preface to volume 1 the *Leitmotiv* of Pieper's presentation is announced: "In the Church of Rome, Christian theology has completely broken down, for there the sole authority of Scripture is denied and the subjective opinion of the Pope is made the real authority."[85] In volume 1 in its

---

78. Brunner, "Evangelium und Papsttum," p. 443.

79. Paul Althaus, *Grundriss der Dogmatik* (Gütersloh: G. Mohn, 1958), p. 81.

80. Paul Althaus, *Die christliche Wahrheit. Lehrbuch der Dogmatik* (Gütersloh: G. Mohn, 1969), p. 505.

81. Althaus, *Die christliche Wahrheit*, p. 505.

82. Althaus, *Die christliche Wahrheit*, p. 233.

83. Althaus, *Die christliche Wahrheit*, pp. 233-34.

84. Franz Pieper, *Christian Dogmatics*, vols. 1-3 (St. Louis: Concordia, 1950 and 1953).

85. Pieper, *Christian Dogmatics*, vol. 1, p. ix.

section on Holy Scripture and commenting on Vatican I, Pieper condemns the infallible authority of the pope as an expression of the "Satanic insolence of him who as God sits in the temple of God and acts as though he were God (2 Thess. 2:4)."[86] The contrast to the authority of Scripture is repeatedly stressed. Accordingly Pieper writes that "the holy father Pope, as the visible head of the church appointed by Christ, is the divine institution in the eminent sense, and thus the supreme authority in the Church rests in the Pope." This explains the concern of Roman theologians "to have the Ego of the Pope acknowledged as the supreme authority in the Church."[87] Pieper adds for the sake of balance that in a similar way the Ego of the theologizing subject has become in modern Protestantism the decisive factor in the church.[88]

In volume 3, dealing with sanctification and with ecclesiology, Pieper continues his biting critique by decreeing that the pope is Antichrist: "By placing his [i.e., the pope's] word as authority beside the Word of God and *eo ipso* above God's Word, the Pope demonstrates that he is Antichrist."[89] This argument is repeated in several places. Referring to the criterion of the highest article, i.e., justification without any merit of men, Pieper holds that this doctrine is officially anathematized by the papacy, and the entire "machinery" of the papal church is geared to oppose and destroy this doctrine. The personal representative of this great apostasy from the Christian religion, the pope, "is truly the worst enemy of Christ and His Church, all the more since he masquerades under Christ's name."[90]

The fact that Pieper does not only use the "high articles" of the Lutheran faith for his arguments but also the liberal individualism (and congregationalism) that is a mark of the Missouri Synod becomes obvious in the following statement: "When the Pope denies to the rest of mankind the right to judge for themselves in matters of doctrine and demands their *sacrificium intellectus et voluntatis* he thereby requires every human being to surrender his own conscience and thus to renounce that faculty which distinguishes man from beast."[91]

Pieper's fury also is directed against those modern Protestants, including Lutherans, who deny that the pope is Antichrist and do so because of

---

86. Pieper, *Christian Dogmatics,* vol. 1, pp. 206-7.
87. Pieper, *Christian Dogmatics,* vol. 1, pp. 225-26.
88. Pieper, *Christian Dogmatics,* vol. 1, p. 226.
89. Pieper, *Christian Dogmatics,* vol. 3, p. 66.
90. Pieper, *Christian Dogmatics,* vol. 3, p. 465.
91. Pieper, *Christian Dogmatics,* vol. 3, p. 65.

their opposition to the *sola gratia* and their liberal attitude toward Scripture. They do not see what an outrage the anathematizing of the doctrine of justification is and "what a heinous offense the Pope is committing by suppressing the authority of the Word of God, and thus of Christ, and supplanting it with his own authority, and that under the cloak of Christ's name and with a great show of sanctity."[92]

I have referred to Pieper's sweeping and often vitriolic judgments rather extensively not only because of the wide influence of his thought in the past and present and beyond his own church, but also because his judgments seem to me the tip of an iceberg of a rather broad popular general Protestant rejection of the office and authority of the pope during the nineteenth and first half of the twentieth centuries.

Conclusion

In 1890 the Erlangen neo-Lutheran **Franz Hermann Reinhold Frank** pointed to a certain parallel between the Lutheran confessional awakening in the nineteenth century and the new Roman Catholic traditionalism and confessionalism — and one could add also the parallel to the Anglican Oxford Movement. Frank writes: "The Evangelical-Lutheran theology made its living home once again in the confession of the Church . . . and on the Roman side there also has been a renewed consideration of the past position of earlier glorious power of the Church, and the claims were renewed which in theory never had been completely abandoned."[93] Forty years later, another Erlangen professor, the Lutheran Barthian **Kurt Frör** published an analysis of Protestant and Catholic thinking since Schleiermacher in which the papacy did not play a role at all. Frör underlines that besides all critique and even rejection "we intend to hear the Word that God addresses to us through the opponent as clearly as we challenge the opponent to self-examination. When we are struggling with Catholicism, one confession is the critique of the other in the sense that both allow themselves being questioned by the other whether they still proclaim (treiben) Christ or something different."[94]

92. Pieper, *Christian Dogmatics,* vol. 3, pp. 467-68.

93. Franz Hermann Reinhold Frank, "Lage und Aufgabe der gegenwärtigen Theologie," *NKZ* (1890): 20.

94. Kurt Frör, *Evangelisches Denken und Katholizismus seit Schleiermacher* (München: Chr. Kaiser, 1932), p. 14.

I conclude with these two voices, and many more could be added even far beyond the collection in Manfred Fleischer's book *Katholische und Lutherische Ireniker*[95] as examples of a different attitude compared to the voices I have surveyed. These other voices point in a broader perspective towards mutual openness and accountability despite necessary critique and even rejection. These voices have come to fruition in recent dialogues while at the same time the other voices — the critical, polemical, negative ones — are still effective in the theological minds and subconscious attitudes of many contemporaries. Consequently, further and patient dialogue efforts are required.

The voices I have surveyed are marked by the spirit of their time and often also by prejudice and rash judgments. But they contain questions and considerations that remain valid beyond their time. I mention a few. There remains the question of the nature, limits, and forms of exercise of papal authority. In what way can it be made clear that this authority stands under and serves the authority of God's Word and the only source of salvation and the only head of the church, Jesus Christ? In what way can it be made clear that papal authority is not the isolated authority of an individual Christian in a high office, but an authority exercised by one in collegial and consultative relations with others? How can a foundation of papal authority in Bible, tradition, and theology be formulated that corresponds to generally accepted results of modern biblical and historical scholarship?

To name such questions that come to us from past Protestant reaction to papal authority immediately makes us aware that these questions have been taken up in studies and dialogues. But it would be an important step forward and a great help for ongoing dialogues if there could be an official Roman Catholic clarifying commentary on the nature of papal infallibility and especially primacy.[96] This would be in line with the request by Patriarch Maximos IV of Antioch, already made at the second session of Vatican II, that the Catholic Church should distance itself from misinterpretations of the Roman primacy in order that this dogma does not become a *"petra scandali."*[97] Indeed, the ecumenical dialogues on the papal office and ministry wait for some form of Roman Catholic reception or recognition of important insights achieved so far. This would be an enormous encouragement for the dialogues and an official sign that the discussion initiated by *Ut unum sint* bears fruit.

---

95. Manfred Fleischer, *Katholische und Lutherische Ireniker* (Göttingen: Muster-schmidt-Verlag, 1968).

96. Also requested by Klausnitzer, *Das Papstamt im Disput*, pp. 523-56.

97. Yves Congar, ed., *Konzilsreden* (Einsiedeln: Benziger, 1964), pp. 55-57.

Historical Development
of Forms of Authority and Jurisdiction:
The Papal Ministry — an Ecumenical Approach

Hermann J. Pottmeyer

A Hermeneutical Suggestion

Anyone who wishes to come to an understanding of the papal ministry cannot avoid dealing with the history of this ministry. The historical facts are not disputed, but their theological evaluation is contentious. Denominational standpoints resulting from diverse experiences, interests, and theological presuppositions have a more dominant effect here than in the case of any other subject in the history of the church.

What pattern forms the basis for many evaluations? Almost always, the current form and exercise of papal primacy is directly compared either with the biblical figure of Peter or with the church of the first millennium. Everything in between is evaluated as the history either of success or of decline. Actually we can distinguish two models.

The first model, quite normal among Catholics for a long time, sees the current form of the primacy as the successful outcome of a consistent development from the biblical beginnings. Its consistent character is explained either as the logical explication of what was implicit, or as organic development, or as the gradual dawning of awareness. The second model is exactly the opposite, seeing here a history of decline: for the Protestants a betrayal of the origins, for the Orthodox a betrayal of the original communion character of the church.

Neither of the two models does justice to the complex facts of the case. Both overlook the fact that, historically, we are dealing with a series of changing shapes that involve discontinuity as well as continuity. Throughout its history the papal office appears both as a convincing ministry of unity and as an abuse of power. Viewed theologically, it is a matter of *historia mixta,* and this does not permit any global verdict of success or failure.

In order to escape the dead-end of these traditional evaluations, I suggest that before we even approach a theological evaluation we should attempt a historical evaluation, referring back to the causes that had an impact on its development and the motives that guided it. Is it possible to discover in the development of papal primacy something like a rationality that makes sense and can at the same time serve as a criterion? If this were the case, that finding could be integrated into the theological evaluation and contribute towards a more subtle differentiation. A methodological hermeneutical approach of this kind could possibly facilitate an ecumenical understanding.

The Pragmatic Conduct of the Church in the Development of Its Leadership Structures

In the development of the leadership structures of the church, we observe three dominant concerns: first, to maintain the constant link with Jesus and his disciples through the true tradition of the witness and the mandate of the apostles; second, to achieve and maintain unity as communion in faith and communion of the faithful; third, to achieve and maintain the independence of this community, initially from Judaism and then from political authorities, at the same time defending itself against the ethnicization of Christianity, which Paul already found it necessary to combat.

These three concerns play an evident role, for example, in the astonishingly early development of the episcopal ministry. This ministry proved to be suited to counter three challenges: *first,* temporal distance from the origins of the church; *second,* the transition from small groups to larger congregations and then to a network of local churches; *third,* the risk to unity presented by heresies and other conflicts. It is sociologically explicable that leadership functions became necessary in the congregations, whether in regard to doctrine or discipline, or to representation to the outside world. In order that these responsibilities could be exercised permanently and in an orderly manner, the functions became offices. Among the various leadership models, that of the monepiscopate prevailed as the most effective. That evolved into the monarchical episcopate as the bishop combined in one individual the functions of the teacher of the congregation, of its leader or pastor, and of its priest, presiding at the celebration of the Eucharist.

The theological legitimization of the episcopal ministry was effected at the same time, since the bishop's authority was dependent on free and faithful recognition. This authority was grounded in the succession and representation of the apostles and their mandate, sometimes in the representation of Christ or God. This foundation had a dual function. It strengthened the bishop's authority, but at the same time formed the criterion for his exercise of authority, which is to follow the example of Jesus and the apostles and the will of God.

So we observe that the needs of the congregation, the necessity for the function, and the evidence of its effectiveness result in the establishment of the office. The simultaneous or subsequent theological legitimization was intended to promote its effectiveness even further. But it also gave expression to the fact that the development of this office was seen as the will of God at work for his church, providing in this way for the well-being and strengthening of his church. So it was the theologically interpreted experience of the episcopal ministry's serving the good of the church that became the motivating reason for the office. The good of the church remained the purpose of this as of all other leadership offices, and a definitive criterion for its exercise.

I have chosen this example of the episcopal ministry because its origins clearly demonstrate the pragmatic conduct of the church in the development of its structures. Something like a rationality is discernible in this conduct, which is oriented towards clear goals and purposes, and theologically examines and justifies the institutions that have arisen. Historians and sociologists refer to the general observation that in the long run the social structures that prevail are mostly those that best foster the life and the goals of a community or society. Whatever explanatory value this finding may have, the conduct of the church does not exhibit conformity to the laws of social Darwinism but instead a thoroughly rational process that is oriented towards the mission of the church, sees in the fulfillment of this mission the good of the church, and recognizes in the episcopal ministry the appropriate means to this end. I have chosen the example of the episcopal ministry because the development of the monarchical episcopate represents an important stage in the development of the papal ministry.

Considering this example further, the question arises whether the impressively consistent development and subsequent durability of the episcopal ministry do not confirm an evaluation model that sees in it nothing but a success story. I would like to respond with both a Yes and a No. Yes, because if this structure had not in fact proved to be helpful again and again, it would not have been regarded by the majority of Christendom as God's will and as perpetually obligatory. No, because if we see it as nothing but a success story, we fail to take seriously the contrary experiences of the Reformers. Although many of them were not in principle opponents of the episcopal ministry, they felt compelled to abandon or redefine the office. This decision too exhibits rationality. Sadly, they found that the office in its contemporary form no longer served the good of the church or its mission. They applied the same criteria that had caused the early church to affirm this office and the later church to retain it.

In fact, the affirmation of the episcopal ministry was accompanied from the very beginning by criticism of its abuse or other forms of misconduct by office holders. The yardstick for this criticism was, in addition to the good of the church, the example of Jesus and the apostles. It is also a fact that there were phases in the history of the church when the episcopal ministry in certain parts of the church became nothing more than the plaything of the nobility in their quest for power. I call this period the "Babylonian captivity" of the episcopal ministry. And that was precisely the situation at the time of the Reformation. But it is important to keep in mind that despite their different conclusions regarding the obligatory nature of the episcopal ministry, Protestants and Catholics were in agreement regarding the criteria they applied to it. The ministry of leadership in the church is not an end in itself, but is to be measured according to whether it serves the mission and the good of the church — the purpose to which it owes its origin.

In my opinion this finding has heuristic value for an understanding today. The question whether the historical episcopate belongs to the *esse* or merely to the *bene esse* of the church is strangely ahistorical. The astonishingly early conviction that this ministry corresponds to or originates in the will of God is indeed based on the experience that it served the welfare, the *bene esse* of the church. The founding experience gave rise to the well-founded tradition.

The Pragmatic-Critical Perspective in the Development of the Papal Ministry

I suggest we ask ourselves whether the same pragmatic and — at the same time — critical conduct can be observed at work in the development of the leadership structures of the universal church. It does in fact become evident that the same concerns and purposes that guided the development of the monarchical episcopate also determined the development of the leadership structures at that level. The same three challenges provided the motivation, with the one difference that here was at stake the transition from a network of loosely connected particular churches to the organization of the universal church, which was to be capable of joint action. The regional synods evolved into the institution of the ecumenical councils. The communion of the local churches was structured as a triarchy of the principal Petrine churches Rome, Antioch, and Alexandria, then as a pentarchy with the inclusion of Jerusalem and Constantinople. Competing claims to the leadership role by the bishop of Constantinople and the Roman bishop, as well as the role played by the emperor of Constantinople in the organization of the universal church, demonstrate the growing necessity of an authority figure for the universal church. The role of the emperor, however, was diametrically opposed to the concern that the church should be independent of all political powers.

As a counterargument against any biblical-theological basis for the papal ministry, the fact is frequently cited that it was only in the fourth century that the Roman bishops began to refer to the succession of St. Peter to justify their claim to primacy of jurisdiction over the universal church. This objection, however, ignores the logic of the historical development of the ecclesial structures, which we have already observed at work in the development of the episcopal ministry. First the need arises, then the function, and then the office develops out of that, accompanied or followed by the theological legitimization of its authority. Only when a ministry of unity became indispensable for the universal church — a ministry capable of action — does the biblically attested authority of Peter acquire its significance for such a ministry of unity.

The Roman bishop's appeal to Peter for his claim to authority over the universal church had a well-founded background. As the place where Peter and Paul, the two most important apostles, had worked, the church of Rome and — following the development of the monarchical episcopate — her bishop were very soon accorded the highest-ranking significance when it became necessary to establish the true apostolic tradition. Whenever splits occurred, from the third century onwards, the important thing was to be in communion with Rome. As witness and teacher of the apostolic tradition, the Roman bishop acquired a prominent status far beyond his sphere of jurisdiction.

In order to establish the true apostolic tradition, the early church applied two criteria: the criterion of antiquity, which was verified by the *consensio antiquitatis,* and the criterion of agreement between the churches, which was verified by the *consensio universitatis.* In the first instance the bishop of Rome was accorded special authority only in regard to the *antiquitas,* and this was in fact shared with the other apostolic churches like Antioch and Alexandria. It was the authority of the witness, the witness to the faith tradition of the Roman church. The site of the *consensio universitatis* was the community relationship between the churches, and in particular instances the ecumenical council. The validity of council resolutions was verified once more by their reception on the part of the particular churches. From the fourth century onwards the claim of the Roman bishops that council resolutions were only valid with their agreement was integrated into this framework.

In the midst of the Arian and Monophysite turmoil the principle of regional autonomy led increasingly to the disintegration of the church's unity into confessional and ethnic regionalism. Synods or councils and the authority of the emperor proved unable to maintain the unity of the church. The Roman bishop was increasingly entrusted with the role of arbitrator and court of appeal.

The churches of the East have, however, never recognized the jurisdiction of the Roman bishop over the universal church. That was also true of the Western churches, apart from Italy, until well into the seventh/eighth centuries. It was among the mission churches of the Anglo-Saxons, Franks, and other Germanic peoples that the primacy of the Roman bishop was initially recognized. For these peoples Rome was not only the sole apostolic church and the church of Peter, for them Rome was still invested with the glory of the *caput mundi.* The eventual Christianization of the Roman *nobilitas,* the political vacuum in the Western half of the Roman Empire, and the real superiority of Roman law over the Germanic — those were the factors that allowed the Roman bishops to carry on the Roman imperial tradition. They saw themselves as the lawgivers of the world. In the image of Peter the motif of Peter as the lawgiver, the Moses of the New Covenant, came to the forefront.

The more predominantly juridical concept of the primacy was becoming visible already in the fourth/fifth centuries. Leo the Great now saw himself not only as the successor of Peter but also as his representative, exercising the plenitude of his powers — in the terminology of Roman law the *plenitudo potestatis.* The first step on the path towards the monarchical primacy had been taken. This development too can be explained not only on the basis of historical circumstances but also in terms of sociological patterns.

In the self-concept of the Roman bishops we can observe a twofold shift: from the authority of the witness of the Petrine tradition to the authority of the plenipotentiary of Peter, and from the charismatic agent to the bearer of the *plenitudo potestatis.* This development followed indeed the laws of any institutionalization. To guarantee its permanence and effectiveness, every institution is presented with the necessity of authoritative leadership that is predictable, rational, and empowered to act. In the political writings of Aristotle and in Roman law the Roman bishops and theologians found the affirmation and justification for the rationality of their conception.

The alliance of the Roman bishops with the Frankish kings, and later with the German emperors, assured not only the continuance of mission activity in the West but also the independence of the pope in relation to the Byzantine emperor. But soon the popes also had to defend the church against the German emperors and Frankish kings, who saw governing the church as an integral part of their politics. In fact, in the course of history the popes did prove to be the authority most capable of effectively asserting the independence of the church. The bishops were often demonstrated to be unwilling or not in a position to do so.

It was their struggle for the independence and reform of the church that motivated the popes to intensify their claim to authority still further in the Middle Ages. The Great Schism with the Eastern church removed an obstacle from this path. In order to implement his reform in the eleventh century, Gregory VII declared himself supreme lawgiver and judge of the church.

The next step was taken by Innocent III in the thirteenth century. He declared that the bishops receive their jurisdiction from the hands of the pope, since the pope was the representative of Christ for the universal church and thereby the visible head of the church. Therefore the pope stands above the college of bishops and the Church. The theological legitimization was delivered, among others, by Bonaventure and other Franciscan theologians, since the Franciscan movement could only assert itself against the opposition of the bishops with the help of the popes. As was often the case, also here the concern for the reform of the church was involved to strengthen the papal authority.

In the same century Innocent IV gave this claim to authority its corresponding juridical framework. He took up the principle of Roman law that the prince stands above the law: *princeps legibus solutus.* The application of this principle to the leadership of the church had been made possible because the canonists had in the meantime created a distinction between the *ius divinum,* to which the pope is also subject, and the *ius humanum,* which the pope can change. The pope cannot of course change the fundamental structure of the church. But otherwise he possesses full freedom of action, even in regard to traditional privileges. According to this theory he had thus become the more or less absolute monarch of the church. For the time being, however, that did not go beyond the theory. Ironically, it was only with the French Revolution and Napoleon that the way was cleared for the theory to be recognized within the church, because they destroyed the old European feudal order.

Just how modern this concept of Innocent IV actually was can be deduced from the fact that both the creator of the modern theory of the state, Jean Bodin in the sixteenth century, and the Ultramontane movement of the nineteenth century took up and developed his concept. The principles of *plenitudo potestatis* and *princeps legibus solutus* became in the hands of Bodin the *puissance absolue et perpetuelle* of the absolute ruler, and that became in turn the modern concept of sovereignty. The Ultramontanists applied this concept to the pope. The internal and external sovereignty of the pope for the sake of the external sovereignty or independence of the church — that was the goal of the Ultramontanists. They therefore demanded the condemnation of Gallicanism, which had for centuries justified the subordination of the church to the king and state, and they demanded the dogmatization of the primacy of papal jurisdiction, which finally was established at Vatican I.

Did Vatican I mean victory for the Ultramontanists? Yes and no! I examined this question last year in my paper at the Farfa conference and in my book *Towards a Papacy in Communion.* Yes, because the Ultramontane concern motivated an anti-Gallican, one-sided formulation of the dogma that seemed to justify the subsequent maximalist interpretation of this dogma. No, because the clarifications demanded by the minority obtained that the dogma remain open to the shift achieved at Vatican II, as well as to a primacy of communion-to-be. Above all, Vatican I affirmed the purpose and the criterion that had from the beginning motivated the development and exercise of the primacy. It has only one purpose and significance, that is, to serve the good of the church. Vatican II has strengthened this affirmation and developed it further.

But the rationality at work in the establishment of a universally responsible ministry of unity got a counterproductive effect as well. In certain situations in which the church, in her unity and independence, was gravely or even extremely threatened, it was indeed helpful that the popes were able to respond to the challenge with a forced exercise of their authority. But when this threat had passed, the increased manner of exercising their authority was not reduced to allow room for communial and collegial structures again. Instead, the expanded form became the normal practice, firmly established as a law forever rather than being seen as an exceptional measure to be applied in case of an emergency. This process, which was criticized already by Johann Adam Möhler, led to a considerable disturbance of the balance of power within the structural framework of the church. What was rational in certain situations, because it served the good of the church effectively, became counterproductive.

It seems to me that this rationality, which I believe I have demonstrated in the history of the papal office, could form the basis of an ecumenical understanding. The joint wish for a ministry of unity for all Christians that is oriented towards the mandate of the church and the example of the apostles could be that basis — a wish that finds expression in the few ecumenical documents that discuss the papal office. Of the two factors that have fostered acceptance of the ministry of unity over the course of history, one is a current reality: the need for such a ministry in a world that is growing closer together. What is still lacking is the second factor: the shared experience that the ministry of unity of the bishop of Rome can and does in fact serve the good of the church. I am therefore convinced that — more than any other efforts — it is incumbent on the Catholic Church itself to give its Petrine ministry a convincing form to make it possible for other Christians to share this experience. Together with Pope John Paul II I am convinced that the Catholic Church needs to seek the advice and assistance of other Christians for this purpose.

The Pragmatic and Critical Elements in the Development of the Leadership Structures of the Church — the Basis of an Ecumenical Understanding?

To conclude these observations on the causes and motives of the development of the papal office, I would like to attempt an evaluation. Like all evaluations it includes a subjective element. It is, however, in accordance with the intention stated at the beginning, not meant to be a theological evaluation. It refers instead to the pragmatic rationality that I believe I have discerned here.

During its history, the papal office has served both to benefit and to harm the church. If the harm had outweighed the benefit, the office would hardly have been accorded such permanence or recognition. The good of the church was the defined purpose against which the exercise of the office was measured right from the start. It was not so much the theological foundations that fostered the recognition of the papal office within the church, but rather the experience that this office was effective in ensuring the unity of faith within the church and its independence. Without it the Catholic Church too would have disintegrated into national churches.

Part of this experience was the fact that this office always served the mandate and the good of the church when it was exercised in accordance with Christ's commission to his disciples and especially to Peter. It caused harm when it was misused in the service of particular interests, when its office holders failed or were mistaken in their view of what served the good of the church.

In the light of this experience, a critical question imposes itself: Is it advisable to leave the assessment of what serves the good of the church here and now to the pope alone, to one individual alone? Together with many of the fathers of Vatican I and Vatican II and in agreement with the tradition of the church I would like to say no. Establishing this assessment on a broader basis is part of the task of the Catholic Church which I have earlier defined as urgent. Despite the efforts it made in this direction, the last council did not succeed. This task can only be fulfilled as part of a more comprehensive task. We were able to observe that the enormous expansion of the primatial claim of the Roman bishop from Leo I via Gregory VII, Innocent III, and Innocent IV to Pius IX produced a one-sided distortion of the weighting within the structural framework of the church. The *Groupe des Dombes* has therefore described this more comprehensive task in its document *Le ministère de communion dans l'église universelle* in the following terms: The essential issue is to arrive at a balance between the communial, collegial, and personal dimensions of the Petrine ministry.

Did Vatican I Intend to Deny Tradition?

Hermann J. Pottmeyer

The Recent Discussion

If one compares theology with a landscape, the theological tradition surrounding the Petrine office resembles a frontier zone between long-hostile countries. At every step, one encounters traces and residues of military conflicts: old trenches and bunkers and — as a particularly dangerous legacy — landmines. It is generally considered that the most dangerous mine lurking here is the dogma of the First Vatican Council concerning the primacy of the successor of Peter. It is no wonder therefore that ecumenical dialogue between the long-hostile churches has until now given this danger zone a wide berth. But if any further convergence is to be achieved, it is imperative that this mine, which has until now seemed an insuperable obstacle, be defused. As with every mine, its de-activation presupposes the will to put an end to the hostility, and demands a method of approach combining expertise and precision.

No other dogma has its identity designated so distinctly by a double hallmark. The same is true of its rejection. Both have been decisively shaped by a polemical debate that reaches back many centuries and has its basis in conflicting human interests rather than in theological distinctions. Both have been equally decisively shaped by the separate evolutionary paths taken by the churches in the East and in the West, as determined by their history and established long before the Great Schism in 1054. To be sure, that schism facilitated the separate evolution of the ecclesiastical tradition in the West, which culminated in the dogma of Vatican I. But even within the ecclesiastical tradition of the West, this dogma bears yet another hallmark. It was also decisively shaped by the religious and political situation in Europe in the eighteenth and nineteenth centuries.

This factor is in turn the reason why controversy surrounds the dogma not only in an ecumenical context. Even within the Catholic Church there is debate, not regarding the primacy of the bishop of Rome itself, but certainly regarding the formulation and interpretation of the dogma, and the form taken by the exercise of the primacy as a consequence of the dogma. To continue the analogy between this dogma and an explosive mine, the explosive effect that this subject has had and continues to have is demonstrated not least by the history of the First and Second Vatican Councils. At Vatican I, the formulation led to the brink of a breach, and subsequently to the secession of the Old Catholics. At Vatican II, the failure of the Constitution on the Church was avoided only by the concession made to the minority by Paul VI with a binding text interpretation. The minority at Vatican I feared the betrayal of the ancient tradition of the Church; the minority at Vatican II feared a betrayal of the dogma of Vatican I.

Therefore, when the Roman Catholic Church today engages in a process of rapprochement on the primacy of the successor of Peter, it should in my view at the same time or — even better — beforehand, clarify those critical questions that have been posed within the Catholic Church itself regarding the longstanding customary interpretation of this dogma, and the exercise of primacy validated by that interpretation. For if we Catholics are convinced that the Petrine office is a gift and an aid which Christ handed down to the community of all Christians, we are called upon to first of all clear away everything that obscures this divine gift and gives rise to misunderstandings.

That does not, however, mean that we should postpone the ecumenical dialogue on Petrine ministry until we have accomplished our own "purification of the memory," which Pope John Paul II invited Catholics to undertake. Rather, we Catholics need the ecumenical dialogue in order to achieve this goal. For it is a common human experience that a different perspective and the experience of others can be helpful in clarifying one's own self-understanding, particularly when the matter at issue is one of common concern, namely recognizing the will of God for his church. This insight forms the basis of the invitation by Pope John Paul II to other churches and other Christians in *Ut unum sint,* to assist him and the Catholic Church in dealing with the pressing question of the primacy. Bound up with this invitation is naturally the hope that the "purification of the memory" by Catholics in ecumenical dialogue may at the same time clear the vision of other Christians regarding this divine gift.

As far as the dogma of Vatican I is concerned, the critical questioning within the Catholic Church was already initiated by the minority at Vatican I. That questioning intensified during Vatican II, and has intensified to an increasing degree since that last Council. Today, a *re-lecture* or re-reception of the dogma of 1870 is demanded within the Catholic Church — a *re-lecture* within the framework of the *communio* ecclesiology that Vatican II wished to re-establish.

That statement identifies the major reason why a discussion of the dogma of 1870 arose within the Catholic Church immediately before, during, and after Vatican II. This was the rediscovery of the sacramental *communio* character of the church, and the *communio* structure and praxis of the as-yet undivided church of the first millennium. The Catholic Church owed this rediscovery to the burgeoning and deepening study of the Bible, of the church fathers, and of the development of the early church. It broke the bonds of the one-sided apologetic and juridical focus of the ecclesiology of nineteenth-century neoscholastic theology. The understanding of the primacy that had prevailed in the Catholic Church since Vatican I, and was grounded in that Council, could only with difficulty be reconciled with *communio* ecclesiology. This problem also set in motion an intensified study of the history of papal primacy. That led in turn to the discovery that the still undivided church was indeed already aware of the primatial position of the bishop of Rome and successor of Peter, but had interpreted and exercised the primacy in differing ways in different epochs, and that the interpretation and the exercise of the primacy at any particular time had been influenced by both the prevailing concept of the church and the contemporary political context.

It was not surprising that the problem experienced by the Fathers of Vatican II in reconciling *communio* ecclesiology with the current interpretation of the dogma of 1870 awakened a special interest in the history of Vatican I. The study of this history led to a twofold discovery. First came the discovery of the degree to which the dogma of primacy and its formulation had been influenced by the historical situation of the eighteenth and nineteenth centuries in Western and Central Europe. The dominant interpretation of the dogma up until Vatican II had not taken this historical factor into account. That interpretation saw the dogma as the result of a logical development of the biblical data and as the perfected formulation of papal primacy. All previous versions were therefore seen as merely preliminary stages in the developmental process of the primacy, and deficient forms of its exercise.

From this perspective, the dogma of Vatican I was indeed irreconcilable with *communio* ecclesiology. It was this interpretation of the dogma that led to the opposition by the minority at Vatican II against the doctrine of the collegial structure of the supreme authority in the church.

At this point a second discovery advanced the discussion. It was established that alongside the longstanding prevailing interpretation, oriented towards the one-sided formulation of the dogma, there had been and still was another interpretation. It is the interpretation of the minority of Vatican I, which — and this can be proven historically — was recognized as legitimate, even if it was virtually ignored following Vatican I. In this interpretation, the dogma of 1870 is open to a *communio* ecclesiology. It therefore appears possible to integrate this dogma into a *communio* ecclesiology.

We have so far sketched in brief outline the progress of the recent discussion within the Catholic Church on the dogma of Vatican I. The results can be summarized as follows: just as we have learned to draw a distinction in the history of the primacy between the abiding commission of Peter and his successors and its changing modes of formulation and realization depending on the current situation, we must also view the dogma of Vatican I in a similarly differentiated manner. In that which it says, it expresses the evolved and abiding belief of the Catholic Church regarding the primacy of the successor of Peter. But the manner in which the Council formulates this belief is guided by a particular situation and intention, which lends its formulation a historical aspect and a certain one-sidedness. This one-sidedness means that the formulation is indeed capable of being overhauled and improved, as are the monarchical structure and the centralist exercise of the primacy, which are supported by that one-sidedness. If the *necessitas ecclesiae,* for whose benefit Christ intended the ministry of Peter and his successors, demands it, we can and must alter the formulation and the exercise of the primacy, without calling into question the truth of the dogma, that is, the perpetual commission of Peter. If the *necessitas ecclesiae* today requires the re-establishment of unity, modeled on the tradition of the still undivided church, then this dogma can and must be integrated into a *communio* ecclesiology.

It is precisely this insight of the recent Catholic discussion on the dogma of Vatican I that found expression in two recent documents of the Catholic magisterium, namely in the encyclical *Ut unum sint* (UUS) of 1995 and in the document *The Primacy of the Successor of Peter in the Mystery of the Church,*[1] which the Congregation for the Doctrine of the Faith published

---

1. Congregation for the Doctrine of the Faith, "The Primacy of the Successor of Pe-

in 1998. In his encyclical, Pope John Paul II distinguishes between "what is essential to the mission" of the primacy and the various ways it is exercised, which are to correspond to the current needs of the church. He refers expressly to the way the primacy was exercised in the still undivided church, which he does not characterize as deficient or as merely a preliminary developmental phase, as was the practice before the last Council (UUS 95).

The Congregation for the Doctrine of the Faith takes up this distinction. It distinguishes between the "unchanging nature of the primacy of the successor of Peter" and its historical forms, the changing ways it is exercised. And it sets down criteria for the forms of exercise appropriate to the particular situation. As criteria it designates on the one hand the intended purpose of the primacy, that is, the unity of the church, and on the other the *necessitas ecclesiae,* which can differ according to place and time.[2] In addition, the Congregation emphasizes that the bishop of Rome should in each instance clarify in fraternal dialogue with the other bishops the appropriate extent of the application of his powers.[3] Beyond that, the document, which is designated as "Reflections of the Congregation," contains initiatives towards integrating the doctrine of papal primacy into a *communio* ecclesiology. It is an attempt to defuse the tension between primacy and collegiality, which was still felt to exist at Vatican II. These reflections by the Congregation have as yet had no effect on the legal structure and practical exercise of the primacy. But they open up perspectives for the future.

The Hermeneutics of the Dogma

The preceding sketch of recent Catholic efforts to evaluate the dogma of 1870 has demonstrated that a perception is beginning to gain ground that this dogma is indeed open to a *communio* ecclesiology. This perception still encounters skepticism, not only outside the Catholic Church. Reservations regarding the possibility of reconciling the two have been raised and still are raised within the Catholic Church itself. I have already mentioned the fears of the minority at Vatican II. And I would also remind you of the discussion aroused by Hans Küng immediately after the Council. He claimed

---

ter in the Mystery of the Church," *L'Osservatore Romano,* English edition, 31 October 31, 1998, p. 7.

2. Congregation for the Doctrine of the Faith, "The Primacy," n. 12.
3. Congregation for the Doctrine of the Faith, "The Primacy," n. 13.

that only the annulment of the dogma could clear the way for a *communio* primacy. Vatican I had defined the primacy as an absolute monarchy of the pope, and papal infallibility as an *a priori* infallibility — concepts that could not be reconciled with the Bible or with the history and tradition of the church. Küng was supported in this by the work of August Bernhard Hasler on Pius IX and the First Vatican Council. Both claimed that the dogma was in fact null and void on formal grounds, because the Council had not been free in its definition.

Küng's thesis did more than simply spark off a vehement controversy. It also prompted a series of studies of the history of Vatican I. The result: Küng's thesis is false. I will mention here only the most comprehensive and detailed study, namely the three-volume work by Klaus Schatz, *Vaticanum I,* which appeared 1992-94. Was Küng's thesis so difficult to disprove that it necessitated such comprehensive studies? In a certain sense, Yes! Catholic apologetics had over a long period presented and interpreted the dogma of 1870 in a way that seemed to confirm Küng's thesis. It is this longstanding prevailing apologetic-maximalist interpretation that to this day determines the image of the dogma both within the Catholic Church and without. An added difficulty arises because the one-sided formulation of the dogma does not make sufficiently clear that this maximalist interpretation does not fully convey the intended meaning of the Council. That meaning can only be inferred from the Council files and from several official documents that followed Vatican I in order to protect the dogma from misunderstanding. In the following discussion I will therefore elaborate on the results of the more recent studies, which demonstrate that the dogma of 1870 did remain open to a *communio* ecclesiology.

The hermeneutics of dogmatic conciliar texts, in this instance those of Vatican I, is well known. To be more precise, the Dogmatic Constitution *Pastor aeternus* of the First Vatican Council deals with two dogmas that are closely linked to one another. The first defines the jurisdictional primacy of the bishop of Rome as the legitimate successor of Peter, the second the infallibility of his teaching office under certain conditions. The interpretation of both dogmas takes as its starting point the respective thetic definitions at the end of the relevant chapters, the canons. The canonical definitions are to be interpreted in the light of the corresponding chapter, which supplies the theological exposition. A further aid to interpretation can be found in the Council files. These consist primarily in the commentaries by the speakers of the responsible commission on the proposals of the Council Fathers and on the concluding text. Important indications of the intended meaning of the

Council can be discerned from these commentaries. Further clarification of the intended meaning of the Council is also provided by the textual history of the two dogmas, and the Council debates.

In order to understand the historical context of the dogma of the primacy, which had a formative influence on its formulation, we will begin with the latter, namely the relevant Council debates and the textual history.

The Struggle between Two Conceptions at the Council

To be clear at the outset: at the Council there was no dispute about two points, *first*, that Christ himself had appointed Peter as the first among the apostles and as visible head of the church here on earth, and *second*, that the bishop of Rome is the successor of Peter, and as such holds the primacy over the whole church. On those points there was undivided consensus. There were, however, critical questions by the Council Fathers regarding the extent and form of exercise of the primacy. How was the relationship of the primacy to the authority of the college of bishops and to the individual bishops to be defined more precisely? These questions were prompted by the fears of the minority that at the Council the pope was to be declared universal bishop and absolute monarch and sovereign of the church, so that the other bishops would be reduced to representatives of the pope.

There were good reasons for these fears, for precisely this concept of the primacy had found broad acceptance in the Catholic Church during the nineteenth century. It did not originate in Rome, but from the so-called Ultramontane movement. Catholic laypeople and clergy in Europe were striving for a strengthening of the papacy because they saw it as the only hope of protecting the church against encroachments by the rulers in the evolving nation-states. For them, only the sovereignty of the pope could embody and guarantee the autonomy and independence of the church from the state.

A brief explanation of this point. The modern state began with the concept of sovereignty and the model of absolute monarchy. Sovereignty meant the absolute independence of the monarch internally, and of the state itself externally. By appealing to its sovereignty, the state claimed the right to direct the church within its territory according to its own interests. That threatened the church with disintegration into national churches. As a countermove, the Ultramontane movement maintained the sovereignty of the pope over the church, that is, the complete independence of his powers of jurisdiction internally within the church, so that it could secure its independence externally. Any claim that the episcopate should also participate in the governing of the universal church was seen as dividing or detracting from papal sovereignty, because that sovereignty had always been interpreted as absolute. The bishops, often bound by national or feudal interests, or exposed to the pressure and influence of the secular powers, were neither in a position nor willing to assert the autonomy of the church.

The classic example of the dominance of the state over the church was France, which is also the land where the modern state originated. The king nominated the bishops and prevented the exercise of papal jurisdiction. Thus, for example, he prevented the implementation of the reforms of the Council of Trent within France. The French Revolution assumed the state's claim to power over the church, as did the restored French monarchy subsequently. Other European states also introduced this system. The ideology of this system was so-called Gallicanism. Gallicanism was therefore the real opponent that the dogma of Vatican I was intended to combat and eliminate. The dogmatization of the papal primacy as sovereignty was at the heart of the Ultramontane strategy in the battle for the freedom of the church.

But it was not only state dirigisme that the Ultramontane movement rebelled against. The intellectual developments in Europe caused no less consternation: rationalism, materialism, atheism, and liberalism called the foundations of the Christian faith into question. In response to this threat too, the Ultramontanes placed their hopes in strengthening the authority of the pope as the representative of the authority of God and his revelation. Therefore the dogmatization of papal infallibility became the second central objective of the Ultramontane movement. Rome did not take the lead in this movement until the time of Gregory XVI and Pius IX.

This brief excursion into the prehistory and the historical context of Vatican I is essential to an understanding of the Council. It was not a lust for power on the part of the popes that led to the two dogmas of the primacy and the infallibility of the pope, but the very real threat to the church, its unity, and its autonomy vis-à-vis the state, and the fact that the faith was in danger. The endeavors to strengthen the authority of the pope were initiated at the grass roots of the church. However, the desire to counter an extreme challenge with an extreme reaction gave rise to a new danger. To declare the pope absolute and sovereign monarch of the church would have meant a break with the divine constitution and the tradition of the church.

That is the background to the fears held by the theologically better-educated of the bishops among the Council Fathers, who formed the minority and rejected the extreme conceptions of the primacy and infallibility of the pope. There was every indication that the Council should and would define these conceptions. It is due to the minority that this was prevented.

The first draft of the text that was presented to the Council Fathers for discussion did indeed take the extreme conception of the primacy as monarchical sovereignty as its starting point. The following critical objections were raised during the discussion of the draft:

- The church is not an absolute monarchy. Beside the supreme authority of the pope there is also the supreme authority of the college of bishops and the authority of the individual bishops, which are no less a part of the divine constitution of the church. The bishops are not vicars of the pope.
- The projected image of the primacy resembles too closely a secular model of power rather than a gift of divine love.
- Not the pope but Christ is the unifying principle of the church. The pope is merely the "visible foundation" of her unity.
- While it is claimed that the primacy defends the rights of the bishops, those rights are nowhere defined, nor are the limits to the exercise of the primacy, or the existence of intermediate authorities.

The focus of the criticism by the minority was the designation of papal jurisdiction as an "ordinary, immediate, and truly episcopal" power. Papal jurisdiction thus appeared to be a rival jurisdiction that superseded the equally ordinary, immediate, and episcopal power of the bishop within his diocese. The minority demanded that the subsidiary character of an immediate intervention by the pope in the local churches should be given prominence. And as far as the definition of papal jurisdiction as an episcopal power was concerned, it must be made clear that the pope was not a universal bishop and the entire church was not his diocese.

Of particular significance for the interpretation of the dogma is the reply of the speaker of the responsible commission to the criticisms of the Council Fathers. It can be summarized in the following points:

- The church is indeed not an absolute monarchy under the pope. The primacy has to observe the divine constitution of the church, including the authority of the college of bishops and the individual bishops, and it must take as its guiding principle the welfare of the church which it has to serve. All of that is assumed to be taken for granted and is not a subject for debate. The sole issue here is the question whether there is any authority beside or above the pope that can limit his authority. That is precisely what is to be excluded.

- It is true that the full and supreme jurisdictional power of the church exists in a twofold manner. On the one hand it pertains to the college of bishops with its head, the bishop of Rome, and also to the bishop of Rome as the visible head of the church, independently of his acting together with the other bishops. For Christ's commission was given both to all the apostles together with Peter, and to Peter alone. This twofold structure becomes problematic only when the two forms, which are bound together by the same apostolic commission and the same sacrament, are considered as separate powers competing with one another, as they are regarded by conciliarism and Gallicanism.

- The definition of papal jurisdiction as "ordinary" power does not mean that it should be considered normal for the pope to constantly intervene in the dioceses. Rather, the word "ordinary" is used as the opposite of "delegated," and means the primacy is grounded not in a delegation by the church, but in Christ's commission to Peter.

- It is designated as "immediate" power because the pope — if the *necessitas ecclesiae* demands — can intervene everywhere within the church, directly and without the mediation or permission of any other authority.

- The designation as "truly episcopal" power is intended to counter the Gallican error that the pope infringes the sacramentally transmitted rights reserved for the responsible bishop when he intervenes in a diocese. The pastoral power of the pope and the bishops is based on the same sacrament, the only difference being that the pope is endowed with the *episcopē* for the entire church and in its supreme form, while that of the bishops is valid only for their diocese and in hierarchical subordination beneath the pope.

These frequently overlooked statements by the speaker of the responsible commission are nothing less than an official commentary on the dogma and a guide to its interpretation. They allow the intended meaning of the Council to become clear. They allow us to recognize what the Council did not intend and what it did intend. The Council did not wish to limit the divinely guaranteed rights of the episcopate, and therefore did not intend to define the primacy as an absolute monarchical sovereignty. But on the other hand, it did want complete freedom of action for the pope when the *necessitas ecclesiae* demanded it, and it wished to teach the inappellability of his decisions. In other words: it did not want to deny the limits to the primacy set by God, but it certainly wanted to establish that no human authority, whether it be a Council or the state, could set limits to his commission.

How was this intention expressed in the definitive text that the Council accepted? To be clear at the outset: what the Council did not wish to deny and presupposed to be true, was written into the prologue to the constitution and the chapters of exposition, but not into the canon itself, as the minority wished. But what it wished to teach as a dogma was expressed in the canon, in order to condemn Gallicanism. In detail it can be summed up as follows:

- The prologue begins with the will of Christ that the church should be one, and with the mission of all the apostles to serve the unity of the church as pastors and teachers.[4]
- This is followed by the mission of Peter and his successors as the abiding principle and visible foundation of church unity, to serve directly the unity of the episcopate, and indirectly — together with the bishops and priests — "the unity of faith and *communion*" (DH 3051). Thus the immediate purpose of the primacy is the unity of the episcopate, and together with them the pope serves the unity of the church, which is designated as a *communio* in faith.
- It is repeatedly stated that the Council wishes to define the primacy and infallibility of the pope with respect for the universal tradition of the church, including the tradition of the still undivided church of the first millennium (DH 3052, 3059, 3065). The Council thereby implicitly acknowledges the plurality of shapes in which the primacy is manifested and realized in the past and in the future.
- A separate paragraph in the third chapter emphasizes that the primacy does not threaten the ordinary and immediate jurisdiction of the bishops — the most important point raised by the minority in its criticism. The fact that this paragraph was inserted into the third chapter, which deals with the nature of the primacy, represents the most important achievement of the minority. The paragraph reads as follows: "This power of the Supreme Pontiff is far from standing in the way of

---

4. Heinrich Denzinger, *Enchiridion symbolorum definitionum et declarationum de rebus fidei et morum*, re-edited by Peter Hünermann, 37th ed. (Freiburg: Herder, 1991), 3050; hereafter cited as DH.

the power of ordinary and immediate jurisdiction, by which the bishops, who under appointment of the Holy Spirit, succeeded in the place of the apostles, feed and rule individually, as true shepherds, the particular flock assigned to them. Rather this latter power is asserted, confirmed and vindicated by this same supreme and universal shepherd; as in the words of St. Gregory the Great: 'My honour is the honour of the whole Church. My honour is the firm strength of my brethren. I am truly honoured, when due honour is paid to each and every one.'" (DH 3061)[5]

For the rest, this chapter clearly states the true objective of the dogmatization of the primacy: It is intended as a condemnation of Gallicanism, because the latter legitimizes the view that the state is permitted to impede the free communication between the pope and the bishops, and to annul papal decrees within its territory (DH 3062). The assertion made by Gallicanism of the possibility of appealing against papal judgments to an ecumenical council meant in practice that state jurisdiction took the place of papal jurisdiction, which was rendered ineffective by this reservation. Because the inappellability of the primacy was therefore the real bulwark against encroachments by the state — that is also made clear by Chapter 3 — the dogma takes aim at precisely this point, but not at the relationship between papacy and episcopate. This is expressed in the corresponding canon, which reads:

> And so, if anyone says that the Roman Pontiff has only the office of inspection and direction, but not the full and supreme power of jurisdiction over the whole Church, not only in matters that pertain to faith and morals, but also in matters that pertain to the discipline and government of the Church throughout the whole world, or if anyone says that he has only a more important part and not the complete fullness of this supreme power, or if anyone says that this power is not ordinary and immediate either over each and every Church or over each and every shepherd and faithful, *anathema sit.* (DH 3064)[6]

---

5. Josef Neuner and Jacques Dupuis, eds., *The Christian Faith in the Doctrinal Documents of the Catholic Church* (New York: Collins, 1983), n. 827.
6. Neuner and Dupuis, eds., *The Christian Faith,* n. 830.

Results of Recent Discussion and Research

It is time to take stock. In judging the dogma of the primacy of the successor of Peter one arrives at a negative and a positive conclusion. The deliberate one-sidedness of the concluding definition is to be assessed as negative. In juridical language — which, it must be said, does serve to make the statement clear — exclusive prominence is given to the primacy, its universality, and its unlimited freedom from any human authority. Neither its intended purpose nor other criteria for an appropriate exercise that respects the jurisdiction of the bishops are mentioned here. This one-sidedness of the definition itself subsequently enabled the maximalist interpretation of the primacy as absolute sovereignty to substantiate its claim on the basis of this dogma.

In turn, the maximalist interpretation justified the increasingly centralist exercise of the primacy as the only form that complied with the dogma of 1870. Finally, the maximalist interpretation influenced the legal structure of the primacy established in the codex of 1917, together with the fact that the pope as the sole authority enacted this binding legal code for the entire church. Conversely, the increasing centralism supported the general impression that the dogma had in fact defined the primacy as absolute sovereignty. Did the pope not in fact intrude upon and regulate the ordinary and immediate jurisdiction of the bishops in enacting the codex as the sole legislator? Such a regulation was indeed fitting. But a greater participation of the episcopate in the legislation would have lent greater credence to the assurance by the Council that the primacy protected and defended the ordinary and immediate jurisdiction of the bishops. That did in fact occur with respect to the state, but less convincingly with respect to the primacy.

As we have seen, it is only the Council files — in particular the commentary by the speaker of the responsible commission — that allow us to infer that the definition's silence regarding the collegial co-responsibility of the bishops for the government of the whole church in no way means a rejection of that responsibility. On the contrary, the doctrine of the simultaneous full and supreme authority of the college of bishops is presupposed as a self-evident component of the tradition. This doctrine was not disputed by anybody. What was disputed on the part of the Gallicans, and what therefore had to be defined, was the simultaneous full and supreme authority of the pope, which empowered him to act independently of the collaboration of the episcopate. For this reason, any proposals by the minority that wished to have the appropriateness of the collaboration of the episcopate also mentioned in the canon were rejected. Such a reference was not rejected because of any intention to deny that appropriateness, but because it was feared that such a reference could be understood in the sense of Gallicanism.

There is yet another reason for this silence that was not intended to be a rejection. The doctrine of the episcopal office and the college of bishops was to be dealt with in a second constitution on the church. This second constitution did not come to pass, because the Council was suspended ahead of time because of the Franco-Prussian War. But we know the draft for this constitution. In it, the full and supreme authority of the college of bishops is designated as *"fidei dogma certissimum."* When the responsible commission rejected the corresponding proposals of the minority, it had in mind that the collegial co-responsibility of the episcopate was to receive due recognition of its rights in the projected second constitution.

Even more important for the interpretation of the dogma are of course the preceding chapters and the prologue. These texts contain sufficiently clear signals that the dogma did not intend to detract from either the tradition of the church or the rights of the bishops and the college of bishops. The citation from Gregory the Great referred to was a sentence with which that pope had refused the proposed title of *universalis papa.*

Nevertheless, the fact remains that the one-sided formulation of the dogma itself and the maximalist interpretation, based on this one-sidedness, by those for whom the strengthening of papal authority could never go far enough, gave rise to the impression among the general public that the Council had in fact declared the pope to be the absolute and sovereign monarch of the church. That is precisely what the German Imperial Chancellor Bismarck maintained in his circular of 1872 to the European governments. He warned them that the bishops in their countries had by this dogma been made mere tools of the pope. That prompted the German bishops to issue a collective declaration in 1875 in which they rejected this accusation. They declared expressly that this dogma had not made the pope an absolute sovereign of the church, nor the bishops papal officials without any personal responsibility.

This document is also important for the interpretation of the dogma, since Pius IX twice gave it official approval, in an apostolic brief of 1875 (DH 3117) and in a consistorial address of the same year (DH 3112). The collective declaration of the German episcopate states: "It is a complete misunderstanding of the Vatican decrees to believe that because of them 'the episcopal jurisdiction has been absorbed into the papa,' that the pope has 'in principle taken the place of each individual bishop,' the bishops are now 'no more than tools of the pope, his officials, without responsibility of their own'" (DH 3115).[7]

On the positive side, we can therefore draw a threefold conclusion.

- The maximalist interpretation of the dogma of 1870 and a centralist exercise of the primacy cannot be substantiated by Vatican I. That is confirmed by Vatican II, which in its Constitution on the Church repeatedly took up the commentary by the speakers of the responsible commission of Vatican I in order to give expression to the coexistence of primacy and collegiality, and to the appropriateness of the participation of the episcopate in the governing of the church.
- The dogma of 1870 is open for the possibility of different forms to exercise primacy because it refers also to the tradition and practice of the yet undivided church of the first millennium.
- The dogma of 1870 is open to a *communio* ecclesiology. In designating the primacy as a "truly episcopal" authority, it binds the pope into the sacramentally instituted *communio* of the college of bishops. As its head, the pope is to serve the unity of the episcopate and together with the episcopate the unity of the church. The pope does not stand above the church but within the *communio* of the church, which is designated by Vatican I as *communio* in faith. The question of how the relationship between primacy and collegiality or synodality was to be structured in concrete terms, the constitution *Pastor aeternus* did not intend to answer. Vatican II therefore wished to confront this question, precisely because it had remained open at Vatican I.

This last point, that is, the openness of the dogma for a *communio* ecclesiology, is confirmed by two recent documents of the Catholic teaching office that have already been mentioned above.

- In his encyclical *Ut unum sint* Pope John Paul II says: "When the Catholic Church affirms that the office of the bishop of Rome corresponds with the will of Christ, she does not separate this office from the mission entrusted to the whole body of bishops, who are also 'vicars and ambassadors of Christ.' The bishop of Rome is a member of the 'college,' and they are his brothers in the ministry" (UUS 95). This lan-

7. Neuner and Dupuis, eds., *The Christian Faith*, n. 841.

guage does indeed differ considerably from the maximalist interpretation of the dogma, but not from the prologue of the Constitution *Pastor aeternus* of Vatican I, nor from the commentary of the speaker of its commission.

- With deliberate one-sidedness the dogma of 1870 gave special prominence to the inappellability of papal judgments according to the principle *prima sedes a nemine iudicatur.* The maximalist interpretation of the dogma had deduced from that the absolute sovereignty of the pope. In contrast, the "Reflections" of the Congregation for the Doctrine of the Faith of 1998 state: "That does not however mean that the pope has absolute power. For it is a characteristic of the service of unity, and also a consequence of the communion of the college of bishops and the *sensus fidei* of the whole people of God, to listen to the voice of the particular churches. . . . The final and inalienable responsibility of the pope finds its best guarantee on the one hand in his integration into the tradition and into the fraternal communion, and on the other hand in trust in the support of the Holy Spirit who guides the Church" (No. 10). This clarification is to be welcomed. It accords both with the characterization of the primacy as a "truly episcopal" authority by Vatican I and the commentary of the speaker of the Council commission, and with the understanding of the minority of the Council.

In a word: the dogma of 1870 did not deserve the bad reputation that its maximalist interpretation in theory and practice has earned it. It is not the insuperable obstacle to the unity of Christians that it has long been considered to be. And one further point: in the "Hall of Fame" of the ecumenical movement, the minority of Vatican I deserves a place of honor, because it was able to win over the Council to keep this dogma open to a future *communio* primacy.

Vatican I and the Development of Doctrine: A Lutheran Perspective

Michael Root

The topic I have been assigned, "Vatican I and the Development of Doctrine: A Lutheran Perspective," calls for the interrelation of three complex elements: Vatican I — an event and the texts it produced; the development of doctrine — an extended historical reality and the modern understanding of that reality under the concept "development"; and Lutheranism — a specific confessional tradition, within which I myself stand. This three-sided topic has within it three binary relations, two of which immediately suggest problems. Vatican I relates to the development of doctrine, the reality and the concept, in a variety of ways. The Council was itself the result of a complex history, but the texts from the Council themselves appear ahistorical in their outlook, oblivious to historical development and change, even though the infallibility they affirm is needed precisely because of the decisions historical change forces upon the church. The second binary relation, Vatican I and Lutheranism, would seem to indicate confessional differences at their sharpest. Not only *Pastor aeternus* but also *Dei Filius* might seem hopelessly at odds with most versions of Lutheranism.

In this essay, however, the focus will fall on the problems located in the third of the binary relations — Lutheranism and the development of doctrine. I have come to believe that a necessary condition for a fruitful discussion between Lutherans and Catholics on the issues set before us by Vatican I is a deeper engagement by Lutheran theologians and church leaders with the

A version of this essay has been published in *Ecclesiology* 2 (2005): 35-51.

question of how doctrine develops over time. I think the recent ecumenical debates among Lutherans on episcopacy (in the dialogue with Anglicans) and on justification (in the dialogue with Catholics) have accentuated this need. After discussing this more limited topic, I will then take up the three-sided question of a possible Lutheran perspective on Vatican I in the context of the development of doctrine.

A Lutheran Perspective on the Development of Doctrine?

The Limitations of "Historical Situationalism" and the Lutheran Understanding of Confession

George Lindbeck began a 1967 survey of "The Problem of Doctrinal Development and Contemporary Protestant Theology" with the statement: "There is little in contemporary Protestant discussions corresponding directly to the treatments of doctrinal development which have proliferated in Roman Catholic circles since the days of Newman and Möhler."[1] My own less-than-exhaustive search of more recent discussions finds that, among Lutherans, this judgment still holds, with the notable exception of Lindbeck's own work and that of his student Bruce Marshall.[2] If one wants to uncover a Lutheran perspective on the development of doctrine, one must look for equivalent discussions carried on using other concepts.

The Lutheran Understanding of Confession

Fruitful hunting grounds for such a search are in the Lutheran discussions of Scripture and tradition and, even more, in the frequent modern Lutheran discussions of the meaning of confession. Confession is claimed as the ex-

---

1. George A. Lindbeck, "The Problem of Doctrinal Development and Contemporary Protestant Theology," in *Man as Man and Believer, Concilium*, vol. 21 (New York: Paulist Press, 1967), p. 133.

2. Lindbeck's work will be cited below. Marshall's is found in Bruce D. Marshall, "The Church in the Gospel," *Pro Ecclesia* 1 (1992): 27-41. A further survey of the topic is in Walter Carl Sundberg, "The Development of Dogma as an Ecumenical Problem: Roman Catholic–Protestant Conflict over the Authority and Historicity of Dogmatic Statements," Ph.D. Dissertation, Princeton Theological Seminary, 1981. With the exception of Lindbeck, the only Lutherans Sundberg discusses in detail are the nineteenth-century figures Vilmar and Baur.

pression of a new Lutheran understanding of church doctrine. This understanding can be summarized on the basis of relatively standard works by such mid-twentieth-century Lutheran theologians as Gerhard Ebeling, Regin Prenter, and Edmund Schlink.

Confession in a Reformation sense "arises as a responsive confessing, as ὁμολογε v, and can only be accepted in this sense."[3] It is "the response of man to the revelation of God in his Word."[4] Confession is made not only *coram deo*, however, but also in a specific situation of challenge to the gospel that calls for a confession of a specific sort. "The Confession as an authoritative document of Church doctrine is bound up with a unique situation of decision-making, where what constitutes a Church, a distinct and concrete church community, becomes visible."[5]

Although historically variable, true confession always, as *homologein*, is the confession of the one dogma — the single, even if complex, Trinitarian content given to the faith.[6] This one dogma is to be found normatively in Scripture, and "a Confession is the comprehensive exposition of the total Scripture."[7] A confession states, in the face of the challenge of a specific situation, the encompassing heart of the scriptural message. For that reason, confession is by its very nature subordinate to Scripture, either implicitly, as is shown in the practice of the earlier Lutheran confessions which lack any statement on biblical authority, but cite Scripture extensively as norm, or explicitly, as in the Formula of Concord's opening statement that "the only rule and guiding principle according to which all teachings and teachers are

---

3. Gerhard Ebeling, "The Word of God and Church Doctrine," in *The Word of God and Tradition: Historical Studies Interpreting the Divisions of Christianity* (Philadelphia: Fortress Press, 1968), p. 176; translation altered ["als antwortendes Bekennen, als ὁμολογε v entsteht und nur in diesem Sinne aufgenommen werden kann"]; Gerhard Ebeling, "Wort Gottes und kirchliche Lehre," in *Wort Gottes und Tradition: Studien zu einer Hermeneutik der Konfessionen* (Göttingen: Vandenhoeck & Ruprecht, 1964), p. 169.

4. Edmund Schlink, *Theology of the Lutheran Confessions* (Philadelphia: Fortress Press, 1961), p. 12.

5. Ebeling, "Word of God and Church Doctrine," p. 176; translation altered ["Confessio als maßgebendes Dokument kirchliche Lehre ist gebunden an die exzeptionelle Entscheidungssituation, in der das, was Kirche zu Kirche macht, scheidend und zugleich konkrete Kirchengemeinschaft in Erscheinung treten lassend neu laut geworden ist"]; Ebeling, "Wort Gottes und kirchliche Lehre," p. 170.

6. Regin Prenter, *Creation and Redemption* (Philadelphia: Fortress Press, 1967), p. 5. Similarly, Ebeling, "Wort Gottes und kirchliche Lehre," p. 173.

7. Schlink, *Theology of the Lutheran Confessions*, p. 15.

to be evaluated and judged are the prophetic and apostolic writings of the Old and New Testaments alone."[8]

The binding force of confession is the binding force of the gospel to which it witnesses and the content of which it states, "The power by which a Confession binds is the power of the Gospel."[9] This understanding both limits and accentuates the authority of a confession. On the one hand, the confession has no authority other than the material authority of its contents. It is not itself a "second authority, alongside the subject matter [*Sache*] which the Word of God concerns."[10] On the other hand, because the authoritative claim expressed in the confessions is that of the gospel itself, it is not a historically passing claim, but a permanent one. Their claim "admits of no limits, either of time or of space."[11] The interpretive task is to "discover and recognize the confessional statements for what they are — statements designed by the church to bind once for all the proclamation of all subsequent times."[12]

"Historical Situationalism"

In his survey of recent Protestant understandings of development and doctrine, Lindbeck found "a widespread — though largely implicit — Protestant consensus that doctrinal development is to be understood in terms of what I shall call 'historical situationalism.'"[13] On the one hand, analogies of organic development, of some sort of "continuous and cumulative growth," are "sharply rejected." On the other hand, historical differences are not ignored, but seen as "the products of the dialogue in history between God and his people and as the historically conditioned and relative responses, interpretations, and testimonies to the Word addressing man through the scrip-

---

8. Epitome, Summary 1, in *Die Bekenntnisschriften der evangelisch-lutherischen Kirchen* (Göttingen: Vandenhoeck & Ruprecht, ⁹1982), p. 767; Robert Kolb and James A. Nestingen, eds., *Sources and Contexts of the Book of Concord* (Minneapolis: Fortress Press, 2001), p. 486.

9. Schlink, *Theology of the Lutheran Confessions*, p. 23.

10. Ebeling, "Word of God and Church Doctrine," p. 178; translation altered [". . . nicht um ein Zweites handelt neben der Sache, um die es im Worte Gottes geht." Ebeling, "Wort Gottes und kirchliche Lehre," p. 171].

11. Schlink, *Theology of the Lutheran Confessions*, p. xvii.

12. Schlink, *Theology of the Lutheran Confessions*, p. xix.

13. He summarizes this understanding in six points; see Lindbeck, "The Problem of Doctrinal Development and Contemporary Protestant Theology," pp. 138-41.

tural witness."[14] The specificity of the Reformation confessions is thus a function of the historical specificity of the challenges of the sixteenth century, as the historical specificity of the Barmen Declaration is a function of its own, significantly different historical situation.

How do these various, historically specific situations of confession relate, not just to their own time, but to their past, which also forms part of the context of confession? Lindbeck notes that while some theologians tend to focus on the immediate situation of confession "to such an extreme as to overlook the elements of continuity and cumulativeness in doctrinal development," most are willing to grant that "doctrinal formulation does not, cannot and should not proceed in a wholly episodic, atomistic and discontinuous fashion."

> Most agree that the church ought to seek to correct its one-sidedness, partiality and distortions by studying and learning how our forefathers in the faith through the whole of history have understood the Gospel. To the extent that this is done, there is a certain progressive enrichment and enlargement of the church's doctrinal formulations and interpretations of revelation. At the same time this development must be regarded not as analogous to organic growth or unfolding in which later stages are contained in and build upon the earlier, but rather as similar to the much weaker type of "progress" in comprehension. This comes from viewing and responding to one and the same object from different perspectives and circumstances.[15]

Problems with Historical Situationalism

Two closely interrelated questions need to be addressed to such a "historical situationalist" understanding of doctrine, especially as it relates to the more specifically Lutheran understanding of confession. These questions are not merely hypothetical, but relate to recent Lutheran ecumenical debates.

The Historical Character of Normative Teaching First, both historical situationalism and the Lutheran embodiment of this understanding in

14. Lindbeck, "The Problem of Doctrinal Development and Contemporary Protestant Theology," pp. 138-39.

15. Lindbeck, "The Problem of Doctrinal Development and Contemporary Protestant Theology," p. 140.

terms of confession must place great weight on some version of a form/content distinction. The use of such a distinction in relation to the issues before us is not new. Luther justified the authority of the creeds along such lines. For him, the creed "is neither a supplement to nor in competition with Holy Scripture. Furthermore, it does not present a development of the teaching of Scripture; 'but, just as a bee gathers honey from many beautiful and happy little flowers, so this creed is gathered from the books of the dear prophets and apostles, that is from all Holy Writ; it is a fine and brief summary for children and simple Christians' (WA 41,275)."[16] By such reasoning, the Reformers could both assert the *sola scriptura* and maintain the authority of the creeds and the Reformation confessions.

Some sort of content/form, *res/forma, Sache/Sprache* distinction is a necessary conceptual tool of understanding. It is particularly necessary for ecumenical reflection on the variety of ways the one faith is realized in diverse forms. Nevertheless, the Lutheran sort of historical situationalism outlined above calls for a particularly precise and thoroughgoing application of such a distinction. Schlink continues his statement quoted above about the task of discovering the permanent claim of the confessions: "This will be done when we single out the positive principles of doctrine from those polemical portions that are directed against dangers which are today no longer so acute."[17] The authority of the confessions seems to reside only in the scriptural gospel they express and summarize and not in any aspect of their historical specificity. The permanently normative aspect of the confessions is related only accidentally, as kernel to husk, to the confessions as historical developments. The historical husk must be stripped away to get at the transhistorical core.

A problem, of course, is that this transhistorical core can only be stated or restated in some historically determinate form. When such emphasis has been placed on the distinction between content and form, can the content then break through its form to function effectively as a doctrinal norm and, if that occurs, how can we know that the content and not the historical form is in fact functioning as norm? Two opposite but parallel developments attest to the difficulty contemporary Lutheran theology and the contemporary Lutheran Church face in making this distinction. To a large degree, doctrinal discipline has become weak, if not absent, in many Lutheran and other mainline Protestant churches. This development has many causes, some of

16. Werner Elert, *The Structure of Lutheranism* (St. Louis: Concordia, 1962), p. 205.
17. Schlink, *Theology of the Lutheran Confessions,* p. xix.

which are non-theological or non-doctrinal. Nevertheless, a historical relativism — rooted in the sense that the specificity of any statement of doctrine sufficiently precise to function as norm might or even probably will be a specificity attributable to the historical situation and not to the truly normative content — is certainly a contributing factor.

In recent ecumenical debates over justification, an opposite tendency can be seen, a tendency to assert the universal and permanent normativity of the historically specific while ignoring its historical specificity. One need not be a devotee of the "New Paul" of E. P. Sanders and James Dunn to agree that the doctrine of justification is a development within Western theology, a response, rooted in Paul, to questions Paul himself did not ask. And yet, a Lutheran theologian such as Eberhard Jüngel can state: "It is only when explained by means of that doctrine [of justification] that Christology becomes a materially appropriate [*sachgemäß*] Christology at all [*überhaupt*]."[18] Not just any doctrine of justification can play this role, of course. As Jüngel's total presentation makes clear, only an evangelical doctrine of justification can play this role. But an evangelical doctrine of justification is not a transcendental reality; it is the product of a certain history. In assertions such as that of Jüngel, the historically specific becomes universally normative, without its specificity being admitted. The problem is addressed to a degree by saying that the doctrine of justification can be present and effective without its specific language,[19] but what does it mean to say that a doctrine is decisive for the *sachgemäß* character of the Christology of a theologian such as John of Damascus, if that doctrine is simply absent from John's writings?[20] When the authority of the confession is so linked to a content distinguishable from any historical form, then either the content volatilizes into shapelessness, or form asserts itself as content.

I would argue that the Lutheran impulse expressed in these claims of Jüngel and others for the permanent criteriological function of the doctrine

---

18. Eberhard Jüngel, *Justification: The Heart of the Christian Faith: A Theological Study with an Ecumenical Purpose* (Edinburgh: T. & T. Clark, 2001), p. 29; translation altered. German original: Eberhard Jüngel, *Das Evangelium von der Rechtfertigung des Gottlosen als Zentrum des christlichen Glaubens: Eine theologische Studie in ökumenischer Absicht* (Tübingen: Mohr Siebeck, 1998), p. 24.

19. Jüngel, *Justification*, p. 21 [Jüngel, *Evangelium der Rechtfertigung*, p. 17].

20. A fuller version of a critique of Jüngel along these lines appears in Michael Root, "The Joint Declaration on the Doctrine of Justification: A Lutheran Systematic Theological Perspective," in David E. Aune, ed., *Rereading Paul Together: Protestant and Catholic Perspectives on Justification* (Grand Rapids: Baker Academic, 2006), pp. 60-76.

of justification requires some sort of understanding of the development of doctrine. The Lutheran claim is best understood as the claim that the development of a doctrine of justification that focuses on the gift character of our righteousness, receivable only by faith, is a permanently valid, irreversible development in the history of the church's understanding of the gospel by which it lives. Such a doctrine of justification is not simply a repetition or summary of Scripture; it is a reading of Scripture from a particular angle, bringing out what earlier had not been seen, but which, once seen, cannot be left behind. It is a development of binding doctrine, in which the historically specific is inseparable from that which binds.

The Binding Character of Past Decisions   Such an understanding of permanently valid doctrinal developments presupposes an answer to a second question: In what sense is the church and its teaching at one point in history bound by the earlier teachings and decisions of the church? Any notion of a development of doctrine assumes some form of authority of past developments for the present and future. Otherwise, there is no genuine development.

Lutheran churches have consistently held to the subordinate authority of the creeds of the ancient church and of the Lutheran confessions themselves. In my own church, the creeds and Lutheran confessions, in a carefully nuanced hierarchy among themselves and beneath Scripture, form a part of the "Confession of Faith" laid out in Chapter 2 of the church's constitution. Any pastor or seminary teacher must swear to preach and teach in accordance with this statement. Even if concrete doctrinal discipline is rarely exercised, the explicit rejection of these standards by an ordination candidate would probably be cause for that candidate's rejection.

When one looks at the warrant offered for these subordinate authorities, however, a certain ambivalence appears. As noted above, the Reformers themselves held to the authority of the creeds as summaries of Scripture, whose authority was tied to their scriptural content. Even on the basis of such an ahistorical account, a question remains: To what degree is the later theologian or the later church bound by the earlier decision of the church that the Nicene Creed in fact *does* rightly summarize Scripture? The question becomes more acute if the historical insight is conceded that the fourth-century church was doing more than simply summarizing Scripture in its doctrinal decisions; it was forced to interpret Scripture in the context of questions Scripture itself did not ask and thus did not explicitly answer. In what sense, if any, can the answers the church has given to questions posed by the Christological and Trinitarian debates of the early church be binding for contemporary theology?

Schlink answers that confession is always made in the name of the one church; it is to be "in consensus with the fathers and brethren."[21] The patristic citations within the confessions are meant to indicate this consensus. "Heeding the voice of the fathers and brethren represented a test and a correction of the understanding of Scripture on the part of the individual authors of the church's Confession." Because they represent a greater consensus, the creeds are "relatively more authoritative than the Confessions of the Reformation."[22]

Schlink is willing to say that the doctrinal decisions of the past do bind the contemporary theologians: "Dogmatics is bound by the Confessions as exposition of Scripture."[23] This binding character, however, must not remain merely formal. "The truth and binding character of a Confession does not rest simply on its claim — no matter how much that claim may be supported by respected church fathers at various times — but in its actual agreement with Scripture which ever anew discloses itself to exegetical study."[24] The task of dogmatics is ever anew to move from formal to material authority.

To what degree, however, do the decisions of the church thus remain mere hypotheses to which the theologian must attend, but which he or she can reject if they appear inadequate? This question is raised by Werner Elert. He argues that in the Formula of Concord, "Scripture is obeyed. The old creeds are received." This reception, however, is and must remain voluntary. He sees the crises of seventeenth-century Lutheranism as rooted "above all in the fact that the reception [of the creeds] was not understood as a task [*Aufgabe*] presented anew to every generation on condition that the authority of Scripture be maintained but was taken into account as an accomplished fact [*abgeschlossenes Faktum*]."[25] But are no interpretive decisions the church has to make about the gospel, no matter how fundamental, ever to be treated as "accomplished facts"? Is the assertion as a matter of Chris-

---

21. Schlink, *Theology of the Lutheran Confessions*, p. 17.

22. Schlink, *Theology of the Lutheran Confessions*, p. 19.

23. Schlink, *Theology of the Lutheran Confessions*, p. 29 ["Die Bekenntnisschriften sind für die dogmatische Arbeit verpflichtend als Auslegung der Heiligen Schrift." Edmund Schlink, *Theologie der lutherischen Bekenntnisschriften* (Munich: Chr. Kaiser, ³1948), p. 58].

24. Schlink, *Theology of the Lutheran Confessions*, p. 29.

25. Elert, *The Structure of Lutheranism*, p. 208 [translation altered: Werner Elert, *Morphologie des Luthertums* (Munich: Beck'sche Verlag, 1952), vol. 1, pp. 183-84].

tian faith that the Logos incarnate in Jesus is "of one being with the Father" or that Jesus is, without compromise, fully human not an "accomplished fact"? Are all decisions of the church reversible?

The decisive question here is whether in fact the authority of creeds and confessions is to be understood simply and only as the authority of their contents, the authority of the gospel to which they witness. Are there subordinate and derivative forms of authority that need to be given greater emphasis, e.g., the authority of Schlink's "consensus of the fathers and brethren" (in effect, the authority of reception)? The authority of the Nicene Creed may ultimately be a function of the gospel it summarizes and to which it witnesses. But does its broad and enduring reception by the church also give it a sort of subordinate, formal authority? Luther taught that every Christian is anointed by the Spirit, so that the body of believers is empowered by the Spirit to judge the teaching of the gospel. If the great mass of teachers and hearers in the church, anointed by the Spirit, have for centuries heard the gospel in the Creed, can the church have a confidence, a confidence approaching moral certainty, that the church of the past did not go wrong in the decisions embodied in this Creed and that the Creed is a permanent contribution to the resources of the church?[26] If the church cannot have such confidence, then can it believe that Christ has in fact sent the Spirit who will lead the church into all truth?

On Reformation grounds, the diachronic and synchronic consensus of the church can be understood as an *authoritative sign* of the material authority the church has encountered and which it believes it will encounter again in the Creed and in the gospel preached in accord with this Creed. The task of theology in service of the gospel of freedom is to move from a reliance on the authority of the sign (accept the Nicene Creed because of the testimony of the church) to the authority of the signified, the authority of the gospel itself (accept the Nicene Creed because it expresses the inner logic of the faith). But the authority of the creed, on this account, is not merely hypothetical until the authority of the gospel within that of the Creed is demonstrated. As the reception of a teaching or decision approaches universality, so the confidence of the church that here the gospel is rightly interpreted and at

---

26. The USA Lutheran-Catholic dialogue agreed that "in the Church universal the harmony between the teaching of the Ministers and its acceptance by the faithful constitutes a sign of the fidelity of that teaching to the gospel." Paul C. Empie, T. Austin Murphy, and Joseph A. Burgess, eds., *Teaching Authority and Infallibility in the Church*, Lutherans and Catholics in Dialogue VI (Minneapolis: Augsburg, 1978), p. 31.

the very least approaches (and perhaps reaches) certainty. Such an understanding would seem to accord with actual Lutheran practice, in which the creeds are not treated hypothetically.

Lindbeck's Rule Theology of Doctrine
and the Development of Doctrine

These last reflections open the door to a brief consideration of the most extensive recent discussion of the development of doctrine by a Lutheran, in George Lindbeck's *The Nature of Doctrine* (1984). Lindbeck presents a theory of doctrines as rules governing the speech and action of a community, rather than as themselves propositions making truth-claims or as expressions of religious experience (although the sentences that state doctrines may also function as truth-claims and as expressions of religious experience). For this theory, "doctrinal definitions are thought of as comparable to grammatical decisions about the correctness or incorrectness of particular usages."[27]

In laying out his theory, he seeks to distinguish different sorts of doctrines. Some are permanent, present from the community's origins and inseparable from the community's identity. Some are conditional upon certain historical developments. Some such conditional doctrines may be irreversible. His example of such a conditional but irreversible doctrine is the Christian rejection of slavery:

> Christians at first shared the consensus of classical cultures that slavery was an inescapable institution (although they differed from many others in thinking of it as unnatural, a result of sin). Once historical developments taught them, however, that societies without institutionalized chattel slavery are possible, they came to think, despite the absence of scriptural commands, that the logic of the biblical story demands not only humane treatment of slaves but struggle against the institution itself. Assuming that history is sufficiently cumulative so that awareness of the possibility of slaveless societies will not disappear, the Christian obligation to oppose slavery is irreversible even though conditional.[28]

When the church makes an irreversible doctrinal decision, however, can it err? Is the church in any sense infallible in making such decisions? A

27. Lindbeck, *Nature of Doctrine*, p. 98.
28. Lindbeck, *Nature of Doctrine*, pp. 85-86.

decision can be irreversible only if the church can be confident that error of at least a certain sort is excluded from such decisions. Lindbeck defines the appropriate sense of infallibility as rather minimal: "To affirm infallibility is simply to claim that the church and/or its magisterium does not mortally violate the grammar of the faith in its solemn decisions on particular issues that are essential to the church's identity or welfare."[29]

Who, if anyone, in the church might make decisions with some such infallibility? In answering this question, he applies the analogy between doctrine and grammar. Could the consensus of competent speakers of a language be wrong about its grammatical constructions? If all competent speakers of German put the verbs at the end of subordinate clauses, could they be wrong? Analogously, could the *consensus fidelium* be wrong about an essential matter of the faith of the church?

> The reliability of their [the faithful's] agreement in doctrinal matters may not improperly be called infallible. This suggestion is intended as an empirical description, not as an affirmation of faith. Think, for a moment, of what it would mean outside the Christian sphere. . . . A virtually unanimous and enduring agreement among flexible yet deeply pious mainstream Muslims throughout the world on some at one time disputed point of Koranic doctrine would constitute empirically indisputable evidence from a detached, non-Muslim scholarly point of view that the doctrine is not in contradiction to the inner logic of Islam.[30]

That the *consensus fidelium* has rightly grasped the truth is an assertion of faith; that such a consensus has rightly grasped the sense of the Christian faith, at least to the extent that it does not mortally violate its grammar, Lindbeck takes to be almost analytic.

Lindbeck intends his analysis to be non-confessional, both in the sense that it does not derive from any particular confessional perspective and in the sense that it is compatible with at least a wide range of such perspectives. Nevertheless, he does note that such an emphasis on the *consensus fidelium* as a subject of infallibility is reminiscent of Orthodox teaching.[31] I would add that it also parallels at least certain emphases of Lutheran theology, viz., that the community as a whole is anointed by the Spirit to judge doctrine

29. Lindbeck, *Nature of Doctrine*, p. 98.
30. Lindbeck, *Nature of Doctrine*, pp. 100-101.
31. Lindbeck, *Nature of Doctrine*, p. 102.

and that the church as a whole will never fundamentally err in its teaching. Lindbeck's position is thus open to the suggestions made in the last paragraph of the previous section — that the consensus of the church constitutes an authoritative sign that the gospel has been rightly interpreted and is thus authoritative for the later tradition of interpretation.

Conclusion

In summary: Recent Lutheran theology has not given great attention to the question of the development of doctrine, even though typical Lutheran statements about the normativity of the Reformation understanding of justification would seem to demand such attention. The way recent Lutheran theology has understood confession and the authority of confession has tended to militate against an understanding of the development of doctrine by emphasizing the exclusive authority of the gospel within the confession in a way that forces an emphasis on a distinction between evangelical content and historical form. There are resources within Lutheran theology, however, for a more robust understanding of the formal authority of the doctrinal decisions of the church, although that formal authority will be grounded on the *consensus fidelium* as authoritative sign of the material authority of the gospel. Such an understanding parallels that developed by George Lindbeck's rule theory of doctrine.

Vatican I and a Lutheran Perspective on the Development of Doctrine

How might Vatican I and in particular its claims of papal primacy and infallibility appear to such a Lutheran perspective on the development of doctrine? I will focus narrowly on this question and not on a more general Lutheran appraisal of Vatican I, which I presume will be given in other presentations.[32]

32. On the specific issue of infallibility from a Lutheran perspective, I find particularly helpful, besides the two relevant rounds of the USA Lutheran-Catholic dialogue, Harding Meyer, "'Suprema auctoritas ideo ab omne errore immunis': The Lutheran Approach to Primacy," in James F. Puglisi, ed., *Petrine Ministry and the Unity of the Church: "Toward a Patient and Fraternal Dialogue"* (Collegeville, MN: Liturgical Press, 1999), pp.

The Importance of Reception

Most immediately, the sort of Lutheran perspective on doctrinal development outlined above emphasizes the significance of reception as an authoritative sign of the material authority of the gospel in various doctrinal developments. In this respect, the argument given so far parallels portions of the argument in the most significant ecumenical discussion of authority and infallibility to date, that of the Anglican–Roman Catholic International Commission, both in the two statements on authority in its *Final Report* of 1981 and in its more recent *The Gift of Authority.* These statements have not, of course, encountered unqualified affirmation from either Anglican or Roman Catholic officialdom. The rather cool Vatican response to the *Final Report*'s discussions of authority,[33] however, should not block Lutheran-Catholic discussions from taking up the ARCIC analysis. Fr. William Henn of the Angelicum, in an insightful analysis of *The Gift of Authority,* argues for the compatibility of ARCIC's discussion of the significance of reception even with Vatican I.[34]

Like the ARCIC reports, the proposal made above is that reception constitutes not a juridical condition of authoritative teaching, but an authoritative sign that the material authority of the gospel is expressed in some teaching. Oddly enough, the Lutheran resistance to an overestimation of the importance of any formal authority means that Lutherans ought to concede that, when the bishop of Rome truly teaches in accord with the gospel, his teaching is authoritative *ex sese, non autem ex consensu ecclesiae.* If *all* authority is finally the authority of the gospel and is not subject to formal, juridical conditions, then *a fortiori* the same must hold for the teachings of the bishop of Rome, when he teaches in accord with the gospel. This observation may seem more problematic than helpful, since it would seem to undercut the formal authority of papal teachings. It might indicate, however, that the worry over subjecting authoritative teaching to juridical conditions expresses what should also be a concern for Lutherans.

15-34; and George A. Lindbeck, "Infallibility (1972 Père Marquette Lecture)," in James J. Buckley, ed., *The Church in a Postliberal Age* (Grand Rapids: Eerdmans, 2002), pp. 120-42.

33. This response can be found in Christopher Hill and E. J. Yarnold, eds., *Anglicans and Roman Catholics: The Search for Unity* (London: SPCK, 1994), pp. 156-66.

34. William Henn, "A Commentary on *The Gift of Authority* of the Anglican–Roman Catholic International Commission" (1999), http://www.anglicancommunion .org/documents/authority/commhennenglish.html.

The Reception of Papal Primacy and Infallibility in the
Development of Doctrine

For the remainder of this presentation, however, I wish to focus on the question of the conditions under which Lutherans might be able to see Vatican I as a legitimate development of doctrine. Is such a Lutheran perception of Vatican I possible?

To answer that question, one must ask, not just about how a Lutheran might view the development of doctrine in the abstract, but about how a Lutheran might view the development of the particular doctrine of the papacy and papal authority. Not all developments are legitimate: How is this particular development to be understood?

As noted, Lutherans (and some contemporary Catholics)[35] have rejected organic analogies for the development of doctrine. But if the history of some doctrine is to be the history of a development and not just a chronicle of how some issue was discussed at different historical moments, then that history must constitute some sort of unified narrative, even if a narrative with many twists, turns, and apparent dead-ends. One of the strongest unifying elements of most narratives is a plot, a tension-resolution scheme in which, over time and through a coherent series of events, some tension or problem reaches release or solution.[36] A murder is committed; the murderer is apprehended by the clever detective; the Rhinegold is stolen and, hours of Wagnerian music later, the Rhinegold returns to its resting place. Historical narratives rarely have the focused plot of fictional narratives, but they are often organized in plotlike ways. Some problem confronts the church — how to understand the relation between divinity and humanity in Jesus; how to organize decision-making in the church — and the historical narrative recounts a variety of attempts to deal with this problem, until closure is reached when some relatively stable solution is achieved.

Histories of the papacy often do exhibit plotlike structures. For example, Hermann Pottmeyer's recent *Towards a Papacy in Communion* outlines a shift from a first-millennium paradigm of the church as witness to a second-millennium paradigm of the church as decision-maker and legislator, a shift

---

35. For example, Jean Tillard, "Dogmatic Development and Koinonia," in Bradley Nassif, ed., *New Perspectives on Historical Theology: Essays in Memory of John Meyendorff* (Grand Rapids: Eerdmans, 1996), pp. 172-85.

36. On narrative and plot within theology, see Michael Root, "The Narrative Structure of Soteriology," *Modern Theology* 2 (1986): 145-58.

brought about by a change in the church's situation and self-understanding.[37] In addition, Vatican I itself is placed in the context of the specific tensions of the eighteenth- and nineteenth-century Catholic Church. Vatican I is thus fitted both into a large, millennium-spanning development and into a narrower, centuries-spanning development.

A Lutheran understanding of the development of the post-Reformation doctrine of the papacy that might at least possibly see it as a legitimate development would, I think, need to be different in one significant aspect from such accounts as that of Pottmeyer or of Klaus Schatz in his *Papal Primacy: From Its Origins to the Present*. For neither of the accounts from these Catholic scholars is the Reformation a particularly significant event. More important, for both, Lutherans and other non-Catholics simply depart from the stage once they are no longer in communion with Rome. For Schatz and Pottmeyer, the post-Reformation development considered is a Catholic development. I would think that there is little hope that Lutherans might come to see the post-Reformation development of the papacy, culminating in Vatican I, as in some sense a valid development unless the specific development of Lutheranism is also seen as part of the narrative. The specific experience of the Lutheran churches cannot be simply ignored. The question is, how might we see the post-Reformation history of the papacy and the history of Lutheranism together in a single narrative?

How one sees the emergence and resolution of problems shapes how one periodizes history or, at the very least, where one makes chapter breaks in books about that history. Klaus Schatz is typical, I think, in the way he divides the four sections of his history of papal primacy: early patristic; late patristic in East and West; the medieval West (ending with the settlement of the conciliar controversy in the late fifteenth century); and the modern era (beginning with the Reformation). Like much church historiography, he closes off one section of the story just before the Reformation begins and then starts a new episode with the early sixteenth century.

But can this organization adequately encompass the development of the doctrine of the papacy as part of a single narrative encompassing Lutheran and Catholic histories (and, potentially, the history of others)? Is the standard periodization of church history and of the history of this topic an artifact of confessionalization, an expression of the defensive self-understanding of entrenched divisions, a periodization that serves division?

---

37. Hermann J. Pottmeyer, *Towards a Papacy in Communion: Perspectives from Vatican Councils I and II* (New York: Crossroad, 1998).

Does it make more sense to see the Reformation as the final playing out of the problems that dominated the late Middle Ages, reaching a kind of stability only with the end of the wars of religion on the Continent and in England around the middle of the seventeenth century? Steven Ozment, for example, deals with the period 1250-1550 as a unit, with problems set by the thirteenth century only finally being settled (though in different ways) in the Catholic-Protestant divisions of the Reformation.[38]

The question of periodization is not trivial, for it shapes how one understands the problems and solutions being worked out in any alleged development. If we are going to see together the post-sixteenth-century histories of Catholics and Lutherans in relation to the papacy, then what plot structure, what scheme of tension and (potential or still outstanding) resolution will hold the narrative together? Let me make a suggestion, though it can here be nothing other than a suggestion.

The late medieval church was disturbed by an intermittent series of crises that together go by the name of the conciliar controversy. The issues centered on the interrelation of the pope and bishops gathered in council for the governance of the church. The standard picture is that, after a period of apparent victory for the conciliarists, the papal party finally triumphed. But did it? Schatz notes that the concessions made by the papacy to various princes and kings in the course of the controversy were such that "the true winner was the established religion of the emerging modern princely states."[39] The later importance of Gallicanism is the most important consequence of this victory of the state.

But I would press the issue further. Were the issues of authority and governance, of papacy and episcopacy, that were at the center of late medieval debates and struggles ever really settled? Can the rejection of conciliarism in the second half of the fifteenth century be seen as definitive if the settlement that resulted so radically failed its first major test, viz., the Reformation? The structures of governance and authority that emerged successfully from the conciliar struggles were not able to settle the controversy over justification and not able to hold together the Western church. The Ref-

---

38. "Rather than being a perfect norm form of which later medieval thought strayed, the scholastic synthesis of reason and revelation in the thirteenth century was a chief source of both the intellectual and ecclesiological conflicts of the later Middle Ages." Steven Ozment, *The Age of Reform 1250-1550: An Intellectual and Religious History of Late Medieval and Reformation Europe* (New Haven: Yale University Press, 1980), p. 20.

39. Klaus Schatz, *Papal Primacy: From Its Origins to the Present* (Collegeville, MN: Liturgical Press, 1996), p. 110.

ormation can be seen as history's revenge for the unsettled issues of the fifteenth century.

For such a view, the development of the doctrine of the church's jurisdictional and doctrinal authority is radically open-ended. A difficult set of issues was raised for the Western church in the Middle Ages, issues foreshadowed in the relations between East and West in the late patristic and early medieval periods. After an extended period of struggle, a fragile settlement was achieved in the mid-fifteenth century. This settlement proved inadequate; a new, significantly different, far more theologically charged period of argument followed. After a century and a half of theological and armed struggle, a theological, church-political, and political stalemate ensued. We still live with that stalemate. No answer to the underlying conceptual and ecclesiological questions was accepted by a consensus of the Western church, if that church is understood to encompass at least Catholics, Lutherans, Anglicans, and Reformed. Lutherans and Catholics together inhabit a narrative that has not yet reached a close.

I would emphasize two aspects of such a possible Lutheran perspective. On the one hand, I see no reason why Lutherans should not acknowledge that the development of a doctrine of the papacy as realized in the texts of Vatican I and II is the development accepted by the large majority of the Western church. There will be no consensus on the issues of doctrinal and jurisdictional authority in the church without some form of affirmation of that Catholic development, including Vatican I. It thus behooves Lutherans to press such concerns as the possibly non-juridical but still decisive role of reception in the recognition of authoritative teaching, concerns that might open the way to a true *consensus fidelium* on authority that will include the Catholic development in a way that Lutherans might affirm.

On the other hand, such a perspective contextualizes the Catholic development, and particularly Vatican I, in new ways. The Catholic development, however central for the Western church, is historically accompanied by alternative solutions to the authority problem in the Lutheran, Anglican, and Reformed traditions. The Lutheran insistence on the primacy of the material authority of the gospel, and on the role of the reception by the faithful in judging the adequacy of the exercise of teaching authority, are contributions to the total development that, from this perspective, can be ignored no more than Vatican I. The minority Lutheran (and Anglican and Reformed) dissenting voice within the whole of the Western church will need to be taken into account in any truly comprehensive *consensus fidelium*.

The crucial question then becomes how this development goes forward. Narratives are read *towards* their end, but understood *from* their end. Vatican I had already been placed in a new interpretive context by Vatican II. How an inclusive consensus on doctrinal and jurisdictional authority might recontextualize and thus reinterpret Vatican I is simply impossible for us now to say. History, thank God, is open to the new. The task of ecumenical theology is to work toward those possibilities that now appear before us, in the trust that the Spirit will open new possibilities in his own time.

Conclusion

Is there a Lutheran perspective on the development of doctrine that is open to the appearance of irreversible insights into the meaning of the one gospel? I believe that there is. Can such a perspective understand the development of the doctrine of the church's jurisdictional and doctrinal authority in a way that might include the teachings of the First Vatican Council? I believe that such a question remains open. Only time will tell.

The perspective offered here is, I hope, Lutheran in at least the minimal sense of being compatible with the fundamental insights that have constituted and driven the Lutheran tradition. The perspective does ask Lutherans and Catholics to view their own traditions as, to varying degrees, moments within a larger tradition of the Western church. Lutherans and Catholics may have differing degrees of difficulty in accepting such a perspective. But have the ecumenical difficulties of the second half of the twentieth century not shown that something of this sort is needed if we are to break out of our confessionally defined and mutually exclusive identities? I believe so.

SYSTEMATICS

What Ecclesiology for the Petrine Ministry?

Joseph A. Komonchak

In popular Catholic consciousness, at least in the United States, the church is thought of as an institutional apparatus: "a bunch of old Cardinals in Rome making decisions for the rest of us," as one of my undergraduate students recently put it when asked what came to mind when he heard the words "the Catholic Church." Despite the best efforts of Vatican II, as well as of the theologians who inspired it and interpreted it, to recover the notion of the church as the *congregatio fidelium,* "Church" usually is taken to mean the "institutional church," that is, the hierarchy, a term that includes bishops, of course, but since these are seen mainly as appointees, executive agents of the pope, the term usually refers to Rome and to the Roman Curia. It is not much of an exaggeration to say that the Roman Catholic Church is regarded as a vast multinational religious corporation with central headquarters in Rome, branch offices in large cities, and retail shops, called parishes, dispensing spiritual goods. On this view, the pope is seen as the CEO of the firm. This view, I say, is rather widespread, and it can be found, almost taken for granted, among both progressives and liberals, among the laity, and among the clergy, including among some bishops.

There are reasons for this popular conception, of course, mistaken or inadequate as it may be. One of them is the teaching of the First Vatican Council, which defined the supreme jurisdictional authority of the pope and the infallibility of certain exercises of his teaching role. The pope's authority was said to be episcopal, immediate, and ordinary, and learned studies of the *Acta* of that Council have not been enough to dissuade people from understanding those terms to mean that the pope may act as if he is the chief (even sole) bishop of the whole church, that he may bypass the authority of a local bishop, and that he may do this as a matter of course. (And, it is also true that at every point the spokesman for the theological commission at the Council refused to allow any restrictions upon the pope's authority — even ones he acknowledged to exist — to be introduced into the decree.)

A few years after the close of that Council, William Gladstone complained that its decrees meant that the whole realm of duty — that is, as he said, everything except some "dregs or tatters of human life" — had now been handed over to the "supreme direction" of the pope. Responding to this charge, John Henry Newman wrote: "Supreme direction, true; but 'supreme' is not 'minute,' nor does 'direction' mean supervision or 'management.'"[1] Writing soon after Vatican I, Newman could not have known of the great growth of central Roman authority in the century afterwards: what Yves Congar called "the incredible inflation" of the papal teaching office; the replacement of a traditional corpus of ecclesiastical law by a highly rationalized and all-encompassing code of canon law promulgated by the sole authority of the pope; the papal monopolizing of the selection of bishops; the expansion of the Roman bureaucracy; etc. Even the Second Vatican Council has not been able to slow this process; indeed a series of Roman interventions in the last two decades has led more than one person to remark that the "supreme direction" has in fact become minute and that it is being taken to mean not only supervision but management, even micromanagement.

Now there are people who would be quite content to allow this primarily administrative view of the church to continue to prevail and to make do as best they can within it. It does have the advantage, after all, of being clear — you know where you stand — and of being reasonably efficient, at least by organizational standards. But we are gathering for a discussion about the papal role that will include people for whom this structure and style of "supreme direction" are not at all acceptable. The ecumenical problem was illustrated by the remarks made by a great scholar of early Christianity and a committed ecumenist:

> Among the ecclesial bodies that have come to be separated from Rome, the small print of Roman primacy is a deep ravine to those who would dearly like to see the barriers to catholic communion dismantled but [who] then meet the doctrine that normal communion with Rome is

---

1. See Alvin S. Ryan, ed., *Newman and Gladstone: The Vatican Decrees* (Notre Dame: University of Notre Dame Press, 1962), p. 113.

possible on condition of submission to the centralized administration of the Curia. The focus of universal communion is available to those also willing to accept ordinary universal jurisdiction and the imposition of a large measure of uniformity. Or is it possible to be united without also being absorbed? Could communion be restored between Rome and Canterbury without Rome demanding the right to nominate to the see of Durham?[2]

The three issues here mentioned as obstacles — centralization of administration in the Roman Curia; uniformity; ordinary jurisdiction, illustrated by the right to nominate bishops — would all be worth consideration in their own right. But I would like to explore some of the ecclesiological presuppositions that continue to be at work and used to justify the type of ecclesiastical governance that is of concern to the likes of Henry Chadwick.

At the heart of the question of the Petrine ministry in the church lies the question of the relation between the whole church and individual churches. I assume the methodological and substantive point that a theology of ministry must derive from an ecclesiology, rather than deriving an ecclesiology from a theology of ministry — *ministeria propter ecclesiam, non ecclesia propter ministeria.*

The First Vatican Council conducted its work within a universalistic ecclesiology, that is, having chiefly in mind the church as a whole, spread throughout the world and paying little attention to the individual churches. While the Second Vatican Council began its deliberation within the same perspective, by the time it had ended, it had laid important bases for a revalidation of the individual churches. The period since the Council, of course, has seen a great expansion of interest in the local church and a large discussion, not uncontroversial, about the relation between the *Ecclesia universa/universalis* and the *Ecclesiae locales/particulares.*

The terms of this latter discussion were posed by two statements made in *Lumen gentium* 23. On the one hand, the Council said that particular churches, by which here were meant dioceses, are formed *ad imaginem Ecclesiae universalis,* but that, on the other hand, it is in and out of these same particular churches that the one and single Catholic Church exists *(in quibus et ex quibus una et unica Ecclesia catholica existit).* The first of these statements implies a priority of the universal church over the particular churches

---

2. Henry Chadwick, review of Jean M. R. Tillard's *The Bishop of Rome* in the *Times Literary Supplement,* 23 December 1983, pp. 1421-22.

since it provides the "image" in which they must be formed. The second statement implies, however, a priority of the particular churches since it is not only "in" them but "out of them" *(ex quibus)* that the one church exists. While a few theologians have opted for the priority of one element over the other, most ecclesiologists have regarded the question of priority as misplaced, wrongly posed, on the grounds that in principle the church is catholic and can only exist locally and that historically the church born at Pentecost was both local (Jerusalem) and universal (speaking all tongues).

To this consensus, however, the Congregation for the Doctrine of the Faith has been a notable exception. For over two decades it has been putting forth the notion of an ontological and historical priority of the universal church over the particular church. Ontologically, the CDF said, the universal church pre-existed creation and has given birth to the particular churches as to daughters. Historically, the church in Jerusalem already speaking all languages is said to be the universal church, which in time gives birth to individual local churches. The prefect of the CDF, Joseph Cardinal Ratzinger (now Pope Benedict XVI), defended and attempted to clarify these two assertions. On his view, the ontological priority, pre-existence, of the universal church is that of the divine idea of the one Church; he has recently wondered if it would be better to speak of a *teleological* priority. Ratzinger has also clarified the interpretation of the church on Pentecost: this was not a local church in the sense that we speak of individual local churches today. Rather, this universal church composed of the future founders of particular churches first gave birth to the individual local church of Jerusalem, from which all the other local churches have since been born.

In the course of the debate over the last two decades, an argument has been adduced that indicates the relevance of this discussion to the question of the Petrine ministry. In 1988 an *Instrumentum laboris* on the theological and juridical nature of episcopal conferences was sent out for comment to the world's bishops. At one point, the text raises the issue we have been addressing: Even if it is true that the universal church exists in and through the particular churches, inasmuch as it has no reality of its own apart from its realization in them (and it is realized in each of them), it is no less true that the particular churches are in the image of the universal church and not vice-versa (see LG 23a), so that in each of them "the one, holy, catholic, and apostolic church of Christ is truly present and active" (CD 11a). Right from its modest beginnings, the church is first of all a single and universal-catholic reality, the single *"communio,"* People of God, and Body of Christ. The Petrine primacy it-self, understood as *"plenitudo potestatis,"* has no meaning and theologi-cal coherence except within the primacy of the one and universal church over the particular and local churches.[3]

In 2000 Cardinal Ratzinger in the same context said something similar: "As for the ministry and responsibility of Peter, it would not even be able to exist had the universal church not existed first. In fact, he would have been mov-ing in a void and representing an absurd claim." (I overlook the considerable anachronism in the last sentence.)

The two statements come close to implying that if the priority of the universal church were denied, the pope would have nothing to do. They also illustrate the ease with which the universal church may simply be identified with "what the pope presides over." This is to reverse the method I chose at the beginning and to derive an ecclesiology from one's understanding of the ministry. It is only a short step from there, of course, to the identification of the universal church with the Roman Curia, as illustrated recently when a draft paper at the U.S. Bishops' Conference referred to a text issued by a Ro-man dicastery as being "a document of the universal Church."

In these and related arguments for the priority of the universal church, one also senses a tendency to make the universal church, so understood, to be the primary mediator of salvation, all of whose blessings and powers are simply received from it by the particular churches. All the initiative appears to lie with the universal church. Consider, for example, how Cardinal Ratzinger deals with three basic sacraments. Baptism, he says, is a totally theological event, "much more than a socialization tied to the local Church." It does not derive from the individual community; "it is the presence of the only Church, and it can spring up only from it, from the Jerusalem on high, from our mother." Becoming members of this one body should not "be mis-taken for belonging to a local Church. . . . In baptism the universal Church continually precedes the local Church and constitutes it" (pp. 75-76). "Simi-larly, the Eucharist is for every local church the place of insertion into the one Christ, the gathering into one of the universal *communio*. . . . The Eu-charist does not arise out of the local church and it does not end in her. It continuously shows that Christ comes to us from outside, through our closed doors; it comes to us continuously from outside, from the total, unique body of Christ and leads us into it."

3. *Origins* 17 (1987-88): 735.

What Ratzinger calls "this *extra nos* of the sacrament" he applies also to the ministry. That only the ordained may lead the Eucharist is a sign "that the community cannot give itself the Eucharist; it must receive it from the Lord through the mediation of the one Church." The bishop, moreover, belongs first of all to the universal body of bishops, and "in this sense, the episcopal ministry derives from the one Church and leads into it. Precisely it here becomes evident that there is no opposition between the local church and the universal church. The bishop represents the one Church in the local church, and builds up the one Church while he builds up the local church and awakens her particular gifts for the benefit of the whole body."

If all this shows that "there is no opposition between the local church and the universal Church," is it not because the individual church has nearly disappeared from theological view? The three sacraments, it appears, simply take place *in* the local church; they do not take place *by* or *through* the local church; they do not appear to be actions of the local church. Elsewhere Ratzinger denies that baptism integrates into the universal church through the mediation of the local church; the integration is immediate. Here Eucharist is not only said not to end with the local church, but even not to arise within it. The bishop appears simply as a representative of the one universal church; nothing is said of his representing his particular church.

In this text, and in certain recent official texts, the view of the episcopate comes very close to the much-criticized position of Karl Rahner, who saw the episcopate as the supreme board of directors of the church. On this view, a bishop's presiding over a local church has no more significance than presiding over a Catholic university or being the head of a religious order (Rahner in fact suggested that such figures should be bishops). It is not surprising, then, to see episcopal orders being conferred in ever-increasing numbers on bureaucratic agents (a practice criticized by Cardinal Frings at Vatican II), and this fact then being considered an important element in deriving a theology of the episcopate!

All of this makes the universal church oddly distant from the particular church: it is "something else," that from which the particular church must receive all that constitutes its life as a church; it is "mother" to daughters. Perhaps the use of this latter metaphor to describe the relation between the universal church and the particular churches (is this not an ecclesiological novelty?) is helpful in understanding what has gone wrong in this ecclesiology. Yves Congar once noted a certain development with regard to the concept of the church as Mother. The Fathers of the church could say at once that the church was the mother of individual Christians but that individual Christians together were the church as mother.

> To the Fathers the Church was the "We of Christianity." Jerome writes: "The Church of Christ is nothing else but the souls of those who believe in Christ." The juridical ecclesiology of recent times has practically forgotten the viewpoint which considers the Church as formed by the faithful; this it has forgotten in favour of that other aspect which sees the faithful as formed by the Church. The Church is considered as the suprapersonal reality which mediates the salvation of Christ to men. These men are nothing more than her "products"; she is set up over them as a storehouse. Of the two dialectically opposed viewpoints from which the Fathers contemplated the motherhood of the Church, one has been excluded, namely that according to which the faithful are seen as the Church procreating. When the Church is no longer considered as formed by the faithful, but is seen chiefly as a mediating institution, then the mission and motherhood of the Church find their locus in external legal acts, instead of being drawn from her Christian existence of love and prayer by which her members live.[4]

Has not something similar happened on this understanding of the priority of the universal church? The universal church takes precedence at every point; it forms the local church to its image; no attention is given to the fact that it is formed by the local churches. The relationship has ceased to be dialectical. As in Congar's description, suprapersonal motherhood of the church neglected the subjective acts of believers, so today the dimension of the one Church as constituted by the subjectivity of the many churches is being neglected to the degree that the only thing being stressed is their being *ad imaginem Ecclesiae universalis*. The local churches have no substantive subjective reality. That the universal church does not do anything except in and as the local churches is lost from view.

There are, however, other ways of looking at the matter. In his unfortu-

---

4. Yves Congar, "Mother Church," in Joseph Ratzinger et al., *The Church Today* (Cork: Mercier Press, 1967), p. 38. The two viewpoints are the one that sees individual Christians as children of Mother Church and the one that sees all Christians together as Mother Church. See Augustine: *"[Ecclesia] quae sibi est et mater et filii: nam simul omnes, quibus constat Ecclesia, mater dicitur; singuli autem iidem ipsi filii appellantur"*; *Quaestionum Evangeliorum*, I, 18:1; PL 35, 1327.(Bouyer p. 334; ET p. 276).

nately neglected book *The Church of God,* Louis Bouyer has a few pages in which he stresses the inescapably *local* character of the church. "Unless one wishes to indulge in the most aberrant Gnostic speculations and make the Church a pre-existing 'aeon'," Bouyer claims, then one must admit that the church "does not exist, has never existed, and cannot exist except in this 'flesh' of ours. Before existing there, it did not exist, properly speaking, except as a project in the divine thought: his unrealized plan, his Wisdom unexpressed."[5] Catholics can agree with congregationalists, therefore, that the church has no "existence apart from concrete 'congregations' where believers assemble to hear the Word, to pray, to celebrate the Lord's Supper, and thus to commit themselves to a life, indissolubly communal and personal, of faith and of love." With Afanasieff they can acknowledge "that the Church does not exist from the outset as a global organization of worship, evangelization, and Christian charity, but, first of all, in the gathering, necessarily local, of communities of believers who have come together to celebrate the eucharist."

Bouyer hastens to add that all the aberrations that can arise from such considerations should not make us forget

> that the Church does not exist from the outset as a sort of enormous apparatus of global reach, a *"Gesellschaft"* destined to establish branch offices everywhere, which for this purpose would deploy a centripetal network for systematic evangelization, so as little by little to set up a chain of cultic or charity "stations." On the contrary, it proceeds from essentially local communities and, truly speaking, has never had actual existence except in them: in *"Gemeinschaften"* where concrete people concretely live a common life of shared faith, of unanimous prayer, of communion in praise and charity. Everything else in the church is only in the service of these communities and has no real spiritual existence except in their actual life.

And Bouyer adds a note that relates to the theme of our conference:

> To say this is not at all to ignore that the Church was established by Christ in the first place on the foundations of the Apostles, etc. It is sim-

5. Louis Bouyer, *L'Église de Dieu: corps du Christ et temple de l'ésprit* (Paris: Cerf, 1970), p. 334; ET: *The Church of God: Body of Christ and Temple of the Spirit* (Chicago: Franciscan Herald Press, 1982), p. 276.

ply to observe that St. Peter did not found the Church by rushing right away to Rome, as to the center of the ancient world, in order to establish there a network of committees which might then methodically implant their subsidiaries throughout the universe. He founded the Church, on Pentecost, by announcing the risen Christ to those around him, by himself baptizing or having his apostolic collaborators baptize "those who came to believe," by having them share in the first celebrations of the eucharistic banquet, and by thus involving them in a common life of thanksgiving and of charity. The Church of all times and all places was founded, then, in a first local church, the church of Jerusalem, and it has been propagated from then on in other local churches, similar to it, as if by cutting and planting. (Bouyer, pp. 336-37; ET pp. 278-79)

Bouyer's suggestion that Catholic ecclesiology could use a good dose of congregationalism is attractive because it draws attention to actual concrete men and women and to their assemblies in specific times and places. These are the persons and the communities *quibus constat Ecclesia,* to use Augustine's phrase quoted above. If one is interested in the "ontology" of the church, this requires study of the subjectivity by which a person becomes a Christian through faith, hope, and love and of the intersubjectivity by which they are brought together as assemblies. There is no suprapersonal entity above and apart from these believers and their assemblies. The *Ecclesia universa* is the communion of all such believers and their assemblies, and this communion is an event within a shared consciousness, the communion that results from or, rather, consists in, the common faith, hope, and love that God's word and grace enable and effect.

Perhaps the issue can be illustrated by a simple reflection. When Pope John Paul II called the whole church to prepare spiritually for the bi-millennium of the birth of Christ, what did it mean for the church to undertake that task? The task was undertaken if and to the degree that dioceses undertook it, and dioceses undertook the task if and to the degree that parishes undertook it, and a judgment as to whether the Catholic Church spiritually prepared for the bi-millennium cannot be made simply on the basis of what the pope did in Rome but has to include also and above all what the churches did or did not do. The church prepared for the bi-millennium to the degree that the churches did.

In similar fashion, it is fatal to counterpose what the so-called universal church does and what the local church does. The so-called universal church is not an agent of activities apart from the local churches. Baptism is not an event of the "universal church" except as an event of the local church, and to be initiated into the local church is to be initiated into the one and universal church. The Eucharist does not exist except as celebrated in quite specific communities of believers, and in this sense the Eucharist is an event of the local church, an event that includes, as a constitutive element, communion with all other eucharistic assemblies, since Christ is not divided. But the axiom that "the Church makes the Eucharist and the Eucharist makes the Church" is true of the one Church only because it is true in the many churches. The one Church does not celebrate the Eucharist except as the many churches.

The exception would appear to be the case of the apostolic ministry, an exception that brings us back to the theme of this conference. The ordained ministry appears to be an exception because of the present practice in the selection of bishops in the Western church, in which the local church (the diocese) has next to no part. As often as not, at least in the United States, a new bishop is dropped in from outside with neither the local clergy nor the people having had a say in the matter. This may help explain why the bishop is said first of all to represent the one and universal church, but this is only because the local church is not at all represented in his selection. How great a deviation this is from original practice is well known. Where once the adage reigned, *"Nullus invitis detur episcopus,"* the only place where anything similar is reflected today is when what the old Code called the *"odium plebis"* and the new Code the *"aversio in parochum"* can be invoked by a bishop in order to remove a pastor. While no such provision is written in the Code, it appears that this criterion has rightly been employed recently for the resignation and removal of bishops, which raises the question: If the people may have a voice in removing a pastor or bishop, why may they not have a voice in selecting one? Or has something changed in the nature of the church, that what was once commanded by popes is now considered to be the dangerous desire to introduce democracy into the church?

The lack of respect for the integrity and self-responsibility of the local church illustrated in the current practice for the selection of bishops may be taken as emblematic of the principal theological difficulty in the way of an ecumenically acceptable form for exercising the Petrine ministry. This is the failure to give proper weight and substance to the local churches. A theory and a practice that cannot acknowledge the local churches as full subjects in their own right cannot be correct. The arguments pro and con on the question of how bishops should be selected will illustrate what in theory and practice stands in the way of ecumenical agreement on a Petrine ministry.

Papal Ministry in a Communication Ecclesiology: A Search for Some Possible Themes

Sven-Erik Brodd

In the universe of the World Wide Web and mass media, the image of the pope and his office is not only mirrored, but also to a certain extent created by the media. This poses a dilemma, not only for the Roman Catholic Church but also for other traditions that hold a sort of doctrinal understanding, negatively or positively, on papacy or the Petrine ministry. In public opinion, Christian or not, the form and content of the Petrine office becomes increasingly perceived and defined beyond the control of the magisterium or the official teaching of ecclesial traditions.

This perception of the pope and his office, probably in that order, emerges in a dialectic between what the church may possibly influence and what it cannot. The dilemma may be described as a tension between what is beneficial to and what is an exploitation of Christian faith and institutions.

On the one hand, the basis for the appearance of the pope and his office through mass media originates in the Petrine ministry itself, in how it is performed and presented. Basically, the church delivers the material to be interpreted. So, for example, the pope's travels are reported on and analyzed by the mass media in the whole world.[1] His sermons, speeches, and statements are listened to and discussed among Roman Catholics and other Christians alike. The Petrine office benefits from all of this.

On the other hand, the mass media culture is centered on public figures: superstars, politicians, religious leaders. Media speculations about, for

---

1. Alitalia had a special issue about "Il Papa pellegrino," 2000.

example, the health and life of the present pope, are immense.[2] Profit interests of different kinds, outside of ecclesial control, create the mass media superstars. Commercial interests thus exploit the Petrine office.

In spite of this risk, one could easily agree with the North American theologian Brian E. Daley, SJ, who writes: "In an age of increasing electronic unity among all cultures and nations, the late twentieth-century public role of papacy as a symbol of the gospel tradition, as preacher to the world, will undoubtedly remain an indispensable part of the office. Probably few future popes will share the dazzling abilities of the present Holy Father [Pope John Paul II] to communicate with crowds, to speak in other languages, to make an impression on the young. But it will doubtless no longer be an option for the bishop of Rome *not* to be a public figure, however much this will trouble some Christians. Precisely in his role as a communicator and preserver of universal Christian values, of the faith and moral convictions shared by *all* who follow Christ, rather than simply of the traditions of a single strand within the Christian tapestry, the pope will fulfill an indispensable role for all churches."[3]

Thus, if the papacy is at least partly formed by the mass media, this is not only a question for communication theorists; it is fundamentally an ecclesiological problem. It cannot be reduced to a question about the Petrine office *and* mass media. It is about the Petrine office *in* mass media affecting the public's understanding of the Petrine ministry and thereby also the church.

The Petrine Office in Mass Media as an Ecclesiological Theme

The fact that the Petrine office is to a certain extent beyond the church's teaching authorities raises a whole spectrum of ecclesiological questions hitherto unexplored. The answer to this might be a reflection and elaboration on the *communio* ecclesiology put forward as a context for the Petrine ministry.

By *communio* ecclesiology I mean a sort of ecclesiology that is *in-*

---

2. A good example is *The Sunday Times Magazine*, 12 March 2000, that gives substantial attention to the matter on pp. 44-52.

3. Brian E. Daley, "The Ministry of Primacy and the Communion of Churches," in Carl E. Braaten and Robert W. Jenson, eds., *Church Unity and the Papal Office: An Ecumenical Dialogue on John Paul II's Encyclical* Ut unum sint *(That They All May Be One)* (Grand Rapids: Eerdmans, 2001), pp. 27-58, here p. 57.

formed by the mass media culture and communication theory but not, and this is important, *formed* by it. Communication ecclesiology is not a substitute for other ecclesiologies, for example, the church as sacrament or the body of Christ; but if it is well done — not reduced to a set of abstract ideas, as sometimes happens — it may offer *a differently balanced ecclesiology.*

The quest for a communication ecclesiology is implicitly raised by many of the ecclesiologies in use today, for example, the various sorts of *communio* ecclesiologies that demand dogmatically significant structures for internal communication in the body of Christ, the people of God. But such structures are also needed for external communication, i.e., in the dialogue between the church and what could be called the world.

One perspective on the Petrine office in a communication ecclesiology might be offered by the concept of hermeneutical reception, which, at least by some, implies that even if the message contains a core message that is not at the interpreter's disposal, it must necessarily be interpreted.[4] From a secular perspective, the pope receives his primacy and authority from others, not by means of mere assertions of an existing fellowship, but by means of global communication with all people of good faith. He communicates the divine revelation with both Roman Catholics and Christians in general, with all believers who recognize his spiritual authority, whatever church tradition they belong to. The church as a sort of *communio* must be marked by identifiable structures of communication.

When elaborating a communication ecclesiology or ecclesiologies, it is important to avoid ecclesiological docetism.[5] Incarnation necessarily implies that the church takes form in persons and institutions. One temptation in formulating *communio* ecclesiologies is to neglect this in favor of sentiments of "belonging." In communication ecclesiology structures, the means and goals of communication must be properly defined. In classical Christian

---

4. This problem is presented in Angela Corsten, *Påven i spegellandet. Påvens ämbetsutövning via pressen underskt med hjälp av ett historiskt exempel: Pius XII och Johannes XXIII i svenska och tyska tidningar,* 1958 (Stockholm: Diss. University of Gothenburg, 1996). German summary: Der Papst im Spiegelreich. Die Amtsausübung durch die Presse, untersucht mit Hilfe eines historischen Beispiels: Pius XII. und Johannes XXII. in schwedischen und deutschen Zeitungen. Corsten 1996, pp. 225ff.; David Tracy, *The Analogical Imagination. Christian Theology and the Culture of Pluralism* (New York: Crossroad, 1981).

5. For this, see Edmund Schlink, *Ökumenische Dogmatik* (Göttingen: Vandenhoeck & Ruprecht, 1985), p. 687.

faith these are always related to persons, not to anonymous decision-making boards, and not to the power of isolated individuals.

There is a dialectic between *communio* and *communicatio,* both from the perspective of sacramentality and of shared doctrine and learning processes. If the church were a *communio* without given structures this *communio* would remain a principle without praxis, i.e., a theoretically founded practice. On the other hand praxis gives growth to the communion, facilitating it by means of new experiences, delivered by the various contexts in which the church is planted. But ecclesial communion from the perspective of communication implies a content to be communicated. Without dependence on the contents given to the communion by divine revelation, ecclesial communication would be devoid of content. One could say that in the process of *communicatio* the *communio* becomes a *congregatio,* a structurally ordered *communio.* This deliberation could be grounded in communication theory as well as ecclesiology. The *communio*'s basis in communication is founded in the dialogue within the Holy Trinity, a notion that must be explored by ecclesiology.

The word *communication* originates from the Latin *communico,* "to share." It describes a social process referring to the act of imparting, conveying, or exchanging ideas, knowledge, and information. It presupposes some degree of mutual trust and a common hermeneutic, without which communication/sharing is not possible.

In preparing any church communication, ecclesiology communication theory should play an important role in order to avoid all sorts of theological amateurism. Theories about "communication" are *legio,* as are descriptions and definitions of the concept. Even if they heavily influence churches, and the churches depend on them, there has been a surprisingly reluctant attitude from ecclesiologists to take them into account when deliberating on the nature and forms of the church. Some of the remarks one finds in literature strengthen the impression, for example, that the church is based on — and continues to exist in — communicative acts and can thus be understood as a communicative process and even interpreted from that perspective.[6]

But it would be disastrous to any communication ecclesiology if restricted to this perspective. Communication is not only a "function" performed in or by the church, derived from the missionary task or any other

---

6. Barbara Kappenberg, *Kommunikationstheorie und Kirche: Grundlagen einer kommunikationstheoretischen Ekklesiologie* (Frankfurt am Main/Bern: Peter Lang, 1981), pp. 205-6.

task entrusted to it. Communication is an ecclesiological structure, and from a certain perspective the church *is* communication. The church is intrinsically marked by communicative patterns, e.g., *leitourgia, martyria,* and *diakonia,* decisive elements of the *koinonia.*

I have no intention here to describe or even less to prescribe a communication ecclesiology. I would, however, like to give some hints about what may or may not be useful for further conversation. My examples also aim at showing that the church doesn't have to be a victim in the mass media culture, and that a communication ecclesiology in dialogue with communication theory may be possible.

After this alarming introduction, I am dividing my presentation into three parts. The first part concerns ideas already presented by others in various contexts; the second part gives some hints at what could be included in a communication ecclesiology, *formaliter* and *materialiter;* and the third aims at showing how a communication ecclesiology might contribute to a common understanding of the Petrine office. In each of the three parts I will give two examples.

(1) I will start by addressing two approaches I have found problematic in constructing a communication theology. The first one is the description of the church as a "network" and the place of the Petrine ministry in that framework. The other one is the construction of "functional" views on the Petrine ministry and ecclesiology.

The Church as Network

The International Theological Commission of the Congregation for the Doctrine of Faith states: "At the heart of the universal network of particular churches of which the single church of God is made up, there is a unique center and reference point: the particular church of Rome."[7] The commission never returns to the ecclesiologically significant term "network" that would later become a focal point in the debate about the future of ecumenism. "Network" in ecclesiology refers to communication theory. Network ecclesiologies having communication as their heart can be found in various places.

---

7. "Selected Themes of Ecclesiology on Occasion of the Eighth Anniversary of the Closing of the Second Vatican Council," in Michael Sharkey, ed., *International Theological Commission, Texts and Documents 1969-1985* (San Francisco: Ignatius Press, 1989), p. 284.

Describing the church as a network is, however, not unproblematic. In postmodernity a network is a social organization that is "made up of autonomous subjects drawn into certain temporary contacts or fragmentary relationships." They have "no centers and sacred collective representations," and they are not capable of representing anything but the aspirations and desires of each individual or group involved in the network.[8] Postmodernity, which is a reality in the North but not necessarily in other parts of the church, finds unity hard to accept, especially as something that overrules the individual's choice. In Europe people are accustomed to pick and choose from various systems of ideas, creating their own conglomerate of thoughts, sometimes called a worldview. The idea of the unity of the church is hard to digest in postmodernity. The African and North American situation seems to be similar, with a never-ending creation of new ecclesial communities. In some corners of the traditional churches this has been accepted, but is often pronounced as warnings for the ideal of "uniformity" in models of unity.

Thus, even if one could identify church in terms of communication theory, the idea of network includes several ecclesiological problems. These difficulties remain even if it is true that "network has replaced hierarchy as a social model for communication."[9]

In a postmodern situation, as at present in the North (which is sometimes very different from other parts of the world), the papal ministry necessarily must be a counterpower to all sorts of financial and cultural paternalism. Parts of the church are now under pressure to accept European or North American thought paradigms. It should also be noticed that the same postmodern cluster of ideas is to be found among those Roman Catholics who are critical of or negative towards the papacy but do not convert to another ecclesial tradition, as well as among those non–Roman Catholics who recognize the pontiff's spiritual authority without formally converting to the Roman Catholic Church — the pick-and-chose possibility presented by postmodernism. Though postmodernity is criticized as a hindrance to the ecumenical movement because of its disinterest in the late-modern program for church unity, it also offers new patterns for Christian unity that should be considered.

8. Gabriel Bar-Haim, "The Dispersed Sacred: Anomie and the Crisis of Ritual," in Stewart M. Hoover and Knut Lundby, eds., *Rethinking Media, Religion, and Culture* (Thousand Oaks/London/New Delhi: Sage, 1997), pp. 133-45, here p. 135.

9. Robert J. Schreiter, *The New Catholicity: Theology Between the Global and the Local* (Maryknoll, NY: Orbis Books, 1997), p. 8.

Function and Instrument

The way we use concepts in ecclesiology is not at all innocent. "Function" is a good example. It was invented, as we know it today, during the Enlightenment. The aim was to separate the person doing something from what he or she really does — not least in Protestant deliberations on ordained ministry. The important thing is that something is done, not who is doing it. This became obvious, for example, in the responses to the Lima document *Baptism, Eucharist and Ministry* (1982). The *episkopē* was, in many cases, affirmed as an important function in the church while *episkopos* was questioned.

As the Roman Catholic–Evangelical Lutheran dialogue in the USA stated, "The Petrine function of the Ministry serves to promote or preserve the oneness of the church by symbolizing unity, and by facilitating communication, mutual assistance or correction, and collaboration in the church's mission."[10]

From an ecclesiological perspective this idea of function is dubious, while baptism is the fundament for all actions a Christian performs. The presupposition for his or her works is that a person is born in baptism into a new existence in the people of God. By baptism a Christian is initiated into the body of Christ; he or she becomes a new person in Christ — in baptism and confirmation sealed by the Holy Spirit. The rejection of functionalism also becomes important in reference to those who are ordained and who thus have been bestowed with gifts of the Holy Spirit (1 Tim. 4:14). In sacramental categories, the alternative to *function* is *instrument*.

If functions are solely goal oriented and subordinate the person under the expected task, the concept of instrument focuses on the person involved. In ecclesiology a person who is an instrument can also be described in terms of intention and responsibility. The key word for this in Christian theology is "heart." A person acts from the basis of her being; she does not get her identity from what she is doing, but acts from what she is. To quote a late medieval German theologian and Reformer: "A bishop, when he consecrates a church, confirms children, or performs some other duty belonging to his office, is not made a bishop by these works. Indeed, if he had not first been made bishop, none of these works would have been valid. . . . So the Christian who is consecrated by his faith does good works, but the works do not

---

10. "Common Statement of 'Differing Attitudes Toward Papal Primacy,'" in Paul C. Empie and T. Austin Murphy, eds., *Papal Primacy and the Universal Church* (Minneapolis: Augsburg, 1974), pp. 11-12.

make him holier or more Christian, for that is the work of faith alone. . . ."[11] Personal authority is closely associated with personal responsibility, especially for offices that claim to exist *in persona Christi et ecclesiae.*

The mass media culture fosters a sort of leadership ideal that implies high spiritual and ethical standards. All deviations from those standards are hung out for public scrutiny. And it is remarkable to notice the intense connection that mass media expect between an institution and those who represent it. Mass media have a clear understanding of how representation works; hence their interest in the form and exercise of the Petrine office.

The Petrine office, then, should not be interpreted as a function but as an instrument. Function is goal oriented and described in terms of what should be achieved, while instrument in sacramental theology and ecclesiology includes the tool, in this case the person. The being and what is supposedly being done are inseparable. Instrumentally, the subject and the action of the subject can be differentiated but not separated.

(2) The second part of my presentation is mainly about ecclesiological structures that can be found in the mass media culture and await discussion and maybe elaboration by theologians. Once again I will try to give two examples. The first is about the reception of the papal ministry in the wider *oecumene;* the second, in relation to that, is about the representative meaning attributed to that office.

Reception of the Papal Ministry in the Wider *Oecumene*

When the Holy Father in the encyclical *Ut unum sint* invited all Christian traditions to reflect on the papal ministry, that was, of course, a constructive ecumenical invitation to the sharing of insights and experiences of divine revelation. But it was also an accommodation to an actual reality. Not many

---

11. "Episcopus sacer, templum consecrans, pueros confirmans aut aliud quippiam officii sui faciens, non consecratur iis ipsis operibus in Episcopum, immo, nisi ante esset consecratus Episcopus, nullum istorum operum quicquam valerent essentque stulta et puerilia et ludicra. Ista Christianus per fidem suam consecratus bona facit opera sed non per haec magis sacer aut Christianus efficitur: hoc enim solus fidei est, immo nisi ante crederet et Christianus esset, nihil prorsus valerent omnia sua opera essentque vere impia et damnabilia peccata." Martin Luther, *Tractatus de libertate Christiana* (1520), in WA 7: pp. 49-73, here p. 61. Translated by W. A. Lambert and revised by Harold J. Grimm, "The Freedom of a Christian," in *Luther's Works* 31 (Philadelphia: Fortress, 1957), pp. 327-78, here pp. 360-61.

years ago the Petrine office was identified by non–Roman Catholic faithful with juridical supremacy over the Roman Catholic Church; its authority was perceived as limited to that tradition and all claims transcending that tradition were totally rejected. Today the situation is different. On the one hand there is in some quarters of Roman Catholicism a public and clearly identifiable skepticism regarding the authority and place of the Petrine ministry in the church. On the other hand, there is in other traditions a reception of the authority and spiritual leadership of the present pontiff and a recognition of the need for the Petrine office. This seems to be due to three factors: First, the results of ecumenical dialogue that deal constructively with old controversial problems and offer new possibilities. Second, the immense impact the papacy has gotten through mass media. Even if journalists have mostly presented critical articles and radio and TV programs, the message presented by the pope has been positively received and recognized by people in other traditions. Third, there seems to be a growing awareness of the need for Christian leadership that can combine local and universal leadership.

This ecumenical reception of the Petrine ministry is not possible to recognize institutionally but is sometimes labeled the Great Tradition, and is found among almost all traditions. Common for all three factors is the formative role of mass media; either they are used under the control of ecclesial authorities or they are secular in character.

The Papal Office as a Representative for the Whole Church

Christians of all denominations receive leadership from the pope through the mass media, and the mass media take it for granted that the pope is speaking on behalf of the whole church. The mechanisms in secular mass media are easily discerned: the most visible and powerful leader is viewed as worthy of attention. Therefore the pope is treated as the spokesman for Christianity. The long-term consequences of that for ecclesiology should be investigated.

But there is also a need, in the church as a whole, for representation that is theologically grounded. In describing "the Great Tradition," in fact a dynamic ecumenical model, the Norwegian theologian Ola Tjørhom depicts the papal office as a sign and instrument of unity: "The Great Tradition of the Church is . . . open to the possibility that visible community on the universal level requires some kind of unity with the bishop of Rome, the successor of Peter. This should not be perceived as a unity of Rome, but as a unity *with* Rome, in which 'the Western patriarch' has a special responsibility for the Church's universal unity within the framework of a comprehensive collegial and synodal structure."[12] The prepositional attributes "under" and "with" should, of course, be interpreted neither in canonical categories nor as an attempt to play down the need for a magisterium in the church of Christ. It must be interpreted in the context of a *communio* ecclesiology in which the prepositions mark structures of communication. This is even more important if the pope is not only a sign and instrument for truth but also for love. Pointing to the one and same reality — the Lord Jesus Christ — truth and love cannot be separated but are distinctions made for the sake of clarity and understanding and must thus be held together. Therefore the concepts "under" and "with" should not be immediately associated with the traditional contrast made in controversial theology between a juridical primate and a primate of "honor." In communication theory and ecclesiology "under" is easily depicted as a strict and direct "order" in an almost military sense of the word, while "with" is referring to another cluster of communication means. The critique of a "command hierarchy" does not, however, impede either a participatory or an ontological view of hierarchy.[13]

(3) The third and last section in this presentation offers from the perspective of communication ecclesiology two themes related to traditional controversies from the sixteenth and nineteenth centuries. I have chosen interrelated problems, namely the authority of the papal office and the question of hierarchy and democracy.

The Authority of the Papal Ministry from the Perspective of Image

Communication theories of various kinds emphasize that what is communicated in mass media are images. This impression is important because it contributes to the understanding of what is conveyed.

One of the advantages of the papal office in a context of communication ecclesiology is that the church's sacramental ecclesiology may itself be seen as the effective sign and instrument of Christ. From the perspective of

---

12. Ola Tjørhom, *Visible Church — Visible Unity: Ecumenical Ecclesiology and "The Great Tradition of the Church"* (Collegeville, MN: Liturgical Press, 2004), p. 31.

13. Terence Nichols, *That All May Be One: Hierarchy and Participation in the Church* (Collegeville, MN: Liturgical Press, 1997).

mission this becomes clear when considering that images in our time are more powerful communicators than words, and especially abstract doctrinal statements. "The papacy is not merely an essential sacred symbol for the Christian Church, it is also or at least can be an extraordinarily important institution for facilitating the proclamation of the Gospel and for speaking to the conscience of the world from the Christian perspective."[14]

The present pontificate has at least implicitly developed a communication ecclesiology adapted to the global mass media culture. The difference between the present pope [John Paul II] and other internationally public persons is that the interest of the mass media in the individual is always balanced with an interest in the office itself. Even if journalists and authors do not always understand it, the underlying theology remains implicitly a decisive factor in their interpretation of what is happening. If, however, the reports on the individual overshadowed the office, it would be an ecclesiological collapse. In the case of the Petrine ministry and its office holders, the image of them should be a representation of Christ and the church. Contextual communication between churches and ecclesial institutions must take form in personal representations. The persons do not represent themselves, but churches and ecclesial institutions. The ecclesiological implications of papacy as a mass medial image and at the same time an instrument of the church, as image, should thus be thoroughly investigated.

Sacramentality, Democracy, and Hierarchy

The mass media culture in which the churches are deeply involved cannot be the fundament for a communication ecclesiology. That would not reflect either how the Petrine office is conceived by public opinion or the character of the church herself. The church must be able to communicate Christ in the various contexts of the world. That means that the same church should be discernible in all parts of the world, independent of cultures and social context. It must be the same church that is heard and seen. The church is perceived by the mass medial world as claiming to be a sign and instrument of the reign of God, of Christ himself. That is not, of course, elaborated in a theological way, but it becomes obvious when the church is criticized in

14. Andrew M. Greely, "Advantages and Drawbacks of a Center of Communications in the Church: Sociological Point of View," in Hans Küng, ed., *Papal Ministry in the Church* (New York: Herder & Herder, 1971), pp. 101-14, here p. 101 (= *Concilium* 64).

mass media. An embedded connection between ethics and ecclesiology seems to be the basis for both what the church communicates to the world and the ongoing critique of the church by the world. The mass media culture focuses on all the discrepancies between what the church claims and how she lives. It is not only the proclaimed word but also the mere existence of the church, the life of the church, that is scrutinized. The "world" seems to be as relevant for the shaping of the communicative church as the creation is relevant for the shaping of the sacramental church.

The popes and bishops during the late Middle Ages were parts of — and exponents of — the dominant feudal system. The cluster of ideas behind it reached even into the ordination rites. Ancient Roman institutions had been taken over, transformed, and applied by the Latin church in continuity with Roman law. The feudal concept of the papacy that emerged out of the Middle Ages and applied to the monarchic episcopate was also based on a communication theory that can be easily described — not only, as often presumed, simply on specific concepts of power.

The feudal system gives perspective on the integration of human and cultural dimensions in ecclesiology. New and constructive ecclesiologies might benefit from that experience. It would be an inconsistency if the critiques of earlier periods in church history are not be taken into account and applied in principle also in the debate on, e.g., modern democracy.

Today representative democracy, based on liberal political ideas and the ideology of association, is predominant. There are ongoing deliberations on how to adapt the present form of the Petrine ministry to this dominant political structure, as the office formerly adapted itself to feudalism; ecclesiologically there are reasons to do so. From the viewpoint of mass media, however, it is obvious that the hierarchical way of communication has been superseded by the democratic.

The collegial exercise of the Petrine ministry together with the bishops is nowadays structuring the church differently than before. But in the mass media culture, pastoral letters directed towards bishops are read by everyone, Roman Catholic or not, who is interested in the matter. These documents are translated into different languages, which means that by communicating with the bishops the pope is communicating with the world in general. This means too that everyone is now taking part in the reception process; the pope is not just talking directly to Roman Catholics, but also to the faithful in other churches.

Another problem, not usually taken into account by churches, is that mass media often overrule the representative democratic system. They intervene in the ordinary life of the churches by forming opinions and influenc-ing the development of those churches. There is a need for signs and effec-tive instruments of the universality of the Christian faith (not to be confused with European and North Americans claims for normativity). A universal corrective is needed in order to avoid a contextualized faith becoming self-referential and isolated.

It is no longer just local authorities but also international celebrities who influence the local and, for that matter, the international context. This is also obvious in the realm of politics, where "stars," politicians or not, by means of medial interest transcend ideology and define the contents of the democratic system. An additional complicating factor is the role of "charis-matic" leaders in churches who apply democratic styles of leadership and forms of decision-making. The basis for these leaders' importance is, in ef-fect, the mass media.

Summary

I am quite aware of the complexity of communication theory and its role in ecclesiology. I am also conscious of the multitude of elements in a construc-tive ecclesiology that embraces the Petrine ministry as an essential element. My suggestion is not to renounce traditional categories used in describing papacy. My point is that we should try another angle in the process of a deepened understanding of the ecclesiological meaning of the Petrine office today. The point of departure suggested is an inventory of the role of com-munication in ecclesiology, based on two themes, namely the church as *communio* and as a sort of sacrament. Communication ecclesiology is nei-ther theologically possible nor realistic from the perspective of the global mass media culture, without taking into account the office of Peter and the Roman see.

In the literature of communication theory the focus is on "religion," and it has thereby become a task for social sciences, not for theology and ecclesiology. Hence, the study of "religious communication" is based on the abstract noun "religion," which in turn is derived from an idea of the exis-tence of common elements in all religions and the existence of a lowest com-mon denominator. But the church is not a religion and must be interpreted not only by means of modern religious studies, based on the phenomenol-ogy of religion born during the nineteenth and twentieth centuries.

A *communio* ecclesiology demands structures of communication that correspond to the fundamental descriptions or definitions of that ecclesiology. Ecclesiology operates in a context of mass media and is influenced by it. That is my perspective in this paper. And by definition one of the given structures in ecclesiology is participation.[15] The Petrine office becomes more and more perceived as a form of representative participation. It is possible, however, that churches lacking communication ecclesiology might also lack the ability to interpret what that means.

---

15. See, for example, Bernd Jochen Hilberath, ed., *Communio: Ideal oder Zerrbild der Kommunikation?* (Freiburg: Herder, 1999).

The Future Exercise of Papal Ministry in the Light of Ecclesiology: An Orthodox Approach

Metropolitan John (Zizioulas) of Pergamon

The issue of primacy is perhaps the most important ecumenical problem. Its importance is underlined by the words of Pope John Paul II himself, who called his Petrine ministry an obstacle to the restoration of the church's unity. The papal document *Ut unum sint* also makes mention of the seriousness of the problem and invites us to study it and propose ways of resolving it. Needless to say, the issue is of decisive importance for the Roman Catholic–Orthodox relations. Historically the question of papal authority and primacy was the main cause for the gradual estrangement between the West and the East, leading finally to the Great Schism of 1054 and the grave consequences that followed it. The same question lies also at the root of the division between Rome and the churches of the Reformation, although the theological disagreements that led to the appearance of Protestantism were of a much broader nature. In the Roman Catholic–Orthodox relations, too, other theological issues became prominent, such as the *Filioque,* but I regard these issues as less difficult to solve, as is evident from a recent document of the Vatican concerning the *Filioque.*[1] The most important and at the same time the most difficult problem in Roman Catholic–Orthodox relations is undoubtedly that of papal primacy.

---

1. See the Pontifical Council for the Promotion of Christian Unity, *The Greek and the Latin Traditions Regarding the Procession of the Holy Spirit,* edition published in French, Greek, English and Russian (Vatican City: Tipografia Vaticana, 1996).

Historical Method and Theological Approach

There are basically two ways to approach this problem. One is the *historical* method, which has been used in the past extensively and has led to no fruitful result. The question whether the primacy of the bishop of Rome in the church can be justified on the ground of biblical and patristic evidence cannot decide the issue. There is undoubtedly a Petrine "primacy" in the college of the Twelve, as is admitted even by Protestant biblical scholars of the authority of an Oscar Cullmann. But it is difficult to establish on biblical grounds the link between the ministry of St. Peter and that of the bishop of Rome. Oscar Cullmann's point that in fact the ministry of the Twelve is unique and unrepeatable continues to be valid as long as continuity is understood strictly in historical terms, i.e., as a matter of linear historical succession.

An attempt to establish the link between the Petrine and the papal primacy through the fact that Peter died and was buried in Rome can hardly convince the historian that such a link follows by logical necessity. Paul also died in Rome and so did many other martyrs of the church, but there has been no claim of their succession by the bishop of Rome. As is indicated by the controversy concerning the celebration of Easter in the second century, other churches in Asia Minor boasted for having hosted the tombs and relics of apostles in their territory, but none of them thought of using this as a justification for a claim of apostolic succession. As the late Francis Dvorník demonstrated in his work *The Idea of Apostolicity in Byzantium and the Legend of the Apostle Andrew,*[2] it was only much later that the argument of apostolicity on the basis of a church's foundation by an apostle began to be used widely. The historical argument became popular in the Middle Ages, but it had for the most part to rely on historically spurious evidence, as was shown later by historical research. The historical approach to the question of papal primacy has proved to be almost pointless in the debate and can be of very little use in the ecumenical discussion of the issue.

The other way to approach the problem is the *theological* one. This method seems to have been followed in the official theological dialogue between the Roman Catholic and the Orthodox churches, and I personally believe that it can bear fruit if it is followed with consistency by both sides. This method begins by raising the fundamental questions concerning the nature of the church, not in a scholastic way of compartmentalizing ecclesiology as

---

2. Francis Dvorník, *The Idea of Apostolicity in Byzantium and the Legend of the Apostle Andrew* (Cambridge, MA: Harvard University Press, 1958).

a subject in itself, but by placing it in the broader context of Christian doctrine, including our faith in the Trinitarian God, in Christ, and in the Holy Spirit. If the church is "the Church of God," it must be asked of *what kind of God* is she the church. If she is the "body of Christ" and the "temple of the Spirit," her nature cannot but depend on a Christology conditioned fundamentally by Pneumatology. If, finally, the church is revealed in her fullness in the Sacrament of the Holy Eucharist, we cannot form our view of her structure and ministries without taking into consideration the structure of the Eucharist itself. All these considerations are fundamental presuppositions in a theological approach to the question of primacy.

Towards a Theology of Primacy

If we approach the problem with such a theological method, the fundamental theological principles for a theology of primacy in the church can be summed up in the following observations.

1. The Church cannot but be a unity of the One and the Many at the same time

This principle stems from Trinitarian theology as well as from Christology in its relation to Pneumatology. It is also supported by the eucharistic nature of ecclesiology. In the Triune God there is unity, but this unity does not precede multiplicity (the three Persons). The priority of the "One God" over against the "Triune God," which we encounter in traditional dogmatic manuals in the West — and, also, in the academic dogmatic theology of the East — was rightly shown by theologians such as Karl Rahner to be wrong. We do not first speak of the One God (= divine substance) and *then* of the three persons as relations *within* the one substance — a favorite approach of medieval theology. The Trinity is just as primary as the one substance in the doctrine of God: the "many" are constitutive of the One, just as the One is constitutive of the "many."

The same principle applies also to Christology. The fact that Christ is inconceivable without the Spirit makes Pneumatology *constitutive* of Christology. Given that the Spirit operates as a force of *communion* (2 Cor. 13:13) and as the one who *distributes* the charismata and personalizes the Christ-event, Christ as the "anointed one" by the Spirit (Χριστός) is at the same

171

time "one" and "many" — not "one" who *becomes* "many," but "one" who is inconceivable without the "many," his "body." There can be no "head" without a "body"; there is no "one" without the "many," no Christ without the Spirit.

The "one" and "many" principle is also fundamental in the case of the Holy Eucharist. St. Paul makes this clear in the interpretation he gives the sacrament in 1 Corinthians 11. The entire Christian tradition in both the East and the West repeats and supports this view. Every Eucharist is offered in the name and on behalf of the entire world. There is one Eucharist in the whole universal church, and yet this one Eucharist is at the same time many Eucharists. Which comes first, the one or the many? It is absurd even to pose the question. There is *simultaneity* between the one and the many, similar to that found in the very being of God as Trinity and in the Person of Christ as a pneumatic being. This mysterious simultaneity is of crucial importance in our Christian faith. Ecclesiology cannot depart from this, if it is not to become heretical throughout.

2. The Church is local and universal at the same time

There have been theological voices in my own church that tried to reverse the priority traditionally preferred by Roman Catholic ecclesiology (see e.g., Rahner and Ratzinger) according to which the church is *first* universal and only secondarily local. In reversing the position Orthodox theologians such as the late Afanassieff and Meyendorff put forth the view that the local church comes first, both historically and theologically, and it is only in a secondary way, if at all (Afanassieff would not allow even for that, at least until the time of St. Cyprian), that we can speak of the church universal. My own personal view has always been different, and it was so because I have always believed that the nature of the Eucharist points to the simultaneity of locality and universality in ecclesiology, as I have tried to explain. This is precisely the reason that the term καθολική ἐκκλησία (catholic church) is marked in the early patristic sources with the ambiguity of indicating both the local and the universal church. It was only St. Augustine that identified for the first time "catholic" exclusively with "universal" in order to react to the provincialism of the Donatists. St. Cyril of Jerusalem in the East offers a synthetic definition of the term and in Ignatius, the *Martyrium Polycarpi*, Tertullian, and even Cyprian, this term clearly indicated the *local* church. All this is quite instructive, as it shows that locality and universality are interdependent in ecclesiology, just as the "one" and the "many" are interdependent in Trinitarian theology and in Christology.

3. The bishop is both a local and a universal ministry

The bishop is ordained for a particular church in order to be its head and center of unity. In the exercise of his ministry he is the "one" who, however, cannot be conceived without the "many," his community. The bishop is the head, but as such he is conditioned by the "body"; he cannot exercise authority without communion with his faithful. Just as he cannot perform the Eucharist without the *synaxis* of the people, his entire ministry requires the *consensus fidelium*, the "Amen" of the community. The reverse is equally true: there is no community without a head, the bishop; nothing can be done without him.

Now, the bishop may be ordained primarily for a specific local church, and yet he is at the same time a bishop of the church universal. This is indicated by two canonical provisions: (a) ordination to episcopacy requires the participation of more than one bishop (whereas that of the presbyter and the deacon is a strictly local affair). And (b) once a bishop is ordained he is entitled or even obliged to exercise his *synodical* ministry. None, except secular force (cf. the case of certain bishops of the Ecumenical Patriarchate today) can deprive a bishop of his right and duty to be a member of the regional or the universal synod. In the person of the bishop locality and universality meet and form two aspects of one and the same ministry.

4. The synodal system is a "sine qua non conditio" for the catholicity of the Church

There can be no church without a synod — this is a principle followed carefully by the Orthodox Church, albeit not always in a satisfactory way. Why is this principle so important? Some tend to see in the synodal system an expression of "democratic" spirit and a reaction against monarchical tendencies in ecclesiology. The movement of *Konziliarismus* was historically such a reaction against the papacy, and there are still many Orthodox who think that synodality is an alternative to the papal primacy. Such views would imply that there is an incompatibility between primacy and conciliarity, which, as we shall see, is by no means true.

The reason why synodality is fundamental in ecclesiology is that through this institution the catholicity of the local church is guaranteed and protected. This is achieved through a double canonical provision. On the one hand *every* bishop has the right and duty to participate *on equal terms* with all the other bishops in a council, and on the other hand no council has the authority to interfere with the internal affairs of each bishop's diocese. The authority of a council or synod is limited to the affairs pertaining to the communion of local churches with one another. Such was the case, for example, in the early church when canon 5 of I Nicea instituted the convocation of synods in every region twice a year in order to examine cases of eucharistic excommunication: if a certain bishop excommunicated one of his faithful, the excommunicated person could not go to another local church to take communion. This could only be decided by a synod of which the bishop concerned would also be a member. The synod could not in this way become an institution *above* the local church. It would exercise authority only *via* the local church. Equally, the local church could not ignore the consequences of its decisions and actions for the other churches, as if it were a "catholic" church independently of its relations and communion with the rest of the churches. The catholicity of the local church cannot be turned into self-sufficiency, while the condition of communion with the rest of the churches should not lead to a loss of its catholicity through subjection to an institution existing and acting above the local church. This means that through the synodical system we do not arrive at a universal church; we rather arrive at a *communion of churches. Universality becomes in this way identical with communion.*

5. Primacy is also a "sine qua non conditio" for the catholicity of the Church

If the fundamental principles mentioned above are to be followed faithfully, the "one-and-the-many" idea which runs through the entire doctrine of the church leads directly to the ministry of primacy. It also indicates the conditions that are necessary for primacy to be ecclesiologically justifiable and sound. Let us consider this in some detail.

(a) There is a primacy *within* each local church. The bishop is the *primus* at the local level. He is the head of the collegium of the presbyters, but at the same time he is the head of the eucharistic synaxis, which means that he is conditioned in his ministry by the entire community of which he is the head. The fact that there can be no eucharistic synaxis without his presidency (directly or indirectly through the authorized priest) shows that the *primus* is a *constitutive* element in the local church. Equally, however, the fact that the synaxis of the people is a condition for the bishop to function as the head of the community shows that his primacy requires the consent and participation of the community. In a similar manner, the bishop is the only one that can distribute the gifts of the Spirit as the sole ordainer in the church (this includes also Baptism and Confirmation taken together as an unbreakable unity according to the ancient tradition and that of the Orthodox Church). Yet, the fact that the bishop cannot ordain in his study or in his home but only within a eucharistic synaxis indicates that he distributes the gifts only on condition that the community is involved in the ordination. The "many" cannot be a church without the "one," but equally the "one" cannot be the *primus* without the "many."

(b) Similar observations apply also to the *regional* level. The *metropolitan* system in the church developed in close connection with the synodical institution. The bishop of the "metropolis," i.e., the capital city of the region, was automatically the *primus* of the synod and of the region. He was very early recognized as the πρῶτος (the first one) and as the "head" (κεφαλή) of all the bishops of the area, but his primacy was strictly conditioned by the involvement in all his decisions and actions of the rest of the bishops of whom he was *primus*. This is clearly laid down by canon 34 of the corpus known as "Apostolic Canons," which belong in all probability to the fourth century A.D., i.e., to the time when the metropolitan system was taking shape. This canon provides that all the bishops of a region (ἔθνος) must recognize their "first one" (πρῶτος) as their "head" (κεφαλή) and do nothing without him, while he should equally do nothing without them. The canon, significantly enough, ends with reference to the Holy Trinity, thereby indicating indirectly that canonical provisions of this kind are not a matter of mere organization but have a theological, indeed a Triadological, basis.

(c) Mention should be made of a special kind of primacy which although regional in character rose above the metropolitan system to comprise all the metropolitan units of a certain broader area. This is what came to be known as *Patriarchates*. The basis of this institution was political as well as historical and ecclesiastical — never theological in the strict sense. Certain local churches acquired pre-eminence, either because they were important in the political structure of the empire or because they had a historic significance in the establishment of the Christian faith and the emergence of new churches (as mother churches). At the time of Byzantium these centers formed the well-known *Pentarchy*, which comprised the churches of Rome,

Constantinople, Alexandria, Antioch, and Jerusalem. The bishops of these churches rose above the rest of the bishops and became each of them *primus* in his own area.

The Great Schism between Rome and Constantinople in the eleventh century opened the way to further developments in this matter. In the first place Rome, following and developing a tradition that started before the Schism, claimed universal jurisdiction and was not satisfied with the primacy of the Patriarchate of the West. This was not recognized by the churches of the East (the other four Patriarchates of the Pentarchy), who formed their own structure and recognized the bishop of Constantinople as the first one among them — keeping for the rest of them the order of the Pentarchy. In so doing the churches of the East never recognized in their *primus* (i.e., Constantinople) a ministry of universal jurisdiction, but only one in the sense of canon 34 of the Apostolic Canons mentioned above. The patriarch of Constantinople could not interfere in the affairs of the other Patriarchates, but would be responsible for the canonical order within them and intervene only when asked to do so in cases of emergency or disturbance and anomaly of some kind. He would also be responsible for the convocation of councils dealing with matters pertaining to all the Orthodox churches, always with the consent of the other patriarchs. The same principles continued to apply after the creation of the other Patriarchates and autocephalous churches that make up the present structure of the Orthodox Church. With the exception of occasional difficulties in their mutual relations, due mainly to nationalistic tendencies, the Orthodox churches have accepted the idea of primacy as exercised within the Orthodox Church by the patriarch of Constantinople in the spirit of canon 34 by the apostles, as analyzed above. This primacy is sometimes called "primacy of honor," a misleading term since, as we have noted, it is not an "honorific" primacy but one that involves actual duties and responsibilities, albeit under the conditions just mentioned.

6. The Primacy of Rome

We can now address the specific question of the primacy of the bishop of Rome. Is such a primacy necessary ecclesiologically, and if it is, in what sense should it be understood and applied?

Let me begin by repeating what I said at the beginning of this paper. The question for me is not a historical but a theological one. If there is a necessity for the primacy of the bishop of Rome this could not be because history demands it, for even if history demanded it (which in my view is doubt-ful, to say the least), this would not make it a necessary thing for the church's *esse.* The same thing would have to be said if the reasons offered for such a primacy were to be practical and utilitarian. For if this were the case the pri-macy we are considering would not be a matter of the church's *esse* but of her *bene esse,* and this would be less than satisfactory to a theologian. The primacy of the bishop of Rome has to be theologically justified or else ig-nored altogether. Speaking as an Orthodox theologian I can see two possibil-ities for a positive appreciation of the papal primacy.

(a) The understanding of the primacy of the Roman bishop *in the tra-ditional sense of the Byzantine Pentarchy.* This would mean that the bishop of Rome is *primus* only for the West; he is the patriarch of the West and should have no primacy whatsoever over the rest of the world. This would seem to satisfy fully the Orthodox, for it would appear to be a return to the Byzantine Pentarchy from which Rome departed by claiming universal jurisdiction.

Such an understanding of the Roman primacy could lead to a scheme of division of the world into two parts, the West and the East, which would mean that Old Rome would have the primacy over the West (whatever that may involve: certainly the Protestant and Anglican world), whereas the New Rome will have the primacy it now has over the East (i.e., the Orthodox world, including the Oriental and non-Chalcedonians?). The problem that such an "arrangement" presents is that there are now parts of the world that are Christian but were not known at the time of the Byzantine Pentarchy. To whom will these belong in terms of primacy?

But there is also another difficulty. What would be the theological jus-tification of such a division of primacies or of any such primacy at all? The Pentarchy can hardly claim a theological *raison d'être,* and for this reason it was eventually amended and modified and can always be amended and modified in terms of number. There is nothing permanent about the num-ber of the *primi;* the only permanent thing is that of the *sees* that hold the primacy, because these were chosen on the basis of irrevocable historical facts relating to the establishing of churches and their faith. Thus, although the limitation of the Roman primacy to the West would be a solution easily acceptable to the Orthodox, this solution would have its weaknesses.

(b) The understanding of the Roman primacy as a universal primacy. This would appear to be totally unacceptable to the Orthodox at first sight. And it *should* be unacceptable *unless it is fundamentally qualified.* These are qualifications that I think should be applied according to the theological principles presented above.

(i) The primacy should not be *primacy* of jurisdiction. The reason for this is that the exercise of jurisdiction means interference with the affairs of a local church and this means the destruction or negation of its catholicity and ecclesial integrity. This, as we noted, has not been allowed to any institution, be it the Council or the Patriarchate or the metropolitan. The local church headed by its bishop must always be allowed to feel like a "catholic church," totally free to run its affairs as long as this does not interfere with the life of the other local churches. This is part of what it means to call, together with Vatican II, each particular church a full church.

(ii) The primacy should not be the prerogative of an individual but of a *local church*. This means that in speaking of the primacy of the pope we mean the primacy of a see, i.e., the *Church of Rome*. There is a big difference between these two ways of understanding primacy. In an ecclesiology of communion we have not a communion of individuals but of churches. Even when councils or synods are composed only of bishops these bishops are not there as individuals but as heads of churches, and it is this that makes the *reception* of conciliar decisions by the faithful a necessary condition for the final authority of these decisions. The bishops, at least according to Orthodox ecclesiology, are not members of an "apostolic college" standing on its own feet and above the local churches. They are each an integral part of their own local church. So too must be the bishop of Rome, if he is to exercise a primacy.

(iii) The primacy should be exercised *in a synodical context* both locally and regionally as well as universally. This means that the spirit and the provisions of the 34th canon "of the Apostles," as explained earlier, would have to be respected: the *primus* must always act together with the rest of the bishops on matters pertaining to or in common with the other churches outside his own local church, while the bishops in similar cases should always act together with their *primus*.

(iv) Given the established structure of the church the universal primacy of the Church of Rome would mean in the first instance that the bishop of Rome would be in cooperation on all matters pertaining to the church as a whole with the existing patriarchs and other heads of autocephalous churches. His primacy would be exercised *in communion*, not in isolation or directly over the entire church. He would be the president of all heads of churches and the spokesman of the entire church once the decisions announced are the result of consensus. But communion should not be exhausted at the level of heads of churches; it should penetrate deeply into all levels of church life, reaching all bishops and all the clergy and all the people.

A Universal *Primus*

These are some conditions that would make a Petrine ministry of primacy acceptable to me as an Orthodox theologian. Under such conditions the catholicity of the local church is respected and at the same time the unity and oneness of the church in the world is served and manifested. A universal *primus* exercising his primacy in such a way is not only "useful" to the church but an ecclesiological necessity in a unified church.

For such a primacy to be accepted and applied an ecclesiology of communion rooted deeply in a theology — and even an ontology — of communion, would be necessary. I believe that the Second Vatican Council has made a historic advance in this direction, and we can proceed in the deepening of such a theology of communion and apply it to all matters still dividing us, including that of the Roman primacy. The final outcome of our efforts can only be the gift of God. We trust in him and pray with him to the Father in the Holy Spirit that we all may be one, as God the Holy Trinity is One.

Infallibilitas Papae — Indefectibilitas Ecclesiae: A Systematic and Ecumenical Approach

Johannes Brosseder

Almost three years after the conclusion of the Council of Trent, the *Catechismus Romanus*[1] was published in 1566. The book was the result of the negotiations at Trent and its final version was accepted by Pope Pius IV and Pope Pius V. A German version appeared 1568. Even though a growing number of Protestant churches already existed in Germany, Switzerland, the Habsburg Estates, Scandinavia, England, and Scotland, only to mention a few, these churches are not addressed or even mentioned in the text. Nevertheless the *Catechismus Romanus* talks about "Reformers" without mentioning their names. In the preface, they are harshly attacked and labeled as false prophets *(falsi prophetae)* who spoil the minds and hearts of the faithful, their unbelief *(illorum impietas)*, trained in all arts of Satan *(omnibus satanae artibus instructa)*, destroyers of souls *(Seelenverderber)*, heretics, teachers of false doctrine, those who distort the glance of true piety, fornicators, those who with all the tricks of Satan spread the errors of ungodliness, destroyers of the Catholic faith, those who give poisoned drinks [to the faithful]. The *Catechismus Romanus* bluntly describes Protestant doctrine, which praises the greatest possible dissociation from the teachings of the Fathers as true piety, as plague.[2] Generations of Roman Catholic believers have been taught this view of other, non–Roman Catholic churches, at least for the last four

---

1. Adolf Buse, ed., *Catechismus Romanus ex decreto Concilii Tridentini ad parochos, Pii V. Pontificis Maximi iussu editus* (Bielefeld/Leipzig: Velhagen & Klasing, [3]1867). Hereafter cited as CR.
2. See CR, Prooemium, quaestiones V-VII.

hundred years until the Second Vatican Council. The seed of the past still bears some fruit as massive criticism of the first ecumenical meeting of Christians in Germany (1st Ecumenical Kirchentag, Berlin 2003) articulated by Roman Cardinals Meisner and Scheffczyk proves.[3] Likewise other bishops from Trier and Eichstätt disciplined "disobedient" clergy in their dioceses. In contrast, the Fathers of Vatican II speak with regard to the relation between the Roman Catholic Church and the other Christian churches in a different language: ". . . The separated churches and (ecclesial) communities as such . . . have by no means been deprived of significance and importance in the mystery of salvation. For the Spirit of Christ has not refrained from using them as means of salvation *(media salutis)* . . ." (*Unitatis redintegratio,* 3).[4] They obviously see "other," in the meaning of non–Roman Catholic communities and parishes, as "churches." They feel the need for reconciliation and re-establishment of former community with greatest urgency. The quote gives an additional impetus to efforts in that direction. Even though we can joyfully appreciate the many steps forward to more community and common Christian faith, we have to admit that several questions which either had been decided years ago, or which can be answered with little effort, or which should be discussed with more enthusiasm, are stored in the archives of the Roman Curia. As a result, the impression of ignorance, negative visions of future community with other Christian denominations, and finally a retrospective approach to these problems cannot be avoided completely. I will not give further examples for the above-mentioned points. The latter might characterize a large number of ecclesiastical officials and church leaders. Are we — as it was said — witnesses of a slow process of maturing while the first decades of ecumenical euphoria in the late 1960s and 70s cools down and vanishes into the historical past? I have the impression that ecclesiastical officials try to play down documents of growing unity, which are pushed more to the margins of theological dispute and official ecclesiastical doctrine. In fact, only a few Roman Catholic bishops really read with sympathy ecumenical documents and declarations. Within the Roman Catholic Church they do not play an important role. What does it mean when sentences like, "That which the churches have in common is greater and of much more importance than the

3. E.g., Joachim Cardinal Meisner, in *Die Tagespost,* 3 July 2003 (see also www.kath.net/printable.php).

4. The English translation of the documents of Vatican Council II is taken from Norman P. Tanner, ed., *Decrees of the Ecumenical Councils,* vol. 2, *Trent to Vatican II* (London/Washington, DC: Sheed & Ward/Georgetown University Press, 1990).

differences," or, "In comparison to those issues which unite the churches the points of difference and dispute are only a few and of much lesser importance," or, "Fundamentally we can agree about faith and doctrine," and, "The pillars of a collapsed bridge are still standing," are articulated in official statements? Whatever the answers to these highly polemical questions are, and whoever might find his way through the jungle of contemporary ecumenism, this is the context in which we will treat the topic of this chapter.

Church

While the doctrine of the *"indefectibilitas ecclesiae"* belongs to the central teachings about the church of Christ of nearly all the Christian churches, the Roman Catholic claim of the *"infallibilitas papae"* is a special doctrine of the Roman Catholic Church, which is neither shared nor accepted by non–Roman Catholic churches. Nevertheless Rome teaches this doctrine with universal validity. But because the doctrine of the *"infallibilitas papae"* is based on the doctrine of the *"infallibilitas ecclesiae"* we should look for a common understanding of the *"infallibilitas ecclesiae"* that makes the *"infallibilitas papae"* superfluous. We need to discuss some questions beforehand, whose answers are of essential importance for the discussion of our main topic. What do we mean by the "church" whose indefectibility we believe in? Since the Western and the Eastern churches separated in 1054/1204 and since the Occidental church split again into three confessions in the sixteenth century, Roman Catholic theology defined "church" exclusively as an assembly under the rule of the Western patriarch in Rome. Like the Orthodox churches in the East, the Western Reformed confessions were no longer accepted as churches but as heretics and schismatic. Church was understood as the Western, Roman Catholic Church. The Second Vatican Council differentiated a bit more: Chapters I and II of *Lumen gentium* (The Mystery of the Church, the People of God) define the *Church of Jesus Christ* in general and basically theologically; following this description LG 8 says, this church (of Christ) subsists within the Roman Catholic Church: "This church . . . subsists in the catholic church"; LG 8 adds, ". . . although outside its structure many elements of sanctification and of truth are to be found which, as proper gifts to the church of Christ, impel towards catholic unity." The Decree on Ecumenism finally explains in more detail, speaking of the Eastern churches and of ecclesial communities and churches in the West. Even though this implies a break with a more than 1000-year-old tradition, opening up a new quality of dialogue, Vatican II was unable to overcome the doctrine that the church of Jesus Christ fully subsists in the Roman Catholic Church only. The Eastern churches as much as the churches and ecclesial communities in the West exist with a certain deviancy and have different approaches lacking the full community with the Apostolic See in Rome. The paradigm for orthodoxy — and in fact community with Rome — is Rome itself. Nevertheless that lack of community with other churches and ecclesial assemblies endangers the Roman Catholic Church, not allowing it to express its full catholicity. The new quality of this argument can be seen especially when the Fathers of Vatican II define ecumenical community. They no longer expect the return of the separated churches back to Rome, but ask for a common search for the unity which had been given by Jesus Christ in the beginning and which was never given up (UR 4). Next to other activities such as spiritual ecumenism, dialogue, revocation of prejudices, studies of and for a deeper understanding of the other Christian traditions, respect for a certain hierarchy of truth, and a deeper search for the meaning of faith, modern ecumenical consensus has to look for penance, renewal, and reform as main paths toward a reconstruction of the lost unity of the church. Catholics are taught: "But their especial duty (in primis) is to make a careful and honest appraisal of whatever needs to be renewed in the catholic household itself, in order that its life may bear witness more faithfully and clearly to the teachings and ordinances which have come to it from Christ through the hands of the apostles" (UR 4).

Accepting this admonition of the Council, I will ask whether we need a new ecclesiological thinking with regard to the fact that within the last decades community grew between churches on all levels of ecclesial and interdenominational relations. The paradigm of this new ecumenical ecclesiology can be found in a common search for the principles by which the church of Christ is constituted. These principles are the Word of God, the sacraments, conversion, the forgiveness of sins, and service. Because every Christian church is constituted by these principles, every Christian church is able to say that the church of Christ subsists in it.[5] If the Spirit — following UR 3 — uses all these churches as a means of salvation, Roman Catholic theology can no longer deny that these churches essentially are constituted by the same principles as the Roman Catholic Church. This means much more

---

5. See Giovanni Cereti, "Critical Relecture of *Lumen Gentium*," in Johannes Brosseder, ed., *Verborgener Gott — verborgene Kirche? Die kenotische Theologie und ihre ekklesiologischen Implikationen* (Stuttgart: Kohlhammer, 2001), pp. 115-27.

than just accepting — theoretically — the fact that outside the Roman Catholic Church one may find only elements of sanctification and truth, which in the end have their roots in the Roman Catholic Church. With this in mind I respectfully disagree — like Cardinal Kasper — with Cardinal Ratzinger, who publicly defended theses of the ontological and historical priority of the universal church in regard to territorial and local churches. Theologically as much as historically, it can be proven that church is the consequence of an institutionalized service: church is constituted through liturgy and Eucharist, the community of Christians with the risen Christ. The unity of Christians within the church and the churches is grounded in the unity of the participants at Christ's table. The universal church has to be understood as a network of Eucharist-celebrating local and territorial churches.

Another aspect can be seen in an ecumenical understanding of baptism, which has not been thoroughly discussed during the last ecumenical dialogues. Through baptism, Christians become members of the church of Christ, not exclusively of a confessional church, even though the rite is celebrated locally in a confessional church. Baptism constitutes instead a spiritual relation between Christ and the baptized. This establishes the membership within the church of Christ: ". . . baptism establishes a sacramental bond of unity existing among all who have been reborn by it" (UR 22). The unity of the church is fundamentally grounded in baptism. This unity is not theoretical or an ideal, but Christ gave it for real and it does not need to be re-established by ecclesial ministries. The division and differentiation of the churches into confessional entities never spoiled this deeper unity. We have no other choice than to accept and respect this inner unity with regard to other churches. The understanding of this unity is the logical consequence following the above-mentioned principles of the composition of the church. Nevertheless the Petrine ministry is in fact not a constitutional element of these principles as Cardinal Ratzinger claims in his introduction to Christianity.[6]

To sum up, we have spoken theologically to distinguish between the church of Jesus Christ in general and confessional churches in particular in which the church of Christ subsists.[7] In consequence of several divisions and particularizations, a greater part of which were caused by man, all churches

---

6. Joseph Ratzinger, *Einführung in das Christentum* (Munich: Deutscher Taschenbuch Verlag, 1971), pp. 247, 256.

7. The importance of this distinction is discussed by the Groupe des Dombes, *Pour la conversion des Églises. Identité et changement dans la dynamique de communion* (Paris: Éditions du Centurion, 1991).

became in fact confessional churches — including the Roman Catholic Church. It is bizarre to deny responsibility for the sin of separation and the essential gospel either by a hypocritical overestimation of secondary issues of a strategic interest or the lack of tolerance for local or individual preferences that do not essentially endanger the truth of the church and its proclamation of the gospel. How could a reform of the church be accomplished that looks much more to historical developments than to clarifications within dogma and doctrine? Guided by these principles, new insights, a deeper understanding, and a wider horizon could be found. This does not contradict ecclesiastical tradition and its grounding in the doctrine of the church. On the contrary, it would awaken new life within the churches and allow corrections without separation and harm. No church will be able to overcome the developments of the last centuries in the way these have been established. We need new ways out of the crisis.

We may conclude the first part of our discussion with the thesis that *"indefectibilitas ecclesiae"* can be proven for the universal church of Jesus Christ only. It cannot be said about territorial, local, or confessional churches in which the universal church of Christ subsists. Thus indefectibility does not exclude accidental developments and the full negation of churches within the historical process of their being. Traditional Roman Catholic dogmatic handbooks published before Vatican II also taught this.[8]

Indefectibility

Let's take a closer look at the doctrine of *"indefectibilitas ecclesiae"* as mainstream churches teach it (e.g., the Lutheran churches, the Reformed churches, the Roman Catholic Church, the Anglican Church, the Orthodox churches, etc.). The traditional Roman Catholic dogma discusses the indefectibility of the church as a first essential. Labeled as *"sententia certa,"* the doctrine is as follows: "The Church is indefectible, which means the Church will remain until the end of times as founded by Christ for the sake of eternal salvation."[9] Vatican I speaks of its *"invicta stabilitas,"* or invincible strength,[10] and of the

---

8. See Ludwig Ott, *Grundriss der katholischen Dogmatik* (Freiburg: Herder, ³1957), p. 357.

9. See e.g., Ott, *Grundriss der katholischen Dogmatik*, pp. 357-59.

10. Heinrich Denziger, *Enchiridion symbolorum definitionum et declarationum de rebus fidei et morum,* re-edited by Peter Hünerman, 37th edition (Freiburg: Herder, 1991), 3013; hereafter cited as DH.

fact that the church will stand fast until the end of times (*ad finem saeculorum usque firma stabit;* DH 3056). Pope Leo XIII describes the Church as unique and everlasting (*unica et perpetua, in: Satis cognitum,* DH 3303). These texts, however, describe the Roman Catholic Church as representing the church exclusively. Vatican II respects the changes within the traditional ecclesiology challenged by the developments of the last century even though it teaches the church's indefectibility (LG 48). On the Protestant side, the Augsburg Confession says in article VII that the church will last eternally (*"una sancta ecclesia perpetua mansura sit"*) as Luther had described it in the Schwabach Articles. The Reformed tradition also knows about the *indefectibilitas ecclesiae.* The Heidelberg Catechism asks, "What do you believe about the holy universal Christian Church?" The answer is, "that the Son of God has elected from humankind a certain assembly . . . which is gathered, protected, and held by the Spirit and the Word of God in the unity of faith from the beginning of the world until its end" (question 54). What does "continuous existence of the church" mean? In his "Ecumenical Dogmatic" the famous systematic theologian Edmund Schlink from Heidelberg explains:

> The continuous existence of the Church does not mean that the Church exists at a certain place on earth. The Church does not have the promise of an earthly Canaan or Jerusalem as it was given to the folk of the old covenant. In some areas where the Church existed through the centuries, today it has disappeared. Continuous existence also does not imply a permanent growth and development. The Church might shrink. Continuous existence finally does not mean that the gospel will be preached in all times at every place with the same perspicuity and power and that in consequence the grace of Christ would be manifest in the full meaning of the word. There are always dark and light, rich and poor times in the history of the Church. It neither means that in all times all ministries are witnesses of the truth — nor that ecclesial unity will be established in the community of teaching and working together in the Church. Nevertheless, there is at any time a people of those who live in faith from the Gospel and through the sacraments, those whose new creation is an essential part of God's plan of salvation. There is always a holy, catholic, apostolic Church. The Church will exist continuously because God will not give up overcoming Christian errors and weakness with his power and his eternal truth. The Church will exist continuously because Christ's kingdom cannot be overthrown. He had suffered and was elevated to the Lord for the sake of his brethren and sisters, who suffer with

him to receive the final victory. As the risen Christ, he will gather them to cleanse them and to empower them and to hold them forever. The Holy Sprit does not end his activities, for the effusion of his power will continue until the end of times. The Spirit will manifest his power by leading men to Christ, to make them Christ's property and to keep them within this relation. Thus the Church will exist continuously, for it is the place where God fulfills his new creation through the Spirit, which he had started in Christ.[11]

To exist continuously also has to be explained as a permanent relation rooted in Christ. To make this clear, the church has collected the sources of apostolic times and added them to the Scriptures of the Old Covenant — the canon of Scripture. The church also developed the doctrine of Christ in its historical setting and context with regard to contemporary discussion and heterodox challenges. Thus the church was able to establish a certain order in close relation to contemporary questions and developments to proclaim the gospel appropriately and correctly. The necessity of this manifestation of ecclesiastical order is rooted in the eucharistic assembly of the faithful, to which it always has to be related. This has to be adjusted to the challenges of the times but should never give up its essentials. Traditional neoscholastic, Roman Catholic doctrine discusses the doctrine of *indefectibilitas ecclesiae* with regard to its temporal immortality as much as with regard to its doctrinal purity (doctrine, cult, and order).

Karl Rahner once discussed extensively the question of the church's indefectibility in his essay "The Church and the Parousia of Christ" (1963).[12] He distinguished between the church as fruit of salvation and the church as a medium for salvation or an institution of eternal glory. The fundamental ecclesiological category for Rahner is the church as fruit of salvation, to which the church as the medium of salvation is related continuously. The "faith which hopefully awaits the return of Christ is not merely something which the Church teaches and mediates to individual men for their individual salvation, but is a constitutive element of the Church as such," "an essen-

---

11. Edmund Schlink, *Ökumenische Dogmatik. Grundzüge. Mit Geleitworten von Heinrich Fries und Nikos A. Nissiotis* (Göttingen: Vandenhoeck & Ruprecht, 1983), pp. 626-27.

12. Karl Rahner, "The Church and the Parousia of Christ," in Karl Rahner, *Theological Investigations* (London/New York: Darton, Longman & Todd/The Seabury Press, 1974), vol. 6, pp. 295-312.

tial element of the Church" (vol. 6, p. 297). "The Church would therefore understand herself falsely as a mere saving institution and only as a means of salvation, were she not to think of herself as the community of those who hope, those who are waiting, of pilgrims who still seek their own homeland, of those who understand and master their present in terms of the future" (p. 297). The Church, he says, has to be understood as provisional and as overcoming herself. "Therefore the Church . . . is living always on the proclamation of her own provisional status and of her historically advancing elimination in the kingdom of God towards which she is expectantly traveling as a pilgrim" (p. 298). Without ignoring the permanent and indestructible presence of final salvation within the church as it is given by proclaiming the Word of God and by administering the sacraments, a presence that is only accessible to the eyes of faith and hope, the church has "even this permanent and indestructible element . . . in a really historical form which changes, which must always be sought anew, which must be endured in its historical originality and contingence, and whose transformation . . . is yet never adequately calculable in advance" (p. 298). By the presence of the final salvation within the Word of God and the sacraments, "the Church" thereby "is constituted as the community of those who believe and confess that God's grace as love which forgives and communicates God himself is really victorious in the world and that its victory in the free acceptance of that love by man is itself the work of God's self-communication in grace. Insofar as this faith confessing the eschatological victory of the grace of God is itself an element in this victory and not merely a polite answer on the part of man to an act of God which as such does not yet include this reaction of the creature but is synergistically added to it, the Church believes and confesses that this eschatological victory of God's communication of himself happens, even if not exclusively in her, yet precisely *also* in her and upon her. For the Church is the community whose faith proclaims this victory and this in such a way that the proclamation of the final and irrevocably initiated victory of God, and not merely the victory itself, can no longer disappear from the history of mankind. But if this proclamation of faith in the victory, as that faith made concrete in history, is itself invincible and an inner constitutive element of the victory itself and at the same time of the Church, then the Church must necessarily be one which confesses of herself in praise of God's grace that in her the acceptance of the divine self-communication, that is the justification of man, is indefectible and that her faith in it as the historical presence of this victory can never disappear. To this extent therefore the Church professes of herself an indefectibility of her holiness and faith" (pp. 301-2).

Now the question arises, "What exactly is the relationship of the Church as institution and official ministry to the Church as eschatological entity?" Karl Rahner explains it as follows: We have to "assume in the Catholic understanding an indefectibility of the official ministry in *all* its functions; but at the same time it is permissible to view . . . this indefectibility . . . of the institution . . . as a peripheral instance *(Grenzfall)* of the Church, instead of, as it is usually done in Catholic theology, developing this indefectibility only in relation to the teaching office of the Church and then setting up that indefectibility as the normal case and interpreting other acts of the teaching office which are lacking in that indefectibility (which in the case of teaching is called infallibility) as peripheral instances."[13] The indefectibility of the historically tangible form of the church, of the church as institution, roots in the indefectibility of the church as an eschatological community of salvation. Even when the teaching office of the church defines an article of faith, its infallibility is not necessarily evident or given by the act itself. Karl Rahner's clear distinction between defectible and indefectible self-realizations cannot be found. Even "infallible decisions of a Pope or of a Council" cannot be clearly distinguished from its fallible historical context and thus do not participate in the principle of indefectibility. Rahner summarizes:

> The doctrine of the indefectibility of the teaching and ruling office does not imply at all that the Church and the individual Christian wander idly from one clear certitude to another. Despite this indefectibility, Church and Christian must laboriously make their pilgrimage through the obscurity of this aeon, and for both there ultimately remains only one thing: trust in the grace of God alone. The Catholic doctrine of the indefectibility of the official ministry and its acts in determinate circumstances does not therefore in any way imply that this area can be so circumscribed as to make it from every possible viewpoint utterly and clearly distinct from all that is defectible in the Church, that according to the Catholic understanding there is, so to speak, a piece of the Church which is clearly distinct from everything else as purely the divinely founded Church of sure salvation and of the absolutely unobscured truth and love of Christ.[14]

13. Rahner, "The Church," vol. 6, pp. 305-7.
14. Rahner, "The Church," vol. 6, pp. 309-10.

In consequence this means for me that the church as an institution manifests itself only in parts and broken as the indefectibility of the eschatological church. The institution is a historical entity developing within a historical process. Thus it has to be explained as *ecclesia indefectibilitate et defectibilitate permixta*. The indefectible church can be seen when liturgy and Eucharist mirror the eschatological church of Christ. It seems evident that Rahner's understanding of the *indefectibilitas ecclesiae* matches what Schlink had explained with regard to its biblical, dogmatic, and legal hermeneutics (Canon, Christology, Order of the Church). This understanding seems to be compatible with our topic, the church of Christ, which subsists in each confessional church.

Infallibility

The doctrine of infallibility of the church is — in a strict sense — nothing more than the doctrine of indefectibility of the church on a doctrinal level. That means the church has the promise of support through and of the Holy Spirit. The Spirit helps the church stay within the apostolic tradition and not to err even though individual Christians, parts of the church synods, and even bishops may fall astray as history shows. The doctrine of the infallibility of the church traditionally distinguishes between an *infallibilitas in docendo* and an *infallibilitas in credendo;* a second traditional distinction is given by the *ecclesia docens,* which is infallible teaching, and the *ecclesia docta,* which as a result of this infallible teaching is infallible believing. Both distinctions are inappropriate. John Henry Newman discussed this problem in 1859 in his essay "On Consulting the Faithful in Matters of Doctrine":[15]

> . . . but I mean still, that in that time of immense confusion [the fourth century] the divine dogma of our Lord's divinity was proclaimed, enforced, maintained, and (humanly speaking) preserved far more by the *Ecclesia docta* than by the *Ecclesia docens;* that the body of the episcopate was unfaithful to its commission, while the body of the laity was faithful to its baptism; that at one time the Pope, at other times the patriarchal, metropolitan, and other great sees, at other times general councils, said what they should not have said, or did, what obscured and compro-

15. John Henry Newman, *On Consulting the Faithful in Matters of Doctrine,* ed. John Coulson (Glasgow: Collins, 1986).

mised revealed truth; while, on the other hand, it was the Christian people who, under Providence, were the ecclesiastical strength of Athanasius, Hilary, Eusebius of Vercellae, and other great solitary confessors, who would have failed without them.[16]

Even though Newman later explained that he wrote his essays from a historical point of view, which cannot be interpreted dogmatically, he recalls with certainty that the continuation of a life in truth is an issue for the whole church. If we take the sentence seriously, "That which separates the churches is negligible in comparison to those issues which bind the churches," we should — with regard to the major shifts within modern ecclesiology since Vatican II and with regard to the growing community between churches and denominations — relate the doctrine of infallibility of the Roman Catholic Church to that of the universal church of Jesus Christ, which subsists in the plurality of churches. An exclusive identification of the Roman Catholic Church with the infallible church is excluded by such an interpretation. Later discussion may show whether we will find an opportunity for a broader common understanding of ecclesiology between the confessions.

With the dogmatization of the infallibility of the pope, which according to Roman Catholic theology can take place within a very close framework of prerequisites, the Roman Catholic Church developed a separate doctrine, which neither existed before Vatican I, nor was present in the faith of that church. Thus no other Christian church accepted it, neither the Oriental nor the Occidental churches. Many Roman Catholic Christians do not believe in the infallibility of the pope even though they see him as a unifying symbol of Christianity, as Hermann J. Pottmeyer described it correctly. It is not necessary to explain within this paper the history and theology of Vatican I. The well-known works of Klaus Schatz and Hermann Pottmeyer and all of those who argued with or against Hans Küng, especially Heinrich Fries and Karl Rahner and many others, have already done this. I will concentrate on the question of whether there is an opportunity to mediate the doctrine of the infallibility of the papacy contextualized in the doctrine of the indefectible church of Christ within an ecumenical horizon, and on how this could work.

Let me start with some remarks on the theological issues of this dogma, on the problems of its inner Roman Catholic reception, and on its relation to the question of papal primacy as a question of jurisdiction. The

16. Newman, *On Consulting,* pp. 75-76.

traditional common Christian teaching of the *infallibilitas ecclesiae* was totally convinced of that also; when something new had to be formulated, the old belief of generations past would be defined in an appropriate contemporary manner. Different from this tradition, the doctrine of the *infallibilitas papae* was defined in a way that extended the traditional understanding and added new sentences to the traditional belief. Karl Rahner[17] discusses that critically and in addition he speaks about the logical peculiarities of the dogma of the infallibility of the pope: "It is a proposition which . . . renders the *other* dogmatic propositions infallibly sure. . . . The only proposition to which this does not apply is that concerning the infallibility of this doctrinal authority itself."[18] The infallibility of the pope cannot be based upon the infallibility of the pope. "And if we say that it invokes the infallibility of a council, or that of the Church, then we are merely shifting the problem a stage further back, for even this proposition can be arrived at only on the basis of other propositions which we already believe in. And our belief in these is not itself in turn based on the validity of the proposition of infallibility."[19] This dogma of the First Vatican Council is characterized by a strange logic: the not-infallible dogma of infallibility is guaranteeing new dogmatic propositions as infallibly true. In short: fallibility is able to create infallibly true propositions. Aphoristically Philipp Schaff[20] realized this logic when he said at the assembly of the World Parliament of Religions in Chicago 1893, that the pope should infallibly declare his fallibility. Rahner's summary:

> The dogma of infallibility is one individual proposition immanent within a system, and not the foundation of the system itself. The system of the Christian and Catholic truths of faith taken as a whole, and the subjective acceptance of it, are not based upon the statement of infallibility. On the contrary this is objectively and subjectively sustained by the system. From this basis its function is confined to that of a relatively secondary checking-point within the system applicable to secondary cases of conflict, and in this it depends upon the system itself as its prior

17. Karl Rahner, "On the Concept of Infallibility in Catholic Theology," in Karl Rahner, *Theological Investigations* (London: Darton, Longman & Todd, 1976), vol. 14, pp. 66-84.

18. Rahner, "On the Concept," vol. 14, p. 76.

19. Rahner, "On the Concept," vol. 14, p. 76.

20. Philip Schaff, "The Reunion of Christendom," in Walter R. Houghton, ed., *Neely's History of the Parliament of Religions and Religious Congresses at the World's Columbian Exposition* (Chicago, 1893), vol. 2, pp. 1192-1201, esp. p. 1196.

condition and does not itself call this in question in any direct sense. From this point of view it would be possible to say that this dogma is not itself infallible (i.e. not sustained by the infallible authority of the Church *quoad nos*), but merely renders other propositions infallible.[21]

The doctrine of infallibility within Roman Catholic theology can only be accepted because the greater majority of matters of faith and revealed truth had been accepted previously, i.e., without a logical relation to the above-mentioned dogma. This means that one has to be a Christian — a Roman Catholic Christian — before one can negotiate the truth of infallibility of the papacy. In fact, the doctrine of an infallible pope has more or less a secondary function. It contains a sentence that needs a fixed system. It does not stabilize or fix the system in its weak parts. Karl Rahner explains "system" as the essentials of Christian belief that are common to all Christians. Individuals did not existentially question this common doctrine. Thus it was discussed on the basis of logic whether there is a need for such an article for the Roman Catholic doctrine in total. This cannot be claimed today. The existential challenge to being a Christian in a secular world at the beginning of the third millennium is too great to waste time with questions of secondary importance. These facts impact the newer history of the doctrine of infallibility. The Roman see decided through Vatican I questions of faith without consulting Christians or related churches. The decision was later claimed as of universal importance. At this point we reach the limits of Vatican I. The doctrine of papal infallibility can be given up as a result of a major shift within Roman Catholic ecclesiology and a growing community of churches at the grassroots. Simultaneously the churches should invest time and effort to develop visions of how an authoritative teaching in the community of churches can be possible. If answers to these questions can be found — regardless of the details — rules for the interim could be left to the individual church bodies. The secondary function of the doctrine of infallibility might emerge in this process. But this is no longer the topic of my paper.

21. Rahner, "On the Concept," vol. 14, pp. 76-77.

Is Papal Infallibility Compatible with Ecclesial Indefectibility?

Peder Nørgaard-Højen

Allow me to start with two introductory remarks:

(1) Already more than thirty years ago at the occasion of the centenary of the definition of the dogma on infallibility of the First Vatican Council, Yves Congar wrote that the topic of *infallibilitas* had been treated from every possible perspective and had resulted in such a fullness of literature, that approximately everything that could be said about it had actually been said.[1] It may, therefore, appear as a rash enterprise, when someone looks at the topic from outside (and as a non-specialist must observe it from outside) and mixes up and interferes with the debate. Commitment and insight are here certainly not in equilibrium. What I may hope, however, is that my personal engagement might promote some insight into one of the most burning ecumenical issues of our time.

(2) The following reflections do not discuss the total scope of the Petrine ministry, nor do they even slightly touch on the increasingly debated (in my view, however, ecumenically premature) reflections on a Catholic reform and a possible Lutheran recognition of this ministry. In my estimation we are only at the beginning of a long, probably not easy dialogue about the

---

1. Yves Congar, "Infallibilität und Indefektibilität. Zum Begriff der Unfehlbarkeit," in Karl Rahner, ed., *Zum Problem Unfehlbarkeit. Antworten auf die Anfrage von Hans Küng* (Freiburg/Basel/Wien: Herder, ²1972), pp. 174ff. For obvious reasons I do not enumerate the vast literature referring to the issue of *infallibility, papal office,* and *Petrine ministry.* It is, however, a matter of course that by preparing this contribution I have profited immensely from the pertinent parts of this literature.

theological questions pertinent to the Petrine and papal office. I know of the remarkable contributions that have already been made to the elucidation of this complex problem. Nevertheless, I dare claim that the theological debates in this area have certainly been initiated, but have so far not gone beyond a mere beginning. My considerations, short as they must be, should be understood as a contribution to illuminate a theological issue significant for the definition of the Petrine office as well as for the critical verification of the question, whether the infallibility of the pope by necessity corresponds to the conviction of the indefectibility of the church that is shared by Catholics and Lutherans alike. In other words: whether the institution of an infallibly teaching office, especially of an infallible head of the church, is theologically compatible with a firm belief in an *ecclesia indefectibilis*. Although the question is not new, it deserves not least in an ecumenical context renewed interest — the more so, as exactly here in the eyes of non-Catholic churches and Christians the offensiveness of the papal office becomes luminously visible.

The socio-political, cultural, and theological development of our time shows increasingly — in fact across the confessions — the need of the churches to comment on burning and controversial issues of all sorts. Albeit not always uncontested, ecclesial statements are (to an extent recently unknown) welcomed as guidance for orientation in a world that has become more and more uncertain and hesitant in matters of faith and moral challenges. For that reason alone, the possibility of authoritative ecclesial decisions is vehemently and unmistakably, though throughout the different confessions dissimilarly, debated and contended. Confronted with the challenges of the time, the world is all the more longing for stimulation and instruction on the part of the churches, even as these — at least in some parts of Lutheranism — tend little towards or are even perhaps directly opposed to responding to this request.

The Theological Concern of the Doctrine of Infallibility

With this we have already objectively touched on the matter of infallibility, although *infallibility* in the strict sense of the term (which according to the decisions of the First Vatican Council is applied only to definitions of doctrine and moral principles) is not usually ascribed to church statements and comments on current issues. The yearning of many for the advice and the voice of the church and the resulting tendency to regard the church as a serious authority in all areas of life may remind us of the fact that the understanding of the church as the column and foundation of truth even in a secularized and non-churchly age has survived to a remarkable extent, and among believers has in no way fallen into oblivion. The conviction that the church has somehow been guaranteed a remaining in the truth and is fundamentally kept from error nourishes (in spite of every actual critical and distant reservation) a positive expectation, and places confidence in church statements that would otherwise be hardly transparent.

Anyway, with the claim of infallibility one pursues the theological concern that if ecclesial faultlessness and indeceptibility is divinely promised to the church, then she must also be given the possibility of concretizing that same indeceptibility and expressing it authoritatively. To this effect, other Christian confessions (including Lutheranism) also share the Roman concern: together with the Catholic Church, Christians of all denominations confront the challenges in dogmatics and ethics; and Lutheranism and Catholicism also share, as we shall see, the common conviction of the church's remaining in the truth. At present the controversial question is not whether and what authoritative teaching is necessary and indispensable, but only the way *in which* the church teaches authoritatively.

The conviction of the perennity of the church has in Roman-Vatican theology assumed a form that not without reason met with such vehement resistance that this issue developed into *the quaestio disputata* and over the years became a regular stumbling block not only, but above all, in relations between Rome and Wittenberg that were all the more strained and difficult to disentangle. This is not surprising news, and recent popes — notably John Paul II — have been painfully aware of this. Though determined to keep the Petrine ministry of unity and not to abandon the communion of all particular churches with the Roman church and the bishop of Rome as "an essential requisite of full and visible communion [sacramentally tangible in the common Eucharist],"[2] the pope appeals again and again distinctly and with reference to "the real but imperfect communion existing between us" to all responsible leaders in church and theology "to engage with me in a patient and fraternal dialogue on this subject, a dialogue in which, leaving useless controversies behind, we could listen to one another, keeping before us only the will of Christ for his Church."[3] The will to conversion, renewal, and reform (cf. *Ut unum sint* 15ff.) is doubtless strong on the Catholic as well as on

---

2. John Paul II, *Encyclical Letter* Ut unum sint *on Commitment to Ecumenism* (Vatican City: Libreria Vaticana, 1995), §97.

3. John Paul II, *Ut unum sint,* §96.

the Lutheran part and in the Roman Catholic Church even highly official. Whether this development will be constructive remains so far the subject of all hopes; only time will tell, however. Whether a consideration of the concept of ecclesial indefectibility over against the idea of papal infallibility could bear fruit in this situation is the topic of the following reflections.

The Church's Maintenance in the Truth

Against the Vatican doctrine, according to which the pope by virtue of the promise given to the apostle Peter possesses "that infallibility, with which the divine redeemer wanted to see his church endowed in cases of defining matters of faith and morals,"[4] even Catholic theologians have had serious misgivings. They have not rejected the theological concern pursued by Vatican I. Yet they have emphasized that this concern might possibly be better served if the ambiguous concept of *infallibilitas* were avoided and thus the risk of provoking connotatively fatal interpretations, and the notion of *indefectibilitas ecclesiae* — as already stated in the introduction — were reinforced, not least in the interest of a growing church rapprochement and an awareness of the considerable ecumenical detriments caused by Vatican I. Originally the two concepts were distinguished from one another, the *indefectibilitas ecclesiae* thereby marking the permanence of the apostolic church institution, and the *infallibilitas* indicating the application of this permanence to issues of doctrine and morals.

The indefectibility guarantees that the church remains identifiable with her apostolic origin in unbroken continuity and, thus, as a definitive institution of salvation. As column and foundation of truth she partakes in the Holy Spirit and is, therefore, undeceivable and enjoys faultlessness in matters of faith and morals.[5] If she should not in this sense be faultless, she would cease to be the church of Jesus Christ. By virtue of the merciful election of God, the church is holy and called to conversion and renewal, through which she remains holy; but conversely it is also true that thanks to the divine fidelity she can never fail to convert to an extent that she loses this grace and perish. The church will never fail so fatally or commit apostasy to

---

4. Heinrich Denzinger, *Enchiridion symbolorum, definitionum et declarationum de rebus fidei et morum,* ed. Peter Hünermann (Freiburg/Basel/Rome/Wien: Herder, [37]1991), n. 3074.

5. Congar, "Infallibilität und Indefektibilität," pp. 174ff.

such an extent that God abandons and leaves her in the lurch. The gates of hell will never prevail (Matt. 16:18; cf. Matt. 28:20 and Luke 22:32); on the contrary, the Spirit of truth will lead her into all truth (John 16:13; cf. John 14:16). We are here confronted with *faits accomplis* of faith: the church is characterized by (in the strict and definitive sense) a constancy, imperturbability, and firmness in the truth that cannot be seriously attacked and destroyed, although she may in dark times — as once the people of the Old Covenant — turn her back on God and betray, mock, and dishonor him and thus promote her own internal and external decline.[6] The church's remaining and being kept in the truth does not exclude concrete mistakes and errors, but implies on the other hand, however, that the church as a whole remains protected against loss of substance. This holds true because she is and remains also — and primarily — the church born and supported by the promises of Christ and not only an earthly institution built by humans and upheld by their responsibility.

Without many comments Lutheran theology too could share this interpretation of the *indefectibilitas ecclesiae* as a *being kept in the truth* that is, in the last analysis, based on God's promise. In another language, though indeed faithful to the universal church tradition, the Lutheran Reformers represent the conviction that "una sancta ecclesia perpetuo mansura sit"[7] and thus formulate their version of the ecclesial indefectibility. To this perspective all of Protestantism, including the Reformed and Anglican traditions, have adhered, and even a modern Reformed theologian emphasizes the infallibility of the church as necessary for belief in the Holy Spirit, although he admittedly applies infallibility to the Christian truth and finally to God himself.[8]

---

6. Yves Congar formulates it in the following way: "Indefektibilität meint Unzerstörbarkeit des Glaubens, auf dem und durch den die Kirche aufgebaut ist. Sie erlaubt ein zögerndes Sich-vorwärts-Lavieren, sogar eine Art Zickzack-Kurs, wie es uns die Geschichte zeigt. Sie gestattet Verdunklungen, partielles oder momentanes Vergessen, ja teilweise oder zeitweilige Irrtümer." Congar, "Infallibilität und Indefektibilität," p. 186.

7. *Confessio Augustana*, Art. 7.

8. "Il serait . . . contraire au Saint-Esprit et à la foi de dénier à la vérité évangélique le caractère d'infaillibilité. . . . Le concept d'infaillibilité est . . . , en substance, nécessaire en théologie, pour marquer l'une des connotations essentielles de la vérité évangélique, qui est d'être vraie non seulement au moment où elle est reconnue comme telle, mais pour tout l'avenir. Reconnaître que l'Evangile est vrai, c'est reconnaître *ipso facto* qu'il sera vrai. Si l'on ne reconnaît pas qu'il sera vrai, l'on n'a pas non plus reconnu qu'il est vrai. Le concept d'infaillibilité ne fait ainsi qu'exprimer l'aspect majeur de l'une des perfections de Dieu, qui est d'être fidèle, fidèle à lui-même et fidèle à ses promesses déjà

Infallibility as Securing and Stabilization of the *Sensus Fidelium*

In the light of these reflections the doctrine of Vatican II — according to which the body of the faithful as a whole, thanks to the *sensus fidei* bestowed on it by the Holy Spirit, cannot err in matters of belief — is hardly able to disturb the Catholic-Lutheran relationship.[9] There is probably also agreement on both sides that a *sensus fidelium* that manifests itself in adjusting church doctrine is only imaginable in a differentiated sense. That the factual belief is not without significance for the formulation of ecclesial doctrine may — though in detail it remains theologically difficult to rationalize — possibly be immediately convincing. But what is *in concreto* the general belief of the church that expresses itself in the *sensus fidelium,* over against the fact that the faith of the people of God often appears fragile and fragmentary and that the individual members from top to bottom including pope and bishops succumb to heavy errors and fail to apprehend or even betray the truth? The claim of infallibility is really so often directly and vehemently contradicted by the concrete statements and actions of the church that the conviction of an infallible *populus Dei* merely appears plausible, when this people is taken in its totality and in a long historical perspective.[10]

The *sensus fidelium* only becomes really controversial, however, if it is conceived not merely as actualization of the *indefectibilitas ecclesiae* but is instrumentally, concretely, and authoritatively defined and communicated in the *infallibilitas papae.* In other words: it becomes controversial when the faith in the imperturbability of the church results in a possibly canonically based (i.e., endowed with a questionable primacy of jurisdiction) practice of an infallible ministry or even an infallible individual. Lutheran theology raises objections where indefectibility is perverted into infallibility, where the

---

manifestées en Jésus-Christ." Jean-Louis Leuba, "L'infaillibilité, nécessité de la foi et problème de la raison," in Enrico Castelli, ed., *L'infaillibilité. Son aspect philosophique et théologique* (Paris: Montaigne, 1970), pp. 214-15. In this perspective the summary dismissal by H. Barion appears premature — to say the least: "Die Kirchen der Reformation lehnen die I[nfallibilität] in allen ihren Formen ab." RGG III (3. Aufl.), 749.

9. "Universitas fidelium, qui unctionem habent a Sancto . . . , in credendo falli nequit, atque hanc suam peculiarem proprietatem mediante supernaturali sensu fidei totius populi manifestat. . . ." *Lumen gentium* 12.

10. Yves Congar puts the case very clearly: "Der Gedanke der Unfehlbarkeit der Gesamtheit der Gläubigen ist nur haltbar, wenn man sie in ihrer Totalität und während einer ausreichenden Zeitdauer betrachtet." Congar, "Infallibilität und Indefektibilität," p. 180.

fragmentary and the approximative are absolutized, and where the historicity of the church and the truth is in this way rejected in favor of an ahistorical fixation and codification, where normativity is misunderstood statically instead of historical-dynamically. The church or rather the truth is infallible, not the pope — neither as authority nor (even less) as an individual.[11]

The concept *infallible* seems meaningfully applicable only to that truth, which people and human institutions — among them also the church that despite her divine origin and as a *realitas complexa* (cf. *Lumen gentium* 8) is not capable of escaping the historicity of all finality — must not only apprehend but also under specific circumstances formulate. The church is, however, only capable of doing so as an entity deeply and inescapably rooted in history and with a final eschatological reservation. The concept of *infallibilitas* runs an unnegligible risk of de-eschatologizing the truth, which remains historical and becomes only tangible and perceptible in history, and of wresting the truth-finding process from history and thus of depriving God, i.e., truth itself, of the final word.[12] The truth thus deprived of its nature, and its capacity for critical, constructive, and disquieting discernment is now perverted into ideology. The unhappy confusion of human and divine word seems unavoidable. One may, to be sure, assume that the vehement emphasis on papal infallibility was intended to underscore and serve the concern of ecclesial indefectibility. As things have actually developed, however, *infallibilitas papae* and *indefectibilitas ecclesiae* are not corresponding, correlative, or mutually exchangeable concepts, especially because the claim for jurisdictional primacy has ideologized the infallibility that has, thus, been exploited by a system totally immune to history, which disrespects the provisional and preliminary nature of the truth-finding process and, consequently, the fundamentally approximative and fragmentary character of truth.[13]

---

11. Cf. the remarks of the Apology of the Augsburg Confession (VII, 25): "Nec est ad pontifices transferendum, quod ad veram ecclesiam pertinet, quod videlicet sint columnae veritatis, quod non errent." *Die Bekenntnisschriften der evangelisch-lutherischen Kirche* (Göttingen: Vandenhoeck & Ruprecht, ³1956), p. 240.

12. Referring explicitly to the biblical concept of truth, Yves Congar clarifies: "So ist das Volk Gottes aufgerufen, nicht nur in der Wahrheit, sondern auf die Wahrheit hin zu leben. Und dazu hat es die Verheißung des aktiven Beistandes Christi und des Heiligen Geistes empfangen, welcher nicht umsonst der Geist der Wahrheit genannt wird." Congar, "Infallibilität und Indefektibilität," p. 184.

13. Lukas Vischer criticizes overtly the ahistorical and immovable character of the infallible papal office and the resulting weaknesses: "The claim [of infallibility] makes it

The concept of pontifical infallibility appears meaningful and helpful as expression of the belief in the *ecclesia semper mansura* only if it is interpreted in the sense of ecclesial indefectibility. In that case, however, it is a superfluous concept that serves a hopeless confusion rather than a helpful clarification of concepts and the pertinent theological matter. Historical development since Vatican I shows that the Catholic Church with the definition of papal infallibility gained a fatal ecumenical point of departure and deprived herself of the possibility of correcting the truth that will always remain merely fragmentary and approximative. This development has given rise to even more serious and alarming worries. What has occurred in the Catholic Church in the last forty years of reform and renewal — and this is in fact highly remarkable — happened, indeed, in spite of and often in open or implicit opposition to the Vatican dogma and as a consequence of a reactive revival of episcopalism and conciliarism. This indicates, in fact, what could be the true correlate of and alternative to ecclesial indefectibility.

Conciliarity as Implication of Indefectibility

The understanding of the church as *communio sanctorum* corresponds to the indefectibility and the *sensus fidelium*. The communion of believers in its totality has received the promise to be guided by the Spirit in its search for truth on its earthly pilgrimage. However, to avoid its degenerating into mere theory without any reference to everyday life, this promise must become efficient in the current and concrete life of the church and its members. To this effect the institution of papal infallibility is, as already mentioned, an attempt to comply with the necessity of a corresponding authority. We also saw, however,

---

almost impossible to admit that popes have at times defended errors and taken dubious decisions. The ministry is so to say placed under the obligation to have been right throughout the centuries. The claim of infallibility leads almost inevitably to the institutionalization of being in the truth or more precisely of 'always having been in the truth.' . . . Roman Catholic theologians spend an unproportionate amount of time for providing the evidence that the utterances of the magisterium were, at least in the context of their time, in harmony with the truth of the Gospel, and perhaps even more, that new insights gained by the Churches are not really new but correspond, at least implicitly, to the teaching of all times." Lukas Vischer, "The Ministry of Unity and the Common Witness of the Churches Today," in James F. Puglisi, ed., *Petrine Ministry and the Unity of the Church: "Toward a Patient and Fraternal Dialogue"* (Collegeville, MN: Liturgical Press, 1999), pp. 148-49.

that the Catholic Church has had an unlucky hand in establishing an infallible teaching ministry that has, moreover, turned out to be exceedingly tied to the person of the pope. *Infallibilitas* and *indefectibilitas* are, as stated above, not compatible concepts. Congar is right, when he traces the necessity of an ecclesial teaching authority back to the fact that the people of God, though in this aeon still subject to historical conditions, have already now entered into the eschatological age and are, therefore, dependent on a teaching ministry whose decisions must be assured of the guidance of the Holy Spirit and by their very nature be unerring and unfailing.[14] Though he does not overtly say so, Congar is obviously referring to the teaching ministry of the pope. The question is, however, whether one could perhaps think of an institution that would be better in accord with the concept of indefectibility.

On the face of it, the general council — in a Lutheran context and in accordance with Martin Luther himself — reflects an obvious implication of a *communio* ecclesiology and the corresponding indefectibility of the church. In the council, the church fundamentally endeavors to formulate the continually new confessing of her universal and ecumenical faith. The definition of the ecclesial confession (the turning of actual confessing into formal confession) is according to common and centuries-old practice, but also for fundamental theological reasons most naturally the task of an ecumenical council. The conciliarity corresponds to the nature of the church as *communio* (koinonia) and is thus able to form the context within which the search of the churches and Christians for truth and their attempt to give this truth concrete shape in word and action can best be promoted and facilitated. On the other hand, conciliar assemblies not being infallible, council decisions are not necessarily expressions of truth. They are, therefore, in need of a corrective authority, which, as it were, receives and by receiving guarantees the truth and, thus, the binding character of the conciliar decisions. This authority may be defined as the universal priesthood of all believers, who are authorized through baptism to exercise their priestly ministry and in the Spirit endowed with the *sensus fidelium.*

The question of who and what is the authority of ultimate appeal in cases of doubt or controversy and, thus, able to define what is valid as true

---

14. Yves Congar mentions a teaching office, "das den Beistand des Geistes hat, damit es seine Rolle im Organismus der Kirche spielen kann, und deren feierliche Feststellungen, die die Wahrheit der Bundesbeziehung betreffen, die Garantie des Nichtirren-Könnens oder Unfehlbarkeit genießen." Congar, "Infallibilität und Indefektibilität," p. 187.

confession in word and action, is as old as Christianity itself. However, the most persistent tradition in Christendom maintains the claim that the collective search for and formulation of the truth is most convincingly entrusted to councils, at which representatives of the churches meet in prayer and under the guidance of the Holy Spirit in order to discern what, in the given situation and under the prevailing, invariably new circumstances, might be interpreted as the will of God. Altogether, the council renders possible the process in which the church is apprehended as the community, in which God's way is recognized in common, and as a comprehensive, yet provisional and therefore fundamentally fragmentary ecclesial authority. No other ecclesial authority can plausibly contend for serious precedence with the general council as representative of the universal believing people of God.

The council *is* the church, and in this sense it has as a matter of course also the privilege of authoritatively formulating the confession of this church and its ethical implications. That the council and its decisions, on the other hand, are not in themselves and without any further dispute valid and conclusive, is another matter. Conciliar conclusions are only considered to express an ultimate authority, if and when they are received and accepted by the people of God represented by the council. As mentioned above, the faithful are anointed with the Holy Spirit (cf. 1 John 2:20-21, 27) and apprehend thus, as it were, infallibly — or rather: unmistakably, i.e., indefectibly — all the matters of faith. The *sensus fidelium* and the conciliarity are correlative concepts to the effect that a confession and/or doctrinal statement remains to be considered a merely private (possibly episcopal) opinion as long as it has not been confirmed and received by the *populus Dei*, to whom the guidance of the Holy Spirit in the truth-finding process is divinely promised.

The *Status Confessionis* as the Locus of Indefectible Decisions

The fronts between the churches and denominations run differently today than previously. The controversial theological issues that led to the disruption of Christendom and to the denominational divisions are partly overcome and have simply lost their separating power, as is also clear in the relationship between Catholicism and Lutheranism. Anyway, the traditional controversial issues increasingly seem to have lost their interest and the attention of the lay level of our churches. All the more intensively, churches and Christians turn their minds towards other contemporary burning issues, primarily those of social and political character, which present a challenge to the confession of faith to such a degree that they could possibly even today turn out to be church-dividing and, therefore, threaten to provoke the formation of new denominations. What this is all about are first and foremost questions of ethical decisions and structural problems of the church that currently mainly threaten to tear apart the body of Christ. Almost unsolvable difficulties have in recent years been part of the agenda, not only of political institutions but also of the churches (besides questions of human rights, also problems of the disastrous concentration of multinational power and economy, human exploitation [in whatever form], political power structures, urgent environmental challenges), and when attempting to overcome these serious problems the churches are, more often than not, confronted with violent clashes that leave deep cleavages that can be difficult to bridge.

When it comes to overcoming or even solving such problems, Lutheranism has traditionally shown a reluctant attitude, although here too signs of change are sometimes evident. In some especially trackless situations one has more and more realized that the confession must be repeated ever anew and therefore demands an explicit reformulation. What in our tradition has been called a *status,* that is, a *casus confessionis,* arises. Decisions necessary in such situations are in many ways comparable and equivalent to the infallible statements of the papal office of the Roman Catholic Church. Exceptional circumstances and an extraordinary situation may give rise to expectations to the proclamation and teaching authority of the church far beyond a mere repetition of the confession within the continuity of tradition, and may require an explicit consideration of the specific historic situation. A specific constellation of problems may develop, demanding a renewed reflection on the content of the confession and, accordingly, a reformulation of the confessional text. Such a revision, which in this sense has been shown necessary, by no means makes the traditional confession obsolete or even meaningless, but indicates that the transmitted text does not reflect the new situation and its difficulties, because it owes its historical shape to divergent conditions and different challenges. This does not, however, exclude the possibility that *implicitly and essentially* it may offer solutions to the challenges of faith that have been evoked in and by present circumstances. In case of acute emergency those in some measure hidden or not yet unfolded truths of faith must be uncovered, unveiled, activated, and *expressis verbis* reworded in a new, so far never seen, authoritative statement of faith that essentially and without doubt confirms the creedal identity of the church. Such an emergency is usually called a *status confessionis* (or maybe better a *casus confessionis*), which may be defined as an extraordinary (in terms of category and complexity) and previously not-experienced situation that calls for an exceptional decision and claims a new version of at least some of the traditional confessional statements, lest the credibility — or even the very existence — of the church as a community of faith and obedience should be endangered. The declaration of a *status confessionis* is one of the important means by which the church is maintained in the truth. "Maintenance in the truth requires that at certain moments the Church can in a matter of essential doctrine make a decisive judgment which becomes part of its permanent witness. Such a judgment makes it clear what the truth is, and strengthens the church's confidence in proclaiming the Gospel. Obvious examples of such judgments are occasions when general councils define the faith. These judgments, by virtue of their foundation in revelation and their appropriateness to the need of the time, express a renewed unity in the truth to which they summon the whole Church."[15]

The concept of *casus confessionis* — so ambiguous and evanescent as it may appear — seems after all to delineate that at its actual declaration the authoritative and binding character of an ecclesial testimony before the world is at stake — a testimony that is experienced as unavoidable and based on the indefectibility of the church. The concept refers to such phenomena that under normal circumstances play no overwhelming role in matters of confession and faith (the so-called adiaphora, for instance, problems of politics, economics, and morals). In political and comparable issues a person may normally adhere to one opinion or another without his or her status as a Christian being disputed. Situations may, however, develop in which political points of view are all but indifferent, because they negatively imply assumptions obviously in opposition to the Christian church and theology (for instance, the Nazi persecution of the Jews, peace and disarmament, refugees and foreigners, sexual and racial discrimination, ecological questions). On such occasions, issues normally classified as adiaphora turn into dogmatic *necessaria* that claim to be accepted lest the affiliation of the believer with the Christian community should be questioned and endangered.[16] The

---

15. ARCIC Agreed Statement on *Authority in the Church* II, 1982, par. 24.

16. The difficult relation between the *casus confessionis* and the concept of sin remains unclear in Lutheran theology. As much as any premature classification of all moral violations as sin (as was especially in the Lutheran tradition often the case) renders ethics ecclesiologically and dogmatically harmless, just as much must the level of doctrine (and

church is certainly always called to testify to her faith in word and action, but now and again, i.e., when the confession to Christ is actively contradicted in words and/or actions and the Christian confession is, therefore, disfigured and perverted, a specific confessing is demanded. From such phenomena normally categorized as insignificant (or rather: from the attitude of the faithful towards such phenomena) flow new sources of confession. The adiaphora create renewed possibilities and hitherto unseen necessities of re-formulating the confession and redefining the obedience; they become confessiogene, "pregnant" with confession.

It is hardly possible to establish criteria by means of which a *casus confessionis* can be unequivocally defined and declared. On the other hand, the awareness of the urgent, inescapable, and confessiogene problems will certainly continue and urge an authoritative and binding decision. Because of the inevitable ambivalence of the respective context, a *casus confessionis* can indeed never be unambiguously determined, but all the more be prophetically proclaimed. This prophetic testimony demands unanimity on the part of the whole community with regard to the imperative obedience of faith, although the church cannot await a full consensus among all its members. Important as such consensus may be and in fact is, it can never be the fundamental basis of its unity, which is founded solely on the faithfulness of God in the Holy Spirit. Where the people of God are guided by the Spirit, they have in fact obtained the necessary consensus.[17]

Where the appeal to authoritatively binding unanimity is heard, there also a call for discernment of spirits is obvious. The aim is by no means to excommunicate those who do not accept a definitive and final ecclesial decision, but to appeal to and convince them that such an act is conclusive — and because of the guidance of the Holy Spirit, is infallible.[18] It is assumed

---

— when violated — of heresy) as the basis of ethics be distinguished from that of simple violation and sin. Here we mean sin as the obstinate perseverance in an erroneous doctrine, which may possibly be manifest in ethical decisions, that is, lack of decisions results in heresy and the declaration of the *casus confessionis*. Where this is not emphasized the relationship between law and gospel threatens to break asunder.

17. ". . . die Kirche wird niemals warten können, bis ein vollständiger consensus unter all denen erreicht ist, die sich zu ihr zählen. Denn die Einheit der Kirche ruht nicht auf unserm consensus, sondern darauf, daß der lebendige Herr seiner Kirche die Treue hält und wir ihm angehören: wo wir seiner Stimme folgen, sind wir auch im Zeugnis eins." "Theologisches Gutachten zur Frage der atomaren Bewaffnung," *Zeitschrift für die Evangelische Ethik* 3 (1959): 242.

18. "Wo sich innerhalb der Kirche einzelne Glieder dem jeweils notwendigen kon-

that whoever commits himself belongs to the church, while others who, for example, do not really realize the confessional relevance of apartheid questions, are living outside the community. Although the declaration of the *casus confessionis* does not intend a church division, it can certainly unmask an already virulent schism and expose it as compromising to ecclesial unity. The authentic confession to Christ can in no way endanger the unity of the church, but on the contrary consolidates and strengthens this unity. The truth does, indeed, not break the unity of the church of Christ, but draws a necessary borderline between light and darkness, between God and his opponent, between inconvincible impenitence and faithful obedience. Yet, how unanimity is reached about a given *casus confessionis,* declared by the universal *communio sanctorum,* remains in Lutheran ecclesiology controversial. However, the forum in which the struggle for finding and formulating the truth primarily resides remains in principle the conciliar assembly as a correlate to the ecclesial indefectibility and as an instrument of the *sensus fidei,* as it has been the prevailing procedure since the first beginnings of the Christian community.

Concluding Theses

Let me conclude by adding a few remarks in terms of summarizing theses:

(1) Christ has promised to be with his church always until the end of the world (Matt. 28:20), and he has promised that his Spirit shall guide it into all truth (John 16:13). Thus it is the common conviction of both Catholics and Lutherans that the church as a totality of believers *(communio sanctorum)* shall be held in and never fall out of the truth *(sensus fidelium).* It may fall victim to all kinds of errors and defeats and even betray its Lord and Savior, but it will never cease to be the church. This fact of faith is expressed in the traditional concept of *indefectibilitas,* that is, *perennitas ecclesiae,* and in the Lutheran context in the notion of *ecclesia mansura.*

---

kreten Zeugnis entziehen, kommt es an ihm um seiner unausweichlichen Verbindlichkeit willen zur Scheidung der Geister. Diese jeden einzelnen zur letzten Entscheidung rufende Verbindlichkeit, und nicht eine Exkommunikation derer, die diese Entscheidung gar nicht oder noch nicht einzusehen vermögen, *das* ist der Sinn des Begriffes 'status confessionis.' . . ." *Zeitschrift für die Evangelische Ethik* 3 (1959): 242.

(2) From this indefectibility results the obligation of the church to actually define what it means *in concreto* to be held in the truth. The Roman Catholic Church responds to that challenge through the infallible
teaching ministry, the Lutherans on the other hand by means of declaring a *status confessionis.* Thus both confessions, though differently,
teach authoritatively and testify to their Christian faith over against
the world *(munus propheticum ecclesiae).*

(3) The theological concern of the doctrine of papal infallibility — parallel to the institution of *status confessionis* — is to underline the necessity of having an authority able to authentically formulate ultimate
binding definitions of truth. Among Lutherans and Catholics it is not
controversial that authoritative teaching is necessary, but the way in
which this is actually done is highly disputed.

(4) Whereas Catholicism ties the *sensus fidelium* so vehemently to papal
infallibility that the prophetic office is at risk of becoming a voice immanent to the ecclesial system, the Lutheran churches are in danger of
individualizing the *sensus fidelium,* with the result of rendering authoritative teaching impossible. Whereas Catholicism exercises authority too vigorously and rigidly, thus ideologically censuring and si-
lencing the voice of the people of God, Lutheranism recedes from
energetically exercising any kind of authority and leaves so much
room to the individual that definitive decisions are made impossible.
Both extremes should be avoided.

(5) Papal infallibility appears to be theologically meaningful and possibly
ecumenically acceptable only when interpreted in the hermeneutic
context of ecclesial indefectibility and thus applied to the church.
However, *indefectibilitas ecclesiae* and *infallibilitas papae* are not immediately compatible concepts.

(6) From the indefectibility of the church results the universal council as
the forum in which the truth-finding process first and foremost takes
place, and in which the church ever anew identifies herself as the
communio sancta et apostolica, remaining in the truth and living towards the truth. As implication of the indefectibility, the council is
open and attentive to the motions of the Spirit and remains, therefore,
faithful to the truth that has been developed by history and is always
developing in history, thereby continually remaining the same and
identical with itself.

(7) This points to another way of finding and defining the truth than that
of infallible papal decisions, which shows more coherence with the

common faith in the indefectibility of the church and takes the *sensus fidelium* and the historicity of truth seriously. Ultimate definitions of truth are taken in and by the general council, but certainly not without the pope. He would, however, according to centuries-old traditions have lost the possibility of defining such ultimately binding doctrines without the council.

I am painfully aware of the fact that such a rethinking is at present hardly possible — primarily because it presupposes the establishing of a *concilium vere oecumenicum.* And such a consideration is definitely not an issue of consensus. On the other side, I remain convinced that we never really make progress in our endeavors for unity unless we join our efforts and summon such a free Christian council in common.[19] The credibility of the churches is at risk. If we recognize each other as churches — and I assume we do! — such a step should, as untraditional and unusual as it might appear, not be impossible. Love urges us; conversion renders it possible. I believe, by the way, that already Martin Luther once expressed a similar wish.

19. Promising attempts could already be observed (the pan-European ecumenical assemblies in Basel and Graz as well as, recently, ecumenical synods) that were determined to testify in common to the Christian truth before the world and thus certainly also to contribute to the recovery of doctrinal unity.

ECUMENICS

Introductory Considerations in the Ecumenical Dialogue on the Petrine Ministry from a Catholic Viewpoint

Walter Cardinal Kasper

I

The ecumenical movement has made great progress in the last century or so, for which God be thanked. But there are still issues that need to be resolved between our churches, of which the thorniest is the question of the claim to primacy by the bishop of Rome. It is one of the most difficult issues ecumenically, but also one of the most important for ecumenism. Both Pope Paul VI and after him Pope John Paul II clearly recognized, and openly stated in words, that for non-Catholic Christians the papacy is the greatest hindrance on the road to unity.

In speaking of the pope we are not confined to a few theoretical theological and canonical problems. Just as, for Catholics, saying yes to the pope is a mark of their identity as Catholics, so also, for many non-Catholics today, rejection of the papacy is still part of their identity as Orthodox or Protestant Christians. Thus the issue of the papacy, whether pro or con, arouses emotional reactions.

In the last century or more certainly something has changed. The churches are still a long way from a consensus on this. But in many places the atmosphere and the climate in which the issue is discussed have been transformed. The insight that, especially in today's world of globalization, there should be something like a "Ministry of Unity" in the church is growing in the ecumenical community. In various ecumenical dialogues the question of a visible center for unity is being explicitly formulated. But the role of the primacy, in its present concrete form, does not appear to be acceptable to all the other churches.

Pope John Paul II sought to resolve this tension, in his 1995 encyclical *Ut unum sint,* by taking what was, for a pope, a revolutionary step.[1] He said he was aware that "the Catholic Church's conviction that in the ministry of the Bishop of Rome she has preserved . . . the visible sign and guarantor of unity" represented "a difficulty for most other Christians, whose memory is marked by certain painful recollections." He did not hesitate to say, "To the extent that we are responsible for these, I join my Predecessor Paul VI in asking forgiveness."[2]

Since the pope was aware of having "a particular responsibility" for the unity of Christians, he declared himself open to the request to "find a way of exercising the primacy which, while in no way renouncing what is essential to its mission, is nonetheless open to a new situation." He expressed the prayer to "the Holy Spirit to shine his light upon us, enlightening all the pastors and theologians of our Churches, that we may seek — together, of course — the forms in which this ministry may accomplish a service of love recognized by all concerned."[3] Finally, he invited other Christian leaders to join with him in "a patient and fraternal dialogue on this subject."[4] He subsequently repeated this invitation and request several times, adding that "We have no time to lose."

What is this dialogue about? Undoubtedly the pope does not intend to present his partners with dogmas about the primacy and infallibility of the pope. His intention is rather, without giving up what is essential, to look for new forms for the exercise of primacy. The encyclical thus distinguishes between the essence that remains valid and the changing forms. But even making such a distinction is a problem. It raises the question, what is this essence of the Petrine ministry, and what are its forms that can change? Thus we are not speaking only of external, practical questions, but also of a very fundamental theological problem.

---

1. This step had been prepared for by various previous statements by Pope Paul VI, as well as Pope John Paul II himself. See John A. Radano, "*Ut unum sint:* The Ministry of Unity of the Bishop of Rome," *Angelicum* 73 (1996): 327-29.

2. *Ut unum sint,* 88.

3. *Ut unum sint,* 95.

4. *Ut unum sint,* 96.

II

When we consider this question, our reflections do not have to start from zero. Even before the pope's invitation to a dialogue on it, there was discussion on the Petrine ministry. I am thinking not only of centuries-old controversies, but also of the more recent ecumenical conversations before, during, and immediately after the Second Vatican Council. Since the encyclical appeared, this discussion has swelled from a brook to a mighty river. There have been official responses from churches, and there have been theological articles aplenty in books and journals, at conferences and symposia. Even in the various dialogues that we are conducting with other churches and ecclesial communities the question has been taken up. Finally, soon after the encyclical appeared, the Congregation for the Doctrine of the Faith and the Pontifical Council for Promoting Christian Unity held several symposia and published the results.

Since then, the Pontifical Council for Promoting Christian Unity (PCPCU), with help from the Johann Adam Möhler Institute in Paderborn, has collected all these contributions and made its own analysis, which it presented to the PCPCU Plenarium of 12-17 November 2001 for discussion.[5] This report marks the end of a first phase of the discussion and the beginning of a second, more thoroughgoing one. In concluding the first phase, the aim was to analyze and state the problems precisely; in the second phase, which is now beginning, the aim will be — if possible — to proceed, step by step, towards a solution. As far as human judgment can tell, it will not be an easy road.

III

The following reflections are not intended to propose possible concrete solutions. I shall be concerned with something more fundamental, that is, the question of whether it is a promising undertaking even to discuss this issue and expect to find solutions. Many doubt that it is. They say that at the First and Second Vatican Councils the Catholic Church committed itself to certain dogmas, and that the primacy (of the pope) is a constitutive element of the church. The other churches in turn have committed themselves *de facto* to opposing Rome's claim to primacy. So what scope is there for movement, when neither the one side nor the other is willing to give up its identity?

---

5. *Information Service* n. 109 (2002/I-II): 29-42 (with a fairly complete bibliographical overview).

I can answer only for the Catholic viewpoint. The Catholic Church can and will not give up the dogmas of the First Vatican Council. It regards the Petrine ministry as having been founded by Jesus Christ and as the Lord's gift to his church. The way forward ecumenically is through a rereading of the doctrine of primacy from the First Vatican Council. Rereading, of course, does not mean some trick of interpretation. Instead, the aim is to interpret the doctrine from the First Vatican Council on the primacy and infallibility of the pope according to the "normal" rules that are generally regarded as valid for hermeneutics of dogma. According to these rules, the dogmas are to be kept in mind in which the church has previously stated its position.[6] But in the Catholic mind this does not mean an irrational, fundamentalist clinging to a formula; instead, especially since the First Vatican Council, faith and understanding are supposed to go together. Catholic doctrine countenances progress in recognizing and understanding the truth which has been handed down once and for all.[7] There is a history of dogma in the sense of a history of understanding and interpretation, and for this there are theological rules for understanding.[8]

It is in this sense that Joseph Ratzinger (now Pope Benedict XVI) spoke of the necessity of rereading,[9] and Yves Congar and others spoke of a re-reception, of the First Vatican Council.[10] Such a re-reception does not question the validity of a council's definitions; but reception does not mean mechanically adopting a text either, but rather a lively and creative process of appropriating it into the faith — and the understanding of faith — of the church.[11]

---

6. "*Hinc sacrorum quoque dogmatum, is sensus perpetuo est retinendus, quem semel declaravit sancta mater Ecclesia, nec umquam ab eo sensu alterioris intelligentiae specie et nomine recedendum est.*" [Hence also that meaning of sacred dogmas is perpetually to be retained which our Holy Mother Church has once declared, and there must never be a deviation from that meaning on the specious ground and title of a more profound understanding.] Heinrich Denzinger, *Enchiridion symbolorum definitionum et declarationum de rebus fidei et morum*, re-edited by Peter Hünermann, 37th edition (Freiburg: Herder, 1991), 3020; hereafter cited as DH; English translation is taken from Joseph Neuner and Jacques Dupuis, eds., *The Christian Faith in the Doctrinal Documents of the Catholic Church*, 3rd ed. (Bangalore: Theological Publications in India, 1978). Cf. DH 3043.

7. DH 3020; DV [*Dei verbum*, Vatican II] 8.

8. Cf. Walter Kasper, *The Methods of Dogmatic Theology* (Glen Rock, NJ: Paulist Press, 1969).

9. Joseph Ratzinger, *Das neue Volk Gottes* (Düsseldorf: Patmos, 1969), p. 140.

10. Yves Congar, *Diversity and Communion* (London: SCM, 1984).

11. On the concept of reception, cf. Yves Congar, "La réception comme réalité

1. A first rule for such a re-reception and rereading is the integration of a dogma, in this case the primacy (of the pope), into the overall doctrine of ecclesiology. This rule was formulated by Vatican I itself. It says that the mysteries of the faith are *"e mysterium ipsorum nexu inter se,"* that is, to be understood on the basis of their inner coherence with one another.[12] Vatican II expressed the same thing with the help of the doctrine of the hierarchy of truths.[13] Thus no dogma may be viewed in isolation from the whole doctrine of the faith, but must be interpreted within and on the basis of the entire doctrine.

Such an integration of the primacy (of the pope) was already the intention of Vatican I. In the preamble to the constitution *Pastor aeternus,* the Council described the meaning of the primacy. It says that, according to God's will for the church, all the faithful should be held together through the bond of faith and of love; it then cites the classical text for today's ecumenical effort, *"ut omnes unum essent"* (John 17:21). The Council text then continues, in the words of Bishop Cyprian: *"Ut episcopatus ipse unus et indivisus esset,"* the Apostle Peter was appointed as *"perpetuum utriusque unitatis principium ac visibile fundamentum."*[14] This statement was emphasized,[15] in a book published just recently by the Congregation for the Doctrine of the Faith, as fundamentally significant for a *theological* interpretation of the *legal* formulations of the doctrine of primacy. Primacy is therefore about the unity of the church.

It is true that Vatican I, due to the outbreak of war between Germany and France, was unable to carry out its intention to show the place of pri-

---

ecclésiologique," *RSPhTh* 56 (1972): 369-403; Alois Grillmeier, "Konzil und Rezeption," in *Mit ihm und in ihm: Christologische Forschungen und Perspektiven* (Freiburg: Herder, 1975), pp. 309-34; Wolfgang Beinert, "Die Rezeption und ihre Bedeutung in Leben und Lehre," in Wolfgang Pannenberg and Theodor Schneider, eds., *Verbindliches Zeugnis,* vol. 2: *Schriftauslegung — Lehramt — Rezeption* (Freiburg/Göttingen: Herder/Vandenhoeck & Ruprecht, 1995), pp. 193-218; Gilles Routhier, *La réception d'un concile* (Paris: Cerf, 1993).

12. DH 3016.

13. UR [*Unitatis redintegratio,* Vatican II] ["When comparing doctrines with one another, they should remember that in Catholic doctrine there exists a 'hierarchy' of truths, since they vary in their relation to the fundamental Christian faith."]

14. DH 3050-51. ["In order that the episcopate itself might be one and undivided . . . [H]e placed St. Peter at the head of the other apostles, and established in him a perpetual principle and visible foundation of this twofold unity. . . ."]

15. Pedro Rodríguez, "Natura e fini del primato del Papa: Il Vaticano I alla luce del Vaticano II," in Congregazione per la Dottrina della Fede, *Il primato del successore di Pietro nel ministero della Chiesa* (Vatican City: Libreria Editrice Vaticana, 2002), pp. 81-111.

macy in the ecclesiology of the church overall. The doctrine remained incomplete, since it only went as far as defining the primacy and the infallibility of the pope. The result was a false orientation.

Vatican II took up the unfinished work of Vatican I and tried to integrate primacy into the entire doctrine of the church and into the entire doctrine of the collegiality of bishops. Moreover, this last Council made clear the significance of the local church, the sacramental understanding of the office of bishop, and above all the understanding of the church as *communio*. This led to a revival of synodal elements in the church, especially synods and bishops' conferences.

However, the Second Vatican Council did not succeed in every way in communicating what is new, although it is in truth the older tradition, in the statements of the First Vatican Council. Many things were left standing side by side but remained relatively unconnected. Here and there people spoke rather too pointedly of finding two ecclesiologies expressed in the Council text. This led, after the Council was over, to a quarrel that is still ongoing over the interpretation of the relation between primacy and episcopate, the universal church and the local church. The process of integration and reception is by no means concluded. To this extent, Vatican II also was a Council that did not complete its task.

2. The second principle for the hermeneutics of dogma is that which directs us to reread the First Vatican Council on the basis of the entire tradition, and to integrate it into the entire tradition. This procedure as well is recommended to us by the texts of Vatican I themselves. In its preface to the dogmatic constitution *Pastor aeternus*, the Council declared its intention to portray the doctrine of primacy *"secundum antiquam atque constantem universalis Ecclesiae fidem"* and to defend it against opposing errors.[16] Statements by earlier popes and by earlier councils are expressly included.[17] The Council even refers to the consensus between the Eastern and Western churches.[18]

By noting these aspects, we have brought out an important point, which is valid for all councils. The church is the same, throughout all the centuries and all the councils; therefore every council must make its interpretations in the context of the entire tradition. The Holy Spirit, which

16. DH 3052 [". . . according to the ancient and constant belief of the universal church . . ."].

17. DH 3059.

18. DH 3065.

guides the church, cannot, of course, contradict himself. Something that was right in the first millennium cannot be false in the second millennium. Therefore the older tradition is not to be seen only as an earlier stage in something that has since developed further, but the reverse is also true: The later development, concretely the First Vatican Council, must be interpreted on the basis of the older and longer overall tradition. The *communio* ecclesiology of the first millennium, brought out and recognized anew by Vatican II, therefore sets the hermeneutical framework for Vatican I.

The significance of the first millennium in setting standards of interpretation has in the meantime, especially since Joseph Ratzinger's lecture in Graz, been widely recognized in Catholic theology.[19] Of course it depends on this hermeneutical framework being properly understood. It is clear that we cannot simply go back to the first millennium, and thus the ecumenical movement is not a movement backward.[20] Even in the first millennium there were differing concepts; to that extent the first millennium does not simply hand us a recipe. On the other hand, in the second millennium there were developments on every side.[21] Today, on the threshold of the third millennium, we cannot turn back the wheel of history. But we can interpret the differing developments of the second millennium in the light of the first millennium which were common to all the churches, and thus open up these developments for one another, so that they will leave the way clear for fellowship among the churches in the third millennium. The Second Vatican Council has already begun to do this, by interpreting Vatican I within the wider context of *communio* ecclesiology.

19. Joseph Ratzinger, *Principles of Catholic Theology: Building Stones for a Fundamental Theology* (San Francisco: Ignatius Press, 1987), esp. p. 199: ". . . Rome must not require more from the East with respect to the doctrine of primacy than had been formulated and was lived in the first millennium." (First published as "Schisme anathématique. Les conséquences ecclésiologiques de la levée des anathèmes," *Istina* 20 [1975]: 87-111; similarly Louis Bouyer, "Réflexions sur le rétablissement possible de la communion entre les Églises orthodoxe et catholique. Perspectives actuelles," *Istina* 20 [1975]: 112-15.) Cf. also Michele Maccarrone, ed., *Il primato del vescovo di Roma nel primo millennio* (Vatican City: Libreria Editrice Vaticana, 1991).

20. Joseph Ratzinger, *Church, Ecumenism and Politics: New Essays in Ecclesiology* (Slough, UK: St. Paul, 1988), pp. 76-77, 81-82.

21. On the Orthodox side this is true especially since the end of the Roman and Byzantine empires and the rise of autocephalous national churches and patriarchates, and the fact that the majority of Orthodox Christians today live in the diaspora in the West (especially in the USA, Canada, and Australia).

Such a re-reception does not mean a mechanical adoption, but rather a lively and creative process of appropriating the older tradition of the church, especially that of the Eastern church. In the process, the tradition of the Eastern church would be enriched; it would experience greater unity and greater freedom from dependence on national traditions. But the Latin tradition too would be freed from ways in which it has become narrower during the second millennium. The church as a whole would be able, as Pope John Paul II said several times, to breathe with both lungs.

While the mutual reception of East and West is frequently discussed, I have the impression that until now there has been less reflection on the extent to which concerns of churches of the Protestant tradition can be constructively brought in. This also includes the question on the other side, of whether and to what extent the Protestant churches are open to receive the Catholic tradition.

3. At this point a further hermeneutical principle comes in: historical reinterpretation. As with all dogmas, with Vatican I a distinction has to be made between the content, which remains binding, and the form, which is historically determined.[22] Thus it would be a misunderstanding to regard the formulations of Vatican I as the only possible way of expressing the substantive meaning of the Petrine ministry and what remains binding therein.

The church fathers of Vatican I were subject to very particular historical conditions, which caused them to use the formulations as we have them.[23] The majority of the Council saw the church as encircled on all sides and in a well-nigh apocalyptic situation. The Council wanted to make sure that the church would remain capable of action even in extreme situations. So the response was to fall back to the modern concept of sovereignty and to define primacy in the sense of an absolute sovereignty.[24] Thus their statements on the primacy (of the pope) were conceived for exceptional and emergency situations.

Yet the understanding of primacy in the sense of sovereignty, even as Vatican I has it, does not mean that the pope has unlimited authority. By nature his authority is limited in various ways: through revelation and the

---

22. GS [*Gaudium et spes*, Vatican II] 62: "for the deposit of Faith or the truths are one thing and the manner in which they are enunciated, in the same meaning and understanding, is another."

23. Hermann J. Pottmeyer, *Towards a Papacy in Communion* (New York: Crossroad, 1998).

24. Pottmeyer, *Towards a Papacy*, pp. 51-52.

binding tradition, through the structure of the sacraments and episcopal constitution of the church, as well as by God-given human rights. The pope is bound by all these things. So Vatican I wrote that the primacy (of the pope) does not abolish the proper and immediate authority of a bishop, but rather affirms, strengthens, and defends it.[25] Pope Pius IX explicitly confirmed this when he affirmed the declaration of the German bishops against Bismarck's circular letters.[26] Finally, Vatican II recognized this in reference to the Eastern churches, that they have the right to govern themselves according to their own ecclesiastical law.[27] Thus the pope wants to honor the Eastern churches' synodal and patriarchal structures, and limit himself, as was customary in the first millennium in the case of important decisions, to the right to ratify them. This is also largely the intention in the new ecclesiastical law for the Eastern churches that are united with Rome.

Thus the problem is not the dogma as such, but its maximizing interpretation by its Ultramontane advocates as well as its critics.[28] In this way something that was intended for use under exceptional conditions has become the normal condition. So we must agree with Joseph Ratzinger's observation that

> the centralistic picture which the Catholic Church presented until the Council does not derive entirely from the Petrine ministry. The unified ecclesiastical law, unified liturgy and unified process of appointing bishops from the central see in Rome — these are all things which are not necessarily prescribed by the primacy [of the pope] as such.[29]

If one separates the statements about the primacy of jurisdiction from the historically determined form in which they are expressed, then their content, which remains binding, is that the pope is free to act in accordance with the changing needs of the church, and with those needs as they are at any particular time. Therefore the (papal) primacy must be interpreted and applied

---

25. DH 3061.

26. DH 3112-17.

27. UR 16.

28. Pottmeyer, *Towards a Papacy,* pp. 76-77. The tendency of critics to consider the maximalist interpretation to be the only possible one, and to base their criticism thereon, is also true of Hans Küng's critique of the dogma of [papal] infallibility in Vatican I, which cannot be discussed in this context.

29. Ratzinger, *Das neue Volk Gottes,* p. 142.

in accordance with the needs of the church at the time.[30] Pope John Paul II is speaking in this sense in *Ut unum sint* about finding ways of exercising his primacy in accordance with the changed ecumenical situation of today.

We can go one step further and say, in the sense of the preamble to Vatican I, which was in large part taken over word for word by Vatican II, that the *theological* meaning of the *legal* formulations of Vatican I is that the Petrine ministry is to be understood as *episkopē* (oversight).[31] Pope John Paul II took up this interpretation in *Ut unum sint*. It constitutes an important approach in understanding, which transposes legal formulations into a biblical and theological context.

4. A fourth and final hermeneutical principle consists in interpreting the *Petrine ministry in accordance with the gospel*. This challenge is posed particularly in dialogue with Lutherans. The Catholic side also is fundamentally in agreement with it.[32] The church can only claim validity for that which is not just a statute made by human beings, but is also founded on the gospel. This is what is indicated by the difficult concept *ius divinum*.[33]

---

30. "Il Primato del successore di Pietro nel ministero della Chiesa," in Congregazione Dottrina della Fede, *Il primato del successore di Pietro. Atti del simposio teologico, Roma, dicembre 1996* (Vatican City: Libreria Editrice Vaticana, 1998), pp. 501-2; cf. in the same volume the articles by Walter Brandmüller, "Natur und Zielsetzung primatialer Interventionen im zweiten Jahrtausend," esp. pp. 377-78. Cf. also comments by Donato Valentini, in *Il primato*, pp. 381-82.

31. See Pedro Rodríguez, "Natura e fini del primato"; Philippe Goyert, "Primato ed episcopato," in Congregazione per la Dottrina della Fede, *Il primato del successore di Pietro nel mistero della chiesa*, pp. 133-34.

32. DV 21 [Vatican II] describes the Sacred Scriptures as "the supreme rule" for the faith of the church. ". . . like the Christian religion itself, all the preaching of the Church must be nourished and regulated by Sacred Scripture." Vatican II emphasizes also that Scripture, tradition, and church belong together: see DV 7-10.

33. A one-sided, positivist understanding requiring an explicit, historically obtainable saying of Jesus as its basis is no longer needed today. It is generally understood today that the *ius divinum* is conveyed historically and concretely through *ius ecclesiasticum* and *ius humanum*. It contains that which, on the basis of the Holy Scriptures, through the history of the church under the guidance of the Holy Spirit, has become valid for the church. Cf. Karl Rahner, "Reflection on the Concept of '*Ius divinum*' in Catholic Thought," in *Theological Investigations*, vol. 5: *Later Writings* (Baltimore/London: Helicon Press/ Darton, Longman & Todd, 1965), pp. 229-43; the articles by Arthur C. Piepkorn and George A. Lindbeck in Paul C. Empie and T. Austin Murphy, eds., *Papal Primacy and the Universal Church* (Minneapolis: Augsburg, 1974), and by Avery Dulles in *A Church to Believe In* (New York: Crossroads, 1982), pp. 80-102; J. Freitag, "*Ius divinum — ius humanum*," *LthK* 5 (1966): 697-98.

In the original meaning of the word the gospel is not a book, but rather that which is proclaimed and believed in the church. That means that though historical exegesis has its permanent place, the Scriptures must not be separated from the tradition. For the issue we are discussing here, this problem of Scripture and tradition is especially important, as the task of a spiritual and theological hermeneutics.[34]

Such a spiritual and theological interpretation begins, without doubt, with the well-known passages where Peter appears (especially Matt. 16:18-19; Luke 22:32; John 21:15-17), and then the whole Petrine tradition of the New Testament; thus we can pose the question of how the primacy is to be substantiated, in the light of the tradition, on the basis of the biblical witness to the position of prime importance given to the apostle Peter. Beyond this formal basis for the Petrine ministry, there is the understanding of it according to the gospel and the exercise of it according to the gospel, that is, an understanding and an exercise of ministry, not as one who rules but rather as one who serves. The gospel says, "whoever wishes to be first among you must be your slave" (Matt. 20:27 [NRSV]). This aspect was given classic expression in the title, which goes back to Pope Gregory, of the *"servus servorum."*[35]

Pope John Paul II brought out this aspect in a new way. He referred to the martyr bishop Ignatius of Antioch, who described the primate of Rome as "presiding in love."[36] Thus the pope himself gave an important indication of a new interpretation according to the gospel. His interpretation of primacy was no longer legalistic, based on the idea of sovereignty, but rather spiritual, a ministry of service, one that serves the cause of unity and also serves, and is a sign of, compassion and love.[37]

This return to biblical thinking has brought us to speaking less today about the office of pope and the papacy and much more about the Petrine

---

34. See article by Walter Kasper, "Dienst an der Einheit und Freiheit der Kirche," in Joseph Ratzinger, ed., *Dienst an der Einheit* (Düsseldorf: Patmos, 1978), pp. 82-88.

35. Quoted from DH 3061.

36. Ignatius of Antioch, *To the Romans*, Prolegomenon.

37. *Ut unum sint*, 88-93. This spiritual understanding is often characterized as pastoral primacy. This is justified to the extent that all ministries of service in the church are to be oriented towards the salvation of souls as the highest rule (CIC can. 1752). Certainly there is a problem with this understanding if pastoral primacy is set over against the primacy of jurisdiction. A serving office that does not also hold authority is of little use in precisely those situations in which it is most needed. Therefore the intention is not to do away with the aspect of jurisdiction, but rather to integrate it into, and interpret it within, the overall context of Scripture, tradition, and the church.

ministry and Petrine service. This change in the way of speaking is significant. Its aim is for the papacy as it has become in the course of history, during which it has acquired some negative baggage, to undergo a new interpretation and a new reception, based on the gospel, which gives up nothing of its essence. Instead, its essential nature is to be brought out anew, through both theory and practice, in a more comprehensive spiritual understanding.

With the help of such a rereading and re-reception in these four ways, according to Catholic understanding, that which remains valid in the dogmas of Vatican I can be preserved, and can at the same time be the foundation for a future spiritually renewed form of Petrine service, which — we hope — will enable ecumenical contacts. As in the first millennium, this could be a form that is exercised in different ways, and nevertheless is recognized by everyone, as a unity in diversity and a diversity in unity. I have no illusions about this. The road to this goal will be, as far as human judgment can tell, a long one. It is my wish that at this symposium we may make at least a modest contribution towards reaching this goal, *"ut omnes unum sint."*

Papal Primacy — a Possible Subject of Lutheran Theology?

Harding Meyer

In his encyclical *Ut unum sint* of June 1995 Pope John Paul II invited all churches and theologians not under his jurisdiction to engage with him in "a fraternal, patient dialogue" about his ministry.[1]

This invitation was followed by a considerable number of theological symposia and publications in which, once again, Roman Catholic and non–Roman Catholic theologians reflected on papal ministry. Nevertheless, and whether this was true or not, one could hear that John Paul himself felt disappointed by the hesitant and weak response to his invitation. It seems that, indeed, many theologians of the various churches but not the non–Roman Catholic churches themselves or their official representatives responded to that invitation. As far as I know this is true also of the Lutheran churches.

It may be premature to ask for the concrete reasons for this silence. But for the Lutheran churches — and for the Reformation churches at large — this has to do with the fact that in their thinking, theology, and spirituality papal ministry appeared to be a "foreign" subject.

Of course, papal ministry has always been, for Lutheran church and theology, an eminently controversial subject, a matter of harsh interconfessional debate. As such a controversial subject it indeed pervades Lutheran theology from its very beginning. But this precisely meant that it was not felt to be a genuine and legitimate subject of Lutheran theology and thus a matter of theological dialogue and inquiry. It was and continued to be a

---

1. *Ut unum sint,* 96.

topic with which Lutheran thinking was confronted, as it were, only "from outside," lacking any authentic place within the horizon of Lutheran perception. Papal primacy as such had no actual relevance, and without controversial motivation it would not have been dealt with at all.

For centuries and up to the present day this merely controversial perspective prevailed. I recall the "cause célèbre" of the Lutheran pastor Richard Baumann in Württemberg who, as recently as June 1953, was removed from his ministry because of his openly favorable attitude towards papal primacy, and whose rehabilitation was refused even after the Lutheran participants of the first international Lutheran–Roman Catholic dialogue in 1972 had affirmed that for Lutherans "the office of the papacy is not excluded."[2] Even the Lutheran World Federation's cautious plea for his rehabilitation remained unheard. To approach papal primacy in anything but a controversial manner seemed to contradict Lutheran thinking. It was simply not a "possible subject of Lutheran theology."

It is true that in our present ecumenically minded era the Lutheran image of papacy has long since lost its blatantly polemical features, and the old "Antichrist" verdict has even been officially retracted. But it would be naïve to deny that the old controversial view, at least in the form of a general and basic attitude, still prevails. One may rejoice that the "stumbling stone" of papacy has lost much of its offensiveness. But even so, this "stone" nowhere really fits into the structure of Lutheran thinking and theology. The recent statement of the Evangelical Church in Germany (EKD) on "Church Fellowship According to Evangelical Understanding" (2001), which says in a rather apodictic manner that the Roman Catholic understanding of papacy "must be rejected,"[3] is only the expression of that general and basic attitude. As long as this attitude prevails, the invitation of John Paul II will be answered only hesitatingly.

Over against this attitude it is the intention of this paper to show why and in what sense papal ministry should be and, indeed, increasingly is being considered a "possible" and even appropriate subject of Lutheran theology. Only when this is recognized, the controversial treatment of this matter between Lutherans and Roman Catholics, which is unavoidable and cer-

2. Malta Report (1972), §66, in Harding Meyer and Lukas Vischer, eds., *Growth in Agreement: Reports and Agreed Statements of Ecumenical Conversations on a World Level* (New York/Geneva: Paulist Press/World Council of Churches, 1984), p. 184.

3. "Kirchengemeinschaft nach evangelischem Verständnis. Ein Votum zum geordneten Miteinander bekenntnisverschiedener Kirchen," *EKD Texte* 69 (2001): III, 2.3.

tainly will continue, can at the same time be transcended towards a genuine theological dialogue.

In this sense I shall, first, deal with the Lutheran Reformation, particularly with Luther and Melanchthon, and then with the present-day Lutheran–Roman Catholic dialogue.

The Lutheran Reformation: Luther and Melanchthon

It is well known that the Lutheran Reformation did not set out with the rejection of papacy. Even if Luther's Ninety-five Theses of 1517 repeatedly spoke of the limits of papal spiritual authority, they did not at all question papal primacy as such. So it remained during most of the two following years. On the contrary, despite the increasing polemic there can easily be found, in Luther's writings, emphatic affirmations of papal ministry and authority. In his writing of June 1521 against Jacob Latomus, who had qualified these favorable affirmations as hypocrisy, Luther emphasized that in his early years he "honestly thought about the pope not differently than the councils and universities usually did."[4] Between his firm adherence to his Reformation convictions and his adherence to the pope he did not see that irreconcilable contradiction which his adversaries saw and which they made the pivotal point of their criticism.

Only very hesitatingly Luther began to question papacy. But soon, although at first only in a hypothetical and conditional manner, this criticism incorporated the idea of "Antichrist." It was during the months of June to October 1520 that this polemical idea of "Antichrist" began to dominate his thinking and writing about papacy. This meant that from that time on, papacy was for Luther a predominantly, almost exclusively controversial subject, and this attitude permeated his writings until the end of his life, taking on very often frightening expressions.

The pope as "Antichrist," his ministry a ministry without secular or ecclesial mandate, even "instituted by the devil" — this was a blatant denial of the question of my paper.

Nevertheless, there are in Luther repeated affirmations that contradict and transcend this merely controversial view of papacy and speak of papal ministry as a *possibility* in the church. Some of these affirmations may be quoted:

4. Weimar Edition of *Luther's Works* (WA) 8, 45.

Particularly interesting is what Luther, in 1533, wrote looking back on the Diet of Augsburg. Although he had blamed the Augsburg Confession for not having spoken about "the question of the pope as Antichrist,"[5] suggesting that he himself was willing to fill this lacuna by a text on the deification of the pope,[6] he said three years later: "Always and up to now, especially at the Diet of Augsburg, we humbly assented to the pope and the bishops not to disrupt their privilege and authority in the church, but to be ordained and governed by them provided that they do not force upon us un-Christian articles (of faith). . . ."[7]

Some time later, in October 1535, Luther, in a letter to the preachers in Soest, said: "I want to say and to admit: If the pope will permit the gospel to be preached freely and purely, as it is his duty to do, I personally shall let him be what he wants to be. . . ."[8]

The most famous affirmations of this kind one finds in Luther's Commentary on Galatians (1531-35). He says that he would be "very willing to recognize the sovereignty of the pope," to "honor him and respect his person, provided he leaves my conscience free and does not force me to offend God."[9] "All we aim for is that the glory of God be preserved and that the righteousness of faith remain pure and sound." And he continues with the often quoted sentence: "Once this has been established, namely that God alone justifies us solely by His grace through Christ, we are willing not only to bear the pope aloft on our hands but also to kiss his feet."[10]

It is true that these and similar affirmations of Luther almost always have a *conditional* character, i.e., they make the possibility of accepting papal ministry dependent upon conditions all of which, in the last analysis, converge in the requirement that the papal ministry frees itself from its "anti-Christian" features and — *summa summarum* — "permits the gospel." It is equally true that Luther doubts that such a renewed papal ministry would ever come about. But even so, these affirmations demonstrate that there is

5. WA Br. 5, 496: ". . . maxime de antichristo Papa. . . ."
6. See WA 30 II, 471.
7. WA 38, 195.
8. WA 38, 397.
9. WA 40 I, 177.
10. WA 40 I, 181. And later on Luther repeats this once again: "I am willing to kiss your feet, pope, and to acknowledge you as the supreme pontiff, if you adore my Christ and grant that we have the forgiveness of sins and eternal life through His death and resurrection and not through the observance of your traditions. If you yield here, I shall not take away your crown and power" (WA 40 I, 357).

underneath his polemic something like a fundamental openness for papal ministry.

Thus, there are in Luther, although with very different emphasis, both attitudes: the radical denial of papal ministry and its conditional acceptance as a possible subject of Lutheran theology. It is a matter of unbiased interpretation of Luther's thinking to recognize and to do justice to his two-sided stance towards papacy with all its inner tension and to resist the general tendency to classify, in view of the almost overwhelming evidence of critical affirmations, his conditional affirmations in favor of papal ministry as irrelevant.[11] To recognize Luther's ambivalent attitude towards papacy is already a first and provisional answer to the question of my paper. It shows that a positive answer can at least *refer* to Luther.

One should, however, not stop at this point. The real and more important question is: How does Luther's occasional but reappearing conditional openness for a renewed papacy relate to the breadth of his thoroughly critical affirmations?

Context-related or vague, psychologizing answers and explanations do not suffice here. What ultimately is at stake is whether Luther considered papacy as a purely controversial matter imposed on him but in which, occasionally and for whatever reasons, he could make superficial "concessions" without thereby revealing his true conviction. Although such an explanation may be conceivable theoretically, it can hardly be substantiated by those passages that speak of his conditional openness for papal ministry.

The only convincing explanation for his two-sided attitude towards papacy has to take into consideration the particular mode of Luther's criticism against papal ministry, which remains the same throughout his writings. And here the "Antichrist" verdict that sums up this criticism is crucial. It is by no means a simple curse word or an expression of profound hate against the pope, as one has said occasionally, nor is it a global and undifferentiated rejection of papal ministry as such. It is rather the biblical abbreviation of or cipher for very clear and specific theological accusations against

11. It strikes me that several recent publications hardly mention Luther's conditional affirmations in favor of a renewed papacy. I am thinking, e.g., of the publications of Scott H. Hendrix, *Luther and the Papacy: Stages in a Reformation Conflict* (Philadelphia: Fortress Press, 1981), of Wolfgang Klausnitzer, *Das Papstamt im Disput zwischen Lutheranern und Katholiken: Schwerpunkte von der Reformation bis zur Gegenwart* (Innsbruck: Tyrolia, 1987), or of Jörg Haustein, "Das Papstamt aus der Sicht der Reformation," in Ferdinand Barth et al., *Papstamt — pro und contra: Geschichtliche Entwicklungen und ökumenische Perspektiven* (Göttingen: Vandenhoeck & Ruprecht, 2001).

the papacy of that time. If one leaves aside such critical objections as the lack of scriptural evidence for papal ministry, the papal claim for secular power, or the papacy's lack of a secular or an ecclesiastical mandate,[12] objections that certainly are important for Luther but do not really constitute the "anti-Christian" character of papacy, there are three decisive and closely interrelated features of papacy that are at the root of the "Antichrist" verdict:

1. The pope "claims for himself the exclusive right to interpret the Scriptures."[13] He has been made in Rome "judge over the Scriptures," who "does not let himself be judged by the Scriptures" since he thinks that "he cannot err."[14]
2. The pope has added to the word of God "new articles of faith," claiming that it is "necessary for salvation to accept them and to place our trust in them."[15]
3. The pope insists that "Christians cannot be saved without his power" and without their "being obedient to him."[16]

These three critical objections constitute the theological kernel of the "Antichrist" verdict. They all refer to features of the papal ministry that are not once for all inherent to that ministry as such, but point to *deformations* of papal ministry and its exercise of which papal ministry was free until the time of Gregory the Great, the "last bishop of Rome," as Luther said,[17] and of which, in principle, it could free itself again.

This also is the meaning and intention of those affirmations in which Luther speaks of a conditional acceptance of papal ministry. These affirmations are an important commentary, which in a crucial way explain and qualify Luther's critique. They clearly show that in the last analysis his rejection of the papal office, in spite of all its harshness, is an *empirical judgment* rather than a *judgment in principle*. It says: The state of things in my time and already

---

12. That papal ministry has neither a secular nor an ecclesiastical mandate is especially emphasized in Luther's writing "Wider das Papsttum zu Rom, vom Teufel gestiftet" (1545, WA 54, 237ff.).

13. WA 5, 339.

14. WA 54, 233.

15. E.g., WA 6, 322; 54, 233 and 237.

16. "Smalcald Articles," II, 4, 10ff., in Theodore G. Tappert, trans. and ed., *The Book of Concord: The Confessions of the Evangelical Lutheran Church* (Philadelphia: Fortress Press, 1959), p. 300.

17. WA 54, 229.

long since is such that I can carry only a radically negative judgment; but it may be that this state of things could change so that my judgment no longer applies, although I personally consider this as a merely hypothetical possibility. At any rate Luther does not exclude the possibility of a renewed papacy that would have a legitimate function in the church. Even in his last and most polemical writing, "Wider das Papsttum zu Rom, vom Teufel gestiftet" (1545), where his rejection of papal ministry seems to become a judgment in principle, he speaks of the possibility of recognizing a primacy of honor to the pope and a ministry of "oversight on doctrine and heresy in the churches."[18]

Melanchthon takes a similar approach to papacy. Here the view opens up also to the Lutheran confessional writings, among which particularly Luther's Smalcald Articles and even more explicitly Melanchthon's "Treatise on the Power and Primacy of the Pope" (1537) speak about papacy. Here, even more consistently than in Luther's private writings, the above-mentioned "anti-Christian" features of papacy are understood as implications or consequences of its claim to be *de iure divino*.[19] Thus, the whole criticism of papal ministry seems to focus on this *ius divinum* claim.

Even so it is exactly here that Melanchthon's "Treatise" shows a rather surprising openness. It is certainly true that Melanchthon starts by questioning the *ius divinum* claim of papal primacy using biblical and historical arguments.[20] Also in the reservation he added to Luther's Smalcald Articles, Melanchthon states that the pope has his primacy only *iure humano*.[21]

Nevertheless, Melanchthon does not deny the *ius divinum* of papal primacy under all circumstances. In two almost identical affirmations his "Treatise" uses a very remarkable argumentation. I quote one of them: "Even if *(etiamsi)* the bishop of Rome did possess the primacy by divine right *(iure divino)*, he should not be obeyed inasmuch as he defends impious forms of worship and doctrines which are in conflict with the gospel."[22] And Melanch-

---

18. "Wider das Papsttum zu Rom, vom Teufel gestiftet" (1545), WA 54, 231.

19. According to Melanchthon's "Treatise" the papal claim to be "by divine right above all bishops and pastors" (§1) implies that the pope "arrogates to himself the authority to make laws concerning worship, concerning changes in the sacraments, and concerning doctrine," that he "wishes his articles, his decrees, and his laws be regarded as articles of faith or commandments of God, binding the consciences of men" (§6), and that he "is unwilling to be judged (neither) by the church," i.e., by the councils (§40), nor by the Word of God (§56).

20. "Treatise," §§7-20.

21. *The Book of Concord*, pp. 316-17.

22. "Treatise" §57. Also "Treatise," §38: "Even if *(etiamsi)* the bishop of Rome

thon refers not only to Galatians 1:8, but also to canonical law according to which a heretic pope should not be obeyed. It is particularly remarkable that Melanchthon explains his position by referring to the fact that even the high priest in the Old Testament who undoubtedly "was the supreme pontifex by divine right *(de iure divino),*" "was not to be obeyed" inasmuch as he had become a "godless high priest," as is shown "in Jeremiah and other prophets."[23]

This argumentation strongly suggests that Melanchthon's criticism of the pope's *ius divinum* claim does not aim at the *ius divinum* claim itself, rejecting it categorically. What his criticism rather is aiming at is an *exaggerated notion or interpretation of this claim,* i.e., a notion of papal *ius divinum* that exempts papal decisions of all criticism and makes them "indisputable" *(unhinterfragbar)* even on the basis of the Holy Scriptures. In this perspective the Reformers' insistence that papal ministry be *de iure humano* is, in its true intention, nothing other than *the emphatic rejection of a maximalist interpretation of the papal ius divinum* claim, which exempts papal ministry from the word of God as ultimate norm.

Here again, although in a somewhat different manner than in Luther, we encounter that differentiation between the papal ministry as such and a rejected notion and exercise of this ministry, a differentiation that permits envisaging a renewed papal ministry which is subordinated to the gospel and which, from the Reformation point of view, would be meaningful and acceptable.

This is in keeping with the famous "reservation" Melanchthon added to his signature of Luther's Smalcald Articles, a "reservation" that takes up Luther's own conditional acceptance of papal primacy but one that Luther had not repeated in his Smalcald Articles. In this "reservation" Melanchthon, at the same time, says what task or function an acceptable papal ministry would have: "I, Philipp Melanchthon, regard the above articles as right and Christian. However, concerning the pope I hold that, if he would allow the Gospel, we, too, may concede to him that superiority over the bishops which he possesses by human right, making this concession for the sake of peace and general unity among the Christians who are now under him and who may be in the future."[24]

---

should possess primacy and superiority by divine right *(iure divino),* obedience would still not be owing to those pontiffs who defend godless forms of worship, idolatry, and doctrines which conflict with the Gospel."

23. "Treatise," §38.

24. *The Book of Concord,* pp. 316-17.

The Roman Catholic–Lutheran Dialogue

This line of thought, which one finds in the Lutheran Reformation and which in spite of all the harsh polemics, could under specific preconditions affirm a possible acceptance of papal ministry, and also characterize the Roman Catholic–Lutheran dialogues of today insofar as they deal with papal primacy. This happens mostly with explicit reference to the Reformation, but with even greater clarity and emphasis on *why* papal ministry is a "possible subject for Lutheran theology."

The result is a peculiar reversal of the overall picture. While for the Reformation the controversial aspect was the general and prevailing framework within which, occasionally, one encountered the idea of a conditional acceptance of papal ministry, this changes in the dialogues. It is now the common concern for the universal unity of the church and its visibility that provides the prevailing framework or perspective. And within this perspective almost necessarily the question arises whether there should not be a *personal* ministry, a Petrine ministry, serving this universal unity of the church, and under which presuppositions the already existing papal ministry could function as that Petrine ministry. Thus, the approach to papal primacy is no longer a primarily controversial one, as it was during the Reformation and the subsequent centuries. The question of papacy is now from the very outset embedded in a fundamentally positive perspective within which, of course, the still existing controversial issues may find their proper place.

In this sense the question of my paper, whether "papal primacy is a possible subject of Lutheran theology," is from the outset and in principle being answered affirmatively. The unity of the universal church cannot be but a legitimate subject for Lutheran theology also, and therefore papal ministry too, understood as Petrine ministry serving the unity and the mission of the church universal, must be considered as theologically legitimate.

This conviction permeates and determines all three Roman Catholic–Lutheran dialogues which, until now, have explicitly dealt with papal ministry: the Malta Report of 1972, with its concise but groundbreaking affirmations,[25] the extensive North American dialogue on "Papal Primacy and the Church Universal" of 1974,[26] and the German dialogue *Communio Sanc-*

---

25. Malta Report (see above, footnote 2), §§66 and 67.

26. Paul C. Empie and T. Austin Murphy, eds., *Papal Primacy and the Universal Church* (Minneapolis: Augsburg, 1974).

torum of 2000, with its section on the Petrine ministry.[27] The following remarks may help to show this.

The Malta Report heading, under which papal primacy is already being dealt with, is significative: "The Gospel and the *Unity of the Church.*"
This is the framework for all considerations about papal ministry, and the
Lutheran participants accept this framework. They recognize "that no local
church should exist in isolation since it is a manifestation of the universal
church." Recognizing the universality of the church and the need for its
unity immediately leads to the recognition of "the importance of a ministerial service of the (universal) communion of churches" and, at the same
time, it makes Lutherans aware of "their lack of such an effective service of
unity." Therefore, the Lutheran participants state that for them, "the office of
a papacy as a visible sign of the unity of the churches is not excluded insofar
as it is subordinated to the primacy of the gospel by theological reinterpretation and practical restructuring."[28]

The North American dialogue, in a similar manner, deals with papal
primacy under the general perspective "ministry and *church unity.*" In the
introduction to the dialogue report it is stated: "Visible unity of the church
has from earliest times been served by several forms of the Ministry," and "it
is within this context that we have considered papal primacy."[29] Looking
back on the preceding sessions of the dialogue, we find the introduction ad-
mitting that "our previous discussions had centered on the service rendered
to the local communities by the Ministry," but "now — it continues — we
focus on the unifying and ordering functions of this Ministry in relation to
the universal church — on how a particular form of this Ministry, i.e., the
papacy, has served the unity of the universal church in the past and how it
may serve it in the future."[30]

Later on in the report the Lutheran members of the dialogue admit
that "generally . . . Lutherans have had no place for papal primacy in their
thinking about the church,"[31] and that papal primacy had been "no possible
subject of Lutheran theology" at all. Therefore, in a retrospective on the dia-

27. Bilateral Working Group of the German National Bishops' Conference and the
Church Leadership of the United Evangelical Lutheran Church of Germany, *Communio
Sanctorum: The Church as the Communion of Saints,* trans. Mark W. Jeske, Michael Root,
and Daniel R. Smith (Collegeville, MN: Liturgical Press, 2004).

28. Malta Report, §66.

29. Empie and Murphy, eds., *Papal Primacy,* Introduction, p. 9.

30. Empie and Murphy, eds., *Papal Primacy,* pp. 10-11.

31. Empie and Murphy, eds., *Papal Primacy,* §31.

logue, they "explain why we have dealt with this issue."[32] And the answer is: "In this day of intensified global communication and international cooperation, the concern for the unity of the entire empirical church is being keenly felt." It is this conviction that compels them to acknowledge the urgent "need for symbols and centers of unity," able "to give concrete expression to our concern for the unity of the whole empirical church."[33]

Within this horizon the question of papal ministry with its "Petrine function"[34] also becomes a legitimate and relevant question for Lutherans. The final answer of the Lutheran dialogue members is almost identical to the affirmations of the Malta Report: "When we think of the question of the church's unity in relation to its mission we cannot responsibly dismiss the possibility that some form of the papacy, renewed and restructured under the gospel, may be an appropriate visible expression of the Ministry that serves the unity and ordering of the church."[35]

The most recent dialogue document, *Communio Sanctorum,* with its chapter on Petrine ministry, comes very close to the two previously mentioned dialogues. It certainly contains a number of additional aspects. Besides the repeated reference to the "*communio* structure" of the church, it is in particular the affirmation of the Lutheran participants that on all levels of the church there is and ought to be an essential "'in and over against' *(in und gegenüber)* of ecclesial ministry and ecclesial community" and that this should be so on the universal level as well.[36] Another particular and noteworthy element of this dialogue document is the vision of "universal church unity" resulting from the dialogue's deliberations on papacy, a vision summarized and described by the Lutheran participants as a "'conciliar fellowship' of all churches in 'reconciled diversity' with a Petrine ministry serving this fellowship."[37]

But essentially the argumentation of *Communio Sanctorum* repeats and thus corroborates the argumentation of the preceding and already mentioned dialogues. The North American dialogue starts by affirming the indispensable service of ecclesial ministry to the unity of the church, which immediately leads to the "question whether and in which manner this ser-

---

32. Empie and Murphy, eds., *Papal Primacy,* §28.
33. Empie and Murphy, eds., *Papal Primacy,* §32.
34. Empie and Murphy, eds., *Papal Primacy,* §33.
35. Empie and Murphy, eds., *Papal Primacy,* §32.
36. Bilateral Working Group, *Communio Sanctorum* (see above, footnote 27), §186.
37. Bilateral Working Group, *Communio Sanctorum,* §190.

vice must and will extend also to the *universal unity of the church.*[38] Thus, the overall framework for dealing with Petrine ministry and papacy is basically the same as in the Malta Report and the North American dialogue. The deliberations, largely historical in character, lead to the affirmation: "A universal ministry serving unity and truth of the church is in keeping with the nature and mission of the church." Prior to this affirmation, however, the Lutheran members of the dialogue had argued that this Petrine ministry should be structured and exercised in such a way that it be no longer exposed to the Reformation criticism as well as to certain Roman Catholic reservations concerning the former and present papal exercise of this ministry. It is here that the controversial questions find their place.

Although this plea for a Petrine ministry rightly exercised sounds very emphatic, the Lutheran dialogue participants, when it comes to the actual installation or adoption of such a ministry, speak as cautiously as in the two preceding dialogues. They say, for example, that one has to "consider" whether such a ministry is "appropriate, possible or meaningful,"[39] that there are at least "no objections in principle," or that the "assignment of this universal Petrine ministry to the bishop of Rome is plausible."[40]

In summary: Very similar to the Lutheran Reformation, the Lutheran participants in the present Roman Catholic–Lutheran dialogue also respond affirmatively to the question of this paper: Since nothing less than the visible unity of the church universal is at stake, papal primacy, understood as Petrine ministry and its right exercise, is for Lutheran theology not only a "possible" but even, if I may for a moment use this unusual wording, a "*necessarily* possible" subject.

---

38. Bilateral Working Group, *Communio Sanctorum*, §153.
39. Bilateral Working Group, *Communio Sanctorum*, §189.
40. *Communio Sanctorum*, §191.

Universal Episkopē and the Papal Ministry:
A Critical Overview of Responses to *Ut unum sint*

Peter Lüning

Introduction

Since the Second Vatican Council the Roman Catholic Church has engaged in a comprehensive ecumenical dialogue — bilaterally and multilaterally — with non–Roman Catholic churches and ecclesial communities. In these dialogues the question of a Petrine ministry has been among the topics on the agenda. The 1970s especially showed both an extensive and intensive commitment in the field of a Petrine ministry.[1] Since then much has been said in this respect.

It was Pope John Paul II whose awareness of this new ecumenical situation made him invite theologians and church leaders from other denominations to enter into a "patient and fraternal dialogue" (*Ut unum sint,* 96) with him on his own ministry. The pope himself gave a new and firm contribution to this dialogue in saying: "I am convinced that I have a particular responsibility in this regard, above all in acknowledging the ecumenical aspirations of the majority of the Christian communities and in heeding the request made of me to find a way of exercising the primacy which, while in no way renouncing what is essential to its mission, is nonetheless open to a new situation" (95). This invitation of the pope is unique in the history of papal ministry after the time of the Reformation. For the first time, Chris-

---

1. Wolfgang Klausnitzer, "Jurisdiktionsprimat und/oder Petrusdienst des Bischofs von Rom. Zu einigen neueren ökumenischen Veröffentlichungen," *ThQ* 178 (1989): 155ff.; cf. H. Leipold, "Papsttum, II. Die neuere ökumenische Diskussion," *TRE* 25 (1995): 676-95.

tians of other denominations are officially and openly asked to participate in dealing with an issue which according to Pope Paul VI is the greatest obstacle on the road to unity and which *Ut unum sint* calls to mind again (8).

Yet, several fundamental theological and ecclesiological questions arise from that invitation. The first series of questions concerns the addressee of his encyclical letter. Whom does the pope invite to enter into a dialogue with him? Does he address theologians and church leaders as individuals or as representatives of their respective Protestant and Orthodox ecclesial bodies on the regional, national, or international level? Does the pope have bilateral or multilateral dialogues in mind? Another question relates to the authority of the dialogue itself. Is it the ecclesial bodies themselves that are officially to be asked to engage in a formal dialogue with the Roman Catholic Church to produce a joint statement on the papal ministry? Or should that proposed dialogue take on the form of informal theological discussions between the denominations at various levels? As these questions have not been precisely answered by *Ut unum sint,* the different form of answers from the various denominations cannot be surprising.

Another, much more important range of questions relates to the encyclical differentiation between the *essence* of the mission of the papal primacy and its *self-opening* to a new situation. Does this differentiation mean a distinction between contents and historical form? Does the pope take up with this phrase the analogical differentiation that one of his predecessors, Pope John XXIII, used with respect to the history of dogma, i.e., distinguishing between the "deposit of faith" and the historical form in which it is transmitted, implying that the first is unalterable and the second historically variable? If the present pope has got this differentiation in mind, some decisive criteriological questions arise: According to which philosophico-hermeneutic, theological, and/or ecclesiological criteria can one distinguish between an unaltering deposit of faith and historical variables within the context of papal primacy, presuming that the papal primacy as such is a matter of faith? Does the term "distinction" mean "separation"? Is it principally possible to distinguish between a material "core" of a teaching and its historical form? Is there something like an essence of apprehended truth as object that can remain unaltered in the ongoing processes of apprehending truth by the apprehensive subject?

If Pope John Paul II does not have this distinction of what is philosophically called "naïve realism" in mind, but a different hermeneutic concept which could be called an *epistemology of critical realism,* then the distinction between the essence of an object (i.e., the papal ministry) and its self-opening to a new situation receives a different meaning. The distinction would then no longer be between unaltering "material" and its variable "form" (Thomistically speaking, this is not possible at all), yet a distinction that is made by the history of apprehension itself concerning the *self-identity of the object in its varying, nonetheless real and identifying apprehensions of the apprehensive subject in different historical contexts.* This would not only do "epistemological justice" to the object remaining itself throughout history but also to the subjective process of really apprehending and thereby identifying the object in various historical settings, yet throwing new and differing light onto this singular object that may lead to *changing and deepening apprehensive insights* into it.

Hermeneutic dialectics between the historical subject and an object analogically corresponds to *ontological* dialectics between the *Being in itself* on the noumenal level and the *appearing Being* on the phenomenal level. As the objective Being in itself really and truly, yet solely presents itself (and not a fake illusion)[2] in the appearing Being within the "lit" subject in its transcendental Being (in contrast to I. Kant, who with his transcendental realism felt obliged to hold the notion of a hiding of the Being in itself),[3] thus in turn the appearing Being is the real, true, and sole apprehensive form of the objective Being to the apprehensive subject. Yet, the apprehensive form underlies the condition of historical change. This means that the object itself cannot be apprehended except through and by its historically changing self-representation on the phenomenal level. We will later see that this is of fundamental importance to the theological issue of (noumenal) universal episkopē, which is according to Roman Catholic understanding (phenomenally) represented in the papal ministry if the pope himself — and this is quite plausible — has implied such hermeneutic and ontological dialectics in his distinction between the essence of his mission and its historical self-opening.

2. Although there are times when the human subject claims to apprehend an object that is, however, not present by itself in the apprehensive process, which then could be called an illusion. According to the ideal the transcendental subject and the object mediate each other in the process of constituting the appearance of the object within the human consciousness.

3. Karl Rahner, "Geist in Welt. Zur Metaphysik der endlichen Erkenntnis bei Thomas von Aquin," in Karl Rahner, *Sämtliche Werke, 2, Philosophische Schriften* (Solothurn/Düsseldorf: Benzinger, 1996). Karl Rahner, *Hörer des Wortes. Schriften zur Religionsphilosophie und zur Grundlegung der Theologie* (Solothurn/Düsseldorf: Benzinger, 1997), thus far differs from Kant, yet agrees with him in the question of the hermeneutically fundamental apprehension by the subject.

It is of equal importance that this fundamental epistemological and ontological concept could also be analogically used as the "hermeneutic clue" to the various reactions from the numerous Christian denominations to this papal distinction, though they differ from each other and from the Roman Catholic position. The common hermeneutic precondition is the question whether and in what way there should be a visible universal ministry of episkopē. The respective answers cast a different hermeneutic light onto the (one) "object" to which the pope has drawn ecumenical attention and apprehension. This is even true in those cases in which theologians or denominations were unwillingly confronted with this Roman Catholic differentiated identification of noumenal universal episkopē and the papal ministry as the concrete, phenomenal "object" of apprehension.

The different and differing answers to this "object" reflect not only the respective denominational positions as such (although there is inner denominational room for a changing apprehension, as we shall later see); but the answers also overtly or covertly reveal the underlying *foundational theological experiences*[4] made with the papal ministry in history forming their respective theological judgments on this ministry. It is through and by these foundational experiences in the form of theological judgments that other denominations fundamentally apprehend the specific "object" of the papal ministry.

Let us now draw our attention to the theological answers coming from different denominations and denominational backgrounds.

Responses to *Ut unum sint*

General Remarks

Before analyzing the different responses to Pope John Paul II's request, we should mention the various ecumenical commissions and reports that dealt with the issue of the papal primacy before *Ut unum sint*, comprised of the Joint International Commission of the Orthodox Church and the Roman Catholic Church, the Anglican–Roman Catholic International Commission (ARCIC), the Lutheran–Roman Catholic Dialogue, the Report of the Disci-

---

4. Burkhard Neumann, "Ökumene und Erfahrung. Zur Bedeutung des Erfahrungsaspekts für Theologie und Ökumene," in Peter Neuner and Peter Lüning et al., eds., *Theologie im Dialog* (Münster: Aschendorff, 2004), pp. 415-30.

ples of Christ and the Roman Catholic Church, the Methodist–Roman Catholic Dialogue, the Joint Working Group of the World Council of Churches and the Roman Catholic Church, and finally the report of the Groupe des Dombes.[5]

Apart from these joint theological reports relevant to the interpretation of the Petrine ministry, we have now got to turn to direct responses to *Ut unum sint.* Answers came from a wide range of Western churches and ecclesial communities (the Old Catholic churches, churches of the Anglican Communion, Lutheran churches, Presbyterian churches, other Reformed churches, and free churches). Geographically speaking most responses came from North America, especially the USA, and from Europe, here again mostly from the British Isles and Germany. Many answers were prepared and delivered by local groups or institutions; the most comprehensive answers were delivered by the House of Bishops of the Church of England, by the Bishops' Conference of the Church of Sweden, and by the Presbyterian Church in the USA. There were no official responses from the Orthodox churches. Some answers were given by ecumenical commissions, such as the Faith and Order Commission of the World Council of Churches; others were handed in by academic institutions (e.g., Konfessionskundliches Institut des Evangelischen Bundes) or ecumenical communities (e.g., the Iona Community). Several symposia had taken place after the publication of *Ut unum sint* to reflect the Petrine ministry in its relation to the papal primacy. Last but not least, a large number of individual theologians of different denominations or denominational backgrounds have made valuable contributions to the issue, including several Roman Catholic authors and some Orthodox theologians who, however, have been mainly living in the West.[6]

Most of the responses and reactions generally agree in emphasizing and explicitly praising the pope's invitation to a "patient and fraternal dialogue" about his ministry. They furthermore value John Paul II's ecumenical commitment and engagement, especially shown in his encyclical letter *Ut unum sint.* Many of the responses appreciate the pope's distinction between

5. "Plenary Meeting of the Pontifical Council for Promoting Christian Unity: Study Documents," in *Information Service* 109 (2002/I-II): 28-47.

6. For a collection of the responses, see Wolfgang Thönissen and Peter Lüning, eds., "Der Dienst des Bischofs von Rom an der Einheit der Christen. Reaktionen auf die Einladung des Papstes zum Dialog über die Form der Primatsausübung nach 'Ut unum sint' von 1995," *Catholica* 55 (2001): 269-309; here 302-9.

the essence of the Petrine ministry and the historical form in which it has been and still is exercised. There is altogether a widespread readiness among the non–Roman Catholic theologians and institutions to respond and enter into the dialogue John Paul II has asked for.

Four general trends among non–Roman Catholic responses relevant to the perception of the papal ministry can be noted:

1. Many reactions reveal a growing awareness of the universal dimension of the church as being essential to its being, and a willingness to reflect its consequences for their own understanding of the church and its ministry.

2. Nonetheless, several reactions show a fundamental opposition to a papal leadership over the church by biblically and ecclesiologically arguing against it. These reactions cannot be confined to a specific denomination. Radically critical responses have come from almost every Protestant denomination (even from within the Anglican Communion and Lutheran churches), although one can of course note the general trend that criticism becomes more fundamental the wider the denominational distance is to the Roman Catholic Church.

3. Many responses mirror an awareness of the ongoing ecumenical debate on the papal ministry as they make use of several of its insights.

4. Looking at the results in general, one can perceive an ambivalent ecumenical situation in that there are those responses that are open to a theological and ecclesiological reflection of the universal dimension of episkopē within the context of the universal dimension of the church, and those who strictly object to a visible form of universal ecclesial oversight that claims to stand in a functional or ministerial continuity with Peter in the New Testament. That means that there is a growing convergence among Protestants and Orthodox towards an awareness of the possibility or even necessity of universal ecclesial leadership on the one hand, and at the same time a transdenominational refusal to accept the notion of visible universal oversight over local churches at all on the other hand. Therefore one cannot record an overall trend of a fundamental ecumenical convergence in the issue of universal episkopē (embodied in the papal ministry), although the ecumenical climate has changed in this direction.

Decisive Theological Questions

In the following section we are going to highlight the decisive critical points that have been put forward in the responses. These points will help to ecumenically clarify the complex issue of universal episkopē in its relation to the papal primacy.

Scriptural or Ecclesiological Argument?

Both Orthodox and Protestant theologians question the possibility of directly founding the papal ministry in the New Testament role of Peter as they perceive it adhered to in a traditional Roman Catholic argument. To them the function or task of Peter to "feed my flock" (John 21:15; cf. Matt. 16:16f.) is exclusively bound to his person and cannot be transmitted in one way or another. The "mandatum clavis" promised to Peter is applied to all the other apostles as well (Matt. 18:18). Therefore a lot of Protestant and Orthodox theologians view Peter in line with Melanchthon's argument as a *representational collective subject* of the apostles, who are the core foundation of the church as a confessing body.[7]

Taking into account the relatively late reference to Peter and Paul(!) of the New Testament by the popes to legitimize their leadership, several Roman Catholic theologians and New Testament scholars[8] are convinced that there was not a *direct* transmission of *Peter's (and Paul's)* unique role to later Christian generations (this is indeed impossible to prove), yet that the last took over the obviously lasting — what was later called — "Petrine function" (and one should add "Pauline function") to bind the local congregations together. The decisive question therefore is whether the task to "feed my flock" had exclusively been bound to the person of Peter among the apostles and analogously to Paul in his teaching and supervising ministry, or whether and how both tasks had been felt as *a need to constantly endure* in one form or another (personally, collegially, or communally) to visibly secure the unity of the universal koinonia of local churches.

If a non–Roman Catholic theologian or even a whole denomination has come to the conclusion that the "Petrine function" as it has been called in the Lutheran–Roman Catholic Dialogue in the USA (1974)[9] should en-

---

7. Günther Wenz, "Papsttum und kirchlicher Einheitsdienst nach Maßgabe evangelisch-lutherischer Bekenntnistradition," *Catholica* 50 (1996): 144-63; here p. 152.

8. Joachim Gnilka, "Der Petrusdienst — Grundlegung im Neuen Testament und Ausprägung in der frühen Kirche," in Peter Hünermann, ed., *Papstamt und Ökumene. Zum Petrusdienst an der Einheit aller Getauften* (Regensburg: Pustet, 1997), pp. 9-24.

9. "Common Declaration on Papal Primacy, 1974," in Joseph A. Burgess and Jeffrey Gros, eds., *Building Unity: Ecumenical Dialogues with Roman Catholic Participation in the United States* (New York: Paulist, 1989), pp. 125-216; par. 4.

dure in a particular form of ministry, then the next question would not be whether this function *should be realized*. It would instead have to be asked, if the historical form in which this function *has actually been realized*, the ministry of the bishop of Rome is an adequate or sufficient realization of the "Petrine function" or not.

Even in those cases in which some denominations prefer to speak of universal episkopē within the broader perspective of a *communio* ecclesiology (and not primarily basing the notion of a universal primate on the scriptural role of Peter) as in the Anglican–Roman Catholic Dialogue,[10] the bishop of Rome can be seen as the bearer of personal universal episkopē in a united church: ". . . we nevertheless agree that a universal primacy will be needed in a reunited Church and should appropriately be the primacy of the Bishop of Rome."[11] On the basis of this argument the Anglican–Roman Catholic Dialogue is able to claim a functional analogy between Peter and the bishop of Rome.[12] Even a few Lutherans could accept such a notion in accordance with the ecclesiologically essential dimension of the universal church, which needs to have some form of historically conditioned supervision under the primacy of the gospel.[13]

This conviction of an inner correspondence of the universal church and a universal primate, which can be found among Anglicans and Lutherans, explains why many free churches and Reformed churches at the same time categorically reject the notion of (visible) universal episkopē as they still adhere to an understanding of the church as solely locally realized, which seems to omit the question of a universal dimension of the church. Yet, the willingness to reflect upon this question is also growing here, although a universal dimension of ministry does not necessarily imply to them a *personal* form of such a ministry, let alone a possible personal transmission of the promise to Peter. For Reformed and free church Christians universal supervision, if envisaged, could take on a collegial and/or communal form as well.

Taking the growing ecumenical willingness to reflect upon a universal dimension of episkopē into account, the question whether there is a scriptural

10. ARCIC, "Authority in the Church I," no. 23, in *The Final Report* (London: SPCK, 1982), p. 64; Gift of Authority, no. 46.

11. "Authority in the Church II," no. 9, in *The Final Report*, p. 85.

12. "Authority in the Church II," nos. 5 and 6, in *The Final Report*, pp. 83-84.

13. Wenz, "Papsttum und kirchlicher Einheitsdienst," *Catholica* 50 (1996): 144-63, esp. 155ff.

foundation to the notion of a *transmission* of Peter's and Paul's supervising functions to possible successors is of secondary importance. Even if Lutherans are more and more prepared to accept the necessity of a universal dimension of church *and* ministry, many of them are reluctant to find a universal ministerial supervision (already) realized in the historical and concrete ministry of the bishop of Rome.[14]

Yet, one should bear in mind what has been said before: *Ut unum sint* implicitly calls for an application of the foundational hermeneutic and correspondingly ontological distinction of the object as Being in itself and the subjectively apprehended historical form of its self-appearing Being to the differentiation of universal episkopē (as the "Being in itself") and the papal primacy (as the "self-appearing Being"). This of course assumes that the historical form of the realization of universal episkopē is solely and uniquely located in the bishop of Rome. From a Roman Catholic point of view therefore the ecumenically most relevant insight is that one cannot talk of universal episkopē, be it primarily grounded in the scriptural role of Peter or not, while omitting or setting apart its solely and historically realized form, the primacy of the bishop of Rome.

Although the Anglican–Roman Catholic Dialogue admits of course that there is a hypothetical possibility of locating a universal primacy somewhere other than in the city of Rome, yet the "continuing exercise of a universal episkopē by the see of Rome presents a unique presumption in its favour."[15] This means that the Anglican–Roman Catholic Dialogue points to the historically *actual* (and not the potential) form of universal episkopē as the basis of its argument. We will later see that the historically necessary distinction between the actual and the potential does not imply the notion that the *potential* form of universal episkopē is *unreal*, even if it has not yet been actualized, as a potential of the dialectic between "subject" and "object" contains real possibilities.

The decisive question is then, not whether there should be some form of universal episkopē *at all* (unless one has got an understanding of the church restricted to the local level), but whether the present form of the papal primacy is the (most) apprehensively adequate historical realization of

14. Bilateral Working Group of the German National Bishops' Conference and the Church Leadership of the United Evangelical Lutheran Church of Germany, ed., *Communio Sanctorum: The Church as the Communion of Saints* (Collegeville, MN: Liturgical Press, 2004), nos. 194; 197; 199.

15. "Authority in the Church," Elucidation, no. 8, in *The Final Report*, p. 76.

such "objective" episkopē. This seems to be the underlying question of many responses from the Anglican and Lutheran sides.

The Papal Primacy as Part of God's Design for His Church?

If one follows this philosophical argument down to its concrete theological conclusion, one is faced with the question whether the historical realization of universal episkopē in the form of the papal primacy is to be viewed as *de iure divino* for the church or whether it is entirely a human means of ecclesial supervision, being *de iure humano*. According to the Lutheran–Roman Catholic Dialogue in the USA this traditional distinction fails to provide usable categories for a contemporary discussion of the papacy. It instead states that "It is God's will that the church has the institutional means needed for the promotion of unity in the gospel."[16] At the same time the Roman Catholic participants of this dialogue are aware that "there are many ways of exercising papal primacy."[17] This means that there is and should only be one actual realization of universal episkopē fundamentally located in the primacy of the bishop of Rome as part of God's plan for his church to effectively promote the unity in the gospel within the universal koinonia of believers.

This is in line with the philosophical dialectic of the apprehensive process between the object and its subjective apprehension. As the apprehensive process is not merely hermeneutic subjectivism, so is the papal primacy not merely a human institution. According to Roman Catholic understanding it is God himself through his Spirit who guides his church through space and time by making use of several invisible and visible means, one of which is the primacy of the bishop of Rome. This conviction can be philosophically expressed by pointing to the *self-constituting* appearance of the "object" within the process of its subjective apprehension. The primacy is therefore not an (admittedly) necessary invention by humans but a non-optional institutional gift from God — to be, however, subjectively grasped within space and time.[18]

At the same time the subjective apprehensive process in turn constitutes the "appearing Being" of the object, as there is no other possibility of

---

16. *Common Declaration on Papal Primacy*, 1974, par. 42.

17. *Common Declaration on Papal Primacy*, 1974, par. 42.

18. "Subjectively" here refers to the collective "subject" of the universal koinonia of believers who in turn cannot be separated from the individual religious subjects in their own subjective right.

apprehending the object than by the subject in its historical transcendental Being grasping and thereby forming the present object. This means that anthropological, sociological, and ecclesiological requirements make the object of primacy change in the history of the apprehensive process within the church as the potential of this object in the sense of real possibilities is *actually (ecclesially) formed.* Therefore one can perceive a dialectic between the primacy as part of God's design for the church and its concrete form as a result of historical processes of *actually apprehending its "objective"* potential. This in turn implies the idea of an always bigger essential potential of the primacy (the Being in itself) than its actual realization (the "appearing Being"), as the last one is characterized by *historical contingency.* The God-given primacy can in fact unfold and has indeed unfolded itself in various ways through space and time.

Universal Jurisdiction and Papal Infallibility: A Matter of Essence or Mere Contingency?

The most negative criticisms of Protestant and Orthodox theologians have focused on the Roman Catholic doctrines of the universal jurisdiction and the infallibility of the papal primacy. These two doctrines are regarded by almost all of the Protestant and Orthodox responses as a deviation from the gospel and therefore as part of corrupt historical contingencies, failing to do justice to the gospel message and to the essence of the primacy itself. The difficult question could thus be raised whether universal jurisdiction and papal infallibility belong to the essence of the primacy or whether they represent historical contingencies based on the judgment of either being optional for the church's ministry or even contrary to it.

Those on the Roman Catholic side who analogously favor a form of papacy that finds its full and adequate realization in the way it was exercised in the first millennium have to be asked if one can legitimately omit theological insights that have originated from the later history of the papacy. Should one not keep the full history in one's theological mind in order to grasp an ever more deepening understanding of the papal primacy? This does not in turn legitimize every single aspect of the papal primacy throughout history, but it tries to avoid the notion that the apprehensive faith in the *second* millennium has not at least *in principle formed its own legitimate history of apprehension* of the primacy as an "object" of faith.[19] One cannot turn back the

19. Wolfgang Beinert, "Endechrist oder Zeichen der Barmherzigkeit? Die Möglich-

wheel of the history of apprehension. There is a certain legitimacy and necessity of historical apprehension with regard to the ongoing process of grasping an object of faith.

Yet, this does not exclude but does instead include the possibility and necessity of apprehending an "object" of faith constantly *anew,* thereby gaining new and different insights into the potential of that "object," which form and "re-form" the actual appearance of it as it has been handed down in the process of apprehension.

Cardinal Kasper,[20] referring to the hermeneutic of dogmas, once called them *"offene Formeln, . . . in ein grenzenloses Geheimnis hinein"* ("open formulae into a boundless mystery"). This corresponds to the hermeneutic insight that historical forms of foundational apprehensions of an appearing "object" have got a lasting meaning not in preserving them as they are, but in transcending them time and time again towards the ever bigger potential of the object (in) itself.

There can, however, be deficient forms of apprehension that need to be corrected when seen in a new light coming from a new apprehension of the object. Is such a possibility also true for the realm of faith? The answer is yes and no; yes, in that there is a *history of dogma* (in the wider sense of the word) that shows not only evolutionary interpretations and reinterpretations of past insights, but also implicit rejections and dismissals of some of them; no, in that at least the Roman Catholic Church is convinced that *foundational* insights into an "object" of faith cannot err. The decisive question therefore is whether the universal jurisdiction and the infallibility of the papal primacy are part of these foundational or essential insights into the primacy itself or whether they are non-foundational and therefore part of historical contingency, leaving legitimate room to adhere to them or not. Even if the Roman Catholic Church is convinced that these two teachings are essential and thereby inerrant and binding apprehensions of the primacy, they in turn *as "objects" themselves underlie a historical process of apprehension as well.* They are therefore not the solution (not even a Roman Catholic solution) to the hermeneutic problem of the papacy, but a decisive part of it that calls for its constantly new apprehension — retaining the foundational insights of them, yet grasping them anew in changing contexts.

---

keit einer ekklesiologischen Konvergenz zwischen Lutheranern und Katholiken über das Papsttum," *Catholica* 50 (1996): 121-43.

20. Deutsche Bischofskonferenz, ed., *Katholischer Erwachsenenkatechismus. Das Glaubensbekenntnis der Kirche* (Kevelaer: Butzon & Bercker, 1985), p. 57.

It is easy to comprehend that non–Roman Catholic churches and ecclesial communities differ in the theological evaluation of the two doctrines. Yet, even in those rare cases in which the non–Roman Catholic responses have shown a growing awareness of the corresponding insights of them (being analogous to Roman Catholic proposals to differentiate more clearly between the various tasks of the Roman see, being the bishop of a local diocese, the patriarch of the Western or Latin church, and the universal minister of unity within the wider context of ecclesial synodality and collegiality)[21] — almost all of the responding non–Roman Catholic theologians and churches remain unwilling to accept the two specific doctrines as universally binding, i.e., as they have been apprehended up until now by the Roman Catholic Church. This calls for a Roman Catholic reappraisal of their actual apprehension in the church, comprehending the so-called "theory" and "praxis" of both doctrines without questioning their apprehensive validity *in principle.*

The interdenominationally still different evaluation of the universal jurisdiction and the infallibility of the papal primacy also calls for a Protestant (and Orthodox) *reappraisal of the late post-Reformation or respectively the second-millennium era of the exclusively Roman Catholic experiences of the papal primacy.* This needs an openness on the side of Protestant and Orthodox churches and ecclesial communities to possibly gain new and lasting *positive foundational experiences* of a newly apprehended papal primacy as its precondition.[22]

Final Remarks: Old Deadlock Anew?

How can the ecumenical situation be theologically described concerning the invitation of the pope to other churches and ecclesial communities to recon-

---

21. The Anglican participants of the Anglican–Roman Catholic International Commission have moved the farthest in this respect. See "Gift of Authority"; cf. "Authority in the Church I," "Authority in the Church I, Elucidation," and "Authority in the Church II."

22. The Anglican-Methodist Dialogue, *Sharing in the Apostolic Communion: Report of the Anglican-Methodist International Commission to the World Methodist Council and the Lambeth Conference* (Lake Junaluska: World Methodist Conference, 1996), nos. 78 and 84, analogously draws attention to an openness on the Methodist side to gain new positive foundational experiences with episcopacy, which would mean a reappraisal of this institution to the Methodist tradition.

sider his ministry together with him? The analysis of the different responses has shown that the ecumenical partners still seem to "stumble" at the last "stumbling block," the papal primacy, on the road to unity in reconciled diversity. Even if there are partial theological convergences in the question of universal episkopē as some Protestant and Orthodox theologians come to accept the essential nature of the universality of the church, they nevertheless reject the papal claim to universal jurisdiction and infallibility as necessary and God-given instruments of his ministry. Yet, this means that they reject not only two single and specific doctrines of the papal primacy on their own, but the *actual form* of that primacy as such being formed by the two.

Has the ecumenical dialogue therefore reached a new deadlock? Or has it reached an old deadlock anew, making us aware of the remaining biggest obstacle to church unity? The hermeneutic and corresponding ontological differentiation of the Being of an object (in) itself and its subjective apprehension in the form of its "appearing Being" may show a possible way out of this seemingly old impasse. The decisive task in the future should then be to promote a twofold ecumenical process, on the one hand reconsidering traditional apprehensions of the primacy within the Roman Catholic Church and on the other hand opening oneself to possible new foundational experiences of the papal primacy within the Orthodox and Protestant churches and ecclesial communities in order to form a new, then *joint apprehension* of the primacy. *Ut unum sint* and the responses to it have already initiated such a necessary and promising process.

Does the Joint Declaration on the Doctrine of Justification Have Any Relevance to the Discussion of the Papal Ministry?

André Birmelé

In the *Joint Declaration on the Doctrine of Justification* (JD) there is no mention of papal ministry. No matter how you look at it, it would be useless to try to read something into it that is simply not there. The JD is concerned with a different subject. It even deliberately excludes any ecclesiological subjects.[1] The ecclesiological consequences of the JD will be addressed later.[2]

The question of papal ministry is by no means irrelevant, however, as the JD works out an ecumenical methodology from the issue of justification. With a basic consensus already existing on the subject of justification, it was important, however, to single it out and set an example for future ecumenical declarations.

In this sense I understand the task of this paper as a depiction of the methodological approaches of the JD with a view to examining whether this method is also applicable to the question of papal ministry. The first part will focus on the former, i.e., depicting this methodology. In the next few days we will take to the task of considering the possibility of applying the method used in the JD also to the Petrine ministry. The second part will deal with two fields in which the JD breaks new ground that may be relevant to our subject. In the third part conclusions will be drawn.

1. See note 9.
2. Paragraph 43.

Part I: The Model of Differentiated Consensus

The main object of controversy in the debates preceding the signing of the JD was not so much the common understanding of justification as the definition of "consensus." The JD, breaking new ground in this regard, proposes a "differentiated consensus."

Four postulations constitute the background of this approach:

1. The JD never claims that the Lutheran doctrine of justification is identical with the Catholic one, or vice versa. Its conviction is that "consensus" does not mean a single or monolithic doctrinal statement, just as unity is not synonymous with uniformity. What is a fact in the Lutheran or Catholic families is also valid in ecumenical settings. Yet there are doctrinal presentations that are not identical in every aspect. Melanchthon and Luther, for example, dealt with the issue of justification with different accents. There was, however, a consensus necessary and sufficient for the maintenance and progress of church unity so that the existing differences were not divisive, but "justified" differences. Likewise each tradition has had different approaches to the doctrine of justification. The simultaneousness of these two statements, the reality of the consensus and the diversity of doctrinal presentation, are essential for the JD.

2. Against this historical backdrop, the JD understands the consensus as the relationship between two statements that are not church-dividing because they are two different explanations of one basic truth. By definition consensus is intrinsically "differentiated" or "differentiating," i.e., it can recognize and accept diversity. Diversity is no deficit, but a characteristic of the very life of every church, a koinonia of believers that is the image of koinonia, which is itself of the Triune God. As a matter of fact, this proposal is not new; it is a conception of dialogue developed within the ecumenical movement over many years. Without this approach no declarations leading to church fellowship would have been possible among Lutherans, Reformed, Anglicans, Methodists, etc.[3] What is new here, however, is the fact that the Catholic Church also partakes in such an understanding of consensus.

3. A significant example of this is the Leuenberg Agreement adopted in 1973 between the Lutheran, Reformed, and United churches in Europe. On the basis of a succinct statement of the basic truth taken up by both traditions, the Lutheran and Reformed churches declared mutual church fellowship, putting emphasis on the fact that they remain "churches of different confessional positions" (§29), *Agreement between Reformation Churches in Europe (Leuenberg Agreement)* (Frankfurt am Main: Lembeck, 1993) (trilingual version).

3. Such a "differentiated consensus" requires distinction between the elements belonging to basic truths and those arising justifiably from different ways of presenting them. Distinction should be made particularly between two different dimensions: basic truths on the one hand and the ways of presenting these truths on the other hand. While basic truths require a common understanding and statement, they are explicated by means of words, ways of thinking, and theological judgments that find expression in a legitimate, salubrious diversity.

4. The JD knows that the differences cannot be reduced to linguistic structures and forms. The criticism of the JD as repeatedly expressed in the debate in Germany, which was taken up even in the Roman response, that the JD tries to reduce all the remaining differences to a simple question of emphasis or language, however, fails to do justice to the text of the declaration.[4] The JD clearly points out that the challenges are greater: it is concerned with the forms of "theological elaboration and emphasis in the understanding of justification" (40) that "are no longer occasion for doctrinal condemnations" despite "the remaining differences in its explication" (5). The JD presents a "differentiated consensus" capable of withstanding theological differences.

Against this backdrop, the "differentiated consensus" is unfolded in the JD. A meticulous analysis of the consensus presented in the JD leads to three planes of distinction.

1. The first plane concerns the common basic statement. After referring to the biblical message, the JD describes in several short paragraphs (14-18) the shared understanding of the doctrine of justification. This approach calls to mind the Christological affirmation of the dialogue in the United States that was in turn taken up in the dialogue in Germany. The JD knows, however, that the simple depiction of the common conviction, which is itself a remarkable progress, is not sufficient, as church-dividing statements may still refer to this very common statement as evidenced by the dialogue in the United States. The JD does not content itself therefore with claiming that this basic statement is in a position to lay a foundation for the differences remaining on the plane of particular elaborations.

2. The JD introduces a second plane of basic consensus. With this, it treads on virgin soil, distinguishing itself from many other contemporary ecumenical declarations. This additional plane tackles, one after another, the points that have led to the condemnations between the two families. The main

---

4. See the manifest of the German Theology Professors, *EPD-Dok.* 7 (1998): 1 and par. 5 of the response of Rome.

part of the JD, paragraphs 18 to 39, serves the purpose of examining the reality of the general basic consensus in terms of its application in the seven fields that were the main points of controversy over the doctrine of justification.

For each of these points the JD presents a new common basic statement of both traditions. In other words, the general basic consensus is completed on the plane of particular elaborations by means of a second basic consensus relevant only to this point that was once the object of doctrinal condemnation. Only after this new common statement has been made does the JD present the particular elaborations of each tradition, trying to show that these elaborations depicting the different theological approaches arising merely from different forms of thought and language express legitimate differences because they are borne by a double basic consensus, a general one and a particular one.

This double consensus is judged as being sufficient to the extent that even the concrete formulations condemned by the other tradition of former times may now be taken up in the Lutheran or Catholic particular elaboration without offending the other, for the double consensus of today sets out a frame that enables such a statement and renders it acceptable for the partner. In this manner four statements condemned by the Council of Trent were taken up in the Lutheran Formula of Concord. Likewise one of the catholic convictions refuted by the Lutheran Formula of Concord appears in the Catholic statement.[5]

3. After achieving this double consensus, the JD advances to the third plane, the lifting of doctrinal condemnations. It is the direct consequence of the two preceding planes. The JD holds that it is possible today to lift the doctrinal condemnations. In other words, the doctrine presented here by the one tradition does not fall under the condemnations from the other (cf. 41). The idea of lifting the doctrinal condemnations is not new; it has been the core and center of the dialogues in Germany, without any mention of consensus. What is new here is the close link between the removal of condemnations and the declaration of consensus achieved by the JD.

For the JD, the interconnection of these three planes is essential as pointed out already in its preamble (5). The doctrinal condemnations being the expression of lacking consensus, a new situation had to be brought about that would justify the affirmation that the doctrinal condemnations no lon-

5. They are the Lutheran statements of mere passivity (21), *sola fide* (26), concupiscence as real sins, assurance of salvation (35), and the Catholic statement on the growth in grace (38).

ger apply to the current teachings of the church condemned at that time. The JD's approach is to seek and verify the "double" common understanding of justification necessary for the removal of each point of condemnation. Once this proof is available, the consensus not only can but also must be testified. The fact that the doctrinal condemnations can be lifted indicates the extent to which a consensus was reached. These two planes of common statements and the removal of the condemnations are inseparable and mutually dependent. Together they form the consensus through complementarity and mutual dependency.

For this reason, the conclusions of the JD (40 and 41) connect both problems very closely to each other and ask the churches to approve these two at the same time: the declaration of consensus and the lifting of doctrinal condemnations. This understanding of consensus presented by the JD arises from theological and ecclesiastical requirements. Concluding its thirty-year work, the Lutheran-Catholic dialogue does not present a theoretical paper on the understanding of "consensus," but explains it by means of its application in a specific case. The doctrine of justification represents an excellent space for the development, examination, and application of this access to the "consensus."

The authors of the JD are convinced that its application in this field may open new perspectives on the questions in which dialogue is even more difficult, especially on the questions of ecclesiology, sacraments, and ministry (see 43).

The question to be tackled in the course of this conference is now raised of its own accord: Is this ecumenical methodology used in the JD also applicable to the dialogue on papal ministry?

This question cannot be answered with a clear yes or no. It can only be answered at several levels. It is necessary to list the fields of classical debates on the Petrine ministry and scrutinize them in the dialogue as meticulously as possible. In doing so, the papers given in this symposium will prove useful. Another task will be to search for new ways as formulated by John Paul II himself in his encyclical *Ut unum sint*. Its object is not exclusively the current shape of this ministry in the Roman Catholic Church, but the universal ministry of unity necessary for the church in general. It is also necessary to identify the fields that require a common statement and those in which differences — not only in linguistic forms but also in theological elaborations — are not merely tolerated but rather desirable. This will have to take place in future dialogues.

It seems to me not only possible but also desirable to apply the procedure of the JD analogously to the question of papal ministry. This position can be backed up by the following points. To conclude this first part, I'll name two reasons that demonstrate the necessity of this step:

1. The applicability of this methodology with regard to the papal ministry is not only important for the question of the Petrine ministry but also for the JD itself. The method used in it won't be able to prove its strength unless it is applicable to other fields. If it proves applicable to the papal ministry, its validity will be confirmed and at the same time the JD itself and the whole process leading to it will be given a significant additional authority in the reception of this procedure.

2. The method used in the JD must not fail to prove its validity in the field of ecclesiology. In his first — very critical — commentary on the JD, E. Jüngel deplores that the consensus has no ecclesiological consequences.[6] Justification in Lutheranism is not a doctrinal statement alongside others, but *the* criterion of the whole church's life, so for Jüngel it is inconceivable to declare a consensus on justification without any immediate ecclesiological consequences. He wishes to add a fourth plane to the three complementary planes describing the "differentiated consensus" as presented by the JD: the ecclesiological consequences. Jüngel does not refute the understanding of consensus in the sense of the JD, but considers it incomplete because of the lack of ecclesiological consequences that would bring a lasting change to the relationship between Lutherans and Catholics. Accordingly, no consensus can be declared unless this additional threshold is overcome. The authors of the JD would of course have wished for the declaration of consensus to entail immediate ecclesiological consequences, as was the case with the declaration of church fellowship among the Reformation churches. They forwent it, however, well aware of the fact that the Lutheran-Catholic dialogue was not yet in a position to undertake such a step. This does not mean that such an additional step is unnecessary. Quite the contrary! Achieving it on the question of the Petrine ministry would mark a great breakthrough.

6. Eberhard Jüngel: "Um Gottes willen — Klarheit! Kritische Bemerkungen zur Verharmlosung der kriteriologischen Funktion des Rechtfertigungsartikels — aus Anlass einer ökumenischen Gemeinsamen Erklärung zur Rechtfertigungslehre" [For God's Sake — Clarity! Critical remarks on the underplaying of criteriological function of the article of justification — on the occasion of an ecumenical common declaration on the doctrine of justification], *ZthK* 94/97, pp. 59-65 (p. 64). This argument also appears in the first paragraph of the statement of the German professors, but has not been taken up in the decisive second part of the text, which defines the consensus as uniformity of doctrinal statements.

Part II: Two Subtopics

Following these fundamental explications on the understanding and nature of consensus, two fields are to be addressed in a second part in which the JD takes a course that may bear fruit also in the issue of papal ministry.

The Question about the Instrumentality of the Church in God's Saving Work

Ecumenical research has known for the last twenty years that there is a common denominator in the field of ecclesiology that summarizes the specific differences. Cardinal Walter Kasper asked as early as 1980 whether "the holiness of the church is suitable enough to permit it to act through its members in a holy and sanctifying manner? Or does the church possess this holiness only in the form of a promise or qualification?"[7] In other words, can the church, which is hallowed not on its own initiative but by God, do things whose actor is itself and that hallow its members in view of their salvation?

For instance, the dialogue on "the Lord's Supper" attained a broad consensus and showed that the remaining major divergence was about the Catholic understanding of the eucharistic offering by the church as being more than a thank offering.[8] There is an agreement on the uniqueness of Christ's sacrifice, but divergence remains with regard to the church, which is, despite its complete submission to Christ, the originator of the action that brings salvation to believers. The delineations between the saving work of the church and its office bearers are occasion for this divergence, as confirmed also by the dialogue on ministry.[9] The consensus is obviously larger than initially intended. The ministry stands in the service of word and sacraments, in the service of the sole mediator Jesus Christ. This is indispensable

---

7. Walter Kasper, "Gegebene Einheit — bestehende Schranken — gelebte Gemeinschaft," *KNA. Ökumenische Information* 52 (1980): 5-7 and 53/54 (1980): 7-10.

8. Gemeinsame römisch-katholisch/evangelisch-lutherische Kommission, *Das Herrenmahl* (Paderborn/Frankfurt am Main: Bonifacius/Lembeck, 1978); also in Harding Meyer et al., eds., *Dokumente wachsender Übereinstimmung: sämtliche Berichte und Konsenstexte interkonfessioneller Gespräche auf Weltebene* (Paderborn/Frankfurt am Main: Bonifacius/Lembeck, 1983), vol. 1, pp. 271ff. Hereafter cited as *DWÜ*.

9. Gemeinsame römisch-katholisch/evangelisch-lutherische Kommission, *Das geistliche Amt in der Kirche* (Paderborn/Frankfurt am Main: Bonifacius/Lembeck, 1978); also in *DWÜ*, vol. 1, pp. 329-57.

for the church. Catholics recall that the Lutheran ministry is marked by a *defectus sacramenti ordinis,* which is based not only on the lack of integration in the apostolic succession, but is also due to a different understanding of the ways and means of the clergy's involvement in God's work. Protestant theology knows rather an instrumental assistance; Catholic theology recognizes a more active participation of the ordained ministry in the priesthood of Christ.[10] The office bearer fully submits himself to Christ as the single source of salvation, but he is hallowed, according to the Catholic understanding, to the extent that he possesses a special character that equips him for sanctifying action, a trait enabling him to preside over eucharistic celebrations. The same problem also emerges in the well-known dispute on the Scripture and tradition. The divergence concerns the way in which authority is endowed in the Scripture, and especially the role of the church and its teaching authority for the established interpretation of the Scripture. We are now dealing with the two most difficult questions relating to the exercise of papal ministry today, the question of the infallibility and the primacy of jurisdiction. Is the church — especially the bishop of Rome — hallowed by God to the extent that it is in a position to decide over the truth?

In order to eliminate every single misunderstanding, two specifications are necessary.

1. It is clear that in Reformation theology the church is understood as God's co-worker for the salvation of human beings. This cooperation is not merely passive and instrumental. Nor is the church simply a visible instrument of the invisible work of God. Whenever the church preaches, baptizes, gives absolution, and celebrates Eucharist in Christ's name, God himself is at work. He has decided to work in and through the concrete ecclesiastical work and through the office bearer entrusted with it. Nevertheless he alone remains the originator of grace and salvation. The church's own work is basically receptive, characterized by a creative passivity of faith, in accordance with the image of the life and work of a Christian justified by faith alone. In this manner, every work of the church lets the work of God, the only source of salvation, shine through.

2. Furthermore it is essential to remember that Catholic theology centers around the differentiation between the primary instrumentality of God and the secondary instrumentality of the church as well as the foremost position of the uniqueness of God's work. B. Sesboüé, a French Catholic theo-

---

10. Second Vatican Council, LG *(Lumen gentium)* 10 and PO *(Presbyterorum ordinis)* 2.

logian, specifies this as follows: "The church becomes the subject of the saving work of God in Christ neither in the sense that it would add a causality of the same kind as God's, nor in the sense that it would intervene in God's work, but only as long as it discharges an instrumental causality which is imbued by the main causality, in other words it acts under grace."[11]

The focal point addressed by the open questions is not easily identifiable. For both traditions, the church's instrumentality is secondary with regard to the primary mediatorship of Christ, and the church's mediatorship can never be elevated to the height of the prime instrumentality of Christ. The issue is the status granted by the respective church to its office bearers within the Christian mystery. The difference can be shown in comparative terms only. In Catholicism the church seems to be more central and its instrumentality more effective than in the Reformation tradition, according to which the church is less primary without being secondary.

Can the JD — which admittedly leaves aside ecclesiology — be of any help in this matter? There are some factors pointing in this direction.

The relationship between human beings and God is the focal point of particular elaborations of the Lutheran and Catholic positions in the JD. For both traditions, justification is endowed in and through baptism (JD 28). In the moment of baptism God interrupts the sinner's life and declares him or her to be his child. Catholic theology insists on the ontological changes that take place through baptism. It says that baptism marks the end of the person's state as a sinner; original sin has been removed. The believer is now the abode of grace, equipped to do good deeds and called to grow in this state of grace towards an ultimate justification that will take place at the end of time. The road to salvation depicts a linear progress, with baptism marking the moment of crossing to another existence, the moment of conversion. Every severe sin that throws the baptized back to a former state requires the sacrament of absolution, which brings the sinner back to the path of salvation. Each Catholic statement of the JD, read one after another, points to the faithfulness of the Catholic partner to this theological tradition. This understanding of salvation as a progress in small steps represents a theological and anthropological decision that, driven by its inner logic, gives room for some serious caveats in the light of the following points: (1) the baptized remains a sinner as his state has changed, (2) the baptized attains the certitude of salvation as he has not reached the end of his road yet, (3) there is no certain in-

---

11. Bernard Sesboüé, "Y a-t-il une différence séparatrice entre les ecclésiologies catholique et protestantes?" *NRT* 109 (1987): 3-30 (here 10-11).

volvement of the believer in his salvation, and (4) good deeds, which symbolize the progress along the road to salvation, have no meritorious character. This linear understanding was repeatedly challenged by the Lutheran partner, who questioned the notion that the door to salvation could be opened by good deeds. They are certainly not the reason of baptism and justification, but the growth in grace takes place, according to this understanding, through good deeds for which the person could take pride before God.

The decision of Lutheran theology is different. Without denying the ontological change effected by baptism, it suggests a radically different approach. Luther's principal decision is marked by a different understanding of God's righteousness. Righteousness is an attribute of God. Instead of setting off an active righteousness intended to punish the unrighteous, God opts for a passive righteousness which is his mercy. This new divine righteousness is received by the believer as a gift and work of God.[12] As a divine attribute this righteousness cannot become a human quality or attribute. It is given to the believer in the relationship that binds the believer to God and, in and through faith, permits participation in a reality that changes the person fundamentally and remains extrinsic. In this relationship, the believer's faithfulness is the work of the Holy Spirit and constitutes an equivalent to God's faithfulness. Particular Lutheran statements in the JD, read one after another, show this Lutheran theological tradition. This radically relational understanding of salvation of the relationship *coram Deo* is very reluctant (1) to insist on the believer's good deeds, as it sees them as consequences and never as prerequisites of this new relationship; (2) to consider the possibility of the human's active involvement in salvation; (3) to declare that the believer is not righteous before God and at the same time sinful, as he or she always turns away from God; and (4) to deny the certitude of salvation, which is understood not as a future gift but as a present reality whose plenitude will be revealed at the end of time. This relational conception of salvation was repeatedly challenged by the Catholic partner, who suspected that it did not sufficiently testify to a real change in the person, neglecting personal salvation and relieving the believer of all responsibility during the earthly life.

The overall procedure of the JD consisted in bringing these two approaches up for discussion without confusing them. Without leaving the persisting differences aside, it tried to reach an agreement on a certain number of statements meant to overcome the exclusive and thus divisive charac-

---

12. Cf. the foreword of the first edition of his works in Latin, in which Luther explains his Reformation-related discovery regarding this notion, WA 54, 185f.

ter of either approach and to show that both approaches, in their diversity, aim to bear witness to the unique work of God for the benefit of humankind. The JD shows that the main concerns of one partner are not contradicted by the other, but rather shared by both. This was to be examined and reiterated on the basis of the involvement in salvation, the true change of the believer, faith alone, the significance of the double *simul,* the scope of the law, the certitude of salvation, and the necessity of good deeds as consequences of justification. Therefore, according to the subscribing churches of the JD, "the Lutheran and the Catholic explications of justification are in their difference open to one another and do not destroy the consensus regarding the basic truths" (JD 40).

The decisive breakthrough of the JD is due to the insight that these fundamentally different approaches in human understanding of God do not impede the consensus. They were once occasion for division, but have lost their dividing character. They constitute rather an integral part of the consensus and declare that different theological decisions can testify to one and the same truth, viz., the work of God who offers his salvation to humankind.

Could what was achieved in the realm of the doctrine on salvation also be made to bear fruit for ecclesiology? I would like to offer the following thesis for discussion:

The Lutheran understanding of humans *coram Deo* leads to an understanding of justification — the Lutheran explication in the JD — that has a certain ecclesiology as a result, an ecclesiology that assigns an instrumentality to the church, laying the main emphasis on God's action analogous to the action of the justified, while being very cautious towards any claim on a saving work of the church. On the contrary, the Catholic understanding of justification as presented in the JD conceives of an active participation of the justified, which finds expression in an active instrumentality of the church. The latter is authorized by God to act in a saving way on behalf of God. The ultimate expression of this capacity of the church is logically the special ministry of the bishop of Rome and his special capabilities for the whole church. If this thesis is true, a close link is established between the understanding of the being of the church as an instrument of salvation and the issue of justification. The progress in the realm of justification can therefore be made to bear fruit also in view of the instrumentality of the church, especially the papal ministry.

The question is whether this link between justification and ecclesiology can be declared in such a way.

The Lutheran theologians raise the same questions. What is valid for the justified believer is also valid for the church as a community of believers. This understanding of *coram Deo* also applies to the church. The church is, just like the believer, righteous and sinful at the same time: righteous in its lasting relation to God who lets the one work of God show in its every single action, sinful the moment it turns towards itself thinking that it can sanctify the world on God's behalf. It then loses its raison d'être. The question about the nature of the church's instrumentality is the same as the question about justification. It involves the human being and the church *coram Deo.*

In Catholic theology, the matter is not so simple, as it probably avoids setting an analogy between the justified and the church, which marks the Lutheran approach. The church is not only the community of believers celebrating word and sacraments. Its integration in God's secret certainly embraces this dimension too, but also transcends it. The church is "in Christ like a sacrament or as a sign and instrument both of a very closely knit union with God and of the unity of the whole human race" (LG 1). The understanding of the very nature of the church cannot be expressed in brief here; it is a central field of contemporary theological research into this tradition.

The analogy between soteriology and ecclesiology must be tackled in dialogue.[13] It should be kept in mind that the question of *cooperatio* of the justified is today not a church-dividing hindrance. If the thesis just mentioned is true, then we can gain from the JD some crucial pointers that may help us advance in all ecclesiological questions, especially in the question of papal ministry.

The Question about the "Criterion"

Thoughts regarding the way of correlating soteriology and ecclesiology bring us to the second question of this second part, the question about the "criterion." I take up here the term used in JD 18, well aware of the difficulty of this term. One can only agree with W. Pannenberg, who regrets that the first version was discarded in which the message of justification is given "a comprehensive critical and normative function."[14] The term of the criterion, inserted at the request of the German churches, only caused confusion.

13. Cf. Roman Catholic/Evangelical Lutheran Mixed Commission, *Church and Justification: Understanding the Church in the Light of the Doctrine of Justification* (Geneva: Lutheran World Federation, 1994).

14. Wolfhart Pannenberg, "Neue Konsense, entschärfte Gegensätze und protestantische Ängste," *EPD-Dok.* 11 (1998): 39-41 (here 40).

This paper cannot enter into detail concerning the problems of JD paragraph 18.[15] This paragraph addresses the question as to whether the message of justification is the only criterion for all truths of faith, as Lutherans assert, or if there are also other criteria obliging the churches, as Catholics claim.

It is interesting to see that in the whole debate over the JD it was only in connection with this article that the question about the papal ministry was raised. In his first reaction, E. Jüngel asked tauntingly whether papal infallibility might be held as one of these other indispensable criteria.[16]

Let's just take note of what is declared in this paragraph:

On the one hand there is a common statement. The doctrine explaining the biblical message of justification is not one of the statements, but "stands in an essential relation to all truths of faith, which are to be seen as internally related to each other." Therefore it is "an indispensable criterion" for all the teachings and practice of the church. Its application does not depend on the good will of theologians and church leaders. It cannot be qualified by other criteria, nor should it be called into question by other aspects of the whole body of doctrinal statements that characterize a church family. This applies of course to the realm of ecclesiology too, including the question of papal ministry.

However, this common statement also expresses dissonance. Of course, Lutherans would have welcomed using the definite article for "criterion." Catholics are opposed to this option. Well aware of this difficulty, the JD adds that Catholics, unlike Lutherans, "see themselves as bound by several criteria." These other criteria are not named, but can be conjectured from tradition and church history, and also the understanding of ministry and church. It is evident that this difference in the understanding of the

---

15. JD 18: "Therefore the doctrine of justification, which takes up this message and explicates it, is more than just one part of Christian doctrine. It stands in an essential relation to all truths of faith, which are to be seen as internally related to each other. It is an indispensable criterion which constantly serves to orient all the teaching and practice of our churches to Christ. When Lutherans emphasize the unique significance of this criterion, they do not deny the interrelation and significance of all truths of faith. When Catholics see themselves as bound by several criteria, they do not deny the special function of the message of justification. Lutherans and Catholics share the goal of confessing Christ in all things, who alone is to be trusted above all things as the one Mediator (1 Tim. 2:5f.) through whom God in the Holy Spirit gives himself and pours out his renewing gifts."

16. Eberhard Jüngel, "Um Gottes willen — Klarheit," *EPD-Dok.* 46 (1997): 59-65 (here 62).

criteriological function of justification entails the impossibility of drawing any ecclesiological consequences directly from the common understanding of justification right at the outset.

This convergence and dissonance are not surprising, as they are mere repetition of the difficulty shown already in the national and international dialogues.

The theological challenge is about the place occupied by the doctrine of salvation in the presentation of Christian teachings, a place worthy of being generally referred to as "special" even if it lacks agreement on its unique character and significance. As in the preceding paragraph, what counts here is also the very definition of church and salvation as well as the manner in which the ecclesiological contexts are and should be submitted to this hermeneutic key describing the message of justification.

In this debate everything boils down to the papal ministry, which appears as the tip of the iceberg and results in pointing to a far-reaching problem that is, however, still open. It is related to what the Lutheran tradition calls the "main article," and the Catholic the "hierarchy of truths." These two concerns are certainly not identical. Their theological objects are different. Their basis or rather their center — the reconciliation given to humans by God — and their goal — the concern to make clear the interrelation of all truths and thus the history of the church and churches — can be directly compared. A comparison illustrates the various ways of understanding the hierarchical ministry for the being of the church. Many examples could be given here for the clarification of this problem, the ultimate concern of JD 18. Let me refer to the last encyclical of John Paul II. In article 35 of the *Ecclesia de eucharistia,* it is expressly underlined that the community of the church is the "communion in the teaching of the Apostles, in the sacraments, and in the Church's hierarchical order."

The term of the "main article" is an object of animated discussion in Lutheranism, and that of the "hierarchy of truths" in Catholicism. In ecumenical theology, the difficulty emerges in identifying the relationship between these two, specifically in the light of a well-known problem, the necessary and sufficient conditions for the true unity of the church.

In the Reformation tradition it is agreed that "agreement in the right teaching of the Gospel and in the right administration of the sacraments is the necessary and sufficient prerequisite for the true unity of the Church."[17]

---

17. §2 of the Leuenberg Agreement, in *Agreement between Reformation Churches in Europe (Leuenberg Agreement)* (Frankfurt am Main: Lembeck, 1993) (trilingual version).

This is simply due to the fact that, according to the Reformation understanding, preaching of the word and celebration of the sacraments are the instruments granted by God to offer himself to sinners and justify them. By justifying sinners, God assembles them to his body, the church. The same instruments of grace through which God justifies the individual are constitutive for the church — the assembly of believers celebrating the word and sacraments — and ground their unity. No further conditions can be added to them. Therefore, the agreement on the message of justification, which has a decisive and exclusive significance for the salvation of each and every human being, will have the necessary and sufficient condition for a common understanding of the church and thus the necessary and sufficient condition for the unity of the church, as soon as it finds expression in a consensus on word and sacrament. This approach was implemented in the dialogues between the families forged from the Reformation, leading to many "declarations of church fellowship" between the Lutheran, Reformed, Anglican, and Methodist traditions.

Catholics and the Orthodox generally demand the complementing of this approach to unity with a corresponding treatment of the ecclesiological aspects, especially with the same understanding and common exercise of the church's ministry. Protestants certainly do not deny that the church's ministry is constitutive for the being of the church, but they do not attach the same degree of importance and authority to the structures of church and ministry that have come into being in church history. Catholics add in turn that it is the same concern of proclaiming the salvation in Christ, which causes these elements to come into being in the Old Church and later. Limiting the criteria to the celebration of word and sacraments eclipses other factors that need to be considered in order to do justice to the wealth of ecclesiastical mystery. Since 1984 the international Lutheran-Catholic dialogue has spoken about a "certain 'asymmetry' in the more precise definition of the theological values assigned to the ministry, particularly of the historic episcopacy in the understanding of the church."[18] The dialogue *Church and Justification* (1994) in turn differentiates between what is necessary for salvation and what is necessary for the church.[19] No agreement has been attained to

18. The Joint Lutheran–Roman Catholic Commission, *Facing Unity: Models, Forms and Phases of Catholic-Lutheran Church Fellowship*, para. 94.2 (joint statement, Rome, 1984).

19. The Joint Lutheran–Roman Catholic Commission, *Church and Justification*, 1994, par. 210-11.

date about how a consensus on certain church structures, particularly on ministries, is necessary for unity. For the Reformation churches, church unity does not demand the same theology of ministries as long as it does not contradict the "main article." For the Catholic Church, such a diversity calls the very being of the church into question. The question about the "criterion," which remains open in JD 18, depends on an even more difficult, still open ecclesiological issue that inevitably condenses to the question about the significance of the papal ministry for the being of the church.

Summarizing Remarks

By way of summary some conclusions may be drawn regarding the link between the JD and the papal ministry:

- The subject of papacy, or Petrine ministry, is not handled in the JD.
- The method used in the JD, particularly the understanding of consensus made clear through this method, should always be applicable to other questions. Only by proving its worth, first and foremost in ecclesiological questions, will it provide this process with the necessary authority.
- The JD's results can be made to bear fruit also in terms of the contents. This is especially true of the manner in which the JD clearly shows in the end that two different anthropologies, two understandings of human beings *coram Deo,* express one and the same truth. It is not least related to the involvement of human beings in God's saving work as well. Is this applicable to the church? It would be important to know, because the question about how the church is instrumental has proved to be a point of crystallization of all unsettled questions in the Lutheran-Catholic dialogue. For Lutherans, what is possible in the doctrine of salvation should also be applicable to ecclesiology. This should also prove exemplarily true with regard to the papal ministry.
- The question of "criterion" is more difficult because this remains an unsettled question in the JD too. Whereas the Lutheran side understands the message of justification as the main article and thus as the hermeneutic principle for ecclesiology as well, the Catholic side has a more reserved view. For the latter, a different kind of order reigns among the elements decisive for the understanding of the church. It is above all in the understanding of the church that what is an expression

of a legitimate diversity for one party is the point of division for the other party. What is deemed an essential and inescapable demand of faith for one party is, for the other party, important but not necessarily pivotal. At this juncture the question is raised about the structuring principles that apply in each tradition. Papal ministry is the point where the compatibility of varying hierarchies of truths becomes clear as a remaining task.

Against this backdrop, two questions are to be raised to round up the whole matter and step up the contemporary ecumenical efforts of the Reformed-Catholic dialogue.

1. The first question is addressed to the Catholic tradition. With the JD the Roman Catholic Church signed a declaration in which it admits that basic truths can be expressed in a form and manner other than the usual in its own tradition. What matters here is not only wordings and linguistic forms, but also various theological decisions and emphases. This is a crucial novelty. This has not been possible until now (at least in the Western dialogue). This has considerable consequences also in the inner-Catholic setting. The question to be raised by Lutherans to Catholics is hence the following: Is what was possible in the question of justification also possible in the realm of ecclesiology? In other words: Is it conceivable that Rome acknowledges another church with different traditions, forms of piety, structures of ministry, and theological approaches as a true expression of *una sancta catholica et apostolica ecclesia?* Certainly there will have to be many dialogues to fathom the possibilities of such a step. The fundamental question has to be raised though. At the moment everything boils down to it. In view of the papal ministry it signifies the acknowledgment of a church in which the universal sole ministry is understood and exercised differently than in Rome. It would be a differentiated consensus, which obviously means that the Roman way of exercising this ministry is also acknowledged by the partner churches, after the necessary theological dialogue, as a true expression of this sole ministry.

2. The second question is to be addressed to the churches of the Reformation. Here too, everything is converging to one point. The declarations of church fellowship between the Lutheran, Reformed, Anglican, and Methodist families are increasing in number. However, difficulties arise at the moment that this new community is to be given a visible shape. Participants seem to be content with a spiritual unity and often advocate a "congregationalism" of the old confessional and national ecclesiastical identity. They have doubts about every effort to create a binding entity that would chal-

lenge the autonomy of the established identities. In theological terms this involves none other than catholicity. Therefore these traditions must be questioned as to whether they are prepared for and capable of catholicity. This inevitably needs a ministry of unity that transcends local (and national) boundaries, a ministry that should be exercised collegially, personally, and synodically. In these traditions too, the question about the universal ministry of unity in contemporary ecumenical situations is more crucial than is generally assumed. The JD makes no mention of it whatsoever. Nevertheless, also for the sake of Reformation traditions, this should be understood as a direct consequence of the JD.

A Ministry of Unity in the Context
of Conciliarity and Synodality

Eero Huovinen

Introduction

1. Regarding the theme of this consultation, there is an anecdote making the rounds in Finland about the late, highly respected bishop of the Roman Catholic Diocese of Finland, Paul Verschuren (1925-99). When Bishop Paul went to Rome from the northern boundaries of the church, Pope John Paul II asked him: "What, in your opinion, is the greatest impediment to ecumeny [sic]?" With a charming grin, Bishop Paul answered in his characteristic open manner: "You yourself, Holy Father."[1]

The answer was not offensive, as it was neither focused on Karol Wojtila nor on John Paul II. The answer was directed towards the Petrine ministry as an ecumenical issue. Bishop Paul honestly expressed what we all know. On the one hand, the Roman Catholic Church holds that the ministry of the successor of St. Peter is a ministry of service for the unity and communion of the church. On the other hand, this ministry is, in the opinion of many, the greatest obstacle to unity.

2. Throughout history, various weighty attributes have been linked to this ministry of the unity of the church. These attributes both defend and assail the office. In some sense, the way one regards the papal ministry has become a shibboleth, a pet phrase Christians have used to evaluate one another.

In the Middle Ages, the Catholic teaching ministry defined subordina-

---

1. As a matter of fact, Pope Paul VI had, in 1967, expressed the same idea in discussion with the representatives of the Secretariat for Promoting Christian Unity.

tion *(subesse)* to the pope of Rome as an absolute prerequisite for salvation.[2] The First Vatican Council appears to have adhered to this concept. Priests and believers of all rites are bound to the pope's juridical authority *(potestas jurisdictionis)* in hierarchical subordination *(hierarchicae subordinationis)* as regards the doctrine(s) of the church, morals, on questions of order and administration: "This is the teaching of the catholic truth, and no one can depart from it without endangering his faith and salvation" *(a qua deviare salva fide atque salute nemo potest).*[3]

For their part the Lutheran Reformers accused the pope of being the Antichrist, the opponent of Christ. This abusive word has been used by the members of other churches as well, from the Orthodox monks of Mount Athos to "free church" Christians. We can hardly hold viewpoints on the Petrine ministry that are farther apart than those represented by these words. But can we approach each other, come together?

3. It is the gift of God that, in general, during the last fifty years the Christian churches have not only been able to approach each other but have also learned to better understand the variety of views on the Petrine ministry.

What has been particularly encouraging in the development within the Roman Catholic Church is that the Second Vatican Council dealt with the Petrine ministry specifically as an episcopal ministry and as part of the collegium of bishops. Although Vatican II approved of the teaching of the First Vatican Council on the papacy, it also balanced this teaching by emphasizing the bishop of Rome as a servant of unity and as part of the college of bishops.[4]

2. Boniface VIII, Bulla *"Unam Sanctam"* (1302): *"Porro subesse Romano Pontifici omni humanae creaturae declaramus, dicimus, diffinimus omnino esse de necessitate salutis"* (Denzinger 875).

3. The Dogmatic Constitution *Pastor aeternus*, chap. 3 (Denzinger 3060), English edition, Norman P. Tanner, ed., *Conciliorum oecumenicorum decreta: Decrees of the ecumenical councils* (London/Washington, DC: Sheed & Ward/Georgetown University, 1990).

4. It is true that Vatican II states of the pope's supreme authority: "In virtue of his office, that is as Vicar of Christ and pastor of the whole Church, the Roman Pontiff has full, supreme and universal power over the church. And he is always free to exercise this power." But it also admits that the supreme authority resides in the collegium of bishops: "The order of bishops, which succeeds to the college of apostles and gives this apostolic body continued existence, is also the subject of supreme and full power over the universal Church, provided we understand this body together with its head the Roman Pontiff and never without this head." This tension in the relationship between the primacy and the bishops is explicated in the session of 16 November 1964, and the exposition of this, *Nota explicativa praevia*, published with the imprimatur of the pope at that time. In addition, *Ut unum sint* emphasizes the pope's connection to the college of bishops: "When the

4. As a young student at the University of Helsinki, I was given the task of researching Karl Rahner's concepts of the relations of the papacy and the episcopacy. I remember being intrigued by Rahner's speculative skill. In one respect, he attempted to be obedient to the Catholic tradition and to the First Vatican Council. In other respects, he searched for a theological interpretation for the primacy of the pope as part of the college of bishops. And while the pope is infallible *"ex sese, non ex consensu Ecclesiae,"* as taught by Vatican I, still he is, even alone, connected to the college of bishops. Between the college of bishops and the primacy of the pope, there prevails a paradoxical "identical difference."[5]

According to Rahner, in one Church, where one office has one vested authority, the supremacy cannot be used by other than one subject. The pope is the pope only as the head of the college of bishops. And the episcopal collegium does not exist other than with the pope and subordinate to him. Between the pope and the college of bishops there exists an essential unity. Neither has authority from the other but only directly from Christ.

Although the pope and the college of bishops essentially form one entity, they nevertheless can act separately. Of the two subjects, Rahner differentiates two modes of activity: the collegial act *(der kollegiale Akt)* and the papal act *(der Akt des Papstes)*. The most visible form of collegial activity is an ecumenical council; other forms are the episcopal conference *(Bischofsrat)*, the act of selecting the pope, or a possible "council by correspondence." The pope neither "ratifies" nor "approves" the decisions of collegial acts, as he does not remain external in relation to the collegium, but is part of it. Thus, a collegial act always includes a papal act.

The pope, for his part, is always a member of the episcopal collegium, and its head. Nevertheless one can speak of particular papal acts. In these acts, the pope alone as head of the collegium exercises the authority residing in the entire collegium. Although the pope in his own act may function

---

Catholic Church affirms that the office of the Bishop of Rome corresponds to the will of Christ, she does not separate this office from the mission entrusted to the whole body of Bishops, who are also 'vicars and ambassadors of Christ'" (*Lumen Gentium, 27*). "The Bishop of Rome is a member of the 'College,' and the Bishops are his brothers in the ministry" (*Ut unum sint, 95*).

5. Eero Huovinen, "Karl Rahner's concept of the relation of the episcopacy and the papacy," M.Th. thesis, University of Helsinki, 1970. The concept "identical difference" is used by Tuomo Mannermaa in his Ph.D. dissertation, *"Lumen fidei et objectum fidei adventicium.* Die Spontaneität und Rezeptivität der Glaubenserkenntnis im frühen Denken Karl Rahners," University of Helsinki, 1970.

physically separately from the collegium, he is nevertheless always essentially the head of the collegium. Thus, an act of the pope is always at the same time an act of the collegium. In practice, the collegium influences the activities of the pope through charismatic and paracanonical measures.

5. Where Lutheran theology underscores the collegiality of the bishops, the cause of this is not so much the admiration of Greek democracy or the psychological fear of the abuse of power, but the theological doctrine of Christ as head and high priest of the church, under whose authority every believer, priest, and bishop must bow.

In the Smalcald Articles, Luther's stand is both theologically and pastorally surprisingly close to what we presently desire to interpret as the collegiality of the bishops: "Consequently the church cannot be better governed and maintained than by having all of us live under one head, Christ, and by having all the bishops equal in office (however they may differ in gifts) and diligently joined together in unity of doctrine, faith, sacraments, prayer, works of love, etc."[6]

6. We Lutherans have indirectly arrived at a situation where we have to ponder the problematics of the papacy, as in our own churches we have been asked what type and form of spiritual leadership we hold to be correct. In many Lutheran churches around the world, the pastoral significance of the episcopacy has been rediscovered. The direction of advancement is delineated in the classic words of the title of the book: *Kirchenpräsident oder Bischof?*[7] It is to be noted that in the Nordic countries the Lutheran Reformation preserved the episcopacy as an essential part of the church order.

The office of a bishop is by its theological nature a spiritual and pastoral ministry. Even under a heavy burden of practical tasks, the office may not be narrowed down to administrative and bureaucratic duties. A bishop is not primarily a chairman of councils and committees; his most important tool is not the gavel, but the missal, breviary, or hymnal. The proper see of a bishop is not a chair in an office or a seat in an official car. His true see is in the church before the altar or in the pulpit.

7. There has been a growing appreciation of the ecumenical role of the

6. Smalcald Articles II, 4, 9 (Theodore G. Tappert, ed., *The Book of Concord: The Confessions of the Evangelical Lutheran Church* [Philadelphia: Fortress, 1959]).

7. Ivar Asheim and Victor R. Gold, eds., *Kirchenpräsident oder Bischof? Untersuchungen zur Entwicklung und Definition des kirchenleitenden Amtes in der lutherischen Kirche* (Göttingen: Vandenhoeck & Ruprecht, 1968). English translation: Ivar Asheim and Victor R. Gold, eds., *Episcopacy in the Lutheran Church? Studies in the Development and Definition of the Office of Church Leadership* (Philadelphia: Fortress Press, 1970).

Petrine ministry. Rather more often the Catholic Church underlines the fact that the bishop of Rome and his ministry already have ecumenical significance. The statements of the pope are read in all the churches and explained everywhere in the media. Thus we Lutherans must also take this invitation to dialogue on the Petrine ministry as a serious challenge to the members of other churches.

Pope John Paul II in his encyclical *Ut unum sint* called upon even the members of other churches for a "fraternal dialogue" to search for a praxis for the ministry of the bishop of Rome that would be "open to a new situation" and would serve the unity of Christendom and the benefit of all Christians.

"Could not the real but imperfect communion existing between us persuade church leaders and their theologians to engage with me in a patient and fraternal dialogue on this subject, a dialogue in which, leaving useless controversies behind, we could listen to one another, keeping before us only the will of Christ for his Church?"[8] This important and valuable invitation also forms the basis for our joint consultation here.

8. Although Lutherans and Catholics have not treated on the papacy more broadly, yet certain important initial steps have been taken. To start with, Lutherans have confessed that although we believe we have preserved all the true marks of a church *(notae ecclesiae),* nevertheless "no local church should exist in isolation since it is a manifestation of the universal church."[9] Within our own tradition there have been congregational and provincial emphases that have viewed the spiritual communion of individual Christians or communion between local congregations as being the most important.

---

8. "Whatever relates to the unity of all Christian communities clearly forms part of the concerns of the primacy. As Bishop of Rome I am fully aware . . . that Christ ardently desires the full and visible communion of all those Communities in which, by virtue of God's faithfulness, his Spirit dwells. I am convinced that I have a particular responsibility in this regard, above all in acknowledging the Christian Communities and in heeding the request made of me to find a way of exercising the primacy which, while in no way renouncing what is essential to its mission, is nonetheless open to a new situation. . . . This is an immense task, which we cannot refuse and which I cannot carry out by myself. Could not the real but imperfect communion existing between us persuade Church leaders and their theologians to engage with me in a patient and fraternal dialogue on this subject, a dialogue in which, leaving useless controversies behind, we could listen to one another, keeping before us only the will of Christ for his Church and allowing ourselves to be deeply moved by his plea 'that they may all be one . . . so that the world may believe that you have sent me'? (John 17:21)" (*Ut unum sint,* 95-96).

9. Malta Report 1972.

9. An excellent example of the development of the Lutheran churches towards universal communion has been the discussion over the name of the Lutheran World Federation.

Whereas the Allgemeine Evangelisch-Lutherische Konferenz, founded in the nineteenth century, was a free world conference of Lutherans, the Lutheran World Convention, formed in 1923, was a form of confederation. The Lutheran World Federation, in 1947, was to begin with "a free association of Lutheran Churches." On the initiative of Peter Brunner, in the 1960s there was great debate as to whether the LWF was a free association or a confessional communion. In the Curitiba Assembly, 1990, it was decided that the LWF was both "a communion of churches which . . . are united in pulpit and altar fellowship" and "an instrument of its autonomous member churches." At the Winnipeg Assembly of 2003, the intent was to complete the name as "Lutheran World Federation — A Communion of Churches."

10. Whenever considering the Lutheran churches as they seek visible unity with other churches, it is good to recall the slow internal development of Lutheranism and the many difficulties incurred. Ecclesiology has not always been the strongest or most characteristic area in Lutheranism. Discussion on doctrine as well as contact with other churches can also assist us in understanding what Lutheran ecclesiology is. Even the discussion of papal status can shed light, e.g., on what *communio* and collegiality truly mean.

11. No longer do the Lutheran churches in a pre-conciliary fashion demand complete revocation of the papacy as an absolute prerequisite for unity. On the one hand, Lutherans have attempted to promote and serve the unity of the universal church through ecumenical organizations. On the other hand, in the minds of many Lutherans the Petrine ministry correctly understood and properly exercised could possibly serve unity.

The Malta Report states that the papacy subordinated to the "primacy of the gospel" is not excluded: "The office of the papacy as a visible sign of the unity of the churches was therefore not excluded insofar as it is subordinated to the primacy of the gospel by theological reinterpretation and practical restructuring."[10] If this holds true, it is no small matter. It is quite a different af-

---

10. "It was recognized on the Lutheran side that no local church should exist in isolation since it is a manifestation of the universal church. In this sense the importance of a ministerial service of the communion of churches was acknowledged and at the same time reference was made to the problem raised for Lutherans by their lack of such an effective service of unity. The office of the papacy as a visible sign of the unity of the churches was therefore not excluded insofar as it is subordinated to the primacy

fair to come together to discuss the reinterpretation of the papal office and the proper exercise of its ministry than to demand its unconditional abolishment.

12. At the same time, we must state that the Malta Report did not hold unanimity on papal status to be a condition determining altar fellowship and the recognition of ministerial offices: "It was nevertheless agreed that the question of altar fellowship and of mutual recognition of ministerial offices should not be unconditionally dependent on a consensus on the question of primacy."[11] How does this statement relate to the new encyclical *Ecclesia de Eucharistia?*

In place of a disapproving attitude our ecumenical duty is to ponder, "in a patient and fraternal dialogue," those possibilities that are contained within the spiritual realization of the papal ministry. In spite of the wounds of the past, our task is to think courageously of what the papacy would be, "subordinated to the primacy of the gospel," and what is intended by "theological reinterpretation and practical restructuring." In the same breath we Lutherans must ask ourselves if we have always placed *ourselves* under the primacy of the gospel.

The Papacy and the Lutheran Reformation

13. In order for us to move forward in the ecumenical dialogue on the Petrine ministry, we Lutherans, for our part, must be capable of patiently evaluating what, during the time of the Reformation, was really being stated, what they desired to say. The past cannot and should not be erased, but it can be understood. At the time of the Reformation, what were the foci of various critiques of the papacy?

14. First, the rift between the Lutheran Reformation and the pope of Rome was not born of theories regarding the papacy, but of practical problems. In looking at the dispute historically, the true first cause was not what was *taught* regarding the papal office but *usus*, i.e., how the office was exercised.[12]

---

of the gospel by theological reinterpretation and practical restructuring" (Malta Report 1972, 66).

11. Malta Report 1972, 67.

12. See Scott Hendrix, *Luther and the Papacy: Stages in a Reformation Conflict* (Philadelphia: Fortress, 1981). According to Hendrix, two abuses, namely, (1) the acceptance of the trade in indulgences and (2) the confirmation of the medieval understanding of peni-

When the young Luther began to oppose the trade in indulgences by publishing his famous theses in 1517, he believed he was defending catholic truth and combating abuse. He believed he would win the pope over: "In my own mind, I could have been assured that in this matter [i.e., the trade in indulgences] I would have the pope as my protector, in whom I could thus place all my trust, because in the decretals he with the utmost clarity condemns the tax collectors [with this term he denoted the mendicant monks who sold indulgences] to shame" (free translation).[13]

When it gradually became apparent that the disciplinary measures undertaken by Rome were not focusing on the trade in indulgences but on Luther himself, his criticism became sharper, until it final centered on the foundations of the papal office. The order of events was, nevertheless, as follows: The dispute began over practical matters, the way in which the papal office was exercised. Only later did the dispute spread to the theological bases of the office itself.

15. Martin Luther's critical relation to the pope was not a set theory but rather a process that culminated and developed by degrees. When he was young he said he was an "archpapist" and a "frenetic supporter of the pope," who even criticized Erasmus of Rotterdam for his adverse comments about the pope.[14] In the discussion on the trade in indulgences he believed he would receive the support of the pope. In his theses on indulgences he did not place into question the pope's primacy *iure divino* but simply reminded the pope that the power of the keys did not extend to purgatory (Thesis 26).

16. When Luther began to be accused of denying the primacy of the pope, six months later he attempted to clarify the arguments of his theses on indulgences by making the classical distinction between office and person. As a private person, anyone, including the pope, can err on doctrine or lapse morally. Therefore, the pope must speak as regards his office in accordance with tradition, to which he is subordinate: "I listen to pope as pope, that is, when he speaks in *(in Canonibus)* and according to the canons *(secundum Canonibus)*, or when he makes a decision in accordance with a council *(cum concilio determinat)*," but not when he speaks according to his own head *(secundum suum caput loquitur)*.[15]

---

tence (i.e., that only true and perfect "contrition" justifies the forgiveness of sins) by Pope Leo X, were the first two matters that roused Luther against the pope.

13. WA 54, 180, 5ff. (Preface to the Latin version).
14. WA 54, 179, 22-23; WA 38, 267, 23-27; WA Tr 4, 25, 10-15.
15. WA 1, 582, 14-26.

The pope cannot speak *secundum suum caput* but *secundum Canonibus*. That means that doctrinal decisions must be made in accordance with the Holy Bible, the church fathers recognized by the Catholic Church, and the church's canons and decretals — and in this order.[16] Because the Bible and the canons speak simply of binding on earth, "anything you bind on earth" (Matt. 16:19), the power of the keys of the pope cannot therefore extend to purgatory. Besides which, if this power did extend there, in Luther's opinion the pope would have a duty to empty and close purgatory.[17]

In all this Luther's true intention is not focused primarily on the church's system for making decisions but on the concept that the Christian faith would preserve its original, apostolic contents. He is aware that the pope can (and he is obliged to) guard the pureness of the apostolic belief but also that under one office and person, the purity of the faith is in danger of becoming distorted. Even the pope needs criteria, foundations for evaluation.

In the same year, 1518, in his letter to Pope Leo X, Luther expressed his obedience to the pope. But between the lines, he also reminds the pope of his duties to be obedient to Christ: "Most Holy Father, I prostrate myself at your feet and before your Holiness I bring all that I am and all that I possess: let me live or slay me, call or disown me, approve or deny me, as you will" (free translation). "I will listen to your voice as the voice of Christ reigning and speaking in you."[18]

17. In the next phase in this development, i.e., March 1518, Luther took still another step. According to him, the primacy of the pope cannot be derived from Christ's words to St. Peter (Matt. 16:18-19), because according to two other Bible texts (Matt. 18:18; John 20:23) and several church fathers, Christ did not give the keys to Peter alone but to all the apostles. The biblical basis for the primacy should be the thirteenth chapter of Romans, which states: "Everyone should obey the government that is over him, because there is no government except that which is put there by God. God has ordered our government to be over us" (Rom. 13:1).

Luther still refrains from denying the papacy *iure divino*, while he derives the papal power as being on the same level as any authority or position

---

16. WA 1, 529, 33-530, 1.

17. WA 1, 574, 30-35.

18. "*Quare, Beatissime Pater, prostratum me pedibus tuae Beatitudinis offero cum omnibus, quae sum et habeo. Vivifica, occide, voca, revoca, approba, reproba, ut placuerit: vocem tuam vocem Christi in te praesidentis et loquentis agnoscam.*" WA 1, 529, 24-25.

of authority that is set by God.[19] Luther states that he respects and follows the Church of Rome in all matters and that he opposes only those who hold that the pope's statements are the sole criteria of the Christian faith.[20]

18. As the dispute over the papacy deepened, Luther, in the next phase, took a larger step by denying the supremacy of the pope *iure divino*. The doctrine that universal supremacy belonged to the successor to St. Peter *de iure divino* did not receive adequate support from the New Testament ("Petrine texts") or from church history. The issue was not whether the bishop of Rome would be a bishop *de iure divino* but whether he had supremacy, i.e., universal jurisdiction *de iure divino*, with regard to other bishops.

Luther's counterargument can be summarized from here on in two parts.

First, *ius divinum* primacy is problematic because it appears to render heretical and schismatic all those churches of Eastern Orthodoxy that have always preserved the true marks of Christ's church but have never been subordinated to the primacy of Rome. Boniface VIII, in the bull *Unam sanctam* (1302), appeared to judge people from those churches to be outside of salvation.[21] This historical theology argument was extremely important in the Reformation not only regarding the pope's universal jurisdiction but also for questions on the justification of child baptism. At the same time, this demonstrated that *sola scriptura* was never alone *(sola scriptura numquam sola)*.

Second, *ius divinum* primacy is held to be ecclesiologically and psychologically problematic as it appears to place the pope above and beyond the reach of all criteria.[22]

19. WA 2, 20, 27-32 *(Acta Augustana)*.

20. WA 2, 22, 22-27 *(Acta Augustana)*.

21. "Zemlich ist die sach, ob das Bapstum zu Rom, wie es in beruhiger besitzung der gewalt ist uber die gantz Christenheit, wie sie sagen, herkummen sei von gotlicher odder meschlicher ordnung, und wo dem szo were, ob man Christlich sagen muge, das alle andere Christen in der gantzen welt ketzer und abruninger sein, ob sie gleich die selben tauff, sacrament, Evangelium und all Artickel des glaubens mit uns eintrechlichklich halten, aufzgenommen, das sie ihre prieser und bischoffe nit von Rom bestetingen lassen oder, wie izst, mit gelt kauffen und wie die Deutschen sich essen und narren lassen, als da sein die Moscobiten, weisse Reussen, dier Krichen, Behemen und vil andere grosse lender in der welt." WA 6, 286, 30–287, 9 *(Von dem Papsttum zu Rom)*. Quoted in Old German.

22. "I fight for only two things: First, I will not tolerate that men establish new articles of faith and scold, slander, and judge as heretics, schismatics, and unbelievers all other Christians in the whole world only because they are not under the pope. It suffices that we let the pope be pope. It is not necessary for his sake to slander God and his saints

For Luther, the "head" of the church is always Jesus Christ. The pope is simply *iure divino* the bishop of Rome: "The pope is not the head of all Christendom by divine right or according to the Word of God, for this position belongs only to one, namely, to Jesus Christ. The pope is only the bishop and pastor of the churches in Rome or of such other churches as have attached themselves to him voluntarily."[23]

20. Was Luther then ready to approve of the primacy of the bishop of Rome on the basis of the law of man *(iure humano)*, perhaps even to recognize this primacy? Does Christendom need one visible head?

Luther's position on the primacy *iure humano* was ambivalent. On one side, in the Smalcald Articles he feels that this primacy is possible: "to whom all others should adhere, in order that the unity of Christendom might better be preserved against the attacks of sects and heresies." On the other side, he doubts that this will work.[24] Thus the outcome seems to be that Christ is the head of the church and that all bishops must be equal: "Consequently the church cannot be better governed and maintained than by having all of us live under one head, Christ, and by having all the bishops equal in office (however they may differ in gifts) and diligently joined together in unity of doctrine, faith, sacraments, prayer, works of love, etc."[25]

21. At last his relationship to the papacy became so inflamed that during his final years Luther held that the papacy was unnecessary, even a condemnable office.[26] There is no use denying that behind Luther's polemic words there was also a personal disappointment in the pope whose ban had made of him an outlaw. Yet, Luther's critique contains so many theological viewpoints that it cannot be dismissed simply as personal bitterness.

22. At the same time, we must note that, in practice, Luther — and the

---

on earth. Second, I shall accept whatever the pope establishes and does, on condition that I judge it first on the basis of Holy Scripture. For my part he must remain under Christ and let himself be judged by Holy Scripture. . . . If these two things are granted, I will let the pope be; indeed, I will help to elevate him as high as they please. If they are not granted, then to me he shall be neither pope nor Christian." *Von dem Papsttum zu Rom*, WA 6, 321,31–322,22 (Jaroslav Pelikan and Helmut T. Lehmann, eds., *Luther's Works* [St. Louis/Philadelphia: Fortress, 1958-86], vol. 39, pp. 101-2).

23. Smalcald Articles II, 4, 1.

24. Smalcald Articles II, 4, 5-8.

25. Smalcald Articles II, 4, 9.

26. In his writing *Wider das Papsttum zu Rom vom Teufel gestiftet* (1545), Luther condemns even the papal office as damnable *(verdamter und lesterlicher Stand)*. See WA 54, 265, 6-8.

Wittenberg theologians — himself exercised an episcopacy. He was truly less than the pope but much more than an ordinary bishop of a diocese. The Reformation congregations throughout Europe sought from Luther — and from Wittenberg — a common "evangelical" course and policy as well as advice on a wide variety of issues, e.g., regarding liturgical controversies and the handling of the elements remaining after the celebration of the mass.

23. The Lutheran Reformation never surrendered its hope for a universal council. The hope for peace, unity, and unanimity was further linked to the hope for a reformed papacy. This thought can be found, e.g., in the stipulation added to the close of the Smalcald Articles by Melanchthon and the priests from the Hamburg region: "I, Philipp Melanchthon, regard the above articles as right and Christian. However, concerning the pope I hold that, if he would allow the gospel, we, too, may concede to him that superiority over the bishops which he possesses by human right, making this concession for the sake of peace and general unity among the Christians who are now under him and who may be in the future."[27]

This piece of evidence is important, although its handling of the primacy of the pope *iure humano* did not correspond to the Catholic concept. This expresses the Lutheran doctrine of the primacy of the gospel — "if he would allow the gospel" — and yet the hope for peace and concord with Rome — "for the sake of peace and general unity." This hope has never been extinguished.

The Collegiality of the Episcopacy in the Porvoo Common Agreement

24. In spite of our differences of theological opinion over the papacy today, we all have to face the same problem as the Reformers did. The issue is what the renewed ministry of leadership in accord with the gospel would be. For one, we ask how, in practice, the pope cares for his ministry. For another, we ask what leadership the Lutheran episcopacy embodies in our own churches.

The activities of episcopacy have been evaluated in analogical fashion in many ecumenical documents. I will refer to only three of these: *Baptism, Eucharist and Ministry,* the Porvoo Common Agreement, and the German Catholic-Lutheran *Communio Sanctorum.*

According to BEM, "the ordained ministry should be exercised in a

---

27. Smalcald Articles III, signatories.

personal, collegial and communal way."[28] The Porvoo Common Agreement applies the same triad to the ministry of oversight,[29] but it takes the BEM concepts a bit further. What does this triad mean?

25. When the Porvoo Common Agreement touches upon the episcopacy, even the subheadings reflect the concept of the bishop as a *servant* of the apostolicity of the church (IV Episcopacy in the Service of the Apostolicity of the Church, §§34-35). It is characteristic of Porvoo that it emphasizes the continuity of the entire church (The Apostolicity of the Whole Church, §§36-40). The episcopacy functions in the service of the apostolicity of the entire church and therefore *under* it: "Thus the primary manifestation of apostolic succession is to be found in the apostolic tradition of the Church *as a whole*."[30]

Within the apostolicity of the *whole* church there is, firstly an apostolic succession (§40), secondly an apostolic ministry (§41), and thirdly a ministry of coordination and oversight (§42). In this last item, Porvoo handles the ministry of oversight, *episkopē*, which is responsible for "a caring for the life of a whole community, a pastoring of the pastors and a true feeding of Christ's flock, in accordance with Christ's command across the ages and in unity with Christians in other places. Episkopē [oversight] is a requirement of the whole Church and its faithful exercise in the light of the Gospel is of fundamental importance to its life."[31]

Following these sections, Porvoo deals with the episcopacy as important in exercising oversight and in *serving* the apostolic succession (The Episcopal Office in the Service of the Apostolic Succession, §43).

Within this idea there is a certain hierarchy. The gospel and the apostolicity of the whole church come first, followed by ministry as one form of the apostolicity. And only then is there the episcopacy as one form of the ministry and serving it.

The Gospel
The Apostolicity of the Whole Church

---

28. Faith and Order Commission, *Baptism, Eucharist and Ministry* (Geneva: World Council of Churches, 1982), M26. Hereafter cited as BEM.

29. Porvoo Common Agreement in *The Porvoo Common Statement: Conversations between the British and Irish Anglican Churches and the Nordic and Baltic Lutheran Churches: Text Agreed at the Fourth Plenary Meeting, Held at Järvenpää, Finland, 9-13 October 1992* (London: The Council of Christian Unity of the General Synod of the Church of England, 1993), §44. Hereafter cited as Porvoo.

30. Porvoo, §39 (italics: Eero Huovinen).

31. Porvoo, §42.

The Apostolic Ministry (the threefold ministry)
The Ministry of Oversight (*episkopē*)
The Episcopacy

The Upper Subsumes the Lower

26. In accord with BEM, and slightly rounding out the concept, Porvoo declares that "The ministry of oversight is exercised *personally, collegially and communally*":

"It is *personal* because the presence of Christ among his people can most effectively be pointed to by the person ordained to proclaim the gospel and call the community to serve the Lord in unity of life and witness.

"It is *collegial*, first because the bishop gathers together those who are ordained to share in the tasks of ministry and to represent the concerns of the community; second, because through the collegiality of bishops the Christian community in local areas is related to the wider church, and the universal church to that community.

"It is *communal*, because the exercise of ordained ministry is rooted in the life of the community and requires the community's effective participation in the discovery of God's will and the guidance of the Spirit. In most of our churches today this takes *synodical* form. Bishops, together with other ministers and the whole community, are responsible for the orderly transfer of ministerial authority in the Church."[32]

27. The concepts of BEM and Porvoo on the three modes of realization of the episcopal office may, I submit, also be applied to the discussion of the papal office. *Communio Sanctorum* takes this discussion even further.

Communio Sanctorum also treats on the three classical tasks of the episcopacy. Further, it asks how the understanding of these tasks can help us to comprehend the nature of the papacy. A bishop and in his special manner also the pope have tasks of teaching *(magisterium)*, administration *(iuris dictio)*, and ordination to church office *(potestas ordinis)*.

At present, it would seem that the pope has factually some form of magisterium even for other churches; his voice is heard throughout the world, both obediently and critically. However, it is more difficult to determine what type of authority belongs to the teaching office of the pope in relationship to the other churches. In a world growing ever smaller due to the

---

32. Porvoo, §44. To a great extent this conforms to the wording of BEM, M26.

influence of the media, the voice of the pope will, necessarily, be heard everywhere. The reception of his voice will, as we know, vary.

Finally, in addition to the above, the issues of authority for ordination *(potestas ordinis)* and of jurisdiction are both theologically and practically complex, as well as sensitive. At the moment it is difficult to imagine how they would, even in theory, be received or accepted in the other churches. And yet, the discussion of these matters can help us all as we consider how the Christian church is to be led not only personally but also collegially and synodically.

A Primatial Ministry of Unity in a Conciliar and Synodical Context

Geoffrey Wainwright

In his ecumenical encyclical of Ascension Day 1995, Pope John Paul II invited the leaders and theologians of other churches and ecclesial communities that he regarded as being in real, if imperfect, communion with the Roman Catholic Church to engage with him "in a patient and fraternal dialogue" on the claims of the primatial Roman see to a universal ministry of unity, in order to help "find a way of exercising the primacy which, while in no way renouncing what is essential to its mission, is nevertheless open to a new situation" (*Ut unum sint*, 95-96).

On Different Grounds?

In its 1986 Nairobi report, *Towards a Statement on the Church*, the Joint Commission for dialogue between the World Methodist Council and the Roman Catholic Church made an early, and no doubt premature, attempt to treat the question of what Catholics call "the Petrine office."[1] After a section on "Peter in the New Testament," the historical and systematic discussion begins sociologically:

1. The report is accessible in Jeffrey Gros, Harding Meyer, and William G. Rusch, eds., *Growth in Agreement II: Reports and Agreed Statements of Ecumenical Conversations at the World Level, 1982-1998* (Geneva/Grand Rapids: WCC/Eerdmans, 2000), pp. 583-96. Citations of this and other similar reports will be made according to paragraph numbers, in order to facilitate reference to other editions.

48. In looking at the question of universal primacy, one may begin with the desirability of unity focused around leadership.

49. All local churches need a ministry of leadership. In early church development, such leadership came to be exercised by the bishop, who was a focus of unity. Eventually, churches were grouped in provinces, regions and patriarchates, in which archbishops, primates and patriarchs exercised a similar unifying role in service to the koinonia.

50. Analogously, the question arises whether the whole Church needs a leader to exercise a similar unifying role in service to the worldwide koinonia.

51. Given this context, one then has to face the claim that the Roman see already exercises such a ministry of universal unity. . . .

Then, after a brief narrative of the Roman development, it is concluded that "the primacy of the Bishop of Rome is not established from the scriptures in isolation from the living tradition. When an institution cannot be established from scripture alone, Methodists, in common with other churches which stem from the Reformation, consider it on its intrinsic merits, as indeed do Roman Catholics; but Methodists give less doctrinal weight than Roman Catholics to long and widespread tradition" (55).

The Roman Catholic members of the commission affirm that "being in communion with the see of Rome has served as the touchstone of belonging to the Church in its fullest sense" (56), and it is made clear that "for Roman Catholics, reconciliation with the see of Rome is a necessary step towards the restoration of Christian unity" (57). For their part, it is claimed on behalf of Methodists that they "accept that whatever is properly required for the unity of the whole of Christ's Church must by that very fact be God's will for his Church. A universal primacy might well serve as focus of, and ministry for, the unity of the whole Church" (58). Indeed, "it would not be inconceivable that at some future date in a restored unity, Roman Catholic and Methodist bishops might be linked in one episcopal college, and that the whole body would recognize some kind of effective leadership and primacy in the bishop of Rome. In that case, Methodists might justify such an acceptance on different grounds from those that now prevail in the Roman Catholic Church" (62).

No more was said in the 1976 report about what the Methodist grounds might be; but it may be possible, by looking at what Methodists view as their own most characteristic structures of ecclesial government, to discern what such grounds might be and to turn those structures into a positive contribution towards a new manner of exercise for the papal office without changing its entire conception. The Methodist features in question are "the Conference" and "the Connexion." The Conference may be taken as the Methodist form of synodality, and the Connexion as the Methodist form of conciliarity.

If it is asked why I have chosen to address our themes of primacy, synodality, and conciliarity so markedly from a Methodist, and even a British Methodist, perspective, I will offer three reasons. First, it is important that a contribution be made to the discussion, ecclesiologically, from the "free church" tradition; and, culturally, from the "Anglo-Saxon" world and in a relatively "modern" form. Lessons may be learned, positively and negatively, from our strengths and weaknesses, particularly in the matters of synodality and conciliarity. Second, it may be useful to show that elements of primacy are not totally foreign to my own Methodism and perhaps the Protestant area more generally. And third, the international Methodist-Catholic dialogue has been characterized by a strongly pneumatological interest. Attention to that dimension may help to avoid the routinization and bureaucratization of charisma that always threatens primacy, synodality, and conciliarity, all three; and in that way, all three features, also in their interplay, may remain open to the renewing, and sometimes surprising, energies of the Holy Spirit.

Conference and Connexion in Methodist History

Some historical review of Methodism is necessary. Time and culture have, of course, brought changes, but the principal features of Methodist life and structures have remained remarkably firm, certainly in Britain (on which I shall concentrate) and to a considerable extent also in the United States. I will begin with the Conference and work "downwards" in terms of "oversight." Then, in a reverse movement, I will show how the "conciliarity" evident in the "societies" (as the local congregations were characteristically called) permeates the whole Connexion. At each stage and level, we shall look for appropriate signs of "primacy" present in the Methodist system itself. After an interlude on the vocabulary of "personal," "collegial," and "communal" in the work of WCC Faith and Order, I will in a further step trace what use has been made so far of the historic Methodist features in the dialogue between the World Methodist Council and the Roman Catholic Church as the joint commission has tackled questions concerning the structures and ministries of unity that should obtain in a reintegrated church. I will end with some personal reflections on future possibilities.

The Conference as a structural feature in Methodism dates from John Wesley's annual calling together of preachers who were, in eighteenth-century terminology, "in connexion with" him; some were parish priests of the Church of England, but an increasing number were laypeople with gifts for evangelism, who were expected to "itinerate" throughout the country. It was evident to the first Conference, held in London in 1744, that "God's design, in raising up the Preachers called *Methodists,*" was to "reform the nation, more particularly the Church," and to "spread scriptural holiness over the land."[2] The Conference regulated points of doctrine, discipline, and practice ("what to teach, how to teach, what to do").[3] The Franciscan historian Maximin Piette called the Conference the "General Chapter of the Methodist Order."[4] Yet Wesley himself had no doubts about his own "primatial" role, which indeed he attributed to his "providential" vocation in the Methodism that God had "raised up":

> I myself sent for these [namely, the traveling preachers whom he summoned to the Conference] of my own free choice; and I sent for them to *advise,* not to *govern* me. Neither did I, at any of those times, divest myself of any part of that *power,* which the Providence of God had cast upon me, without any design or choice of mine.[5]

2. See *Minutes of the Methodist Conferences,* vol. 1 [from 1744 to 1798] (London: The Conference Office, 1812), p. 9.

3. *Minutes of the Methodist Conferences,* p. 4.

4. Maximin Piette, *John Wesley in the Evolution of Protestantism* (London: Sheed & Ward, 1937), p. 384; originally *La réaction de John Wesley dans l'évolution du protestantisme,* Universitas catholica lovaniensis: dissertationes ad gradum magistris in Facultate Theologica, series 2, vol. 16 (Bruxelles: Lecture au Foyer, 2e éd. revue et augmentée, 1927), p. 536.

5. So amid his defensive statements in the Minutes of the Leeds Conference of 1766, in *Minutes of the Methodist Conferences,* vol. 1, pp. 58-61; here p. 60. Further, against the charge of "making yourself a Pope": "The Pope affirms, that every Christian must do all he bids, and believe all he says, under pain of damnation. I never affirmed any thing that bears any, the most distant resemblance to this. All I affirm is, 'The Preachers who choose to labour with me, choose to serve me as sons in the gospel.' And 'the people who choose

"Wesley's authority," says Piette with perhaps a little exaggeration, "was always decisive; his word went without appeal at all the annual Conferences."[6] At the Bristol Conference of 1774, one observer considered that "Mr. Wesley seemed to do all the business himself."[7]

In 1784, John Wesley made legal provision for the continuation of the Conference in Britain after his own death, by a "deed in chancery" that established a hundred of the most senior Methodist preachers as "the Legal Conference"; and "the Legal Hundred" remained at the core of the Wesleyan Conference, even when the numbers attending increased. In the nineteenth century, the Conference became regarded as "the living Wesley." Within this corporate "succession," a president was elected annually for that year's session. In the British Methodist Church, this pattern of presidency endures. The president sits in "Wesley's chair" and uses Wesley's "field Bible." It is more than a presidency of honor, since the president can act in some matters for the Conference during the ensuing year; moreover, it is customary for past presidents also to preside at ordination services beyond their year of office.

Wesley held a strong view of pastoral authority. In Sermon 97, titled "On the Duty of Obedience to Pastors," he traces a "mean" between "the Romanists," who believe that "implicit obedience ought to be paid to whatever commands they give," and "the generality of Protestants," who "are apt to run to the other extreme, allowing their pastors no authority at all, but making them the creatures and the servants of their congregations." In Wesley's view, pastors are properly understood as teachers, nourishers, and spiritual guides.[8] In 1771, during a dispute in Dublin, Wesley made it quite clear

---

to be under my care, choose to be so, on the same terms they were at first'" (p. 61). As late as the friendly account of William L. Doughty in 1944, *John Wesley: His Conferences and His Preachers* (London: Epworth Press, 1944), the terms of the description are amusingly symptomatic: "There could be no question about the Presidency. *Jure divino* it was John Wesley's" (p. 22); "*Concilium locutum est* (or should it be *Johannes Wesley locutus est?*); *causa finita est*" (p. 31). The traveling preachers are almost portrayed as paying "*ad limina*" visits to Wesley on the occasion of Conference: "It is no matter for surprise that to the Preachers he became a father in God, and their annual journey to meet him was a kind of spiritual pilgrimage, with the Conference town an earthly Jerusalem, 'whither the tribes go up, even the tribes of the Lord'" (p. 18). Especially in his later years and after his death, Wesley's soubriquet among Methodists was "our venerable Father."

6. Piette, *John Wesley,* p. 466 (p. 633 in the French).

7. See the letter footnoted in the standard edition of Nehemiah Curnock, ed., *The Journal of John Wesley [1915],* vol. 6 (reprinted London: Epworth Press, 1938), p. 35.

8. Albert C. Outler, ed., *Works of John Wesley,* bicentennial edition, vol. 3 (Nashville: Abingdon Press, 1986), pp. 374-83.

that final decisions on discipline were the sole responsibility of "the assistant," that is, a supervisory traveling preacher appointed by Wesley as *his* assistant or, in later terminology, the "superintendent" appointed by the Conference.[9] As Methodism, after Wesley's death, assumed more of an existence independent of the Church of England, the traveling preachers in effect functioned as presbyters, even though it was not until 1836 that their admission "into full Connexion" by the Conference was regularly sanctioned by ordination-with-the-laying-on-of-hands.[10] In the period dominated by Jabez Bunting (secretary of the Conference 1814-19 and 1824-27, and four times its president: 1820, 1828, 1836, and 1844), "high Wesleyanism" in Britain maintained a very elevated view of "the pastoral office."[11]

By about 1746, Methodism was organized geographically into "rounds" or "circuits." The traveling preachers, appointed each year by John Wesley at the Conference, were to work in one of these specified areas. At first, there were seven such circuits, but over the years they increased in number and decreased in size; one traveling preacher "superintended" each circuit, where in fact he might, as time went by, have others as colleagues. In 1791, the circuits were grouped into "districts," each with (from 1792) a "chairman" who, until the creation of "separated chairmen" in the 1950s, retained direct pastoral duties in one of the circuits. In British Methodism, the Conference retains final responsibility for the "stationing" of ministers in the circuits, and the ministers remain under a discipline of itinerancy; these are the factors that have done most to maintain consistency of doctrine and discipline throughout the Connexion as well as favoring the personal *disponibilité* and mutual support needed in evangelism and mission.

At the local level, Methodist life was from the start organized in "soci-

---

9. See David Carter, *Love Bade Me Welcome: A British Methodist Perspective on the Church* (London: Epworth Press, 2002), p. 163, note 46. Carter's book provides a valuable survey of the broadest questions in Methodist ecclesiology from the beginning until the present.

10. See A. Raymond George, "Ordination," in Rupert E. Davies, A. Raymond George, and E. Gordon Rupp, eds., *A History of the Methodist Church in Great Britain*, vol. 2 (London: Epworth Press, 1978), pp. 143-60. Ordinations took place in the United States already from 1784 onwards, according to the ordinal that John Wesley provided for the North American Methodists following their political independence from the British crown and their ecclesiastical independence from the established Church of England.

11. See John C. Bowmer, *Pastor and People: A Study of Church and Ministry in Wesleyan Methodism from the Death of John Wesley (1791) to the Death of Jabez Bunting (1858)* (London: Epworth Press, 1975).

eties," which "met" for preaching, fellowship, and worship (though not, by Wesley's intention, in competition with the offices and sacraments of the Church of England's parishes, which he encouraged Methodists to attend and enliven). The classic *Collection of Hymns for the Use of the People Called Methodists* of 1780 shows the themes and functions of Methodist gatherings: a section devoted to "beseeching and exhorting" an initial "return to God" is followed by prayers for "repentance," "conviction," and "recovery" from "backsliding"; and then the two main sections are "for believers: rejoicing, fighting, praying, watching, working, suffering, groaning for full redemption, brought to the birth, saved, interceding for the world," and "for the society: meeting, giving thanks, praying, parting." The advantage of the societies was that the members could "watch over one another in love, build one another up, and bear one another's burthens."[12] Within the societies, there was an even closer mutual accountability embodied in the meeting in "classes" under lay leadership, and (more intimate still) in "bands."[13]

We have worked "down" from Wesley and the Conference to the local societies, but we can broaden out. "Each society," writes David Carter, "saw its intensity of communal experience of the renewing and transforming grace of God as the manifestation of the one Church of Pentecost within its community, an experience that they knew to be replicated in all other Methodist societies since the Methodists were 'one people the world over.'"[14] "The sense of providential interconnectedness," Carter continues, "emerged out of the symbiosis of Wesley's skill in developing new and flexible forms of interdependent church life and the experience of communal spiritual renewal that developed within these interdependent communities."[15] Thus it becomes possible, in giving an account of Methodist connexionalism, to work back "up" from the local societies — through the geographically widening circles of circuits and districts — to the Conference itself.

While class meetings fell largely into disuse, other forms of small-group association have been a recurrent feature of Methodist life at the local level. From about 1753 onwards, "quarterly meetings" brought together the preachers of a circuit, both itinerant and local, as well as the lay "stewards,"

12. From the manuscript minutes of the 1748 London Conference; see Rupert E. Davies, A. Raymond George, and E. Gordon Rupp, eds., *A History of the Methodist Church*, vol. 4 (London: Epworth Press, 1988), p. 91.

13. See the Minutes of the 1744 Conference, in *Minutes of the Methodist Conferences*, vol. 1, pp. 10-12.

14. Carter, *Love Bade Me*, pp. 18-19.

15. Carter, *Love Bade Me*, p. 19.

who were responsible for finances in the societies and the circuit; the "assistant" or "superintendent" chaired these meetings as well as having responsibility for the preaching plan and the exercise of pastoral discipline. In the Wesleyan Methodist Connexion, the "district committee" or "district meeting" convened annually in May (and, for long, in September also), assuming by 1892 the official name of "district synod." The Conference continued to meet annually.

In *John Wesley: His Conferences and his Preachers,* W. L. Doughty writes of the early decades: "Conference steadily grew in influence and popularity and speedily became the focal point of Methodist religious life, a position it has never forfeited. Its meeting places were London, Bristol, and Leeds, and the Methodists in those areas eagerly anticipated its coming and shared joyously in its many public ministrations. Round it gathered the loving, reverent thoughts, and for it rose the prayers, of the Methodist people everywhere. It became the symbol of their unity, the grand climax of their year, an incentive to more intense missionary enterprise, and the fount of inspiration for a deeper personal consecration."[16]

Whether in spite or because of the focal role played by the Conference in the Methodist mentality, laypeople came to look for a share in the government and deliberations of the body to which they belonged. Lay assertiveness played a major part in several intra-Methodist schisms in the course of a nineteenth century that was marked both by a general spread of education

---

16. Doughty, *John Wesley,* p. 27. Russell E. Richey affirms much the same for American Methodism, not only for "the annual conference, the basic unit of Methodist structure," but also "the quarterly meeting and, after it emerged in 1792, the [quadrennial] general conference" (*Early American Methodism* [Bloomington: Indiana University Press, 1991], p. 66). American Methodism differs from British Methodism in two chief respects: first, the sheer size of the United States made it necessary to distribute some functions between the annual conference and the quadrennial general conference, with the latter holding supremacy in doctrinal decisions; and second, American Methodism has bishops, who retain some of the functions of a general superintendency of the entire "connection" such as Wesley envisaged for Coke and Asbury, but who have long been "resident" in particular areas and preside over particular annual conferences. These bishops do not claim an "apostolic succession" in the sense that Catholics and Anglicans do; but the Americans may perhaps be viewed as standing in some kind of succession from the ordinations that John Wesley, considering himself a "presbyter-bishop," performed for North America in September 1784. In 1784, at the "Christmas Conference" held in Baltimore, the principal American body took the name "Methodist Episcopal Church." The vicissitudes of later divisions and partial reunions do not directly concern us here, although of course their occurrence is not irrelevant to the question of a "ministry of unity."

and by the development of democracy in the culture at large.[17] From 1878 on-wards elected laypeople became members of Conference, even in the pre-dominant Wesleyan Methodist Connexion.[18] (In 1897 the Wesleyan Method-ist Connexion for the first time officially referred to itself as the Wesleyan Methodist Church; this body became the principal component in the re-union of 1932, which brought almost all Methodists in the land together as the Methodist Church of Great Britain.)[19] Laypeople played increasingly prominent parts also at district level. District synods as well as the Confer-ence met in two modes: ministerial session and representative session, the lat-ter including both ministers and laity. Some matters were reserved to the ministerial session, though these decreased in number over the course of the twentieth century. It is the Conference in representative session that bears fi-nal authority in the interpretation of doctrine. Only candidates approved by the Conference can be ordained to the presbyterate. The imposition of hands is performed by existing presbyters, led by the president or a past president of the Conference.[20]

In sum, the Connexion stands in Methodist terminology and experi-ence for the complex tissue of conciliar fellowship and mutual accountabil-ity that obtains *at* the various (geographical) levels of church life and *be-tween* those levels, allowing for the exercise of oversight by a divinely authorized and endowed ministry that itself submits to a synodical disci-pline in which laypersons also have now long played a constitutive part.[21]

17. See, briefly, Carter, *Love Bade Me*, pp. 63-67.

18. See Carter, *Love Bade Me*, pp. 44-46, 61-62; Martin Wellings, "Making Haste Slowly: The Campaign for Lay Representation in the Wesleyan Conference, 1871-8," in *Proceedings of the Methodist Historical Society* 53 (May 2001): 25-37. The process took place slightly earlier in the Methodist Episcopal Church in the United States, with the compli-cating factor of Civil War issues: the Methodist Episcopal Church, South approved lay representation at the Annual and General Conference in 1866, and the Methodist Episco-pal Church followed suit at the level of the General Conference in 1872; see Russell E. Richey, *The Methodist Conference in America: A History* (Nashville: Kingswood Books, 1996), particularly pp. 118-19, 140-47, and 281, note 52.

19. See Carter, *Love Bade Me*, pp. 70-76.

20. Or by a bishop, in the American system. Here too, only candidates approved by the Conference may receive ordination. The bishop, advised by his or her "cabinet" (dis-trict superintendents), appoints preachers to their stations.

21. See a pair of articles, grounded in both history and recent practice, from a for-mer secretary and president of the British Methodist Conference: Brian Beck, "Some Re-flections on Connexionalism," *Epworth Review* 18 (May 1991): 48-59, and 18 (September 1991): 43-50. Another constructive study co-authored by an American and a British writer

While the language may have changed over time, Methodists would still characteristically endorse John Wesley's dictum that "the end" or purpose of "all ecclesiastical order" is "to bring souls from the power of Satan to God, and to build them up in His fear and love."[22]

Faith and Order

Faith and Order's Lima text, *Baptism, Eucharist and Ministry,* declared that "the ordained ministry should be exercised in a personal, collegial and communal way":

> It should be *personal* because the presence of Christ among his people can most effectively be pointed to by the person ordained to proclaim the Gospel and to call the community to serve the Lord in unity of life and witness. It should also be *collegial,* for there is need for a college of ordained ministers sharing in the common task of representing the concerns of the community. Finally, the intimate relationship between the ordained ministry and the community should find expression in a *communal* dimension where the exercise of the ordained ministry is rooted in the life of the community and requires the community's effective participation in the discovery of God's will and the guidance of the Spirit. (M 26)[23]

---

is Bruce W. Robbins and David Carter, "Connexionalism and Koinonia: A Wesleyan Contribution to Ecclesiology," *One in Christ* 34 (1998): 320-36.

22. Letter of 25 June 1746, to "John Smith," in Frank Baker, ed., *Works of John Wesley,* bicentennial edition, vol. 26 (Nashville: Abingdon Press, 1982), here p. 206.

23. Faith and Order Commission, *Baptism, Eucharist and Ministry* (Geneva: World Council of Churches, 1982). In its own commentary to paragraph 26, the Lima text declares that "an appreciation of these three dimensions lies behind a recommendation made by the first world conference on Faith and Order at Lausanne in 1927": "In view of (i) the place which the episcopate, the council of presbyters and the congregation of the faithful, respectively, had in the constitution of the early Church, and (ii) the fact that episcopal, presbyterial and congregational systems of government are each today, and have been for centuries, accepted by great communions in Christendom, and (iii) the fact that episcopal, presbyterial and congregational systems are each believed by many to be essential to the good order of the Church, we therefore recognize that these several elements must all, under conditions which require further study, have an appropriate place in the order of life of a reunited Church." Of course, the Roman Catholic Church, with its particular understanding of primacy, was not yet part of the ecumenical movement in 1927.

In the interim statement from the later ecclesiological study, *The Nature and Purpose of the Church* (1998),[24] these three qualities or dimensions were developed in a manner that, though at times confused in argumentation and rather minatory in tone, was on the whole helpful.

First, "communal" or "conciliar": "All the baptized share a responsibility for the apostolic faith and witness of the whole Church. . . . Communal life sustains all the baptized in a web of belonging, of mutual accountability and support" (para. 98). "Conciliarity is present at all levels of the life of the Church. Conciliarity is already present in the relations which exist among the members of the smallest local communities" (107). Thus the terms "communal" and "conciliar" are said to describe "the ongoing life of the whole Church and not merely particular structures and processes which serve its ongoing life" (box, p. 53). (The text itself appears to make also "synodal" synonymous with "communal" and "conciliar," but I think it would aid linguistic clarity to use "synodal" rather in relation to the "collegial" dimension of BEM.)

Second, "collegial" (and, as I would say, "synodal"): collegiality is defined as "the 'communion' of all those who exercise oversight" in the churches (96); and "collegiality is at work wherever those entrusted with oversight gather, discern, speak and act as one on behalf of the whole Church" (105).

Third, "personal": "God calls out persons for the exercise of the ministry of oversight" (101). "Those who exercise oversight have a special duty to care for the unity, holiness, catholicity and apostolicity of the Church. . . . In their special responsibility for maintaining the unity and continuity of the Church, they exercise discipline" (102).

From a Methodist standpoint, "conciliarity" and "community" are our connexionalism; "collegiality" or "synodality" is manifested in the corporate exercise of oversight at all levels, from the Conference through district synods and quarterly circuit meetings to (historically) the "leaders' meeting" in each local church; the "personal" dimension is present, at appropriate levels, in presidents of Conference, bishops (in those Methodist churches that have them), district chair(wo)men, circuit superintendents, presbyters in pastoral charge, and leaders of classes. To bring the three "dimensions" together: Methodism is a connexional system in which government and pastoral care are exercised in a collegial way by persons who at various levels function in primacy (leadership). That is a top-down description, but we were also able

24. Faith and Order Paper No. 181 (Geneva: World Council of Churches, 1998).

to redescribe it bottom-up: Methodism is a connexion of societies whose representatives gather synodically at ever wider levels until the Conference is reached.[25]

Before moving on from the Faith and Order discussion, one final point may be picked up from *The Nature and Purpose of the Church:* "Primacy, wherever it exists, is an expression of the 'personal' mode of ministry. It is a service of presidency to be exercised in a spirit of love and truth. Primacy is inseparable from both the collegial and communal dimensions of the Church's life. It strengthens the unity of the Church and enables it to speak with one voice" (103). The interesting move then comes when, at least in one of its "problem boxes" (p. 55), the 1998 document goes on to make a link between primacy and eucharistic presidency. This latter concept and term, thanks to the twentieth-century Liturgical Movement, became ecumenically acceptable across a wide range of the ecclesial spectrum. Thus in *Baptism, Eucharist and Ministry:* "In the celebration of the eucharist, Christ gathers, teaches and nourishes the Church. It is Christ who invites to the meal and who presides at it. He is the shepherd who leads the people of God, the prophet who announces the Word of God, the priest who celebrates the mystery of God. In most churches this presidency is signified by an ordained minister" (E 29). The idea then floated in *The Nature and Purpose of the Church* is that of a universal primacy in terms of presidency at the Lord's table:

> Most churches accept that a Eucharist needs a president. Among these, there are some who would go on to say that it follows that a gathering of eucharistic communities at a regional and world level similarly need a president, in the service of communion. In this perspective, conciliarity implies primacy, and primacy involves conciliarity.[26]

---

25. There is a quite close similarity between our three "dimensions" and what Russell Richey calls the "community, fraternity, and order" that were characteristic of "early American Methodism." See *The Methodist Conference,* pp. 1-20.

26. This last notion comes very close to a combination of two statements made from the Catholic side in the dialogue between the Roman Catholic Church and the World Methodist Council: "*Koinonia* and *episkopē* imply one another. In a Catholic perspective this mutual implication reaches its culmination when the bishop presides over liturgical worship, in which the preaching of the Gospel and the celebration of the Lord's Supper weld together into unity the members of Christ's body" (Singapore report, paragraph 92); and "just as each bishop is a focus of unity in his own diocese, so the bishop of Rome is such a focus in the communion of dioceses of the whole Church" (Nairobi report, paragraph 61).

Methodists and Catholics in Dialogue

Now we may return to the dialogue between the World Methodist Council and the Roman Catholic Church, picking up from the Nairobi report of 1986. The dialogue is arranged according to five-year periods, so that the commission's report may be made to the quinquennial meetings of the World Methodist Council as well as being presented simultaneously to the Vatican. On the Methodist side, at least, the reports are known by the place at which they were presented to the WMC. Thus the ensuing ones are the Singapore report of 1991 *(The Apostolic Tradition)*, the Rio de Janeiro report of 1996 *(The Word of Life: A Statement on Revelation and Faith)*, and the Brighton report of 2001 *(Speaking the Truth in Love: Teaching Authority among Catholics and Methodists).*[27]

The Nairobi report, in introducing to Methodists the "unfamiliar" concept of primacy, asserted that "historically, John Wesley exercised a kind of primacy in the origins of Methodism. In his day this was carried out in the context of his Conference of preachers; today's Conference continues to embody certain elements of this function" (37). Clearly, much more precision would be required in relating any Methodist experience of primacy to "the possible exercise of the ministry of the Bishop of Rome among Christians who do not at present accept it" (60). In a first look at "the primacy which [in Catholic eyes] the Bishop of Rome has among other bishops in virtue of his special relation to Peter and the special position of the Church in Rome deriving from the witness of Peter and Paul," the two "aspects" that first caught attention were papal "jurisdiction" and "infallibility" (60). In any exercise of his "ordinary . . . immediate episcopal jurisdiction" throughout the church, the pope "is required to respect each local church and the authority of each bishop," and "Catholics recognize that theological exploration of the relation between the authority of the Pope and that of the local bishop remains unfinished" (61). In the matter of "authoritative teaching," Methodists could and would, as paragraph 64 implies, agree with the Catholic statement that "to the extent that the Church in any era teaches the truths of salvation that were

---

27. The Singapore and Rio reports may be found — though under place-names nobody knows them by — in *Growth in Agreement II*, pp. 597-617 and 618-46. The Brighton report, like all previous ones, was originally published in the *Information Service* of the Pontifical Council for Promoting Christian Unity and as a brochure by the World Methodist Council's Lake Junaluska office. Periodicals such as *One in Christ* have also regularly carried the reports.

originally taught in the Scriptures, that teaching is binding" (66). Then comes
the difference: "Roman Catholics believe that the bishops of the Church enjoy the special assistance of the Holy Spirit, when, by a collegial act with the
Bishop of Rome in an ecumenical council, they define doctrine to be held irrevocably" (68), and that "in carefully defined and limited circumstances, the
Pope exercises this capacity in and for the whole Church" (69) — and in neither case can the "assent" of the faithful then be lacking (66; 70). In Methodist
eyes, the Roman Catholic understanding of infallibility "seems to imply a discernment of truth which exceeds the capacity of sinful human beings":

> Methodists are accustomed to see the guidance of the Holy Spirit in
> more general ways: through reformers, prophetic figures, church leaders
> and Methodist Conferences, for example, as well as through general
> Councils. Methodist Conferences, exercising their teaching office, for-
> mulate doctrinal statements as they are needed, but do not ascribe to
> them freedom from error. Nevertheless Methodists always accept what
> can clearly be shown to be in agreement with the Scriptures. The final
> judge of this agreement must be the assent of the whole people of God,
> and therefore Methodists, in considering the claims made for Councils
> and for the Pope, welcome the attention which Roman Catholic theolo-
> gians are giving to the understanding of the reception of doctrine. (72)

In the 1991 Singapore report on *The Apostolic Tradition,* the church is
seen as "a living Body" and, insistently, a "community." "The same Spirit operates among all the baptized and across all the generations," and this is the context for seeing "the specific charism received by those who are called to the ordained ministry": "This charism is directed toward the ordering and harmony
which must prevail in the exercise of all the gifts" (60). More precisely:

> Chosen from among the people, the ordained ministers represent the
> people before God as they bring together the prayers of the community.
> (71)

> In the pastoral care that is extended to them, the faithful perceive them-
> selves to be led by the Good Shepherd who gave his life for the sheep.
> (73)

> The function of oversight entails on the part of the ministers a solicitude
> for all the churches: they are charged to ensure that the community re-

main one, that it grow in holiness, that it preserve its catholicity, and that it be faithful to apostolic teaching and to the commission of evangelization given by Christ himself. (74)

Among the "unresolved" questions (87; 94) are "the sacramentality of ordination" (88-91) and "the forms of succession and oversight" (92-93). The former matter will persist into the 2001 Brighton report, where the question is phrased as that of a "guaranteed reliability" of "human instrumentality" in "ministries and institutions" (Brighton, 68, 82, and 120). As to *episkopē:* Catholics and Methodists agree that "an ordained ministry which exercises *episkopē* is vital for the life of the Church. Without the exercise of this gift of oversight, disorder and therefore disunity are inevitable. *Koinonia* and *episkopē* imply one another" (Singapore, 92). On the Catholic side, "this mutual implication reaches its culmination when the bishop presides over liturgical worship, in which the preaching of the Gospel and the celebration of the Lord's Supper weld together into unity the members of Christ's Body" (Singapore, 92). On the Methodist side, much is made of the personal *episkopē* exercised by John Wesley, and it is claimed that "his appointment of Francis Asbury and Thomas Cook to the superintendency in America was rooted in his belief that the Holy Spirit wished to bestow the gift of *episkopē* at that time and in that place for the sake of maintaining unity of faith with the Church of all ages. It was part of a fresh and extraordinary outpouring of the gift of the Spirit who never ceases to enliven and unify the Church" (93).

In the 1996 Rio de Janeiro report, *The Word of Life,* the most important paragraphs for our main question are those in the section on "Faith" that deal with "The Discernment of Faith" (53-72), and those in the section on "Koinonia — Communion" that deal with "The Church Universal" (126-30). The "criteria for discernment" are named as "fidelity to Scripture," "*sentire cum Ecclesia*" ("an inner harmony" between the "spiritual instinct" of the faithful and "the teaching of the Church"), "reception" ("One criterion by which new developments in Christian teaching or living may be judged consonant with the Gospel is their long-term reception by the wider Church"), and "the flowering of spiritual holiness" that comes from "conformity to Christian doctrinal and moral truth." The "agents of discernment" are located at several levels: scripturally, the discernment of God's will and truth "is the task of the whole people of God." Yet, at times in the history of the people of God, when "shepherds and flock have gone astray," God has "through prophets called his people back to the way." Again, "there are times when the Church needs a formal decision about whether some doctrines are right or wrong, or which actions are appropriate to the needs of the time as well as to the calling of the Church." At this level, "it is the common belief of our churches that there are those who are authorised to speak for the Church as a whole and who, having carefully listened to Scripture and Tradition and the experience of believers trying to live out the Gospel, and after a reasonable and prayerful discussion, may say 'It has seemed good to the Holy Spirit and to us.'" Both Methodists and Catholics reckon "the first Ecumenical Councils" among those so authorized, but further discussion will be needed, given that the Roman Catholic Church locates the teaching office in "the bishop [being] in unity with the Bishop of Rome," whereas in Methodism, "the teaching office is exercised by the Conferences." Already, however, there is agreement on the need for "convergence in discernment" even *within* the respective bodies of Catholicism and Methodism during their current existence in separation:

> Every formal expression of pastoral authority, whether the teaching office of the bishops or the power of councils, synods and conferences, and every expression of prophetic challenge, is to serve the upbuilding of the whole people of God under the lordship of Christ himself. This should lead to a growing interdependence and mutual recognition of those who exercise pastoral authority within the Church, those who offer prophetic vision, and all those who, by their response to revelation and their inspiration through the creative love of God, participate in the active tradition of the Gospel and compassionate discernment of the will of God for his Church and the world. (72)

Regarding "The Church Universal," the Rio report declares that "Christian communion is more than the fellowship of the members of the same congregation or the same local community. The Church of God has universal dimensions in regard to both time and space" (126). Differences are acknowledged between Catholics and Methodists in "our evaluations about what have been signs of faithfulness and perseverance in the Church's history" (127) and in "perceptions about the nature and the theological weight" of the structures that "bind together local churches to testify to the global nature of the Gospel and of the Church universal" (128):

> 129. The Roman Catholic Church relies on the promise which it believes to have been given to St. Peter and the Apostles (see e.g. Mt 16:18) and to have been fulfilled throughout history in the apostolic succession and the episcopal college together with its head, the Bishop of Rome as the

successor of St. Peter. The hierarchical structure of the Church is an important means and guarantee given by God's grace to preserve the continuity and the universality of the Catholic Church.

130. Methodist churches see the continuity of the apostolic tradition preserved by the faithfulness to the apostolic teaching. The teaching office which decides what is faithful and what is not lies in the hands of conciliar bodies, the Conferences.[28] All Methodist churches recognize the necessity of a ministry of *episkopē*, "oversight," and in many Methodist churches this is expressed in the office of bishop. Local churches are bound together by connexional structures which have to mediate the needs of local churches and of the Church as a whole. Methodists anticipate that more unity and a growing communion between churches of different traditions may be achieved by new conciliar structures. . . .

The Rio report concludes soberly that "Roman Catholics and Methodists share a common concern regarding the Church universal as an expression of communion in Christ. But they differ widely in their beliefs about the means that God has given to attain or preserve this goal. These differences may be the greatest hindrances on the way to full communion" (130). Accordingly, the commission looked forward to addressing "the related topics of pastoral and doctrinal authority, the offices of oversight in the Church and succession in them, and the offer made by Rome of a Petrine ministry in the service of unity and communion. We should thus be encouraged to pursue, more immediately and at a deeper level, the understanding that we both have of ourselves and of our partners in respect to the one Church of Jesus Christ and the communion which belongs to the body of Christ" (132).

In the next quinquennium the focus in fact fell on teaching authority, and the Brighton report of 2001 was titled *Speaking the Truth in Love*. Within an agreed emphasis on "The Church as Communion" (13-15), it is under the aspect of teaching authority that treatment is made of our questions of conciliarity, synodality, and (rather marginally as far as *interaction* between Catholics and Methodists is concerned) primacy. In a section that newcomers are advised to read first, the report sets out in descriptive fashion the respective histories and current understandings and practices of Methodism and the Catholic Church in these matters (86-98; 99-116). Readers of the present

28. In the terminology I have been using in this paper, "the Conferences" would be called "synodal."

paper will by now be substantially familiar with much of what is there laid out. But by way of summary recapitulation it may be useful to quote what is said on the Methodist side about "the Conference" as an "organising centre of ecclesial life." Six functions of a Conference are listed in paragraph 96:

- It is the gathering point and chief instrument of connexion. There is a family feeling of reunion when Conference meets.
- It exercises corporate *episkopē* and oversees the whole life of the Church, including doctrine and discipline for the sake of mission.
- It has final authority over doctrine. Methodist Conferences have always accepted the Scriptures as the supreme rule of faith and practice, and have been guided in their reading of them by Wesley's *Sermons* and *Explanatory Notes upon the New Testament*. In understanding these authorities, the Conference is the final interpreter.
- It exercises its authority also by approving service books and hymn books to communicate doctrinal matters to the people. Through these the faith is taught and maintained by the local congregations.
- It provides for the orderly transmission of ministry by authorizing ordination. Even where there are bishops, the decision to ordain is the prerogative of the Conference. Ordination takes place during the Conference by prayer and the laying on of hands, invoking the Holy Spirit.
- It elects its bishops and presidents. For most Methodist Churches they serve for a limited time. Some Churches elect their bishops (who serve as Presidents of their Annual Conferences) for life.

For the purposes of progress in ecumenical dialogue on our themes, the most interesting paragraphs in the Brighton report are probably those that describe the differences between Methodists and Catholics on "the participation of the laity in authoritative teaching" and set out the questions that each partner poses to the other:

78. . . . Catholics locate the authoritative determination of teaching in the college of bishops with the Bishop of Rome at its head. Methodists locate that same authority in Conference, where laypeople sit in significant numbers, with full rights of participation and decision-making.

79. Methodists understand that teaching authority is a gift to the whole Church, and suggest that excluding presbyters and laypeople from the place of final decision-making denies them the exercise of that gift,

thereby weakening the Church's ability to discern the faithful interpretation of God's Word for a particular time and place. By having representatives of the whole Church present in the decision-making body they can hope to hear the variety of perspectives and understandings needed to ensure the catholicity of the Church. Laypeople do actively participate and contribute in different ways in many areas of the structures of the Roman Catholic Church, for example in pastoral councils, diocesan synods, and meetings of the Synod of Bishops in Rome. However, Methodists ask Catholics why laypeople could not be more formally involved in decision-making bodies, even when authoritative discernment and teaching is concerned, sharing responsibility in some way with the bishops who nevertheless retain their special ministry of authoritative teaching.

80. Catholics understand that the episcopal teaching function is exercised as a service to the whole Church. Bishops lead communities of faith which are themselves bearers of the truth of the Gospel. They authoritatively discern and proclaim the faith given to the whole people of God. The task of authoritatively ensuring catholicity and apostolicity is entrusted to the college of bishops. Methodists do have an ordained ministry, and a superintendency that has teaching functions. However, Catholics ask Methodists why, in their understanding and practice of the Conference, they do not more formally distinguish the role of ordained ministers, especially bishops and superintendents, particularly where authoritative discernment and teaching are concerned.[29]

---

29. It seems that this last question may concern with particular acuity the United Methodist Church. Its *Discipline* charges the bishops "to guard, transmit, teach and proclaim, corporately and individually, the apostolic faith as it is expressed in Scripture and tradition, and, as they are led and endowed by the Holy Spirit, to interpret that faith evangelically and prophetically" (quoted in the Brighton report, paragraph 75, from the 1996 edition of *The Book of Discipline of the United Methodist Church*, #414.3). But while bishops preside over the sessions of the General Conference, they have no voice from the floor or vote. The standard textbook explains that the presidency of bishops here means "serving as chief parliamentary authority" (Thomas Edward Frank, *Polity, Practice, and Mission of the United Methodist Church* [Nashville: Abingdon Press, 2002], p. 237). Given the very considerable executive power of bishops in American Methodism, it may be that the United Methodist Church has been led to follow the secular Constitution of the United States into a "separation" or "distribution" of powers, whereby "checks and balances" obtain between the executive, the legislative, and the judicial branches of government. Thus the "royal" office in the church would be exercised in a "republican" way.

One final (missing) feature must be mentioned from the Methodist-Catholic dialogue: very little attention has been paid to structures at the universal level within Methodism itself.[30] From 1881, "Oecumenical Methodist Conferences" were held roughly every ten years, until the World Methodist Council was constituted in 1951; this body now meets quinquennially. Administered by a minimal bureaucracy, it has no legislative powers over its member churches but serves for fellowship, mutual information and advice, the management of cooperative programs in evangelization and social action, and the international exchange of pastors. It has acquired a certain "theological" status as the agency through which Methodist churches have engaged in international bilateral dialogues (not only with the Roman Catholic Church, but also with the Lutheran World Federation, the World Alliance of Reformed Churches, the Anglican Communion, and, incipiently, the Orthodox churches); and in 1996 it approved a short statement of "Wesleyan Essentials of Christian Faith." By far the largest of the eighty or so member churches of the World Methodist Council is the United Methodist Church. While having its origin and basis in the United States, the United Methodist Church considers itself a "global" church by virtue of its overseas annual conferences. Delegates from these bodies make for cultural, and sometimes theological, diversity in the quadrennial meetings of the United Methodist Church's general conference. On the other hand, what might be thought of as "daughter churches" of Methodism in the British tradition have almost all acquired fully autonomous status and have regularly sought — sometimes successfully (as, for instance, in South and North India, in Zambia, and in Australia) — to enter into organic unions with other Christians at national level. Among contemporary developments the Brighton report, in paragraph 98, notes cross-representation at the Conferences of some Methodist churches and regional consultations among the bishops and presidents of different Methodist churches for the furtherance of common witness. Churches belonging to the World Methodist Council enjoy, of course, full communion in word and table and the mutual recognition of membership and ministry.

Some Personal Suggestions

Although I have been a member of the Methodist-Catholic international commission since 1983, and since 1986 its co-chairman, it is in an individual

---

30. The only direct treatment occurs in paragraph 98 of the Brighton report of 2001.

capacity as a lifelong Methodist that I now wish to make three suggestions. The first concerns the *communal* location of ministries of oversight, their service of (in Methodist terms) "the Connexion." The second concerns their *collegial* nature, their embodiment of "Conference." The third concerns their *personal* exercise, even to the level of a primacy that may perhaps, greatly daring, be analogously attributed to John Wesley (in the origins of Methodism) and the bishop of Rome (in a universal ministry of unity).

The first reflection springs from experience in relations between the Methodist Church and the Church of England, where the Methodists have on several occasions formally expressed their willingness, for the sake of unity, to accept a "historic episcopate" in the form to which the Anglicans lay claim. In response to a self-framed question, "Is episcopal succession a matter of dogma for Anglicans?," I have proposed the following as an account of the conditions on which a historic episcopate can and should be affirmed:

> Dialectically, bishops in their teaching office become accountable, by the criteria of Scripture and ecumenical tradition, to all other Christians who by their faithful witness and practice bear the truth of the gospel. Thus it becomes a two-way move — between the bishops (individually and collegially) and the rest of the Christian community — when, with paragraph 51 of the *Porvoo Common Statement,* the historic episcopate serves as "a permanent challenge to fidelity and to unity, a summons to witness to, and a commission to realise more fully, the permanent characteristics of the Church of the apostles." The historic episcopate may be affirmed *insofar* as it both fulfils its responsibilities of teaching and maintaining the faith and remains corrigible, in the light of Scripture and the steadfast practices of the church, by the persuasion of believers within the community who have been well taught and bear consistent, courageous, and sanctified testimony to Christ. Incorrigible bishops should be removed from office.
>
> On those terms, it is possible, and indeed desirable, theologically and ecumenically, to "appreciate the episcopal succession as a sign, though not a guarantee, of the continuity and unity of the Church" (*BEM,* M38).[31]

---

31. Geoffrey Wainwright, "Is Episcopal Succession a Matter of Dogma for Anglicans? The Evidence of Some Recent Dialogues," in Colin Podmore, ed., *Community — Unity — Communion: Essays in Honour of Mary Tanner* (London: Church House Publishing, 1998), pp. 164-79; here p. 176.

Second: in the matter of collegiality I have floated the idea of a "perichoretic and peripatetic episcopate."[32] As to perichoresis: the notion of "circumincession" is offered as an answer to the questions broached in the Methodist-Catholic Nairobi report as to whether, in a united church, the varying needs of different spiritual and cultural traditions could be met within a single local congregation, and whether the pastoral care of such groups would require "separate, possibly overlapping jurisdictions" or could be provided by "one, single, local form of *episkopē*" (27). A local college of bishops, perhaps with a rotating presidency, need not be excluded, I suggest, although "a perichoretic episcopate could not stand alone as a statement of cross-cultural and confessionally reconciled unity among Christians in each place: there would need to be ample opportunity for spiritual fellowship, sacramental communion, and joint action among the mutually open communities represented by the council of bishops in each place."[33] The model of a British Methodist circuit was not too far from my mind, typically with its several "societies" and several "presbyters," any one of whom can in principle be appointed as "superintendent minister."

As to *peripateia:* Thomas Coke and Francis Asbury, the first two "general superintendents" or "bishops" of the Methodist Episcopal Church in the United States, made this note to the *Discipline* of 1798:

> Our grand plan, in all its parts, leads to an itinerant ministry. Our bishops are travelling bishops. All the different orders which compose our conferences are employed in the travelling line; and our local preachers are, in some degree, travelling preachers. Everything is kept moving as far as possible. . . . Next to the grace of God, there is nothing like this for keeping the whole body alive from the centre to the circumference, and for the continual extension of that circumference on every hand.[34]

In nineteenth-century Britain, the Wesleyan ecclesiologists James Harrison Rigg and Benjamin Gregory considered the "circulating pastorate" or

---

32. Geoffrey Wainwright, "In Favour of a Perichoretic and Peripatetic Episcopate — Perhaps . . . ," in Harding Meyer, ed., *Gemeinsame Glaube und Strukturen der Gemeinschaft: Günther Gassmann zum 60. Geburtstag* (Frankfurt am Main: Otto Lembeck, 1991), pp. 198-207.

33. Wainwright, "In Favour of a Perichoretic and Peripatetic Episcopate," p. 202.

34. *The Doctrines and Discipline of the Methodist Episcopal Church in America, with Explanatory Notes by Thomas Cook and Francis Asbury,* facsimile edition (Rutland, VT: Academy Books, 1979), p. 42.

the "itinerant superintendency" signs of apostolicity.[35] The ecumenical lesson I would draw is that "any uniting Church should expect to include itinerating evangelists — recognized as performing episcopal, because apostolic, functions — among its structures of communion. Locally proven evangelists, whether already bishops or not, could be appointed or (where necessary) ordained to such a travelling episcopate. Successful itinerants could 'settle' as local bishops, for a time or permanently. Wherever they were, they would be part of a perichoretic episcopate in that place."[36]

My third proposal was made in 1997 in response to Pope John Paul's invitation to "a patient and fraternal dialogue" on primacy as a universal ministry of Christian unity:

> My respectful suggestion is that the Pope should invite those Christian communities which he regards as being in real, if imperfect, communion with the Roman Catholic Church to appoint representatives to cooperate with him and his appointees in formulating a statement expressive of the Gospel to be preached to the world today. Thus the theme of the "fraternal dialogue" which John Paul II envisaged would shift from the *theory* of the pastoral and doctrinal office to the *substance* of what is believed and preached. And the very *exercise* of elaborating a statement of faith might — by the process of its launching, its execution, its resultant form, its publication, and its reception — illuminate the question of "a ministry that presides in truth and love." *Solvitur ambulando.*[37]

I am not thinking here of anything like the formulation of a "new creed" or doctrinal decisions such as would be appropriate to a general Council. Taking for granted an agreement in the basic Christian faith, my model is perhaps closer, in the first place, to that of John Wesley calling together his preachers for the determination of "what to teach, how to teach, and what to do" in the service of evangelization. That cause is dear to the heart of a pontiff who also recognizes that "the lack of unity among Christians contradicts the

---

35. Geoffrey Wainwright, "'The Gift Which He on One Bestows, We All Delight to Prove': A Possible Methodist Approach to a Ministry of Primacy in the Circulation of Love and Truth," in James F. Puglisi, ed., *Petrine Ministry and the Unity of the Church* (Collegeville, MN: Liturgical Press, 1999), pp. 59-82; here pp. 68-70.

36. Wainwright, "In Favour of a Perichoretic and Peripatetic Episcopate," p. 205. My proposal for a peripatetic element in the episcopate has, of course, nothing to do with "*episcopi vagantes*"!

37. Wainwright, "'The Gift Which He on One Bestows,'" p. 82.

Truth which Christians have the mission to spread and, consequently, it gravely damages their witness" (*Ut unum sint*, 98-99). Pope John Paul II, the "traveling preacher," has certainly exercised a peripatetic primacy.

Conclusion

Not wishing to claim the last word for myself, I will co-opt for Methodism the opinion and testimony of Lesslie Newbigin, an ecumenical giant of the twentieth century. Although he began as an English Presbyterian, Newbigin was one of the first bishops in the Church of South India that resulted from the union in 1947 between Anglicans, Reformed, and those Methodists who were the fruit of British missionary labors. Already in his book of 1948, *The Reunion of the Church,* and when he was assuming a prominent role in the newly inaugurated World Council of Churches, Newbigin looked beyond South India to the visible reunion of Christendom:

> However far-reaching may be the transformation required both of the Protestant Churches and of the Roman and Eastern before union can be a matter even of discussion, there ought to be nothing to prevent our looking now towards the restoration to the whole Church of a visible unity with a central organ of unity such as Rome was for so many vital centuries of the Church's history.[38]

Admittedly, Newbigin, in *The Finality of Christ,* sharply criticized the Romanocentric cosmos of Pope Paul VI's encyclical *Ecclesiam suam.*[39] But in a paper on "Ministry" written in the late 1980s, he spoke of "the right balance of personal and conciliar elements in the government of the Church at every level — local, regional, national, universal": "That means that Protestants have to take seriously the Roman Catholic witness about primacy, that Catholics have to take seriously the testimony of Protestants about the role of the church meeting and the synod or council."[40]

---

38. J. E. Lesslie Newbigin, *The Reunion of the Church: A Defence of the South India Scheme* (London/New York: SCM Press/Harper, 1948), p. 189.

39. J. E. Lesslie Newbigin, *The Finality of Christ* (London/Richmond: SCM Press/ John Knox, 1969), pp. 43-44, 73-74.

40. Unpublished paper on "Ministry," quoted from Geoffrey Wainwright, *Lesslie Newbigin: A Theological Life* (New York: Oxford University Press, 2000), p. 407.

It seems, then, that Newbigin would certainly have been willing to engage in what Pope John Paul II called "a patient and fraternal dialogue" on "the ministry of universal unity" which the Roman see wishes to offer to all Christians, especially when that ministry and its cause are geared — as declared in *Ut unum sint* — to the task of evangelization, which was Newbigin's lifelong concern. Newbigin also affirmed the necessity of a teaching authority within the church: the pope saw this as located in the magisterium "entrusted to the Pope and the Bishops in communion with him, understood as a responsibility and authority exercised in the name of Christ for teaching and safeguarding the faith"; in Newbigin's perspective, the free assent of the company of the faithful — in obedience to the living Lord encountered in the church — would remain important. Recognizing also with Newbigin the sin that remains in Christians and in the church, there would be a need to affirm with Vatican II the realization of *Ecclesia semper purificanda*. And anyone with a Reformed streak in him would doubtless keep Lesslie's limerick in mind:

> The Church of St. Peter in Rome
> has a vast and magnificent dome.
> It's spectacular, but
> in a fisherman's hut
> I think Peter would feel more at home.[41]

But let the last word fall to the vision of Petrine ministry that Newbigin captured from chapter 21 of St. John's Gospel:

> In the first part, Peter is the fisherman who (if only he is obedient to the Lord) is able to catch not only a vast number of fish, but also (unlike the putative "evangelists" who leave as their legacy a litter of mutually competing sects) is able to bring them all to the feet of Jesus as one, with no "schism" in the net (21:11). Then Peter is the shepherd to whom the Lord entrusts his sheep, but only because he is assured that Peter loves him, the one to whom the sheep belong. But finally — and this is where the chapter comes to its crucial point — Peter is a disciple. The words "follow me," in the context of all that has gone before (see 13:36-38), constitute the punch-line of the whole chapter. But this decisive word can only

---

41. Quoted in Wainwright, *Lesslie Newbigin*, p. 406, from manuscript collection of limericks.

be spoken because Peter has learned what following means — not his own programme, but the way of the cross (21:18f.). Peter in other words can be a shepherd only if he is a disciple. He can bring others to Jesus and guard them in his ownership only if he is himself following Jesus on the way of the Cross. He can be a leader only as he is a follower — a follower on the way of the cross. Following Jesus on the way of the cross in such wise that others are enabled to follow: this, I believe, is the heart of what the New Testament has to say about ministry.[42]

42. "Ministry" manuscript, quoted in Wainwright, *Lesslie Newbigin,* p. 407.

Towards a Common Understanding of Papal Ministry: A Catholic Critical Point of View

Hervé Legrand, OP

Conclusions must be short and clear, free from chit-chat and even from political correctness. As Cardinal Lehmann pointed out after *Dominus Iesus,*
"the time of bogus politeness is over." Otherwise conclusions are a waste of
time, especially within the kind of meeting we have had here, and which is
becoming a valuable tradition.

Few places, indeed, offer such an opportunity for experienced ecumenists to exchange their insights, with candor, at the high level of scholarship we appreciate in Farfa — and moreover, in a context of deep mutual
trust, friendship, and experienced brotherhood.

The conclusions I wish to offer for the last round of our discussions
shall be definitely, as critical as possible, and first of all critical towards our
own Catholic thinking and practice. Ecumenism should not try to convince
our partners of the truth of our theology. It is not up-to-date apologetics;
neither is it an attempt to disguise our reluctance to reform ourselves by so-
phisticated speculative, historical, or epistemological considerations. Ecumenism is rather an exercise in which we try to convert our hearts and our
minds, standing before "such divisions [that] openly contradict the will of
Christ, scandalize the world and damage the holy cause of preaching the
Gospel to every creature. But, the Lord of Ages wisely and patiently follows
out the plan of his Grace on our behalf, sinners that we are. In recent times
more than ever before, he has been rousing divided Christians to remorse
over their divisions and a longing for unity" (*Unitatis redintegratio* 1).

Therefore the same Decree on Ecumenism requires from us Catholics
that we "undertake with vigor the task of renewal and reform" (UR 4);

"[our] primary duty is to make an honest and careful appraisal of whatever needs to be done or renewed in the Catholic household itself" (UR 4). Further on, if there are "deficiencies in moral conduct or in church discipline, or even in the way church teaching has been formulated (to be carefully distinguished from the deposit of faith itself), these can and should be set right at the opportune moment" (UR 6). It is not an option but a necessity: *"quae renovanda et efficienda sunt."* One way to achieve these rectifications is "to remember that in Catholic teaching there exists a 'hierarchy' of truths, since they vary in their relationship to the fundamental Christian faith. Thus the way will be open by which, through fraternal rivalry all will be stirred to a deeper understanding and a clearer presentation of the unfathomable riches of Christ" (UR 11).

Our meeting here in Farfa is already a fruit of the Decree on Ecumenism. It has allowed us to tackle peacefully and honestly the difficult question of the papacy Pope Paul VI once characterized as "the greatest obstacle on the road of ecumenism."[1] Our consultation has worked out two areas of consensus:

1. *On the theological level,* we can summarize it thus: the dogmas concerning the papacy, as they are generally understood, are unacceptable to all the other Christians, without exception. Only if they are well explained may they become not objectionable, provided that they be set within a better-balanced ecclesiology. For the first time after *Ut unum sint,* we have had a few signs from the Anglican side that the doctrinal authority of the papacy could be accepted, provided it is exercised in both churches through synodal and collegial structures (*The Gift of Authority,* 1999). Professor Geoffrey Wainwright also gave us an impressive overview of the works of the International Methodist-Catholic Commission. On the Lutheran side, the Catholic-Lutheran joint theological commission of Germany issued the declaration *Communio Sanctorum,* containing a plea for a binding canonical interpretation of the two dogmas of universal jurisdiction and infallibility that would put them in the framework of communion and the "submission of the principle of infallibility to the unconditional respect of the Revelation found in the Holy Scripture" (n. 198). The Declaration goes even farther; I quote:

> A universal ministry for unity and truth in the Church corresponds to the essence and the task of the Church which is realized at the local, regional and universal level. In principle, it has to be considered as appro-

---

1. *Documentation catholique* 64 (1967): 870; *AAS* 59 (1967): 498.

priate. This ministry represents all Christians and has a pastoral task towards all local Churches. (n. 195)

Here Catholic theologians have an important role to play: they must recall the original meaning and the limits of the definitions of Vatican I, vis-à-vis the undue maximalist interpretations of that council rereading asked for by Cardinal Kasper and Harding Meyer.

2. *On the practical level,* the everyday practice of the papacy is consistent with the maximalist interpretation of Vatican I and remains unacceptable to other Christians. Paradoxically, after Vatican II, this practice has probably worsened. When we read the present-day Catholic literature about the papacy, we find strong doubts among the theological community about the readiness of the Roman Curia to support reforms in the exercise of the papacy. There is obviously a serious gap between ecclesiology and church life. Our duty as Catholic theologians is to acknowledge it and to note that the present state of affairs does not derive from the Catholic faith; it is also our duty to state that, we, Catholics, are the first to blame when we complain about the slowness of the dialogue: the practice of our church contradicts what we say: "It is our home work" (Pottmeyer).

First Conclusion: For the vast majority of Catholic dogmaticians and historians a theological re-reception of Vatican I is needed and fully legitimate because its definitions are commonly misunderstood within the Catholic Church and because they present shortcomings owing to historical circumstances.

There is a growing consensus nowadays within the milieu of Catholic theologians and historians that stresses the wide gap remaining between the dogmatic contents of Vatican I's definitions, their common understanding, and their institutional implementation.

These definitions have been coined in a highly technical language, mostly canonical. From the beginning this language has been misleading, not only for the common faithful but even for the lower clergy. Leaving aside for the time being the implementation of Vatican I, let us first summarize what Catholic dogmaticians and historians agree about Vatican I's definitions.

Technical versus Common Understanding of Vatican I's Dogmatic Definitions

Universal Jurisdiction

"Full and supreme power and jurisdiction, ordinary and immediate, both over each and all the churches and all the pastors and the faithful."

There is full agreement among Catholic dogmaticians that these words do not convey their ordinary meaning in the definition quoted above. It is useful to recall that they are precise technical and canonical terms.

Ordinary

Bishop Zinelli, speaking for the Deputation of the Faith, Vatican I's theological commission, reminded the bishops, before their vote, that an *ordinary* power is such a power that belongs to an office, and is not received by the office holder through delegation from anyone else.[2] For the Catholic faith, ordinary does not mean at all that the daily government of the church belongs to the pope, or that the pope may have a constant involvement in the life of the local churches.

But we have to recognize that many Catholics, unaware of canon law vocabulary, understand *ordinary* as *daily.* Moreover, even in the revised canon law of 1983, it seems that this misunderstanding has become official since it is said about the cardinals that "they assist the Roman Pontiff especially *in the daily care of the universal church* by means of the different offices they perform."

Catholic theologians agree that this formulation of canon 349 does not express the dogma of 1870.

Immediate

According to the explanation given by the same Zinelli before the vote, "immediate power" means that the holder of such an office does not need the permission of an intermediary power to use it. The pope can exercise his authority without having to go through any intermediary — whether ecclesiastical or civil. The scope of such phraseology was to exclude the necessary assent of many secular powers to enact religious decisions.[3]

2. Mansi 52, 1105.

3. Mansi 52, 1105; Heinrich Denziger, *Enchiridion symbolorum definitionum et*

Truly Episcopal

In common language, this technical wording can also be very easily misunderstood. Here again Zinelli explained *"episcopalis"* in the sense of *"pastoralis."*[4] It is not a claim that the bishop of Rome is also the bishop of every single diocese: this has been clarified by the German bishops in their famous answer to Bismarck in 1875, approved by Pius IX.[5] More important, this expression, which is meant to characterize the nature of the primatial power ("it is *like* the power of a bishop), is not resumed in the corresponding canon, which means that "truly episcopal" is not included in the definition. This nature is then left to theological discussion. Another remark can be made: we do not find here a foundation for the trend of the Roman Curia, which tries nowadays to make the pope an intrinsic component of the dogmatic identity of every diocese.

Full and Supreme

"Full and supreme power over the church" are stronger words, since the council adds *"both over each and all the churches and all the pastors and the faithful."* Bishop Papp-Szilágyi feared he saw there "an absolute monarchy of divine right." Zinelli explained this fullness in terms that were not reassuring: "such a power is meant as having no other boundary than natural and divine law."[6] Here lies the greatest trouble with the definitions. These were understood by non-Catholics in a framework of absolute monarchy, with infallibility making the case even worse. This was also the so-called maximalist interpretation well recorded by Catholic historians and lately by H. J. Pottmeyer.

But the maximalist interpretation stands only when they do not give this power the purpose given to it by Vatican I, which is quite clear from the Prologue:

> in order that the Episcopate might be one and undivided, and that by means of a closely united episcopacy, the multitude of the faithful might be kept secure in the oneness of faith and communion, He [Jesus] set the

---

declarationum de rebus fidei et morum, re-edited by Peter Hünermann, 37th edition (Freiburg: Herder, 1991), 3062; hereafter cited as DH.

4. Mansi 52, 1104.
5. DH 3112-17.
6. Mansi 52, 1108-9.

Blessed Peter over the rest of the apostles, and fixed in Him an abiding principle of this twofold unity.

The object of the papacy is clearly stated in the prologue to the definition: unity among the bishops and unity of the whole church. It is only to pursue this aim that the power of the pope is full and supreme. The Catholic dogmaticians have another criterion to underline the limits of this "full and supreme power." These are given by Vatican I itself, which teaches that this definition has to be understood "in accordance with the ancient and constant faith of the universal Church" (DH 3051) and with "the acts of the General Councils and the sacred canons" (DH 3059), in accordance with "the perpetual practice of the Church" (DH 3065) and with "the Ecumenical councils, especially those in which the East with the West met in the union of faith and charity" (DH 3065).

If this "full and supreme power" is thus limited, one may have the hope of reaching at least a first condition of a re-reception of Vatican I, namely, in a common ecumenical council with the Orthodox Church in order to find a common doctrine on the matter. Perhaps the Orthodox may consider that Vatican I, though defective, was not plainly heretical.

Infallibility

The second definition concerning infallibility raised greater misunderstanding than that relative to jurisdiction. The wording of the definition is carefully thought out and restrictive. But in this respect it is important to repeat that Catholic dogmaticians agree on three points: the meaning of the word *infallible,* the conditions of infallibility, and the meaning of the phrase *ex sese non autem ex consensu ecclesiae.*

The Meaning of the Word Infallible

Declaring that the pope is infallible according to Vatican I, that is to say, expressing in four words what Vatican I has defined in fourteen lines, is certainly erroneous. Vatican I does not speak of the pope's infallibility but of his solemn magisterium, which is completely different. Infallibility is a negative concept meaning error-free, but it does not mean the definition has been worded in the best possible terms and even less that it was timely used.

Infallibility is only concerned with Revelation, to which the pope (the church) cannot add anything.

The Conditions of Infallibility

Only a definition *ex cathedra* can be infallible. There is one requirement added by canon law: "no doctrine is understood to be infallibly defined unless it is clearly established as such" (can. 749, §3). When there is a doubt, there is no infallible definition.

Ex sese, non autem ex consensu ecclesiae

The phrase is often understood as if *non ex* had the same meaning as *without*. The real scope is to exclude the subsequent compulsory ratification of the definition by civil or ecclesiastical authorities to make it valid. It was practical in those days: for instance a decision of Trent (The Decree *Tametsi*) was not received in the Low Countries until 1909 because the civil authorities resisted it.

So far, concerning the consensus among Catholic dogmaticians, the most difficult issue with the First Vatican Council is not the learned reception but the practical reception. But even the learned reception of Vatican I is open to a re-reception. In this matter too there is a consensus among Catholic historians about the limitations of Vatican I.

The Reasons Why a Re-reception of Vatican I Seems Legitimate to Most Catholic Historians and Theologians

The opinion that it would be legitimate and fruitful to re-receive the definitions of Vatican I is widespread among Catholic theologians. It is easy to summarize their reasons:

Vatican I Was a Broken Council

This is true in every sense of the word. Historically the conquest of the papal states by the troops of the king of Savoy put an end to the deliberations. Theologically the Council could not therefore discuss the planned texts on episcopacy. Unwillingly Vatican I produced an unbalanced ecclesiology.

It immediately raises the following question: Did not Vatican II bring the desired balance? The answer is "no," and is given by the latest developments in ecclesiology brought by the Roman Curia, as we shall see.

Vatican I Has Suffered from Theological Limitations of Having to Face the Many Urgent Needs of the Time

The thesis has been well illustrated by Hermann J. Pottmeyer.[7] He analyzes convincingly the traumas suffered by the Catholic Church in the nineteenth century: the control of the national churches by the states (like that introduced by Emperor Joseph II); the ideologies of modern times (liberalism and socialism, the triumph of rationalism); the remembrance of Gallicanism and conciliarism, recently illustrated by the council of Pistoia. All these "attacks" and the near end of the papal states created a sense of extreme urgency. All these tests came in a period when the Catholic Church was not theologically well equipped, after the Enlightenment and the French Revolution.

These fears were not only the fears of the pope; they were also the fears of a great number of priests and laypeople. It explains the success of Ultramontanism, seen as a bulwark against a disquieting modern world, and the broad and popular reception of the papal dogmas.

In such an emergency, it is quite possible, as Pottmeyer suggests, that Joseph de Maistre, who was actually a Freemason and not a theologian, could influence the minds of many by his logically developed idea that the pope needed to be an absolute monarch:

> There can be no human society without a government, no government without sovereignty, no sovereignty without infallibility.[8] . . . Christianity is entirely built upon the sovereign Pontiff . . . no public morality nor national character without religion, no European religion without Christianity, no Christianity without Catholicism, no Catholicism without the Pope, no Pope without the supremacy which belongs to him.[9]

But today, such a candid belief in the value of an absolute monarchy appears for what it is: a prejudice.[10] This belief discloses the poor theological

---

7. In his book *Towards a Papacy in Communion: Perspectives from Vatican Councils I & II* (New York: Crossroad, 1998).

8. Joseph de Maistre, *Du pape* (Genève: Droz, 1966), p. 123. Originally published in French around 1817.

9. *Correspondance* IV (Lyon, 1821), p. 428.

10. In the Congregation for the Doctrine of the Faith, *Reflections on the Primacy of Peter in the Mystery of the Church*, n. 7, one reads that the primacy "cannot be understood like a monarchy of a political nature," *DC* 95 (1998): 1017. Nevertheless in our present

education within the nineteenth-century Catholic Church, and particularly how far we were from the perceptions we may have today through the Lima document:

> Ordained ministry should be fulfilled in a personal, collegial and community mode. Each of these three systems [forms] of Church organization has been acknowledged for centuries . . . we reckon that under some conditions, they will have to play their respective roles simultaneously in the organization of the reunited Church. (n. 26)

From this perspective, the Vatican dogmas necessarily need to be re-received, by being embedded in such better-balanced ecclesiology, far from the ideal of the absolute monarchy.

Vatican I Is Open to a Re-reception Because It Is an Ecclesiological Council

In its dogmas, Vatican I gives a verdict on what primacy must be in the whole church, but paradoxically it does it in the absence of all the other churches. But since the latter are concerned with the terms, we, Catholics, should be all the more open to their reception of these terms. Following Paul VI, who described the council of Lyon II as a general council held in the West, we should welcome a responding document from the East,[11] provided its wording is non-heretical, and as long as it is interpreted in the strictest way.[12]

Second Conclusion: The major responsibilities towards an ecumenical reception of the papacy lie with the Catholic Church. The key towards a change is primarily of a practical and institutional nature.
It seems useless to resume here the consensus of the Catholic theologians and historians on the legitimacy and even necessity to re-receive Vatican I. It

---

canon law, the pope is juridically an absolute monarch, like the bishop in his diocese and the parish priest in his parish, the only difference being that the bishop obeys the pope and the parish priest the bishop!

11. Letter of Cardinal Willebrands on the occasion of the seventh centenary of the Second Council of Lyon, *AAS* 66 (1974): 620.

12. Remember that this is the norm for infallible definitions.

seems just as useless to resume the theological insights found in Vatican II: collegiality, ecclesiology of communion understood as a communion of churches, legitimate diversities, subsidiarity, cooperative exercise of authority on every level. . . .

There is no shortage of light on all these issues. So at the risk of being politically incorrect it is necessary to leave the realm of ideas for that of realities and precisely the institutional realities that the exercise of papacy involves. If not, the proposition of a dialogue on papacy does not stand a chance of being taken seriously.

Indeed for the past fifteen years a careful observer must have witnessed the implementation of Vatican I's maximalist interpretation and not its correction by Vatican II's teachings. Practically speaking, one cannot mention an enhancement of the episcopate or the local churches. In this field one notices regression on both the doctrinal and institutional levels, combined with an expansion of the papal and curial magisterium.

Vatican II's intention, as everyone knows, had been to highlight the role of the episcopate and to reduce the weight of the Roman Curia. Not only has this objective not been reached, but on the contrary, the Roman Curia has experienced unprecedented expansion: the number of bishops in a position of responsibility has quadrupled, growing from fewer than twenty (cardinals included, under Pius XII) to more than eighty today — so much so that they constitute a kind of permanent synod. Its staff has more than doubled. It is no wonder that the Curia has turned into some kind of universal decision-maker and that at the same time collegiality, subsidiarity, and legitimate diversities regress.

This evolution is at work in three main fields: (1) in the Curia's restrictive interpretation of Vatican II's teachings, which allows us to understand *communio ecclesiarum* as *communio ecclesiae;* (2) in a number of canonical measures controlling the episcopate and its authority in a stricter way; and (3) in the quantitative and qualitative expansion of the papal and curial magisterium.

Teachings Intended to Restrict *Communio ecclesiarum* to *Communio ecclesiae*

An Attempt to Balance the Statement of Lumen gentium *23: "In and from the individual churches there comes into being the one and only Catholic Church" by a new teaching about "the ontological and chronological priority of the Universal Church over the particular Churches"*

The clearest assertion in this respect is to be found in *Communionis notio,* n 9. After aptly denying that "the individual Church is a complete subject in itself and that the universal Church is the result of the reciprocal recognition of the individual churches" and after not so aptly stating that the individual churches (the dioceses) are "parts of the unique Church of Christ," *CN* 9 goes on:

> The universal Church cannot be conceived as the sum of the particular churches or as a federation of particular churches. It is not the result of the communion of the churches, but, in its essential mystery, it is a reality ontologically and temporally prior to every individual particular church.[13]

Such wording does not pose any problem: The diocesan church is not a self-sufficient subject and the whole church is neither a federation of dioceses nor the result of their communion. It is clear that if the diocese is legitimately the church of God it does not represent the whole church of God (other dioceses are also legitimately churches of God). Each local church fits into the network of a diachronic *traditio-receptio,* not only a synchronic or geographical *traditio-receptio.* Received as a norm by each diocesan church, the faith of the *Catholica,* through time and space, is the Rule of Faith of each particular diocese (the term is quite rightly underlined in CN). In this sense, there is precedence (temporal) and priority (that could be termed ontological) of the Catholic Church's faith and communion over each particular diocese. The Congregation for the Doctrine of the Faith (CDF) has good reason to remind it.

But the doctrine further developed in n. 9 of CN raises a question of wording and general balance and even seems to distance itself seriously from Vatican II:

13. *Communionis notio,* n. 9.

According to the Fathers, ontologically the Church-mystery, the Church that is one and unique, precedes creation, and gives birth to the particular Churches as to her daughters; she expresses through them, she is a mother and not the end product of particular Churches. . . .

From the Church, which in its origins and its first manifestation is universal, have arisen the different local Churches, as particular expressions of the one unique Church of Jesus Christ. Arising within and without of the universal church, they have their ecclesiality in her and from her. Hence the formula of the Second Vatican Council: The Church in and formed out of the Churches (*ecclesia in et ex ecclesiis*, LG 23) is inseparable from this other formula *(Ecclesiae in et ex Ecclesia)*.

This attempt to amend LG 23 comes up against four immediate and serious difficulties:

1. From the ontological priority of the universal church over the whole singular particular church, one switches to its priority over *all* the churches. The latest formulation no longer allows us to express that the Catholic Church, one and unique, derives its existence from the churches, as LG 23 teaches.

2. This wording compels us to imagine a universal church that could exist prior to any concrete, confessing, and sacramental processes that institute it, and regardless of these same processes, to think that the church could exist without the faithful and the sacraments of the Faith. The pre-existence of the church in God's design cannot justify such a "logical concept." Besides, why shouldn't the simultaneity of the church and the churches also be in God's design?

3. This wording jeopardizes the catholicity of the church by reducing it to universality. Thus one forgets that the diversity of the local churches, every one of which praises God and hears the Good News in its own tongue, contributes in an essential way to the catholicity of the whole church.

4. Turning the universal church into the mother of all the diocesan churches is completely different from the well-known thesis of the maternity of the church for every believer; it is also completely different from the historical filiation in relation to the church that is said to have founded it. The immediate consequence of this doctrinal innovation is the impossibility of conceiving the Catholic Church as *communio ecclesiarum* or as having potential sisters: hence the logical refusal to award the title to the Orthodox Church as we shall see later on.

This type of chronological and ontological precedence results in the weakening of the episcopate and the status of the regional churches on the one hand and the highlighting of the pope's status on the other, and it compromises the prospect of a *communio ecclesiarum*.

1. The body of bishops is disconnected from the communion of churches. *Apostolos suos* (1998), which relies on *Communionis notio,* teaches that *"the college of bishops, as an essential element of the universal Church, is a reality which precedes the office of being the head of a particular Church"* (n. 12). This doctrinal innovation is justified by a very recent empirical fact: *"As it is obvious for all, numerous bishops are not at the head of a particular Church."*[14] We are faced with the *"college of the universal Church's senior managerial staff"* according to a Rahnerian idea that is very unlikely to assert itself in Catholic theology and does not stand the slightest chance of being accepted one day by the orthodox ecclesiology.

2. In so doing one deprives the regional churches of any foundation: their very existence and the forms of existence they assume are left to the sole assessment of the primacy.

Apostolos suos teaches that groupings of dioceses can have neither foundation nor legitimacy in the churches' own right to take initiatives. Thus, concerning conferences of bishops, one can read in n. 13:

> The binding effect of the acts of the episcopal ministry jointly exercised within conferences of bishops and in communion with the Apostolic See derives from the fact that the latter has constituted the former and has entrusted to them, on the basis of the sacred power of the individual bishops, specific areas of competence.

Paradoxically enough, while felicitously innovating by the introduction of the concept of a church *sui iuris*,[15] the 1990 Code of canons of the Eastern churches has nevertheless standardized these churches so much that they have administratively merged canonical traditions as heterogeneous as

---

14. The Annuario Pontificio last edition [2004] gives an idea about it: 43 percent of Catholic bishops (17 percent of whom only are bishops emeritus) are not actually at the head of a diocese (in absolute figures: 4329 bishops for 2667 dioceses). The obvious is the abnormal position of nearly half of the college members, whereas being a bishop does not mean being "the delegate of a centralized system . . . but being the pastor of one's Church," as Joseph Ratzinger reminds us, rightly criticizing Karl Rahner. See *Église, œcuménisme et politique* (Paris: Fayard, 1987), p. 77.

15. Jean-Claude Périsset suggested granting this status to the churches born of the Reformation.

those of Byzantium and Ethiopia or Armenia and Syriac India. Moreover, the Code is written in Latin, thereby opening these Catholics to the suspicion of being Latinized because of their communion with Rome. Finally, the pope alone promulgated it, as if his primatial authority also included being the patriarch or major archbishop of these churches; and besides, some of the clauses of the Code entrust him with maximal power.

3. The same universalist priority turns the pope into an "internal element" of the dogmatic identity of every diocesan church. This idea, lacking in LG 23, 26, and *Christus dominus* (CD) 11, is put forward by *Communionis notio*, nn. 9 and 13, and notably resumed by the reflections of the CDF titled *The Primacy of the Successor of Peter in the Mystery of the Church*. It is claimed (n. 13) that "the ministry of Peter is engraved on the heart of every particular Church," which is hardly coherent with Pius IX's answer confirming that of the German bishops to Bismarck. It is added that "this interiority of the Bishop of Rome to every particular Church is also the expression of the reciprocal interiority between universal Church and particular Church." In this last sentence, the bishop of Rome is equated with the universal church(!) whereas he fulfills his Petrine ministry in the service of the whole church as *communio ecclesiarum* in his capacity of bishop of the local Church of Rome.

The "subsistit in" (LG 8) is in the process of being interpreted as having the same meaning as "est." This is detrimental to the communio ecclesiarum.

Quoting a previous Declaration of the CDF (1985) condemning a book by Leonardo Boff, *Dominus Iesus* asserts that it is "contrary to the authentic meaning of LG 8, that the unique Church of Christ could also subsist in non-Catholic Churches and ecclesial communities." However, according to the documentation available thanks to the *Acta Synodalia*, one is assured that the church fathers' intention when adopting the wording *subsitit in* had been to avoid, as Cardinal Liénart claimed, the exclusive identification of the church of Christ found in a first version of the text, quoting Pius XII himself:

> The Roman Catholic Church is the mystical Body of Christ . . . and only the Roman Catholic Church is entitled to the name of Church.

By interpreting *subsistit in* as the exact equivalent of *est*, one returns to the exclusivism of *Lumen gentium*'s former schema. So it is quite logical that the CDF's secret note sent to all the Catholic bishops in June 2000 should forbid referring to the Orthodox Church as a sister church: "one cannot say that the Catholic Church is the sister of a particular Church or a group of Churches," for "the universal Church is the mother of all the particular Churches."

Concerning similar reasoning, Cardinal Kasper pointed out:

> The wording becomes very problematic if the unique Universal Church is stealthily [*unter den Hand*] identified with the Church of Rome. . . . If such is the case, then the Letter of the Congregation for the Doctrine of the Faith cannot be understood as a help for the clarification of the ecclesiology of communion, but it must be understood as its abandonment [*Verabschiedung*] and as an attempt at theologically restoring Roman centralization.

To sum up, the attempt to revise the impact of *"in quibus et ex quibus"* is far-reaching and makes less likely the prospect of a papacy in the service of a *communio ecclesiarum* in which the churches are not absorbed in the church.

Numerous Canonical Clauses Have Weakened the Bishops' Status and the Expression of the *Communio ecclesiarum*

The doctrine of collegiality is meant to enhance the episcopal body. By conferring the entire power on the college of bishops, and not first and foremost on the pope who would hand it down to the bishops, Vatican II has theoretically changed the place of the pope in the body of the church.

This became possible due to the rediscovery of the sacramentality of episcopal ordination. Differently from Pius XII, Vatican II teaches that the bishops receive responsibility for governing directly from Christ (LG 26). The separation between the power of orders (said to stem from sacrament) and the power of jurisdiction (said to stem from the pope) is thus over in principle. Therefore one must consider the bishops to be "the vicars and ambassadors of Jesus Christ . . . and not the vicars of the Roman pontiff" (LG 27), a formulation that will not unfortunately be resumed by the 1983 Code.

It entails two consequences for the promotion of the local churches and their bishops, who acquire greater leeway:

- First canonically, the pope, in his capacity as primate and for the welfare of all, reserves for himself a number of prerogatives that the bishops could legitimately exercise. In this way, one leaves the regime of "concession" for that of "reserve," and so potentially for a regime in which the local churches are, in themselves, full-fledged subjects. Especially, such a regime is based on and requires the active responsibility of each bishop towards the entire church and first towards the churches of his region, where one of the structures happens to be the bishops' conference, now made compulsory.
- The purpose of the conference of bishops was aimed at giving real expression to the communion of churches within a nation (LG 23), or even several nations (CD 38,5). In this way one hoped to revitalize regional churches and to allow them to voice their opinions within the entire church through the bishops' synod with the pope. But forty years later, the prospects we had caught a glimpse of have not been reached. Let's briefly analyze the canonical measures that have caused the former order to be restored in many areas.

The Curia Has Resumed the Daily Government of the Diocesan Churches and Their Bishops

The 1983 Code and its subsequent legislation have transformed the bishops into civil servants of the pope. This is the term used by Georg Bier to conclude his comprehensive study on the judicial status of the diocesan bishop according to this code.[16] It is a harsh formulation but it seems juridically confirmed.

Thus the Curia settles the issue whether little girls should serve mass and is keen on revising liturgical translations, including languages unknown to its officials. These two examples are proof enough. The testimony of one bishop among many, such as John R. Quinn, former archbishop of San Francisco, can also provide sufficient evidence.

16. Georg Bier, *Die Rechtsstellung des Diözesanbischofs* (Würzburg: Echter Verlag, 2001), p. 376: "rechtlich päpstlichen Beamten."

Episcopal Conferences Have Not Developed
and Their Magisterium Has Been Restricted

According to canon 753 of the 1983 Code "bishops . . . gathered in episcopal conferences are authentic teachers of the faith." But as early as 1985, the prefect of the CDF was of a different opinion; he said to Messori: "No episcopal conference as such has a teaching mission."[17] From *Apostolos suos* onwards (1998), doctrinal declarations must either be unanimously approved or receive the approval *("recognitio")* of the Holy See if approved by two-thirds of the members in order to be published as authoritative documents of the conference. Such a stringent criterion is greater than any required in any other instance of ecclesiastical governance or teaching, on either a local or a universal level.

The requirement of unanimity also creates the impression that there is a deliberate intention to ignore the importance of conferences, because under this statute they would rarely, if ever, be able to propose doctrinal teaching, even of the lowest level.

This distrust for conferences and the policies aimed at limiting them may lead one to deduce that in the Catholic Church we can ignore the bishops. Thus one forgets that fear of centralization is one of the fears that Orthodox and Protestant Christians have in regard to establishing full communion with Rome.

Appointing the Vast Majority of Bishops Remains the
Responsibility of the Pope, the Nuncios, and the Curia

With a few exceptions (twenty dioceses or so in German-speaking countries), our process of selecting bishops is a closed one, with an inconsequential participation of bishops and with little or no participation whatsoever of priests and laypeople. It is not uncommon for bishops to be appointed without having ever been put forward by the bishops of a region or even being known to them.

The matter is not ethical but ecclesiological. If the local church is a communion and the bishops are servants of the communion between the churches, it would be necessary for diocesans to cooperate even remotely in the choice and reception of their bishop while keeping the precious coopera-

17. *The Ratzinger Report* (San Francisco: Ignatius Press, 1985), p. 60.

tion of the Roman see (it is an established warranty of the *libertas ecclesiae*).[18] But the appointment of almost all the bishops by the pope, a very recent practice for that matter, gives other churches a false idea of the papal ministry. Will they deem it right to enter into communion with Rome if giving up the election of their bishops is the price to pay?

The Synod of Bishops Works as an Instrument of the Primacy

The wish was expressed in CD 5 that *"Acting in the name of the entire Catholic episcopate [the synod] of Bishops will at the same time demonstrate that all the bishops in hierarchical communion share in the responsibility for the universal Church."* This wish never took shape.

The synod very clearly appears in its functioning as an instrument of the papacy and not as a representation of the churches. The pope summons the synod and decides on the agenda; preliminary answers from episcopal conferences are not allowed to be made public, or even discreetly shared with other episcopal conferences, and they must be directly sent to Rome where the synod is held; prefects of the Roman curia are members with voting rights; the pope, in addition to the curial members, appoints an additional 15 percent of the membership directly;[19] there is no discussion in plenary,[20] and the bishops are not supposed to address questions that have already been decided on in canon law or are taught by the ordinary magisterium. The synod does not have a deliberative vote; its deliberations are secret. Its recommendations to the pope are secret: even the members do not know the result of their votes; the pope writes and issues the final document a year or so after the synod has concluded and the bishops have returned home.[21]

18. This dossier is more open among the cardinals than one could imagine. For example, in the consistory of May 2001, Cardinal Winning wished for the reform of the process of nominations, while Cardinal Pompedda, Prefect of the Supreme Tribunal of the Apostolic Signature, considered insufficient "current practice of consultation followed in the procedure of nomination of bishops." *Il Regno* 46, no. 12 (2001): 365.

19. Their composition has less and less place for the elected. In the synod for America, only 136 members were elected by their peers; 161 other participants were *ex officio* or by papal designation. Cf. *DC* 95 (1998): 17.

20. For two weeks the bishops are allowed to speak eight minutes, one after another, in five different languages.

21. From 1974, no synod has written its own conclusions. The general description

Even after Vatican II the Roman Primacy
Institutionally Remains an Absolute Monarchy

Non-Catholics consider the pope to be an absolute monarch. In terms of constitutional law, this is true and generally acknowledged by Catholics themselves.[22] According to canon 333,3: "there is neither appeal nor recourse against a decision of the Roman Pontiff."[23]

The competence to determine the extent of his own competence is often ascribed to the pope. In other words, he himself can define the limits of his powers[24] as well as the extent of his infallibility, as can be seen in *Ad tuendam fidem* (1998). It states that the pope can define, without the infallibility granted to him by Vatican I, what has been *definitively* proposed infallible by the ordinary and universal magisterium. This seems to be the case for the non-ordination of women.[25]

But there is no consensus within the Catholic Church about the competence ascribed to the pope to determine his own competence, probably because throughout history more than a few mistakes have been made in this matter, to say the least.[26]

---

of a synod is taken from John R. Quinn, *The Reform of the Papacy: The Costly Call to Christian Unity* (New York: Crossroad, 1999), p. 111.

22. Cf. Klaus Schatz, *La primauté du pape. Son histoire des origines à nos jours* (Paris: Cerf, 1992), p. 238. Antonio Acerbi, "Per una nuova forma del ministero petrino," in Antonio Acerbi, *Il ministero del papa in prospettiva ecumenica* (Milano: Vita e Pensiero, 1999), p. 30; Pottmeyer, *Towards a Papacy*, p. 25: "from witness to monarch"; p. 35: "the process by which the pope was advanced to the position of monarch in the church was neither a logical nor organic development of the Petrine idea . . . it was a one-sided development."

23. This has been recently extended to the decisions of the CDF: *Ratio agendi in doctrinarum examine, AAS* 89 (1997): 834.

24. This is an unknown possibility that allows him to relinquish the absolute exercise of his power. For instance, law could grant bishops a right of initiative or proposal, compelling, for example, the whole church to take up an issue that a continental conference of bishops would have deemed necessary to be dealt with at the level of the church as a whole; similarly the pope could force himself to seek advice from the episcopate or such and such group of bishops before making such and such a decision, or else, on conditions to be specified, the bishops could ask for an ecumenical council to be convened, it being agreed that, in so doing, they would not question the canonical position of the pope. These are the wise suggestions made by Acerbi, "Per una forma," pp. 333-35.

25. See the Explanatory note of Cardinal Ratzinger, n. 11, *DC* 95 (1998): 656; *Catholic International* 9 (1998): n. 9, 407.

26. Let us mention the papal claim to world sovereignty by Boniface VIII and, most

The institutional form the papacy has taken must not be understood only as a theological or canonical issue; it also takes on a cultural form. Working out decisions with those who have to implement them is a must for the primacy. Local and regional churches have to be instituted as interlocutors. If not, taking decisions in a universalist and canonico-administrative pattern will only lead to very superficial adherence entailing permanent tensions. On a deeper level, the question raised by Melanchthon in the sixteenth century is finding some echo: *"non est transferendum ad pontifices quod dicitur de ecclesia."*

The Papal and Curial Magisterium Has Experienced a Great Quantitative and Qualitative Development Ever Since Vatican II

One can easily notice the quantitative increase of the papal interventions.[27] Their doctrinal authority is very diverse. Most of the time the pope expresses himself as the doctor of the Christians he addresses. As a rule, the value of the texts published in the Acta of the Holy See (the only ones to have official value) is easily discernible, thanks to their careful classification according to importance, but this fact remains unknown to the general public and to the other churches' theologians. The curial texts do not belong to the papal magisterium and the obligation to assent to them is less: they very often deal with a particular theology.[28]

disturbingly, the misunderstandings about the extension of their spiritual claims specifically in interpreting the Bible: the Galilei case, the historicity of Genesis, or even in a recent matter the claim of the CDF of the infallibility of papal canonizations, when we know that a figure like Felix de Valois, who owes his existence to false bulls, has been canonized (cf. *Catholicisme* IV, 1156-57; *LfTH*[2], 1222) as well as Jean Népomucène, canonized by error (cf. Paul de Vooght, OSB, *L'hérésie de Jean Hus*, t. II [Louvain: Bureaux de la Revue, Bibliothèque de l'Université, Publications Universitaires de Louvain [2]1975], pp. 955-1010; Roger Aubert, *Jean de Pomuk*, DGHE [Paris, 1998]).

27. The *Insegnamenti di Giovanni Paolo II*, published by the Libreria Editrice Vaticana, usually reach 4000 pages a year, sometimes 5000 pages (4932 pages in 1988).

28. Thus *l'Instruction sur quelques questions concernant la collaboration des fidèles laïcs au ministère des prêtres* (15 August 1997) (signed by the officials of eight dicasteries, and approved in specific form) firmly asserts "the theologically certain doctrine and the age-old practice of the Church according to which the sole valid minister [of the anointing of the sick] is the priest. While confirming that point in the last few centuries, the theological file shows in reality much greater freedom in the field. One shall compare, for example, with Antoine Chavasse, *Étude sur l'onction des infirmes dans l'Église latine du 3e*

Beyond the quantitative aspects, one easily notices a will to regulate theologians that has resulted in a growing number of crises, in the Cologne declaration,[29] in the CDF "Instruction on the Ecclesial Vocation of the Theologian,"[30] and in an exceptional sensitivity to the possibility of public disagreement between theologians and magisterium.[31]

One has already mentioned that the Oath of faithfulness and *Ad tuendam fidem* also presented a qualitative expansion of the teaching of papal magisterium.

Summary

Harding Meyer is right. The possibility for the papacy to become an ecumenical theme does not depend only on its theological reinterpretation; it depends just as much on its practical reorganization. I have particularly emphasized this point: for Catholics, primacy is not a concept; it is practice. And if it were not a practice, it would be pointless. Currently, the Roman primacy works according to an excessive maximalist interpretation of Vatican I. Therefore, its reorganization is the most urgent contribution that we, Catholics, can make. Vatican II had foreseen the task. But it is currently neglected. The recent evolution of the Catholic Church has even forsaken it with a practical and theoretical coherence that we must assess. We will not be able to do it unless we look at ourselves through other Christians' eyes. Since the ministry concerned is that of the unity of all Christians, John Paul II has shown us the good method: "together of course" (*Ut unum sint* 95).

Towards common understanding of the papacy?
It is far too early to assert that we are moving towards a common understanding of the papacy. The conversation has hardly started!

It is even too early to detect true convergences about it among our churches. Let us bear in mind that the refusal of the papacy is at least part of the sociological identity of a great number of these churches. Conversely, it

---

siècle à la réforme carolingienne (Lyon: Librairie du Sacré-Coeur, 1942), who demonstrated more than fifty years ago that the minister of such anointing was often a relative who used oil blessed by the bishop.

29. Signed by 163 professors from the Germanic area, *DC* 86 (1989): 240-42.

30. *AAS* 82 (1990): 1550-70.

31. See the letter published on the subject by the secretary of the CDF, *DC* 94 (1997): 108-12.

appears to me (1) that theologians have just engaged in conversation; (2) that they seem to find it desirable on Christian grounds, and not because of a strong interest in the papacy itself, even if some popes command their respect; and (3) that Catholics, ceasing to be on the defensive, have already become aware of their theological responsibilities but still need to realize that we will not move forward without practical reforms in the papacy.

1. As far as theologians are concerned, the papacy issue is no longer a stalemate: the conversation is starting.

In the eyes of the better-informed and more benevolent Orthodox and Protestant theologians, Vatican I's dogmatic terms still appear to be very odd, with little biblical foundation (if one is Protestant) and/or traditional foundation (if one is Orthodox). These terms are not very balanced and are fraught with various dangers that can be easily illustrated with historical events or current affairs. But today's novelty is that these theologians are now able to accept that these dogmas are not necessarily heretical by considering the very specific context that the nineteenth-century church was steeped in, and considering their strict exegesis in keeping with critical-historical methodology.

This is most important in the long term for the relationships that could one day develop with the Orthodox Church, since, if we are not seen as heretical, it might become possible for us to hold a common council, especially to re-receive Vatican I. Denominationalism would not have prevailed. In regards to the Reformation, one of the most symbolic obstacles on the long path to unity would then have been overcome.

This negative statement on a lack of heresy will not suffice. At the same time, it will be necessary to acknowledge positively that it would be impossible to receive these definitions if they are not integrated into better-balanced ecclesiology. We could meet up by agreeing to the requests of the Orthodox Church about equality between sister churches, and those of the Reformation as expressed by Melanchthon *("non est transferendum ad pontifices quod dicitur de ecclesia")*, and those of the consensus on BEM ratified by the Catholic theologians, on the mutual belonging of synodal and collegiate responsibilities and the personal responsibility that Geoffrey Wainwright has spoken about so well. On our side we will still have to develop even more consistently a pneumatological ecclesiology and a theology of the local churches, precisely in order to better reorganize primacy and collegiality, and a college for the service of the communion of churches. Even though we also lack a theology of canon law, we constantly settle questions canonically.

2. Insofar as theologians are preoccupied with Christian unity, the papacy issue is beginning to offer some interest.

It is rare for the papacy as such to arouse a specifically Christian interest in non-Catholics. Its history is too ambivalent. Catholics themselves acknowledge that schisms did not happen under the best of popes! As Harding Meyer so clearly expressed, it is the concern for the unity of the church of Christ in our world that brings the reality of the papacy into relief. Thanks to it, some Christian realities are made possible and would be much more difficult if the papacy did not exist. We shall draw up a list of theses realities and illustrate each one of them with an example:

- The possibility of a council is considered positively by all Christians: real primacy has made a council such as Vatican II possible, especially when there is no longer a Christian emperor.
- The possibility for the local and regional churches to be questioned on their Christian life would be positive. Real primacy makes the approach possible. With the World Youth Days, doesn't the pope challenge the Western churches, which are virtually afraid of gathering the young?
- The regulation of relationships between churches that are unequal in different ways can be facilitated by real primacy, creating solidarity or protecting the poorer against the richer.
- The protection of the churches against state infringement or ethnic identification could benefit from positive primacy.
- Finally, the possibility for Christians as a whole to be represented on a world scale could be a blessing. This is what was experienced by the churches that sent their delegates to the first Assisi meeting or by Christians who thought John Paul II represented them at the Wailing Wall.

One could continue and conversely underline that the usefulness of a type of service does not ensure its truth. The issue is obvious. By showing a Christian interest in this service, by affirming *"res nostra agitur,"* could not Protestants and Orthodox contribute to making this pre-eminently evident service, already perceived as Christian, even more authentic?

3. Ceasing to be defensive concerning the papacy, Catholic theologians have already initiated a sounder reception of Vatican I. Henceforth they rank foremost the combining of ecumenism, pastoral and institutional revisions.

With his encyclical *Ut unum sint,* John Paul II legitimized Catholic theologians who are no longer defensive on the papacy issue, as they used to be fifty years ago. It has proved true of those who have reflected on primacy, such as Congar and Tillard among the French speakers, Pottmeyer and Schatz in Germany, Acerbi in Italy, Komonchak and Killian McDonnell in the United States. They are all good historians and also concerned with ecumenism and pastoral concerns.

The greatest hopes lie in this characteristic. The ecumenical approach to the papacy has simultaneously turned into a pastoral issue. Even some cardinals admit it. Let us cite the awareness of this hope in the speech of Cardinal Martini, the former archbishop of Milan, at the synod on Europe in 1999. Underlying the need for communication between bishops, within the Catholic Church, in order "to undo some disciplinary and doctrinal knots," he lists "the ecclesiology of communion of Vatican II, the crucial lack of ordained ministers in some places, women's situation in society and in the Church, sexuality, marriage discipline, relationships with sister churches and the fundamental need to revive ecumenical hope."[32] Obviously, pastoral ministry and ecumenism are very similar in mutual exchanges but also in the request for a more cooperative exercise of authority in the church. In that respect, a third Vatican council on the pattern of Vatican II would probably be a mistake. Instead of proposing views on almost every aspect of Christian life, shouldn't "Vatican III" concentrate on a single issue, namely adjusting and improving decision-making methods in the church? Haven't we noticed that Vatican II failed on these aspects for having neglected law, too often exposed as legalism? Ecclesiology, ecumenically oriented ecclesiology in particular, that did not take law seriously would be unrealistic.

There will be neither unity among Christians nor true enculturation without local and regional churches who are the holders of right in the communion. That is the conviction shown by another cardinal, Walter Kasper, in his friendly exchanges with Cardinal Ratzinger about primacy. He concludes one of them as follows:

> My reflections on the connections between the universal Church and the local Church have significant impact on pastoral issues. . . . What appeared to me at the outset to be a pastoral issue specific to the Catholic Church has ever since become a pressing ecumenical concern, for the ec-

32. *DC* 87 (1999): 950-51.

umenical movement is not aiming at a unitarian and uniform Church but a Church reconciled in its diversity.[33]

Without primacy, such an aim cannot be achieved. Will it be better achieved if we have a one-way conception of the papacy? I rather tend to think that it will be all the easier to achieve by maintaining a differentiated understanding of primacy. What appears to be a "cultural must" in a global church[34] also represents, it seems to me, a "doctrinal must" for the communion of churches — which cannot be, I am afraid, a communion of uniform churches.

33. Walter Kasper, "Das Verhältnis von Universalkirche und Ostkirche, Freundschaftliche Auseinandersetzung mit der Kritik von Joseph Kardinal Ratzinger," *Stimmen der Zeit* (December 2001): 795-804, here p. 804.

34. A plain example: after the synod on Oceania, Cardinal Clancy, the archbishop of Sydney, stressed that "our brothers in Rome have not grasped the real situation as we experience it at home . . . after centuries of authoritarian regulations from the different Roman congregations, it is difficult to engage in a genuine dialogue," *Il Regno* 46 (2001): 267. That such remarks should be made by a cardinal from a Western country clearly shows it will never be possible to have "common understanding of primacy." The cultures are too different.

Towards a Common Lutheran/Roman Catholic Understanding of Papal Ministry

Harding Meyer

Three short remarks, to begin with, in order to show how I understand the topic assigned to me and in what manner I intend to treat it.

1. The topic has been carefully phrased. It begins with a preposition indicating the direction towards a goal, towards something that, essentially, has not yet been reached but is still before us: "a common Lutheran–Roman Catholic understanding of papal ministry." It is exactly in this perspective that I shall deal with my subject: How may Lutherans and Roman Catholics, one day in the future, arrive at a common understanding of the papal ministry? What would be required? What could further such a process? On what would it be necessary to agree?

2. I shall deal with these questions, and this should be a matter of course, from a primarily Lutheran point of view. This does not mean that I disregard the Roman Catholic doctrine and convictions. Throughout my paper I will be concerned with how the Lutheran view and "desiderata" relate to the Roman Catholic understanding of papal ministry. But even so, my point of departure almost always will be a Lutheran one.

3. The matter at stake is not something *like* papal ministry, something that does not yet exist, something that — maybe in analogy to papal ministry — still has to be imagined, developed, even invented. Rather, it is papal ministry as it has developed in history and has been defined theologically.

We all know that the Lutheran–Roman Catholic dialogue on papacy has long since started.[1] Do these dialogues and their wider context reveal, at

---

1. The first, rather concise but groundbreaking affirmations of the Lutheran–

least, a first and general direction of what a common Lutheran–Roman Catholic understanding of papal ministry might be? This is what my paper will try to investigate. Given the time limit of such a paper I shall concentrate on three aspects only, but the ones that seem to me the most important.

Papal Ministry as a Ministry of Unity
for the Universal Church ("Petrine Ministry")

One thing, I believe, those dialogues and the concomitant discussions have made fully evident: If ever, after centuries of radical divergence, the trajectory of Lutheran and the trajectory of Roman Catholic understanding of papal ministry should converge, *this will happen only if papal ministry, in its very essence, is being conceived as a personal ministry of unity for the church universal,* a ministerial service that is directed to Christendom itself but also beyond, towards the world and society representing Christendom, its message and its concerns. Such a "ministry of unity for the church universal," which for some time now has been called "Petrine ministry," "Petrine office," or "Petrine function," can be assigned to the papal office also by Lutherans.

For Roman Catholics this Petrine ministry has always been in the center of papal primacy. As bishop of Rome and patriarch of the Occident the pope always understood himself as shepherd of all Christendom. In his encyclical *Ut unum sint* John Paul II speaks of his ministry as a "ministry of

Roman Catholic dialogue about papal primacy are to be found in the Malta Report (1972) of the international Lutheran–Roman Catholic dialogue commission (§§66 and 67, in Harding Meyer and Lukas Vischer, eds., *Growth in Agreement: Reports and Agreed Statements of Ecumenical Conversations on a World Level* (New York/Geneva: Paulist/WCC Publications, 1984), p. 184. Hereafter *GiA*. These affirmations are being reiterated and commented on in the report of the same commission on "The Ministry in the Church" (1981; *GiA*, pp. 269-71: "The Episcopal Ministry and Service for the Universal Unity of the Church," §§67-73). In 1974 the North American Lutheran–Roman Catholic dialogue concluded a number of sessions by publishing a report in Paul C. Empie and T. Austin Murphy, eds., *Papal Primacy and the Universal Church* (Minneapolis: Augsburg, 1974), followed in 1978 by another report in Paul C. Empie, T. Austin Murphy, and Joseph A. Burgess, eds., *Teaching Authority and Infallibility in the Church* (Minneapolis: Augsburg, 1978). Most recently, in 2000, the German dialogue report *Communio Sanctorum* was published, which included an extensive chapter on Petrine ministry (Bilateral Working Group of the German National Bishops' Conference and the Church Leadership of the United Evangelical Lutheran Church of Germany, *Communio Sanctorum: The Church as the Communion of Saints* [Collegeville, MN: Liturgical Press, 2004]).

unity," as "the visible sign and guarantor of unity."[2] Even Vatican I, however one judges its further affirmations about papal primacy, speaks in the same manner.[3] Is it not true that John 17:20f., the great motto of the ecumenical movement, is being referred to in the very first sentences of the dogmatic constitution *Pastor aeternus*?[4]

This vision of papal ministry as Petrine ministry, as a "ministry of unity for the church universal," is the guiding vision also in the ecumenical dialogues on primacy, and not only in the Lutheran–Roman Catholic dialogues. John Paul II in his encyclical letter refers to this fact, quoting the Faith-and-Order World Conference in Santiago de Compostela (1993) which had proposed "a new study of the question of a universal ministry of Christian unity."[5]

For the Lutheran–Roman Catholic dialogues this view was determinative from their very beginnings. I would like to show this somewhat more in detail, since the dialogues also identify the theological and ecclesiological reasons why they endorse this view or vision of papal ministry.

The Malta Report of 1972 deals with primacy under the significative heading "The Gospel and the Unity of the Church." The point of departure and the ecclesiological basis of the entire argumentation is "that no local church should exist in isolation since it is a manifestation of the universal church." It is this view on the church universal and its unity that demonstrates "the importance of a ministerial service of the [universal] communion of churches" and, at the same time, points to the "problem raised for Lutherans by their lack of such an effective service of unity." Therefore, it is said, "the office of the papacy as a visible sign of the unity of the churches [is] not excluded" by Lutherans, "insofar as it is subordinated to the primacy of the gospel by theological reinterpretation and practical restructuring."[6]

The North American dialogue argues in a very similar way. The general framework or "setting of the problem" is church ministry and its relation to the unity of the church. The point of departure and the ecclesiological basis of reflection is the conviction that "visible unity in the

---

2. *Ut unum sint*, §§88-89.

3. Vatican I speaks of Peter as "unitatis principium ac visibile fundamentum" (Heinrich Denzinger, *Enchiridion symbolorum definitionum et declarationum de rebus fidei et morum*, re-edited by Peter Hünermann, 37th edition [Freiburg: Herder, 1991], hereafter cited as DH), 3051.

4. DH 3051.

5. *Ut unum sint*, §86.

6. Malta Report, §66.

church has from earliest times been served by several forms of the Minis-try."[7] After discussions in a previous stage of the North American dialogue that "had centered on the service rendered to the local communities by the Ministry," the dialogue now focuses "on the unifying and ordering function of this Ministry in relation to the universal church." And the question is, how the "Ministry might best nurture and express the unity of the universal church for the sake of its mission in the world."[8] In a retrospective the Lutheran members of the dialogue explain "why they have dealt with this issue,"[9] saying: "In this day of intensified global communication and international cooperation, the concern for the unity of the entire empirical church is being keenly felt. . . . We Lutherans consider the need for symbols and centers of unity to be urgent" in order "to give concrete expression to . . . the unity of the whole empirical church."[10] And this almost immediately implies the question whether the papal ministry with its "Petrine function"[11] could serve as such a symbol and center of unity. The Lutheran answer given is practically identical with the affirmations of the Malta Report: "When we think of the question of the church's unity in relation to its mission we cannot responsibly dismiss the possibility that some form of the papacy, renewed and restructured under the gospel, may be an appropriate visible expression of the Ministry that serves the unity and ordering of the church."[12]

The most recent Lutheran–Roman Catholic dialogue document *Communio Sanctorum,* with its chapter on Petrine ministry, essentially repeats and thus confirms the thinking and the argumentation of the two former dialogues. Its approach to papal ministry is similar to the North American dialogue in that it sets out with *ministry in general and its service to unity.* This, in turn, opens up the question of "whether and in what manner this service must be rendered also to the universal unity of the church,"[13] a question that by itself leads to papal ministry as a possible form of such a ministerial service. The entire chapter on Petrine ministry in *Communio Sanctorum* is rich in content. The North American dialogue also speaks of the New Testament evidence for such a Petrine ministry, a very important aspect that I cannot take up in this paper. Another argument, however,

7. Empie and Murphy, eds., *Papal Primacy,* Introduction, p. 9.
8. Empie and Murphy, eds., *Papal Primacy,* Introduction, p. 10.
9. Empie and Murphy, eds., *Papal Primacy,* §28.
10. Empie and Murphy, eds., *Papal Primacy,* §32.
11. Empie and Murphy, eds., *Papal Primacy,* §33.
12. Empie and Murphy, eds., *Papal Primacy,* §32.
13. Bilateral Working Group, *Communio Sanctorum,* §153.

which is used in the document and which sometimes one encounters also in private publications, should be mentioned. It says: On all levels of the church there is "a fundamental 'in and over against' *(in und gegenüber)* of ministry and community,"[14] and it is argued that this ought to be so on the universal level of the church as well. Thus, the conclusion is that "a universal ministry of unity of the church is in keeping with the nature and the mission of the church."[15]

This overall vision of papal ministry as a ministry of unity for the church universal, grounded in the nature and mission of the church and its ministry, is absolutely fundamental for a common Lutheran–Roman Catholic understanding of papal ministry. It overcomes and leaves behind the merely controversial and polemical treatment of the papacy so characteristic of post-Reformation centuries. Even if Lutheran criticism of the papacy does not fall silent, papal ministry is no longer a "non-topic" *(Unthema)* for Lutherans. Papal ministry, rather, has become a legitimate and important subject of Lutheran theology as well.

This changed Lutheran view of papal ministry is by no means without support by the Reformation. An unbiased examination of what the Reformers thought and said about papacy must concede that their harsh and often excessive criticism repeatedly was interrupted and, as it were, "suspended," by a conditional recognition of papal ministry.[16] (And I am thinking not only of the famous reservation which Melanchthon added to his signing the Smalcald Articles of Luther.)[17] This means that the Reformation's negative judgment on the papal office, in the final analysis, was not a statement of principle *(Grundsatzurteil)* that rejected papal ministry as such and by all circumstances. It rather was a statement of facts *(Tatsachenurteil),* claiming that, as Luther sometimes says: since Gregory the Great whom he considered to have been "the last [authentic] bishop of Rome,"[18] the papal ministry *de facto* was in a state of depravation.

However, this vision of papal ministry as a ministry of unity, so capital

---

14. Bilateral Working Group, *Communio Sanctorum,* §186.

15. Bilateral Working Group, *Communio Sanctorum,* §153.

16. Already in my preceding chapter, "Papal Primacy — a Possible Subject of Lutheran Theology?," and also in several other articles I repeatedly have pointed to this fact, more recently, e.g., in "Das Papsttum bei Luther und in den lutherischen Bekenntnisschriften," in Harding Meyer, *Versöhnte Verschiedenheit. Aufsätze zur ökumenischen Theologie II* (Frankfurt/Paderborn: Lembeck/Bonafacius, 2000), pp. 317-38.

17. *The Book of Concord,* 316-17.

18. WA 54, 229.

for a common Lutheran–Roman Catholic understanding of papal ministry, in a Lutheran perspective is in need of two qualifications. Both qualifications make us wonder how far Lutherans and Roman Catholics are already meaning really the same thing when they speak of papal ministry as "a ministry of unity for the church universal." Both qualifications, therefore, are indications that we still are "on the way towards" a common understanding of papal ministry.

I think — and this is the first qualification — that Lutherans would hesitate very much to affirm that such a Petrine ministry is in the strict sense "necessary" for the unity of the church universal, as *Ut unum sint* maintains,[19] so that without this ministry there could never be such a unity. The Lutheran dialogue members, indeed, do not go so far.[20] What Lutherans would say, even emphatically say rather, is that such Petrine ministry is "meaningful" and "desirable," that it is "appropriate" and "advantageous." In saying so they would point to other elements and factors that also promote the unity of the universal church, such as the canon of Holy Scriptures, the ecumenical creeds, and ecumenical councils. On this point most probably there will remain, as one could say, a "difference in valuation" with regard to papal ministry. This difference in valuation, however, does not necessarily jeopardize a common understanding provided that, just as in the question of justification, one does not insist on a "monolithic" consensus but is open for a "differentiated" consensus.

The second qualification is even more important and more problematic. Lutherans would indeed agree that the Petrine ministry of the pope has to do with the *oneness* of the church. However, they would not admit that it has to do with the *being* of the church. I am fully aware of how difficult it is to distinguish between the being and the oneness of the church. But a common understanding of papal ministry somehow has to imply such a differentiation. This means that also in this respect the common understanding we are striving for would have to be a "differentiated" consensus. If not, papal ministry with its Petrine function would appear to be a *conditio sine qua non* for the church's being, its *esse*, which Lutherans — and most non–Roman Catholic

---

19. *Ut unum sint*, §97.

20. Sometimes in *Communio Sanctorum* it may seem as if the Lutheran dialogue members would consider a universal Petrine ministry as something "necessary" (§§188 and 189). But later on and in contrast to the Roman Catholic members they only state that there are "no fundamental objections" against "a universal Petrine ministry as a pastoral ministry" (§194).

churches — would not admit. To put it more concretely: The bearer of the Petrine ministry, in exercising his service of unity, could not deny the Lutheran churches to be churches in the full sense. It is my conviction that today's general ecumenical openness towards a papal ministry serving the unity of the church universal urges for a differentiation between oneness and being of the church. This general ecumenical openness stands and falls with such a differentiation. If it fails, this openness would vanish again.

A Reinterpretation of the Papal Ministry's Claim to Be *de iure divino*

What is the origin of such a Petrine ministry? Is it the product of a merely historical development in the church, the result of human experiences? Is it desirable, meaningful, appropriate because of sociological considerations that speak in favor of such a ministry?

Or, is this ministry at the same time, i.e., together with historical developments and factors, together with human experiences and sociological considerations, grounded in the God-given nature of the church as people of God, as body of Christ, as temple of the Holy Spirit?

All of us are aware that this is the old and hard controversial question — whether the papal ministry is of divine or of human right, whether it is *de iure divino* as the Roman Catholic doctrine maintains,[21] or only *de iure humano* as the Reformation maintained.

Surely, on the Roman Catholic as well as on the Lutheran side today, one is aware of the ambiguity and the limited usefulness of these categories, *ius divinum/ius humanum*.[22] But we know that the Reformation and the

---

21. Vatican I: ". . . ex ipsius Christi Domini institutione seu iure divino" (DH 3058).

22. See, e.g., the Malta Report, §31, and also the North American dialogue report "Papal Primacy," in Empie and Murphy, eds., *Papal Primacy*, §§42; 50. Mention should be made of the paper "Ius Divinum and Adiaphoron in Relation to Structural Problems in the Church: The Lutheran Symbolical Books," which Arthur Carl Piepkorn prepared for the North American dialogue, printed in addition to the dialogue report Empie and Murphy, eds., *Papal Primacy*, pp. 119-27. Also the article of Yves M. Congar, *"Ius Divinum,"* *Revue de Droit Canonique* 28 (1978): 108ff., which is directly related to the present discussion about papal primacy and in which Congar refers also to the Malta Report, §31, should be mentioned. Congar says about papal primacy: "Il n'y a en elle (dans la primauté papale) que le 'ministère de Pierre.' Jean 21:15-17 en donne une formule très substantielle, mais dont la forme de réalisation a connu bien des variations et peut en

later Protestant criticism of the papal office again and again concentrated on the *ius divinum* claim of the pope. This is true particularly of the Lutheran Confessional Writings and their affirmations about the papacy, be it in Luther's Smalcald Articles or in Melanchthon's "Treatise on the Power and Primacy of the Pope," which argues that all questionable and rejected aspects of the papacy are implications of its *ius divinum* claim.[23] Therefore, one simply cannot disregard and leave aside the *ius divinum/ius humanum* problem if one wants to come, one day, to a common understanding of papal ministry.

It seems to me that in this matter there actually *is* a way towards a common understanding.

One can observe very clearly how the Reformation criticism is not so much directed against the *ius divinum* claim as such, but rather against the consequences and implications of this claim. This is particularly evident in Melanchthon's "Treatise on the Power and Primacy of the Pope." According to Melanchthon the three major reproaches of the Reformation against the pope, which constitute the theological center of the famous "Antichrist" verdict,[24] are consequences or implications of the papal *ius divinum* claim: (1) the papal exemption from all criticism, even by the Holy Scriptures, (2) the authority of the pope to establish new and binding laws and doctrines, and (3) the claim that submission and obedience to the pope is necessary for salvation.[25]

---

connaître encore. Cela ne signifie pas qu'il n'y ait aucun 'droit divin' dans la primauté papale, mais qu'à la prendre en sa réalité concrète, c'est-à-dire dans l'histoire, son âme de droit divin n'existe que dans un corps humain . . ." (121).

23. It is with the papal claim for *ius divinum* that the chapter on the papacy in Luther's Smalcald Articles starts (*The Book of Concord,* 298) and the chapter comes back to it twice (299 and 300). For Melanchthon's "Treatise on the Power and Primacy of the Pope" (*The Book of Concord,* 319-35) this papal claim is even more crucial.

24. Again in my preceding chapter, "Papal Primacy — a Possible Subject of Lutheran Theology?," I have emphasized that the "Antichrist" verdict of the Reformers was by no means an expression of blind hate against the pope, nor was it a total rejection of papal ministry. It rather was the biblical abbreviation of or cipher for very clear and specific theological accusations against the papacy of that time.

25. According to Melanchthon's "Treatise," the papal claim to be "by divine right above all bishops and pastors" (§1) implies that the pope "arrogates to himself the authority to make laws concerning worship, concerning changes in the sacraments, and concerning doctrine," that he "wishes his articles, his decrees, and his laws to be regarded as articles of faith or commandments of God, binding the consciences of men" (§6), and that he "is unwilling to be judged [neither] by the church," i.e., by the councils (§40), nor by the Word of God (§56).

Hence, the approach to the *ius divinum* problem should not be a "frontal" approach, asking whether or not the papal ministry is *de iure divino*. Rather, the endeavor for common understanding has to concentrate on those consequences and implications of the papal *ius divinum* claim. If agreements could be reached here, then the question of *ius divinum* or *ius humanum* would basically be settled; at least, it would be secondary and ought not to be divisive.

What is even more: Also from a Lutheran point of view it should be theologically legitimate to attribute a certain *ius divinum* to papal ministry. If, as the dialogues argue, a Petrine ministry is "in keeping with the nature and the mission of the church," and if it is a specific form of the ministry God has instituted, then such a Petrine ministry shares in the God-given nature of the church and in the divine institution of ministry in general and cannot be considered as an institution that originated in merely human history or only on the basis of sociological requirements. It seems to me that the Lutheran–Roman Catholic dialogues and what they affirm about papal ministry as a legitimate "service to the unity of the church" and as a legitimate form of ministry in the church clearly point in that direction.

It is very interesting to see that Melanchthon's "Treatise" also seems to endorse such a view. It is certainly true that Melanchthon starts by questioning and even denying the *ius divinum* claim of papal primacy using biblical and historical arguments.[26] Also, in his reservation, added to Luther's Smalcald Articles, he stated that the pope had its primacy only in *iure humano*.[27] Nevertheless, it seems that Melanchthon does not intend to deny the *ius divinum* of papal primacy categorically. In two almost identical affirmations, he uses a very remarkable argumentation. I quote one of them: "Even if *(etiamsi)* the bishop of Rome did possess the primacy by divine right *(iure divino)*, he should not be obeyed inasmuch as he defends impious forms of worship and doctrines which are in conflict with the gospel."[28] And Melanchthon refers not only to Galatians 1:8, but also to canonical law according to which a heretic pope should not be obeyed. It is particularly remarkable that Melanchthon explains his position by referring to the fact that

26. "Treatise," §§7-20.
27. *The Book of Concord*, 317.
28. "Treatise," §57. Also "Treatise," §38: "Even if *(etiamsi)* the bishop of Rome should possess primacy and superiority by divine right *(iure divino)*, obedience would still not be owing to those pontiffs who defend godless forms of worship, idolatry, and doctrines which conflict with the Gospel."

even the high priest in the Old Testament who, indeed, "was the supreme pontifex by divine right *(de iure divino),*" "was not to be obeyed" insofar as he had become a "godless high priest," as it is shown "in Jeremiah and other prophets."[29]

This argumentation, which we find twice in Melanchthon's "Treatise," strongly indicates that his criticism of the pope's *ius divinum* claim does not aim at the *ius divinum* claim itself, rejecting it categorically. What his criticism rather is aiming at is an exaggerated notion or interpretation of this claim, i.e., a notion of papal *ius divinum* that exempts papal decisions from all criticism and makes them "indisputable" *(unhinterfragbar),* even on the basis of the Holy Scriptures and their testimony to the gospel. In this perspective the Reformers' insistence that papal ministry be *de iure humano* is, in its true intention, nothing other than the emphatic rejection of a maximalistic interpretation of the papal *ius divinum,* which exempts papal ministry from the norm of the gospel or, to use André Birmelé's argumentation, obscures the necessary "transparency" of papal ministry for the word of God as ultimate norm.

This leads us to the crucial question of papal authority.

Basic Approval but Theological and Practical Limitation of Papal Authority

In his encyclical letter John Paul II emphasizes that it belongs to the nature of the papal "ministry of unity" for it to have a "proper authority" and "power," or *Vollmacht,* as the German text says.[30] Without "the power and the authority . . . such an office would be illusory," he adds. The bearer of the "Petrine office," he says, "has the duty to admonish, to caution and to declare at times that this or that opinion being circulated is irreconcilable with the unity of the faith."[31]

Since Lutherans assign authority and power *(Vollmacht)* also to other forms of ministry in the church, they can and even should assign authority and power *(Vollmacht)* to a Petrine ministry as well. Wolfhart Pannenberg, who should have given this paper, writes: "Without doubt it belongs to a Petrine ministry of unity of the universal church to make declarations about

29. "Treatise," §38.
30. *Ut unum sint,* §92.
31. *Ut unum sint,* §94.

the common faith of the church, doctrinal affirmations which relate to the church at large."[32]

Nevertheless, it is exactly here where the center of Reformation criticism and expectations with regard to papal ministry lies. The only Lutheran confessional writing that is entirely concerned with the problem of papacy is titled "De *potestate* et primatu Papae" (emphasis mine). When, in allusion to 2 Thessalonians 2:4, the Reformers say that the pope, like the "Antichrist," "exalts himself above every so-called god or object of worship," they, in the final analysis, speak of the *authority claim* of the papal ministry. The criticism is a twofold one:

First: The pope has made himself "a judge over the Holy Scriptures" and "does not allow to be judged by them." He establishes new and binding doctrines, "new articles of faith," pretending that "he cannot err."

Second: The pope "claims for himself alone the right to interpret the Holy Scriptures," and thus "transfers" *(transferre)* to himself, to the *pontifices,* what has been promised to the entire church, i.e., the *non potest errare,* the remaining in the truth.

These are affirmations of Luther[33] and Melanchthon,[34] but in substance they occur in the other Reformers as well and, for Protestants, the dogma of 1870 has fully confirmed this criticism.

The question, therefore, is: How could a Lutheran–Roman Catholic common understanding of papal ministry interpret the authority of a Petrine ministry in such a way that this criticism no longer applies? What is at stake are the limits of — basically approved — papal authority.

This is also the main concern of the dialogues. The Lutheran expectation is that papal ministry, in order to be recognized as "a visible sign of the unity of the churches," be "subordinated to the primacy of the gospel by theological reinterpretation and structural restructuring." So the Malta Report.[35] In substance the North American dialogue says the same: "The one thing necessary, from the Lutheran point of view, is that papal primacy be so

---

32. "Evangelische Überlegungen zum Petrusdienst des römischen Bischofs," in Heinz Schütte, ed., *Im Dienst der einen Kirche. Ökumenische Überlegungen zur Reform des Papstamts* (Paderborn/Frankfurt: Bonafacius/Lembeck, 2000), p. 186.

33. See my above mentioned essay on "Das Papsttum bei Luther," pp. 330-33.

34. In the "Apology of the Augsburg Confession" (VII, 25; Latin version in *Die Bekenntnisschriften der evangelisch-lutherischen Kirche* [Göttingen: Vandenhoeck & Ruprecht, ⁶1967], p. 240) Melanchthon states: "Nec est ad pontifices transferendum, quod ad veram ecclesiam pertinet, quod videlicet sint columnae veritatis, quod non errent."

35. Malta Report, §66.

structured and interpreted that it clearly serve the gospel and the unity of the church of Christ, and that its exercise of power not subvert Christian freedom."[36]

It is true that, also for Roman Catholics, the authority of the pope has its precise limits. Vatican I itself very extensively and in a controversial manner has dealt with the "limits and conditions" of papal infallibility. This was the subject of the most extensive speech at the Council and, at the same time, the last speech on papal infallibility — the "Relatio" of bishop Gasser, July 11, 1870. It pointed out that the doctrinal infallibility of the pope was not, as the minority bishops at the Council feared, an *infallibilitas absoluta, privata,* or *separata,* but that it was limited in several respects: with regard to its "subject" *(ad subjectum),* to its "object" *(ad objectum),* and to its "act" *(ad actum).*[37]

However, this interpretation could not dispel the fears of the Council's minority over against the proposed and, finally, accepted and declared definition of papal infallibility. And this was and still is all the more true of Protestant criticism, which insisted and insists on even a sharper limitation of papal authority.

How is it possible, in the endeavor for a common understanding of papal ministry, to advance in this crucial question of papal authority and its limits?

In the attempt to come to grips with this question one has, over the last years, tried to develop something like general perspectives or guidelines that together, though in different ways, point in the same direction. I mention

---

36. Empie and Murphy, eds., *Papal Primacy,* §28.

37. Giovanni Domenico Mansi, *Sacrorum conciliorum nova et amplissima collectio* (Paris: Hubert, 1927), vol. 52, pp. 1203ff., in particular pp. 1211-14 and also pp. 1225ff. This "Relatio" of Bishop Gasser is frequently referred to and interpreted. Hermann Pottmeyer, e.g., says: "Die Unfehlbarkeit des Papstes . . . ist (1) eingeschränkt hinsichtlich des *Subjekts:* nur wenn der Papst als oberster Hirte und Lehrer der Kirche tätig wird. In der Erläuterung dazu heisst es, dass der Papst ausserhalb der Beziehung zur Gesamtkirche das Charisma der Wahrheit nicht besitze. Seine Unfehlbarkeit ist (2) eingeschränkt hinsichtlich des *Objekts:* nur in Sachen des Glaubens oder der Sitten. Ausdrücklich heisst es dazu, der Papst könne keine 'neue Lehre' verkündigen, sondern nur das, was bereits von der Kirche als geoffenbart geglaubt werde. Seine Unfehlbarkeit ist (3) eingeschränkt hinsichtlich des *Aktes:* nur wenn die Entscheidung alle Gläubigen, und zwar endgültig, verpflichten will. Damit ist der Papst gehalten, nur aus schwerwiegenden Gründen auf solche Weise tätig zu werden" ("Der Papst, Zeuge Jesu Christi in der Nachfolge Petri," in Karl Lehmann, ed., *In der Nachfolge Jesu Christi* [Freiburg: Herder, 1980], p. 76).

some of those that are encountered more frequently. For instance, one has referred to the Latin and ancient Roman distinction between *auctoritas* and *potestas*. In this sense papal authority ought to be true *auctoritas,* based not on any kind of coercion but rather on conviction,[38] as the dictum says: "Tantum valet auctoritas, quantum valent argumenta." Something similar is meant when it is emphasized that the authority of a Petrine ministry must be exercised in a "pastoral" manner.[39] Both suggestions, certainly, indicate the right direction to be followed, but they are still in need of further explication and application.

A suggestion of a different kind is the often quoted proposal of Cardinal Ratzinger, that Rome should expect from the other churches not more than the understanding of primacy that was lived in the first millennium.[40] Close to this suggestion comes another one, i.e., the proposal to "disentangle" *(entflechten)* the three papal offices in a way that would allow, e.g., the Lutheran churches to be dismissed from the patriarchal power the pope has over the Latin churches of the West.[41] Both suggestions would imply that the particularly controversial dogma of 1870 would not be binding for the other churches. But both suggestions would also have a serious disadvantage: If the dogma of 1870 continues to be binding for the Roman Catholic Church, a common understanding of papal ministry would not yet be reached.

The appropriate approach, therefore, should be to try to come to a theological definition or interpretation of papal authority acceptable to both sides, which in turn would determine also the practical exercise of papal authority. It is in this sense that the dialogues speak of the need for "theological interpretation" or "reinterpretation" followed by "practical restructuring" of the primacy.

There are two main problems in this approach, each multifaceted in itself.

---

38. Pannenberg, "Evangelische Überlegungen zum Petrusdienst," pp. 175ff.

39. E.g., *Ut unum sint,* §91; Bilateral Working Group, *Communio Sanctorum,* §194.

40. Joseph Ratzinger, "Allgemeine Orientierung über den ökumenischen Disput und die Formalprinzipien des Glaubens," in *Theologische Prinzipienlehre: Bausteine zur Fundamentaltheologie* (München: E. Wewel, 1982), p. 209: "Rom muss vom Osten nicht mehr an Primatslehre fordern, als auch im ersten Jahrtausend formuliert und gelebt wurde."

41. Pannenberg, "Evangelische Überlegungen zum Petrusdienst," pp. 179-80.

Papal Doctrinal Authority and Holy Scriptures

As we all know and as I have mentioned already, it is this relationship between papal authority and the Holy Scriptures which the Protestant criticism first of all aims at. It is the reproach that the pope has made himself "a judge over the Holy Scriptures" and that he establishes "new" and binding doctrines, "new articles of faith," pretending that "he cannot err."

It seems, however, that this criticism is being answered already by Vatican I. Its chapter on papal infallibility includes an important passage that says: In making doctrinal decisions "the Roman pontiffs . . . sometimes by summoning councils or consulting the opinion of the churches scattered throughout the world . . . defined as doctrines to be held those things which, by God's help, they knew to be in keeping with Sacred Scripture and the apostolic traditions. For the Holy Spirit was promised to the successors of Peter not so that they might, by his revelation, make known new doctrine, but that, by his assistance, they might religiously guard and faithfully expound the revelation or deposit of faith transmitted by the apostles."[42]

Why did these clear affirmations of the Council never silence Protestant criticism, or, at that time, the criticism of the Council's minority?

The reason was and still is that these affirmations are affirmations only in the indicative mood. This means: They are only stating what the popes, in making doctrinal decisions, always and actually have done and what, "by the assistance of the Holy Spirit," they will continue to do in the future: They always have "consulted the opinion of the churches"; they have taught and they will teach what is "in keeping with the Sacred Scripture and the apostolic traditions"; they never have and never will "make known some new doctrine" but always "religiously guard and faithfully expound the revelation or *depositum fidei* transmitted by the apostles." This indicative is, one could say, a kind of "pneumatologically guaranteed indicative" that cannot be disputed, that is, *unhinterfragbar*.

For the minority bishops at Vatican I this was not satisfactory and did not dispel their fears. What they insistently demanded was that the commitment of the papal magisterium to the consensus of the church at large and its being bound to the Holy Scriptures and to the apostolic tradition should, in the "definition" of papal infallibility itself, somehow be clearly expressed as a normative commitment. This would have made of the papal authority or prerogative of infallible teaching an authority that, at least in principle,

42. DH 3069 and 3070.

was open for verification and could be judged. But this demand of the Council's minority, which essentially corresponded to Protestant criticism and concerns, was rejected.

Therefore, the question with regard to a common Lutheran–Roman Catholic understanding of papal ministry should be, whether those affirmations of Vatican I that only in the indicative mood speak of the papal magisterium as being bound to the apostolic tradition and to the Holy Scriptures could be interpreted in a clearly normative sense. This would imply that the authority and the authoritative teaching of the papal magisterium, in principle, remains *hinterfragbar* (disputable), i.e., *open for verification*. In other words: Could the legitimate "authority claim" of the papal magisterium and its doctrinal decisions be interpreted in such a way that it includes, at the same time and in a certain manner, an "authority reservation" or "proviso"?

If I understand them correctly, a number of Roman Catholic theologians seem to consider such an interpretation or rereading of the infallibility dogma of 1870 as possible and legitimate. I am thinking, e.g., of Klaus Schatz and Hermann Pottmeyer, two experts on the First Vatican Council. Schatz wonders "whether, at least today, in a later reading of that dogma an interpretation is beginning to prevail which by and large corresponds to the basic concerns of the minority at Vatican I."[43] Likewise and also in reference to the concerns of the Council's minority, Hermann Pottmeyer writes: "The pope must draw upon Scripture and tradition and the consensus of the church in a way which is open for verification and testing. . . . The wording of the infallibility dogma itself is quite open for this interpretation."[44] And Avery Dulles, who some years ago was appointed cardinal (and who, by the way, is not the only cardinal who could be quoted here),[45] pleads for what he calls a

---

43. *Kirchenbild und päpstliche Unfehlbarkeit bei den deutschsprachigen Minoritäts-bischöfen auf dem I. Vatikanum* (Rome: [s.n.], 1975), pp. 492-93.

44. "Das Unfehlbarkeitsdogma im Streit der Interpretationen," in Lehmann, ed., *Das Petrusamt. Geschichtliche Stationen seines Verständnisses und gegenwärtige Positionen* (München/Zürich: Schnell & Steiner, 1982), pp. 98-99.

45. In 1969 Joseph Ratzinger wrote about new insights for the "interpretation of Vatican I" (*Das neue Volk Gottes. Entwürfe zur Ekklesiologie* [Düsseldorf: Patmos-Verlag, [²]1970], p. 144): ". . . Kritik an päpstlichen Äußerungen (wird) in dem Masse möglich und nötig sein, in dem ihnen die Deckung in Schrift und Credo bzw. im Glauben der Gesamtkirche fehlt. Wo weder Einmütigkeit in der Gesamtkirche vorliegt noch ein klares Zeugnis der Quellen gegeben ist, da ist auch eine verbindliche Entscheidung nicht möglich; würde sie formal gefällt, so fehlten ihre Bedingungen, und damit müsste die

"moderate infallibilism." He says: "Perhaps in our day . . . we should recognize that adequate investigation of the sources is a true condition for infallible teaching. This view, proposed by the minority at Vatican I, could, I believe, be integrated into a moderate infallibilism." And with regard to the "validity" of papal doctrinal decisions, Dulles adds: "If grave and widespread doubt were to arise among committed Christians who are orthodox on other points, the definition would have to be treated as dubious and hence not canonically binding. This consequence does not appear to me to be disastrous to the whole concept of infallibility."[46]

Such an interpretation of papal doctrinal authority would be as it were the "cornerstone" of a common Lutheran–Roman Catholic understanding of papal ministry. It would correspond to the often-quoted affirmation of Vatican II: "The Magisterium is not superior to the Word of God, but is its servant."[47]

Finally, what about the second main problem about papal authority?

Papal Authority and the Church

This problem, too, has been mentioned already in my paper. It is the second great focus of Reformation criticism addressed to papal ministry. The pope, the Reformers said, "claims for himself alone the right to interpret the Holy Scriptures," and thus "transfers" *(transferre)* to himself, to the *pontifices,* what has been promised to the entire church, i.e., the *non potest errare,* the remaining in the truth.

With regard to this Reformation criticism, much has happened in Ro-

---

Frage nach ihrer Legitimität erhoben werden." Walter Kasper must have had something similar in mind when he wrote about "acknowledgment" ("Anerkennung") of papal infallibility by the church: "Der Papst kann nur insoweit unfehlbar sein, als ihn die Kirche als den sprechenden Mund und Zeugen ihrer eigenen Unfehlbarkeit anerkennt. Würde sie ihm diese Anerkennung (nicht zu verwecheln mit der vom Vatikanum I abgelehnten nachträglichen Zustimmung zu einer Kathedralentscheidung, wodurch diese erst ihre juristische Verbindlichkeit erlangt) versagen, dann wäre der Papst im Extremfall häretisch oder schismatisch, dann wäre er gar nicht mehr Papst" ("Zur Diskussion um das Problem der Unfehlbarkeit," in Hans Küng, ed., *Fehlbar? Eine Bilanz* [Zürich: Benzinger, 1973], p. 84).

46. Avery Dulles, "Moderate Infallibilism," in Empie, Murphy, and Burgess, eds., *Teaching Authority,* pp. 91-92.

47. *Dei verbum,* 10.

man Catholic theology since Vatican II. It finds its overall expression in a renewed understanding of the church as *communio,* and it is this *communio* church the Petrine ministry is serving. According to this *communio* ecclesiology the church is, certainly under the pope, a communion of local or particular churches with their proper responsibility and authority. Thus, the doctrine of papal primacy is being complemented by the doctrine of episcopal "collegiality," and "the primatial leadership of the church is set in relation to its collegial leadership."[48] Walter Kasper speaks of "an integration of the pope into the church."[49] The principles of "conciliarity," of "collegiality," and of "subsidiarity," but also the principle of "synodality," are now standing side by side with the principle of primacy. And especially the last, the *synodical principle,* which includes of the whole people of God, ordained and non-ordained Christians, is of crucial importance for the Reformation churches.

The application of this view to the papal magisterium and its authority leads to an aspect that is very important for a common understanding of papal ministry. It is the idea of "reception" so much emphasized over the last decades, i.e., the idea of acceptance or recognition of papal as well as conciliar decisions by the church at large. "Reception" is an "ecclesial reality,"[50] an "inner church 'life process.'"[51] It is "in its nature a spiritual process"[52] sustained

48. Walter Kasper, "Das Petrusamt in ökumenischer Perspektive," in Lehmann, ed., *In der Nachfolge,* p. 116. In this sense Joseph Ratzinger can speak of a "communio-Primat" which has its place "in der als Kommunionsgemeinschaft lebenden und sich verstehenden Kirche hat" ("Die pastoralen Implikationen der Lehre von der Kollegialität der Bischöfe," *Concilium* [1965]: 21). Patrick Granfield speaks of the pope as "Mitbischof" and writes: "Sowohl der Papst als auch die Bischöfe sind wesentlich für die Kirche; die Kollegialitätsdoktrin hilft uns, die komplexen Zusammenhänge recht zu erwägen, die zwischen den Teilkirchen und der universalen Kirche und zwischen den bischöflichen und päpstlichen Funktionen existieren" (*Das Papsttum. Kontinuität und Wandel* [Münster: Aschendorff, 1984], p. 77).

49. Lehmann, ed., *Das Petrusamt,* p. 116.

50. Yves M. Congar, "Die Rezeption als ekklesiologische Realität," *Concilium* 8, no. 9 (1972): 500-514. Hermann J. Pottmeyer, "Rezeption und Gehorsam. Aktuelle Aspekte der wiederentdeckten Realität 'Rezeption'," in Wolfgang Beinert, ed., *Glaube als Zustimmung. Zur Interpretation kirchlicher Rezeptionsvorgänge* (Freiburg/Basel/Wien: Herder, 1991), pp. 51-91.

51. Heinrich Bacht, "Vom Lehramt der Kirche und in der Kirche," *Catholica* (1971): 161.

52. Wolfgang Beinert, "Die Rezeption und ihre Bedeutung für Leben und Lehre der Kirche," in Beinert, ed., *Glaube als Zustimmung,* p. 37.

by the Holy Spirit, who animates the whole body of Christ.[53] Although reception does not constitute the formal "validity" of a papal decision, reception very well relates to the "truth substance" *(Wahrheitsinhalt)*[54] of a papal decision, in particular to its "effectiveness" *(Wirksamkeit)*,[55] its "vital power" *(Lebenskraft)*, and its "beneficial nature" *(Zuträglichkeit)*[56] for the "well-being," for the "edification" of the church (2 Cor. 13:10).[57]

By implication this means: Where reception by the church does not happen or is refused papal decisions, as history shows, such decisions do not come to bear in the church even if they have formal validity. They remain ineffective and can be left to collective oblivion.[58] Therefore, reception, since it is always coupled with the possibility of non-reception, contains an element of "judging"[59] and of spiritual "discernment."[60] In other words, reception has a "criteriological meaning," as Pottmeyer puts it.[61]

53. Congar, "Die Rezeption," p. 508.

54. Congar, "Die Rezeption," pp. 508 and 510; Beinert, "Die Rezeption und ihre," pp. 43-44.

55. With regard to conciliar decisions Congar says: "Die Rezeption eines Konzils (ist) praktisch mit seiner Wirksamkeit (efficacité) identisch." Congar, "Die Rezeption," p. 510.

56. Bacht, "Vom Lehramt," p. 162. Also, the Roman Catholic members of the international dialogue on "Church and Justification" (Report on the Third Phase of Lutheran/ Roman Catholic International Dialogue, Paderborn/Frankfurt 1994) state (§218): "These decisions . . . are valid of themselves and do not need any subsequent formal approval, though they of course 'depend on extensive reception in order to have living power and spiritual fruitfulness in the church.'"

57. Congar, "Die Rezeption," p. 507. He agrees with the former Protestant expert on canonical law Paul Hinschius (1835-98) who had argued that conciliar decisions used to find their "*'Bestätigung'* durch die Rezeption." Congar says: "Wir können diesen Begriff akzeptieren, nicht im rechtstechnischen Sinn, wie man beispielsweise von der Bestätigung einer Wahl durch eine höhere Instanz spricht, sondern im Sinne des Zuwachses an Durchschlagskraft (surcroît de puissance), den die Zustimmung der davon Betroffenen zu einem gefällten Entscheid hinzufügt" (p. 511).

58. Bacht writes: ". . . die Nicht-Rezeption [ist] nicht ein Akt formellen Ungehorsams. . . . Vielmehr haben wir es hier offensichtlich mit einem innerkirchlichen 'Lebensvorgang' zu tun, bei dem deutlich wird, ob eine vom hierarchischen Amt getroffene Entscheidung wirklich dem Gemeinwohl dient. Dass . . . diese Rückbindung an das Gemeinwohl für die Akte des Amtes massgeblich ist, dürfte unbestreitbar sein" (see Bacht, "Vom Lehramt," p. 161.).

59. Beinert, "Die Rezeption und ihre," pp. 43-44.

60. Congar, "Die Rezeption," p. 508.

61. Pottmeyer, "Rezeption und Gehorsam," p. 68. Pottmeyer strongly emphasizes

If, in dealing with the authority of the papal magisterium, the idea of "reception" is seriously taken into account, this could be a decisive step towards meeting the Lutheran request that the whole people of God be involved where Christian truth is at stake. Therefore, it would be an important task of further dialogue to examine in detail whether and how far the Roman Catholic emphasis on the necessity of "reception" can be seen as an equivalent to the Lutheran request for *Hinterfragbarkeit* or *Überprüfbarkeit* of papal decisions by the whole church.

Speaking of papal authority and the church brings me back to the first part of my paper, where I dealt with the general view or vision of papal ministry as "ministry of unity for the church universal." It is self-evident that the unity of the church also shares in the *communio* nature and the *communio* structure of the church. Therefore, within the horizon of a *communio* ecclesiology, the unity of the church universal that we are striving for must be understood as a *communio* of churches that, among themselves, are and can be different in many respects but that nevertheless consider and recognize each other as churches of Jesus Christ. The papal ministry understood as Petrine ministry must correspond to this view of church unity. And this means: The Petrine ministry of the pope *must respect the diversity of the churches as legitimate realizations of the church of Christ.* And, therefore, it will have to protect this legitimate diversity and to watch that any tendencies towards uniformization do not suffocate this diversity, or that vice versa, these diversities do not develop into contradictions and thus lose their legitimacy.

This very last observation may show how much we are still "on the way towards" a common Lutheran–Roman Catholic understanding of papal ministry.

---

this "criteriological significance of reception." Without intending to simply separate both (pp. 84-85), he sets "Rezeption aus Einsicht" ("Wahrheitseinsicht") over "Rezeption aus Gehorsam," and he underlines that the former always implies the element of "examining" and "judging": "Prüfung und Urteil sind das Merkmal jeder Rezeption" (p. 88). Theologically he "defines" reception as "gläubige Annahme des Wortes Gottes und die von Einsicht getragene Anerkennung seiner Gegenwart im Zeugnis der Heiligen Schrift, der Glaubenstradition und des Lehramtes durch die kirchliche Gemeinschaft und ihre Glieder" (p. 79). This reception by the people of God "dient . . . dem Ziel, das Wort Gottes in der Kirche wirksam werden zu lassen" (p. 91). Pottmeyer's plea for a "Rezeption aus Einsicht" has clearly critical overtones and is founded in a *communio*-ecclesiology which was in the mind of Vatican II but which still needs further development and deepening.

How Can the Petrine Ministry
Serve the Unity of the Universal Church?

Jared Wicks, SJ

The title of this concluding session of the symposium proposes a work of Lutheran-Catholic collaboration on defining, or redefining, the Petrine ministry in its contribution to universal church unity. Such a work has to be, in May 2004, a continuation and extension (1) of documents from Lutheran/Catholic bilateral dialogues, such as *Papal Primacy and the Universal Church* from the dialogue in the USA (1974)[1] and the section on the Petrine ministry in the recent German study *Communio Sanctorum* (2000),[2] (2) of preceding symposia, with Lutheran participation, on the Petrine ministry held in the wake of Pope John Paul II's encyclical *Ut unum sint* (UUS),[3]

---

1. Paul C. Empie and T. Austin Murphy, eds., *Papal Primacy and the Universal Church* (Minneapolis: Augsburg, 1974), from which the U.S. dialogue moved on to Paul C. Empie, T. Austin Murphy, and Joseph A. Burgess, eds., *Teaching Authority and Infallibility in the Church* (Minneapolis: Augsburg, 1978).

2. Bilateral Working Group of the German National Bishops' Conference and the Church Leadership of the United Evangelical Lutheran Church of Germany, *Communio Sanctorum: The Church as the Communion of Saints* (Collegeville, MN: Liturgical Press, 2004), §§153-200.

3. Johann-Adam-Möhler-Institut, ed., *Das Papstamt. Anspruch und Widerspruch. Zum Stand des ökumenischen Dialogs über das Papstamt* (Münster: Aschendorff, 1996) = *Catholica* 2 (1996), in which the Lutheran contributors were Günther Wenz and Ulrich Kühn. James F. Puglisi, ed., *Petrine Ministry and the Unity of the Church: "Toward a Patient and Fraternal Dialogue"* (Collegeville, MN: Liturgical Press, 1999), with a Lutheran paper by Harding Meyer. Antonio Acerbi, ed., *Il ministero del Papa in prospettiva ecumenica* (Milano: Vita e Pensiero, 1999), in which Marc Lienhard reviewed Reformation

and (3) of "situation reports" on our question, such as those offered by W. Klausnitzer.[4]

Difficulties in Approaching the Primacy
in Lutheran-Catholic Dialogue

Immediately, however, two difficulties come to mind that, at least initially, seem to stand in the way of completing this work of Lutheran-Catholic collaboration.

(1) Regarding the papacy, the respective understandings of Lutherans and Catholics contrast with each other, to the point of appearing logically incompatible. When Lutherans express their fundamental openness to accepting the papal office in service of universal ecclesial communion, they regularly state as a condition of such acceptability that the *office be subordinated to the gospel,* renewed by the gospel, and precisely in this, then, it can render its service to all Christians as believers in the gospel of Christ.[5]

But when Catholics consider what the pope contributes to the church, they assume that as a bishop the proclamation of the gospel is for him a primary duty (CD [*Christus dominus*] 12; *Pastores gregis* [2003] 26), but they also come sooner or later to speak of the faith that he professes and teaches as an important *criterion, or source of convalidation, of what is conformed to the gospel* in present-day teaching and sacramental life. Hence, in the Catholic ecumenical program, it pertains to the Apostolic See, that of the successor of Peter, to judge whether the conditions of full communion in faith, sacra-

---

positions. Carl E. Braaten and Robert W. Jenson, eds., *Church Unity and the Papal Office* (Grand Rapids: Eerdmans, 2001), with a Lutheran view offered by David S. Yeago.

4. Wolfgang Klausnitzer, *Das Papstamt im Disput zwischen Lutheraner und Katholiken. Schwerpunkte von der Reformation bis zur Gegenwart* (Innsbruck: Tyrolia, 1987), continued in "Der Papst . . . ist zweifelsohne das grösste Hinderniz auf dem Weg der Ökumene" (Paul VI). Ist-Stand der theologischen Diskussion und Perspektiven einer Lösung im ökumenischer Absicht," in *Das Papstamt. Anspruch und Widerspruch,* pp. 117-33.

5. According to Wolfhart Pannenberg, Lutherans have expressed their readiness to accept, not only the authority of ecumenical councils, "sondern auch für ein der Norm des Evangeliums untergeordnetes und ihm dienendes päpstliches Amt, das sich von dieser Norm her erneuren läßt und gerade so der Einheit der ganzen Christenheit im Glauben dienen könnte." "Die lutherische Tradition und die Frage eines Petrusdienstes an der Einheit der Christen," in *Il primato del successore di Pietro: Atti del simposio teologico, Roma, dicembre 1996* (Vatican City: Libreria Editrice Vaticana, 1998), p. 473.

mental life, and ministry according to the gospel are fulfilled.[6] The problem the Petrine ministry claims to help resolve is not knowing the apostolic gospel from the New Testament, but rather how to discern what in a contemporary formulation is a proper expression of that gospel in this later age.

Our collaboration has to bring out how an office can be *at the same time* subordinated to the gospel, as Lutherans rightly require, and still can serve as an instance that judges expressions of the gospel in the time of the Church, as Catholics maintain.

(2) Lutherans, based on the Augsburg Confession, article VII, hold that what is necessary for salvation — the gospel and the sacraments of Christ — constitute as well *what is necessary for the church* to be essentially itself.

But Catholic ecclesiology, while recognizing the presence and effectiveness of the means of grace and salvation outside the Catholic communion, maintains that certain *relationships,* including communion with the successor of Peter, are *necessary* for the full manifestation of the universal communion that Christ wills for his Church.[7] The issue for Catholics is not where the gospel is operative and saving grace is given, for the good news and the Holy Spirit are present and active throughout our human family, but the question is rather where one finds the full sacramental expression and ministerial mediation of that grace.

Therefore, our project on the Petrine Ministry is made difficult by our different approaches to applying the gospel of Christ as *criterion* of the elements of church life and by differences over what is necessary for an ecclesial community to be a full manifestation of the church.

To push forward this collaborative project, notwithstanding the difficulties, this paper will offer reflections in two areas, both of which lead to

---

6. On discerning the conditions for full communion, the *Directory for the Application of the Principles and Norms on Ecumenism* (Vatican City: Libreria Editrice Vaticana, 1993), no. 29, refers to a joint responsibility of the college of bishops and the Apostolic See, with reference to the 1983 Code of Canon Law, can. 755, §1. This tension concerning the gospel or the pope as criterion was pointed out succinctly by Angelo Maffeis ("Il ministero di unità per la Chiesa universale nei colloqui ecumenici," in Acerbi, ed., *Il ministero del Papa,* p. 255), who rightly notes that while for Catholics the pope is not in principle the only criterion of conformity to the gospel, the definitions of Vatican I make the papacy relevant to assessing the other criteria.

7. In different moments of the world-level dialogue since 1986, Lothar Ullrich has expressed the Catholic conviction about the episcopate, apostolic succession in ministry, and communion with the Apostolic See of Rome as components of *"notwendiger Dienst am heilsnotwendigen Evangelium."*

fresh considerations of the Petrine ministry. First, it seems helpful to review Catholic convictions about the visible principles and foundations of ecclesial unity in communion. Second, some current rereadings of Vatican I's Dogmatic Constitution on the Petrine ministry, *Pastor aeternus,* also open fresh perspectives, which may well be convergent with more recent Lutheran approaches to the episcopal office and ministry in the church.

The Several Principles of Ecclesial Communion in Catholic Teaching

To begin, I note a small, but suggestive, difference in translating Catholic documents on the finality intended by Christ when he instituted the ministry of unity to be carried out by Peter and his successors. In a standard English translation, we read in the Prologue of Vatican I's *Pastor aeternus* (PA; 18 June 1870), regarding the institution of the papal office, that to maintain the unity of the bishops and of the whole multitude of believers, "he [Christ] set blessed Peter over the rest of the apostles and instituted in him *the* permanent principle of both unities and their visible foundation." But when the same documentary volume presents Vatican II's restatement of this very text, we read that Christ "placed blessed Peter over the rest of the apostles, and in him instituted *a* perpetual and visible principle and foundation for the unity of faith and communion" (*Lumen gentium* [LG] 18).[8]

Of course the original Latin texts of PA and LG had no article at all, neither the definite *the (den, le),* denoting a unique principle of unity and connoting a foundational role that the Petrine ministry *and it alone* carries out, nor an indefinite *a,* whose denotation is open but in connotation can indicate the presence and actual functioning of *several other* principles and foundations of

---

8. Norman P. Tanner, ed., *Decrees of the Ecumenical Councils* (London/Washington, DC: Sheed & Ward/Georgetown, 1990), 812, 863. This is the bilingual edition that incorporates Giuseppe Alberigo, ed., *Conciliorum Oecumenicorum Decreta* (Bologna: Dehoniane, 1972). One finds the same transition, regarding Peter from "*le* principe durable et le fondement visible" (Vatican I) to "*un* principe et un fondement perpétuel et visible de foi et de communion" (Vatican II, LG 18), in the bilingual edition of Denzinger-Hünermann in French. Also in Neuner-Roos, first, "*den* ewig daurenden Ausgangspunkt und die sichtbare Grundlage" (Vatican I, no. 436), but then "*ein* immerwährendes und sichtbares Prinzip und Fundament der Glaubenseinheit" (Vatican II, LG 18, no. 462). But the Spanish bilingual edition in 1999 of Denzinger-Hünermann reverses the articles, from "él [Cristo] instituyó *un* principio perpetuo" (Vatican I) to "instituyó en él [Pedro] para siempre *el* principio y fundamento . . ." (Vatican II, LG 18).

unity and communion. The difference between the articles (definite/indefinite) is due to contingent options made by the translators, but more important, the Vatican II form, *a* principle and foundation, does alert us to a Catholic conviction of considerable ecclesiological and ecumenical importance.

Recognition of Several Ecclesial Principles the Papacy Serves

Catholic doctrine grounds a conviction that being church and being in ecclesial communion do rest on several principles and foundations, not on just a single basis, as some translations of *Pastor aeternus* suggest. These principles, or foundational elements, are then central to situating the ministry of the successor of Peter.

The conviction concerning several principles shaped the account of "full incorporation" of the Catholic faithful into the social-ecclesial body of the church in LG 14 ("by the bonds of profession of faith, the sacraments, ecclesiastical government and communion"). We find a similar plurality structuring the German Lutheran-Catholic dialogue report of 1984, *Kirchengemeinschaft im Wort und Sakrament,* in which the three central chapters treat communion *(Gemeinschaft),* first, in the confession of the one faith *(Bekenntnis* — chap. 2), then in sacramental-liturgical life and celebration *(Gottesdienstliche Feier* — chap. 3), and then in the apostolic office of ministry *(Apostolisches Amt* — chap. 4). At the same time, the second phase of the world-level Lutheran-Catholic dialogue sketched in *Facing Unity* (1985) the realization of ecclesial communion as unfolding in fellowship in three areas: confessing one apostolic faith (55-69), sacramental life (70-85), and "community of service," in ministry and *episkopē* (86-148).

In these documents incorporation into the church and life in ecclesial communion are presented without explicit reference to communion with the bishop of Rome, the successor of Peter. Obviously the Petrine ministry is implicit in Catholic thinking about ecclesial communion, but an accurate and balanced account has to include and examine other principles. In a recent study of the differences between the Eastern and Western traditions on the Petrine primacy, E. Lanne framed this point in a way that has relevance to any consideration of the primatial role of the successor of Peter.

> For the Orientals, just as for Rome, the invisible principle of the unity of the church is the Holy Spirit, but they differ in their concept of the visible principle. The Byzantine tradition does not deny . . . the privileged

role of the Roman see in maintaining visible unity when this is threatened in matters of faith or juridical practice. However, in expressing the visible principle and foundation of unity, this tradition sees it in the *sinfonia* of the pentarchy in the one faith according to Sacred Scripture, in the faith of the Creed of Nicea-Constantinople and the ecumenical councils. This visibility comes to its highest expression in eucharistic concelebration by the hierarchs of these churches.

The East and the West agree that the principle of the unity of the church is the Holy Spirit. But while the East sees the visible principle of unity above all in the common profession of faith, in the agreement of the bishops, and in a common eucharistic celebration, the West — at least since St. Leo the Great — recognizes in the Church of Rome and its bishop, the successor of Peter, a most important visible principle of the unity of the church. But you cannot say that this principle is the only one, because of other elements that — each in its own role and order — are visible principles and foundations of church unity, namely, the creeds professed in the one baptism, the decisions of the ecumenical councils, and, to be sure, eucharistic celebration. Nor can you say that the other principles of unity lead back ultimately to the see of Peter, for each of them has its own consistency in ecclesial life, while certainly Rome does serve as the authority that convalidates the authenticity of these other visible principles.[9]

From this text, for our discussion of the papacy as a *visible* principle of ecclesiality, it is good to be reminded of the divine work of the Spirit poured forth by Christ glorified, through which Christ calls and gathers believers.

It is the Holy Spirit, dwelling in those who believe and filling and ruling over the church as a whole, who brings about that wonderful communion of the faithful. He brings them all into intimate union with Christ, so that he is the principle of the church's unity. (*Unitatis redintegratio* [UR] 2)

We certainly do not want to relativize the visible ecclesial principles of word, sacramental rites, and ministry, for we live and think within an economy of Incarnation and sacramental mediation. But there is more, in both

9. Emmanuel Lanne, "Tradizione orientale del I Millennio e tradizione occidentale del I e II Millennio sullo sviluppo della dottrina del Primato," presented to the Interdicasterial Study Commission on the Exercise of the Primacy (Congregation for the Doctrine of the Faith/Pontifical Council for the Promotion of the Unity of Christians). March 2003, pp. 8-9 and 11-12 (trans. Jared Wicks).

our origins and present lives, a "more" rooted in Christ's saving work and im-
parted by God's grace, as we confessed in our *Joint Declaration on the Doctrine of Justification:* "we are accepted by God and receive the Holy Spirit, who
renews our hearts while equipping and calling us to good works" (15). Here is
a profound unity, a communion in God's saving Spirit, which our visible
words, rites, and offices seek to serve and promote in human lives.

The main point, for our discussion today, is the existence of the other
visible principles and foundations of communion, such as the confession of
faith and the conciliar doctrinal heritage by which we have communion in
professing God's saving work as his word has revealed. Ecclesial communion
is the sharing in the sacraments of our Lord that we celebrate. These are the
principles of unity in the church that the ordained ministry, both
presbyterial and episcopal, serves, promotes, and protects. These principles,
E. Lanne implied, come from Christ and the work of all his apostles, not
simply from the Petrine ministry, even though the latter has for Catholics an
important role in their regard. In fact, these "several other" principles and
foundations mark off an area, with definite limits, *within which* Catholics
hold that the Petrine ministry is being carried out. To use the language of
one of the most famous declarations of Vatican II, that of *Dei verbum,* no. 10,
concerning the magisterium and the written and transmitted word of God,
we can say that the Petrine office is not superior to the confessions and dogmas expressive of the faith of the church, nor to its sacraments and fundamental liturgical forms, nor to the presbyterial-episcopal structure of church
ministry, but it serves these, listening and observing, guarding and protecting, and promoting and expounding what has been transmitted.

Regarding the area of action of the papal magisterium, A. Dulles recently declared succinctly that it is not superior to the transmitted faith:
"The Popes have never made *ex cathedra* pronouncements except to certify
and defend beliefs already professed by the vast majority of bishops and
faithful. The power of the magisterium is used to confirm and clarify, not to
alter the beliefs of Catholics."[10]

Regarding the episcopal structure of ministry in the church, we recall
the clarification given by the German bishops in 1875, heartily approved by
Pope Pius IX, after Chancellor Bismarck's circular letter had declared that

10. "A New Orthodox View of the Papacy," *Pro Ecclesia* 12 (2003): 345-58; here 357.
This is a review-essay on Oliver Clément, *Rome autrement. Une réflexion orthodoxe sur la
papauté* (Paris: Desclée de Brouwer, 1997), now in English as *You Are Peter: An Orthodox
Reflection on the Exercise of Papal Primacy* (Hyde Park, NY: New City Press, 2003).

with *Pastor aeternus* the authority of diocesan bishops had been absorbed into the newly declared supreme papal jurisdiction. The bishops declared this to be a serious misunderstanding: "It is in virtue of the same divine institution upon which the papacy rests that the episcopate also exists. It too has its rights and duties, because of the ordinance of God himself, and the Pope has neither the right nor the power to change them."[11]

From the Several Principles, a Better Grounding of Our Identity as Dialogue Partners

The several other principles of ecclesial communion help to situate, or contextualize, our discussion of the Petrine ministry of unity, but they do more. Their existence also contributes to rightly expressing the ecclesial situation of the Lutherans and Catholics who carry out a dialogue on papal primacy. In a word, we are not simply "separated" or "divided" or "in no way in communion," even though Lutherans do not admit the primacy. Catholic ecclesiological principles, at least, lead to framing our relation differently as dialogue partners.

As is well known, especially after the CDF declaration *Dominus Iesus* of the year 2000, the Orthodox and ancient Oriental churches are for Catholics "churches in the proper sense," because of their faith, their sacramental life centered on the Eucharist, and their presbyterial-episcopal ministry. In these cases, the "several other" principles effectively constitute a dense ecclesial reality, in spite of these churches not being in communion with the successor of Peter and notwithstanding the fact that because of the schism they do not receive the benefits of the Petrine ministry of universal unity.

But many of the same "several other" principles of ecclesial reality and communion are also recognized, by Catholic doctrine, to be present and operative in the ecclesial communities rooted in the Reformation, as Pope John Paul II restated Vatican II's teaching on our true but imperfect communion in *Ut unum sint.*

> By God's grace . . . neither what belongs to the structure of the Church of Christ nor that communion which still exists with the other Churches

---

11. Cited from Jacques Dupuis, ed., *The Christian Faith in the Doctrinal Documents of the Catholic Church* (Bangalore/New York: Theological Publications in India, [7]2001), p. 322, translating Heinrich Denzinger, *Enchiridion symbolorum definitionum et declarationum de rebus fidei et morum,* re-edited by Peter Hünermann, 37th edition (Freiburg: Herder, 1991), 3115; hereafter cited as DH.

and Ecclesial Communities has been destroyed. Indeed, the elements of sanctification and truth present in the other Christian communities, in a degree which varies from one to the other, constitute the objective basis of the communion, albeit imperfect, which exists between them and the Catholic Church.

To the extent that these elements are found in other Christian communities, the one church of Christ is effectively present in them (UUS 11).

It is not the case that beyond the boundaries of the Catholic community there is an ecclesial vacuum. Many elements of great value, which in the Catholic Church are part of the fullness of the means of salvation and of the gifts of grace which make up the Church, are also found in the other Christian Communities. (UUS 13)

For some, this important aspect of the Catholic-Lutheran relationship has been obscured by the language-rule laid down by *Dominus Iesus,* namely, that in Catholic parlance the Reformation confessional bodies are not "churches in the proper sense," that is, according to the logic of predication that rests on Catholic ecclesiology. But this terminological specification does not cancel or revoke what has been affirmed in *Unitatis redintegratio* at the moment when it introduced the designation "ecclesial communities" for the Reformation confessional bodies.

The adjective "ecclesial" did not appear in this context in the 1963 draft of *De oecumenismo,* but at the request of several Council Fathers, including Cardinal Franz König, it was introduced into the emended draft of 1964 and remains in the promulgated *Unitatis redintegratio* (three times in 19, and once in 22). The final section of the Decree, 19-23, bears the subtitle, "The Separated Churches and Ecclesial Communities of the West."

The meaning of the term "ecclesial" in these emendations was given in the official *Relatio* distributed before the Council's Third Period of 1964 to explain the revised text.

It must not be overlooked that the communities that have their origin in the separation that took place in the West are not merely a sum or collection of individual Christians, but they are constituted by social ecclesiastical elements which they have preserved from our common patrimony and which confer on them a truly ecclesial character *(caracterem vere ecclesialem).* In these communities, the one sole church of Christ is present, albeit imperfectly, in a way that is somewhat like its presence in particular churches, and by means of their ecclesiastical elements is in some way active in them.[12]

The "truly ecclesial character" of the Lutheran churches of the world constitutes a significant aspect of the situation in which we discuss the Petrine ministry of universal communion. From their own doctrinal perspective, the Catholic participants do not see their Lutheran dialogue partners as simply persons of good will who are joined in a voluntary association, like a Rotary Club. Many elements constitutive of church, that is, principles and foundations of unity and communion, which come from Christ and are effective by the action of his Spirit, have gathered and formed Lutherans in bodies that are "truly ecclesial" in nature.

The papacy we are discussing has a finality that concerns precisely the elements of truth and sanctification that give Lutheran bodies their truly ecclesial character. The Petrine ministry, Catholics believe, was instituted with regard to them, to promote and serve visible unity in faith, sacramental worship, and ministerial service. The Petrine ministry of universal oversight and vigilance *(episkopē)*, of promotion, and of confirmation and convalidation is essentially related to the elements of word, sacrament, and ministry that Lutherans cherish and Catholics believe to be creative of ecclesiality.

This consideration seems to ground, not simply Catholic respect for the Lutheran confessional bodies, as *ecclesial* communities, but also an invitation by those who cherish the Petrine ministry to Lutherans to enter discussion of this ministry with the conviction, *"Nostra res agitur,"* because it serves the "several other principles" of communion in which we have much in common, that is, word, sacrament, and ministry.

The Petrine Ministry, First, to Ground the Unity and Communion of the Episcopate

For this part of the paper, just as in the previous section, the point of departure is the Prologue of Vatican I's *Pastor aeternus*, which states the finality of

---

12. *Acta Synodalia Conc. Oec. Vaticani II*, III/3, 335. I explained this Vatican II development more at length in "The Significance of the Ecclesial Communities of the Reformation," *Ecumenical Trends* 30 (2001): 170-73; in French in *Irénikon* 74 (2001): 57-66; in Italian in *Studi ecumenici* 20 (2002): 133-42. A summary in *Luther Digest* 12 (2004).

the Petrine ministry in terms that have been little noticed until recently. As an introductory text, the Prologue does not sketch the ministerial actions of the successor of Peter in serving ecclesial unity and communion, since that is to come in the body of the Constitution, but, more important, it specifies *the persons toward whom* these actions are first directed as *the bishops* of the church and then through the bishops the multitude of church members.

The Prologue first refers to Jesus instituting the church, "in order to render permanent the saving work of redemption" in a dwelling place in which "all believers should be linked by the bond of one faith and charity." Our Lord prayed for the unity of those who would believe in him; he sent his apostles; and, "in like manner it was his will that in his church there should be shepherds and teachers until the end of time." Then the text introduces the Petrine ministry in terms of its purpose or finality for the good of the Church.

> In order, then, that the episcopal office should be one and undivided *(ut vero episcopatus ipse unus et indivisus esset)* and that, by the union of the priests, the whole multitude of believers should be held together in the unity of faith and communion, he set blessed Peter over the rest of the Apostles and instituted in him the permanent principle of both unities and their visible foundation.[13]

It is no exaggeration to say that this has been among Catholics, and through them also for their ecumenical dialogue partners, a neglected text. The dialogues have not taken into account the priority of effectively serving the unity of the episcopate as the *means by which* the Petrine ministry serves the unity and communion of all the faithful.

The Lutheran-Catholic dialogue in the USA, in its statement on *Papal Primacy and the Universal Church,* framed the notion of "the Petrine function" as a ministry to the church as a whole (4-5) and it reviewed the New Testament accounts of this function (9-13), but on Vatican I the U.S. dialogue spoke only briefly, not mentioning the pope's ministry to the unity of the episcopate, but instead his full, supreme, ordinary, and immediate jurisdiction over all individuals and churches (19).

Communio Sanctorum gives a valuable sketch of the Petrine ministry as it has changed over the ages of church history (164-75), followed by the

13. Cited from Tanner, ed., *Decrees,* 811-12. DH 3050-51. Dupuis, *The Christian Faith,* no. 818.

Reformation criticism of the papacy and contemporary Lutheran consider-ations (176-91). But the discussion is largely controlled by concern for con-stitutional provisions obligating the successor of Peter to respect collegial and synodal structures of ministerial responsibility, as well as the relative au-tonomy of regional churches, along with assuring an exercise of his magisterium in clear subordination to Scripture and the *sensus fidei* of the whole church (especially 190 and 194). The episcopate as the initial setting and priority of the Petrine ministry is not mentioned.

But the helpful placement given by *Pastor aeternus* to Petrine papal ministry, when it stated its initial finality, is being recalled, and emphasis is being placed on its potential fruitfulness for renewing Catholic presenta-tions of the Petrine role. In fact, one hears calls for the "re-reception" of Vati-can I's doctrine of papal primacy, precisely in terms of making the "episco-pal finality" stated in the Prologue the guiding principle and foundational interpretation of the papal primacy. This recollection and insistence oc-curred at the Theological Symposium, *Il primato del successore di Pietro,* held under the auspices of the Congregation for the Doctrine of the Faith in De-cember 1996.

At the symposium, M. J. Buckley's major paper based its "doctrinal synthesis" concerning papal primacy on the opening paragraphs of *Pastor aeternus.*

> The primacy was to foster initially 1. unity within the episcopate, the unity of the bishops among themselves, 2. and then, by means of that unity *(per)*, the unity of the members of the Church. The unity of the episcopate was the condition and the agency through which the unity of the Church would be realized — a unity specified as that in faith and communion, to which the contradictory would be heresy and schism.

Thus *Pastor aeternus* taught that there are two terms of the relation-ship that is the primacy. First, in his primacy, the pope relates to the episco-pate to foster its unity in authentic faith and effective/affective charity and communion. Second, in his primacy and in and with and through the epis-copate, the pope relates to the faithful by fostering their unity in authentic faith and communion.[14]

The doctrinal synthesis offered by M. J. Buckley takes as its governing

14. "The Primacy and the Episcopate: Towards a Doctrinal Synthesis," in *Il primato del successore di Pietro,* p. 306.

concept or comprehensive principle for understanding papal primacy precisely the unity of the episcopate and the unity of the church within the agency of a united episcopate. It goes on to treat that unity as *communio,* to speak of the instrumental role of primatial and episcopal ministry under the action of the Holy Spirit (UR 2), to describe the properly "episcopal" role of the successor of Peter, and to specify the exercise of this Petrine *munus* in terms of both habitual oversight and extraordinary "substitutional" functions.[15]

At the CDF symposium, M. J. Buckley's option to understand the primacy from the point of departure and governing principle of the unity of the episcopate was accepted as quite correct by the commentator on his paper, F. Ocariz.[16] In another paper of the symposium, P. Rodríguez expanded on the Prologue of *Pastor aeternus* as a valuable expression of the finality of the Petrine ministry, to the point of finding here the *"razón formal"* of the primatial function of the bishop of Rome. For P. Rodríguez, the two-step understanding of the papal ministry of unity opens the way to a valuable reinterpretation of the doctrinal nucleus of chapter 3 of *Pastor aeternus* on papal jurisdiction.[17]

In the 1998 volume of published papers of the 1996 symposium, the Congregation for the Doctrine of the Faith added a set of "Considerations" in fifteen paragraphs, on "The Primacy of the Successor of Peter in the Mystery of the Church," in which the Prologue of *Pastor aeternus* serves, along with *Lumen gentium,* to show the essential correlation between the ministry of the bishop of Rome and that of the other bishops (5). Furthermore, the characteristics of the exercise of the primacy must be understood above all from its service of the unity of the episcopate and its own episcopal nature (8).[18]

This emphasis on the Prologue of *Pastor aeternus* as a promising point of departure in reconceiving the Petrine ministry should not, however, obscure the fact that this Vatican I Dogmatic Constitution is deeply marked by the historical conditions of its origin. In spite of the new light that comes

15. "The Primacy," in *Il primato del successore di Pietro,* pp. 309-25. After the CDF Symposium, Michael J. Buckley published *Papal Primacy and the Episcopate: Towards a Relational Understanding* (New York: Crossroad, 1998).

16. In *Il primato del successore di Pietro,* p. 340.

17. Pedro Rodríguez, "Reazione al testo di Ángel Antón," in *Il primato del successore di Pietro,* pp. 454-66.

18. Hermann J. Pottmeyer highlighted in the "Considerations" a series of hopeful signs pointing toward renewal of the papacy. *Die Rolle des Papsttums im Dritten Jahrtausend* (Freiburg/Basel/Vienna: Herder, 1999), pp. 123-27.

from the Prologue, the doctrinal nucleus of this text clearly needs to be freed from its historic limitations and restated in a new context.[19]

Pastor aeternus, on the papal primacy of jurisdiction and the infallibility of certain strictly defined actions of the papal magisterium, is part of a wider nineteenth-century anti-revolutionary reaction, especially strong in Ultramontanism, which aimed to reassert the principle of authority in human life.

In the Constitution's teaching, the doctrinal context needs explicitation, by placing its teaching within the Third Article of the Creed, on the work of the Holy Spirit sent to animate the apostolic mission of proclamation and to bring to full application in human lives the revelatory and redemptive work of Christ. The comprehensive ecclesiological concept surrounding the papacy needs cleansing of any remaining traces of the church seen as *societas perfecta,* to treat it as a confessional and sacramental *communio,* in which the juridical conceptuality will give way to biblical themes, and account will be taken of the ecclesial reality of particular churches. Much greater clarity is needed in distinguishing the spheres of papal action, namely, jurisdiction in governance and a magisterium of faith and doctrine. To be sure, beginnings have been made in Vatican II's *Lumen gentium,* but it did not address itself directly to the papacy, and its treatment of the church as *communio* is still embryonic, hesitant, and scattered. *Lumen gentium* was also historically conditioned.

The sharply drawn limits on magisterial infallibility in *Pastor aeternus* are well known, as is the essential orientation of papal teaching to the apostolic legacy and to the faith of the church. But papal jurisdiction needs far greater specification, and this not only to state the concept in a manner adequate to a *communio* ecclesiology. Concretely, in view of reunion with the Orthodox and ancient Oriental churches, some mode of stating the limited range of papal governance in such churches is clearly needed, in line with the seed of such an account given by Vatican II.

> For many centuries the churches of the east and the west followed their separate ways though linked in a union of faith and sacramental life; the Roman see by common consent acted as a guide when disagreements arose among them over matters of faith and discipline *(sede Romana*

---

19. See, on this complex of issues, Angelo Maffeis, "Il ministero di unità," in Acerbi, ed., *Il ministero del Papa,* pp. 267-75, who draws especially on the Groupe de Dombes, *Le ministère de communion dans l'église universelle* (Paris: Centurion, 1986).

moderante communi consensu, si dissensiones circa fidem vel disciplinam inter eas orirentur). (UR 14)

Beyond these *desiderata,* there lies the work of reconceiving Petrine ministry as serving first the unity of the episcopate, on which Catholic thinking on the primacy has only recently begun.

This presentation of the primacy, emphasizing the priority of promoting the unity of the episcopate, may seem oblivious to Lutheran concerns. But it is also offered at a time in which Lutherans are taking up for coordination, clarification, and doctrinal elaboration their own position on the "supra-congregational ministry of oversight." This process has already led to some weighty statements concerning the episcopal form of this ministry.[20] For example, in the document just cited:

> By being specially charged to care for the communion of all worshiping congregations with the universal church, the episcopal ministry has the specific task of safeguarding the true nature of the *una, sancta, catholica et apostolica ecclesia* that transcends the boundaries of both space and time. (20)

The episcopal ministry carries responsibility for larger geographical areas of the church than individual congregations or parishes. Therefore, the *ministerium ecclesiasticum* carried out by bishops has certain *propria* that are not shared by pastors at the local level. Bishops are called to guide the life of the congregations in the region under their care, especially through visitation, and to support their life together. They are authorized to ordain pastors and to supervise their teaching and practices. In all of these *propria,* care for the unity of the church universal, and its apostolic faithfulness, is a responsibility to which bishops are especially committed (30).

The personal character of the ministry of oversight cannot be sepa-

---

20. *The Episcopal Ministry within the Apostolicity of the Church* (LWF 2003), a study document, of forty-four concise paragraphs, issued after five regional meetings and a consultation of twenty-five Lutheran participants in world-level ecumenical dialogue held in Malta in late 2002. The central paragraphs, nos. 19-32, treat "The Ministry of Episkopē," introducing it as "the supra-congregational ministry of oversight" (no. 19). The document draws upon previous Lutheran study documents, e.g., on the Episcopal Office (1983), and on common statements made on the occasion of establishing communion with episcopal churches (Porvoo, Reuilly, Waterloo, and "Called to Common Mission" in the U.S.).

rated from its collegial aspect. As a collegium, the ministers of oversight represent and promote the unity and common life of the many local congregations within the church at large. They also represent their churches in the framework of the universal church. The episcopal ministry must also be exercised collegially in cooperation with other ministries of church leadership in the area under the bishop's care (31).

The Catholic contribution to dialogue on papal primacy will, under the guidance of the Prologue to *Pastor aeternus,* treat the Petrine ministry as a service of unity and communion to just such "supra-congregational ministers of oversight" in their responsibilities for congregations and their supervision of local pastors. It will treat the pope as one whose first ministry, in the logic of its finality, arises out of the responsibilities of bishops described in these Lutheran texts. It will also underscore the properly "episcopal" nature of the Petrine ministry in service of the unity and communion of the bishops. Thus, our recalling of recent Lutheran statements on episcopal ministry points out the proper setting for further Lutheran-Catholic dialogue on the Petrine ministry.

The successor of Peter *is* a bishop with the ordinary responsibilities of oversight in the diocese of Rome. His further, universal, oversight has as its first purpose the effective promotion of unity and communion among all the bishops in their witness to the gospel and further teaching, in their sacramental leadership, and in the governance they exercise in the particular churches.

Among his brother bishops, the bishop of the see consecrated by the martyrdom of the two apostles Peter and Paul will have a special responsibility for keeping alive in local bishops that *sollicitudo omnium ecclesiarum* (2 Cor. 11:28) proper to a ministry derived from the unique service of the apostles. The papal ministry of the word is thus especially concerned with the mission of evangelization to all areas and all cultures, to which he will insistently call the other bishops out of the particularities of their regions.

We can break off here, since much in the Petrine ministry is also historically conditioned and many of its concretizations are contingent upon the *necessitas ecclesiae.*[21] About the latter, there is much for the ongoing Lutheran-Catholic dialogue to discuss.

---

21. "Il primato del Successore di Pietro nel Mistero della Chiesa. Considerazione della Congregazione per la Dottrina della Fede," nos. 8-10, in *Il primato del successore di Pietro,* pp. 488-500.